Lions Under The Throne

Lions Under
The Throne

ANTHONY MOCKLER

Frederick Muller Limited
London

First published in Great Britain in 1983
by Frederick Muller Limited, Dataday House,
Alexandra Road, Wimbledon, London SW19 7JZ.

British Library Cataloguing in Publication Data
Mockler, Anthony
    Lions under the throne.
    1. Judges – England – History
    I. Title
    344.207'14   KD7285

ISBN 0 584 10437 5

Printed in Great Britain by
The Anchor press Ltd, Colchester, Essex

Contents

Dedication

To Edmond Joseph, who would have enjoyed
this book, and to Marjorie Mary, with love and affection.

Foreword

Originally this book was planned to begin at the Conquest and proceed to the present day. Like Toad, it swelled and swelled: in size, in complexity, and indeed potentially in expense. It became necessary to deflate – to chop it rather ruthlessly in less than half. Even a Solomon would have found it difficult to decide where precisely to draw the dividing line. I chose to do so at a point where the Lord Chief Justices were beginning to become, it seemed to me, definite personalities in their own right as they had not been since the days of the Justiciars. I doubt, though, whether they ever became, or ever will become, as interesting as the men they tried. For one of the inevitable difficulties in writing a book of this sort, in which trials and particularly treason trials are enormously important, is that the judicial system and those who implement it form as it were the purely mechanical side of a triangle dominated by two opposing dynamic forces: the government and the rebels. In other words, whatever the ostensible subject-matter of this book and however hard I have tried to limit it to its ostensible pro-tagonists the figures that will almost certainly stand out in the end are more those who went to the block or the gallows than those who wore the black cap and sent them there.

The only conclusion I have come to is a very simple one – but it may be as surprising to the reader as it was to me. It is this: that there is no such creature as a 'conventional' or a 'normal' Lord Chief Justice, not by a long chalk. An extraordinary variety of men have held that position, united by nothing, not even by knowledge of the law – in many cases minimal – or by talent – in some cases nonexistent.

To show what sort of men they were I have tried (within the limits of the space available) to write about their lives as a whole, personal as well as public, both before and after they became holders of the office. Yet in order to give the narrative continuity, to set it against the political and general history of the times in which so many of them played such a major part, their lives are interwoven with the lives of both their predecessors and their successors. I do not think this method will be found confusing in practice; though Plutarch, the master of the brief self-contained biography, would certainly not have approved.

Readers will notice that I have used, almost invariably, the family names rather than the titles of peers who first appear as commoners; this is not normal practice but I hope that they will, as I do, find it an easier system to follow.

For the inspiration behind the book I would like to thank Nicholas Thompson's mother; and for fanning the first embers into flame Nicholas Thompson himself. The present Lord Chief Justice, Lord Lane, gave me a welcome, an interview, and lunch; Stephen Oliver Q.C. and Lord Gifford Q.C. assisted with their very different opinions. I am particularly grateful for all their long-suffering help to the staff of the History Faculty Library in Oxford; but my main thanks must inevitably go to my predecessors, to all those who have written biographies of individual Lord Chief Justices or studies of legal history; to them I owe an enormous debt.

Sally Jones typed most of the manuscript with great enthusiasm and flattering interest. Jocelyn Gold rounded it off. To both go my thanks.

Finally I would like to thank my father who suggested that Lord Denning should be fitted in somehow and who made short shrift of my argument that, though Master of the Rolls, Lord Denning had never been Lord Chief Justice. 'Look here,' I was told, 'if anyone objects, you can always say that he ought to have been.'

August, 1982
Milton Manor

Introductory Notes

Any book about lawyers and the law is bound to include a fair number of technical terms. These notes are designed to help the ordinary layman understand the historical background to titles, phrases and procedures that may otherwise be baffling or obscure. They are placed here at the beginning of the book for convenience's sake – to be referred to when needed, not necessarily to be digested whole at a single gulp.

TREASON, ATTAINDER AND IMPEACHMENT

The role of the Lord Chief Justice was, very largely, to preside at treason trials, to make sure that those accused were found guilty of high treason, and to pronounce sentence.

Peers of the realm however were judged by their fellow peers under the presidency of the *Lord High Steward*; though the Lord Chief Justice and his colleagues would sit in as expert advisers on legal points, as *Assessors*.

The law of treason was – and indeed basically still is – governed by Edward III's *Statute of Treason*, of 1352. Previously the term *treason* had been extended to cover almost any offence that offended the King. Whatever the King called treason was therefore, the judges had ruled, treason 'on the King's record' – a frighteningly autocratic system. Furthermore the judges themselves had extended the concept to include such minor offences as 'unlawfully making waste of the King's wards or unlawfully taking venison, fish or other goods.' The Statute, drawn up largely by the Lord Chief Justice of the time, William Shareshull, laid down a long but clear and logical list of high treasons, of which the two most important were 'compassing or imagining' (i.e. bringing about or plotting) the death of the King, the Queen or the Heir to the Throne; and, secondly, levying war against the King or adhering to his enemies.

The penalties for high treason were for commoners both symbolic and excruciatingly painful. Those found guilty were hanged up to be exposed to the public gaze, cut down quickly while alive, disembowelled, had their hearts plucked out and exposed, their entrails burnt and their limbs then quartered. Their various dismembered parts were sent to adorn, as a warning to others, gateways, battlements and bridges all over the kingdom. In such circumstances it meant a great deal to be a peer and to have the right to a simple and relatively painless beheading. But even for peers there were additional penalties – forfeiture of all the traitor's goods to the Crown and the perpetual disinheriting of the traitor's heirs.

On occasions, however, judicial murder – which was what treason trials almost always amounted to – could not be guaranteed. Either those accused of treason were in hiding or abroad or in rebellion, or else their offences very clearly did not fall within the terms of the Statute. In that case the authorities could use the procedure of *Attainder*.

Attainder was judgment by legislation, without even the pretence of a trial. A Bill of Attainder against a person or persons named would be proposed, with a recital of offences, by the Lords, sent down to the Commons for agreement, and assented to by the King. Thereupon the Bill would become an *Act of Attainder* and the victims named would suffer, if caught, exactly the same fate as those found guilty of high treason after a proper trial. It was a vile, extremely useful, device.

As Attainders came into fashion, in 1459, impeachments passed temporarily out of use. *Impeachment* was a milder and considerably less tyrannical form of judgment not exactly by legislation (for there were no Bills or Acts and the King's assent was not needed) but by Parliament. In this case it was the House of Commons that drew up the charges, acting as a joint prosecuting body and hailing the accused – usually favourites or ministers of the Crown – up before the House of Lords. The Lords then, sitting as both judges and jury, heard the evidence, gave their verdict and pronounced their sentence. Impeachment could be for any crime known to the law of England – it was often used in cases of corruption or maladministration and did not therefore inevitably result in death for those found guilty. Furthermore the accused were at least present at the bar of the Lords and allowed to speak in mitigation. It was by no means as tyrannical a procedure as Attainder; but for all that it was, like Attainder, a convenient way of disposing of political enemies.

The last Act of Attainder was passed, disgracefully against Sir John Fenwick after the Glorious Revolution of 1688 that was meant to put an end to tyrannical abuses. Impeachment gradually disappeared as the House of Commons asserted its control over Ministers. Drawing and quartering were abolished. The last public execution, that of Michael Barrett the Fenian, was held in 1868. But high treason remains one of the very few crimes still punishable by death in the United Kingdom.

THE JUDGES OF ENGLAND AND THE LORD CHIEF JUSTICE

Traditionally the King, in practice the *Justiciar*, sat in the judgment seat and gave judgment. The Justiciars headed the post-Conquest judicial system. They were not, however, merely judges but powerful politicians, often highly intelligent and ambitious soldiers and administrators like Odo of Bayeux, the Conqueror's half-brother, or the heroic Hubert de Burgh. Indeed the Justiciar was, after the King, by far the most important person in the realm, 'lieutenant in his absence, chief regent in his presence; prime minister in legal, financial and military affairs.'

Their successors, the first thirty or so Chief Justices, were by comparison (and with certain notable exceptions, like the hated Tresilian) pale, powerless men. By late mediaeval times the very memory of the title of Justiciar had faded from English history, living on only in the Latin origins of the title into which it was transmuted: in 1268 Robert de Bruce, the VI of that name and grandfather of the future King of Scotland, was appointed the first *capitalis justiciarius ad placita coram rege tenenda* – that is to say, chief justiciar for holding pleas (i.e. hearing cases) in the King's presence; in effect *Chief Justice of the King's Bench*.

By the reign of Henry III, a period of increasingly specialised legal activity, two other courts were emerging besides King's Bench itself: the Court of Common Pleas headed by the *Chief Justice of Common Pleas* and the Court of the Exchequer headed by the *Chief Baron of the Exchequer*.

For centuries these three courts continued to function – a triple-headed entity with always two Chief Justices and one Chief Baron in office at the same time. Though the numbers of judges fluctuated, the normal figure was four for each court. The two Chief Justices, the Chief Baron and their *puisne* (assistant) judges together formed a group of immense importance and influence – *the twelve common-law judges of England.*

Judges are often referred to in legal texts not as Mr Justice Smith but more simply as *Smith J.* – a usage which will occasionally be found in the pages that follow.

The Court of King's Bench gradually acquired a position of acknowledged superiority over the other two more specialised courts; and when in the Victorian reforms of 1873–1875 the three courts were amalgamated, it was the Chief Justice of King's Bench who became, officially, the *Lord Chief Justice of England.*

Unofficially the title had often been used by, or attributed to, the Chief Justice of King's Bench in the preceding centuries; and it is therefore with the successive holders of this office and of this office alone that this book will deal.

THE HUB OF THE SYSTEM: THE GREAT HALL AT WESTMINSTER

On the site of a run-down Benedictine monastery, on a gravelly island in the Thames about two miles outside London's City walls, Edward the Confessor built his great Abbey of Westminster, consecrated a few days before his death in 1066. A generation later William Rufus, the Conqueror's son, in the last years of his own reign raised next to the Abbey Westminster Hall, the greatest hall in England and possibly in Europe.

The Great Hall was the central, and oldest, building of the rabbit-warren that the whole palace complex of Westminster later became. The official two-storey buildings that surrounded it, of dull stone on the outside, were full of colour on the inside – the Painted Chamber where King, Lords and Commons would always assemble to open a parliament, the high-timbered White Chamber for the Lords and the Council to meet in, and the very ancient upper and lower chambers where the *Court of the Exchequer*, which specialised in matters of taxation, heard and decided the disputes that came before the Chief Baron and his three puisne judges.

Edward III added a beautiful Council Chamber, the *Chambre des Etoiles*, or Star Chamber. His grandson Richard II lavished thousands of pounds on rebuilding and redecorating the Great Hall itself. Everywhere, on roof and walls alike, his favourite device was carved: the emblem of the White Hart.

The Great Hall at Westminster had from early days become the hub around which the whole legal world revolved. The *Court of King's Bench*, that decided disputes between the King and his subjects, was situated at the far end of the Great Hall on the right. Ambitious young lawyers hoped to win fame and promotion here, either as *attorneys* (the representatives of parties involved in a lawsuit) or as *pleaders at the Bar* – the wooden bar that kept the crowds of litigants from pressing too closely upon the Lord Chief Justice and his court.

Those *apprentices of the law* (students first at one of the numerous Inns of Chancery, then at the Inns of Court) who however, preferred fortune to fame, aimed at practising before the *Court of Common Pleas*, that was situated permanently just by the draughty great entrance doors on the north side of the Great Hall. The Court of Common Pleas was so called because it dealt with lawsuits – *pleas* – between subjects, commoners, in which the Crown was not involved but large sums of money habitually were.

Whereas however *utter* (outer) *barristers* could plead at the Bar in King's Bench or at any other court in the realm after only eight years of training and *special pleaders* (apprentices who had not been called to the Bar) could plead 'below the Bar', only *sergeants-at-law* could practise at the Court of Common Pleas. To qualify as a sergeant-at-law was a long and arduous business, involving sixteen to eighteen years more of study and, on installation, an expensive sergeant's feast. Only the most talented and most serious of the apprentices aspired to this rank.

A third court was situated at the far end of the Great Hall on the left, opposite the Court of King's Bench. This was, as it were, the interloper: the *Court of Chancery* presided over by the *Lord Chancellor* or in his absence by his assistant the *Master of the Rolls*.

The Chancellor had originally been the head of the King's secretariat, or *chancery*, and the *Great Seal*, which was in his charge, was simply the means of imposing the mark by which documents issuing from the royal secretariat could be recognised as genuine. (At certain times no Lord Chancellor was appointed; instead a *Lord Keeper* – Keeper of the Great Seal – , at a lesser salary and with lesser precedence, took his place and fulfilled his functions.)

Gradually the Chancellor's court had grown in importance. Disputes were settled there quickly according to the laws of the Church, canon law, and the principles of natural justice – *equity* – rather than according to the *common law of England* with its intricate precedents and procedures. Edward III enormously increased its scope when he decided that the Chancellors (and the Great Seal) should stay in England rather than follow the King about on his peregrinations. By his command the Chancellor was established on the marble throne in the Great Hall at Westminster – much to the disgust and dismay of the common-law judges.

By the time of Henry VIII the Lord Chancellors far exceeded in magnificence and display their rivals the Lord Chief Justices, the successors of the great Justiciars.

In time equity was to develop its own complexities, to become as costly and as long delayed as common law, and finally to merge with it. But in More and Wolsey's time those who had lawsuits to decide favoured the Court of Chancery. For their part the equity lawyers believed that they were administering real justice, using a system that contrasted utterly with the hideously complicated, desperately slow and horribly expensive procedures of the common law of the realm. It was Coke who three generations later led the counterattack with his combative reliance on learning, tradition, precedence and the letter of the law. The struggle between the two rival systems of thought continues, despite their formal merger, to this day.

The three courts – of King's Bench, Common Pleas and Chancery – sat every day from 8 to 11 in the morning. It is hard to visualise how the judges could have concentrated on their cases or their judgments, for the Great Hall was a noisy bustling place, full of comings and goings, at the very heart of the country's government and administration, thronged not only with visitors, members of parliament, court officials and judges, attorneys, apprentices, pleaders and sergeants but with litigants and their families, and with dozens of stalls selling paper, wax, writing materials and everything else that might be required.

Yet when the new Royal Courts of Justice were opened in the Strand by Queen Victoria on December 4 1882 and the Great Hall at Westminster, the scene of so many tense episodes, fearful decisions and outright melodramas, sank to its present status as a mere empty monument to the past, it was as if history itself had suffered a blow. Justice if more dignified, seemed both colder and more remote.

CRIMINAL TRIALS IN LONDON

Where the Old Bailey now stands, once stood a far more forbidding building: Newgate Prison, the principal prison of the walled City of London. Built in 1190, it was almost as old as the Tower itself. Wat Tyler broke it open in 1381. Almost exactly four hundred years later the Gordon rioters set fire to it and set free, as Wat Tyler had done, many of the prisoners. With garrets above, gallows outside, and dungeons below it was a brutal, barbarous place.

Yet till comparatively modern times imprisonment, even in such a prison as Newgate, was not considered a punishment in itself but merely a staging post on the road to a trial that would end either in acquittal, a money punishment, a moral punishment or an immediate physical punishment, such as death. Arrested by a constable, investigated by a magistrate, the prisoner would be held in prison simply till the time came for his trial.

Trials on serious charges – on allegations of *felony* – were considerably more complicated than they are now. In London the system, which was itself slightly more complicated than in other parts of the country, functioned like this: the two *Sheriffs* of London and Middlesex, who were themselves elected each year under the City Charter by the City burghers, would select a *Grand Jury*, twenty-three freeholders, in practice gentlemen of solid fortune. The Grand Jury, in the presence of the *Recorder of London* (a judge but, like the Sheriffs, elected to his office) would study the *Bill of Indictment* – the list of charges – but would hear only the case for the prosecution expounded. They would then withdraw to consider whether or not the prisoner should be sent to trial. If they found that there was no case to answer, they would write the single word *Ignoramus* (roughly 'we find no case') on the back of the Bill of Indictment and return it to the court; whereupon the prisoner would be released from Newgate. If on the other hand they found that there was a case to answer, they would *return a True Bill*, writing the words *Vera Billa* (True Bill) on the back of the Bill of Indictment and return it to the court.

The next stage, if and when a 'True Bill' had been found, was for the prisoner to be formally *arraigned* – charged and asked to plead. If he pleaded guilty, judgment was given. Many prisoners charged with felonies refused, however, to plead at all. As long as they refused to plead they could not be tried, though they would not be released. As long as they were not tried they could not be convicted as felons. As long as – but only as long as – they were not convicted as felons their goods and chattels were safe from confiscation by the Crown. If a prisoner remained mute, it had to be decided whether he was mute of malice or by visitation of God. If mute of malice, the *peine forte et dure* – pressing – was applied in the Press Yard at Newgate as a method of inducing the prisoner to plead.

If he then pleaded Not Guilty or had originally pleaded Not Guilty, he was asked by what mode of trial he would agree to be tried. 'By God and my country' was the traditional formula for his reply. The *petty jury* – the ordinary jury of modern times still often thought of as 'twelve good men and true' – was then sworn in; its role being to decide the question of guilt or innocence in the trial that followed.

The Grand Jury was restricted to certain cases only in 1933. It was finally abolished in 1948, though the system continues to exist and flourish to this day in the United States of America.

Preamble
The Climax of Treason 1603–1607

'Let judges also remember, that Solomon's throne was supported by lions on both sides. Let them be lions, but yet lions
under the throne: being circumspect they do not check or
oppose any points of sovereignty.'

Francis Bacon,
'Of Judicature',
Essays Civil and Moral

Francis Bacon became a judge himself and, paradoxically for a
man of his vast intellectual powers, practised the traditional
subservience to the throne that he had preached. By way of
contrast his rival Edward Coke won, half-justifiably, an eventual reputation as the most independent-minded judge in England's history. In the end Coke was the Lord Chief Justice who
set the pattern that judges now are assumed to follow: that of
the defenders of individual liberty in the face of the authorities,
of lions not under but against the throne.

It was not however, until his old age, till his professional
career had ended in apparent disgrace and he had ceased to be
Lord Chief Justice, that Coke finally abandoned circumspec-
tion. His early career, as these pages will show, was remarkable
even in an obsequious era for its lack of any sense of decency or
justice.

Almost invariably at this time future Lord Chief Justices rose
to their position in the same way – via election to the House of
Commons and there, in Parliament, via unquestioning subservience to the interests of the Crown. The path of promotion lay
from Solicitor General, the junior law officer, to Attorney
General, the senior law officer. From Attorney General, the
Crown's feared prosecutor, promotion, if it came at all, would
be almost automatically to the eminent position of Lord Chief
Justice, the Crown's most feared judge.

1

Jesuits, Treason and Plot

In the later plot-ridden years of Queen Elizabeth's reign Coke and Popham, two brutal and domineering men, formed as Attorney General and Lord Chief Justice a fearsomly efficient team. It was not their business to catch traitors; the Secretary of State, Walsingham, with his vast network of spies and informers did that. But once traitors were caught they dealt with them. They presided over the examination, which often took place on the Rack in the Tower; then Coke prosecuted the traitor, and Popham sentenced him – or her – to death.

It was, except for noblemen who were mercifully beheaded, a gruesome form of death that traitors suffered. They were not 'hanged by the neck until they were dead' in the famous phrase. They were strung up to be exposed to public view, and if cut down quickly by the 'topman' who sat aloft on the gibbet, they sometimes staggered to their feet and had to be tripped by the executioner or his assistant before the rest of the ghastly business could be carried out. Astoundingly, the wretched victims did not necessarily faint when slit open by the executioner's knife. Dr John Storey, who refused to acknowledge the Royal Supremacy, had to be held down by four men to be disembowelled even after his castration. The executioner of Richard White, a Catholic layman, 'having made a little hole in his belly pulled out of the same his bowels by piecemeal; the which device taking no good success he mangled his breast with a butcher's axe to the very chin most pitifully'. Thomas Pritchard, a seminary priest executed at Dorchester in the year before the Armada, had so wretched a butcher that, according to an eyewitness account, 'the priest raised himself and putting out his hands cast out his own bowels crying out "Miserere mei"'. To round off the disembowelling – the 'drawing' – the entrails were thrown into the fire and burnt, sometimes in front of the still-living victim. Then the heart was cut out 'leaping and panting' in the executioner's hands; and either thrown into the fire or placed in a boiling pan. Finally, before 'quartering', the executioner took an axe, cut off the victim's head and held it high. At this the watching crowd were expected to cheer and cry 'God Save The Queen!'. The head and quarters were parboiled before being publicly displayed.

Who were these traitors whom so grim an end awaited? Papists in the main. Under the continually strengthened Treason Acts 'for the utter extirpation of Popery' it was high treason merely to be a Jesuit or a seminary priest and enter or remain in the Queen's realm, or to assist or shelter such a priest. Still the priests continued to cross the Channel clandestinely from the seminary at Douai, though in the atmosphere of the time it meant almost certain arrest and death. The real antagonists whom the authorities most feared, however, were not the seminary priests but the élite of the exiles, the English members of the comparatively recently founded Society of Jesus, the Jesuits.

The first tiny two-man Jesuit mission had entered the country in 1580. It was quickly eliminated. The idealist Edmund Campion, who in his pre-Papist days had as Orator of the University once greeted the Queen in Oxford with a brilliant Latin speech, was betrayed, paraded through London, racked in the Tower, tried for high treason – with Popham, then Attorney General conducting the prosecution – and in November 1581 executed. His companion the swarthy, self-willed Robert Parsons, an unquiet spirit but a master of English prose, escaped – never to set foot in England again. He became, from abroad, the moving force behind many of the plots of the next few years.

In the summer of 1586 a second two-man Jesuit mission was dispatched from Rome; it was led by Henry Garnet, then aged thirty-one, who had joined the Jesuits eleven years earlier at the same time as Robert Parsons. Parsons was extremely worried at dispatching, as he put it, 'this meekest lamb to cruellest butchery'. With Garnet came the more imaginative Robert Southwell, a young man of the Norfolk gentry, aged only twenty-five. And later that year they were joined by a third famous Jesuit of the 'second wave', John Gerard, son of a Lancashire knight.

Topcliffe the priest-hunter trapped Southwell one Sunday in June 1592. He took him to his own house, next to Westminster's Gatethorne prison, and suspended him from the manacles. It was there that the astute hunchback Robert Cecil, son of the ageing Cecil and soon to succeed his father as the Queen's chief minister, visited him. 'They boast about the heroes of antiquity,' he told his colleagues on the Privy Council, 'but we have a new torture which it is not possible for a man to bear. And yet I have seen Robert Southwell hanging by it, still as a tree trunk, and none able to drag one word from his mouth.' Topcliffe repeated the torture at least ten times. 'It will be as though he were dancing a trick,' he had reported to the Council, 'or a figure at trenchmore'. 'God forgive me, Mr Topcliffe,' Southwell said to his torturer, 'but I do not think there can be another man like you in the whole world.'

Southwell was tried on February 20, 1595 at Westminster Hall, with Popham presiding and Coke constantly interrupting his attempts at defence. Topcliffe joined Coke as assistant prosecutor. The accused was of course found guilty and sentenced to the usual punishments. He was executed next day at Tyburn. Eyewitnesses noticed, however, that when he was cut down the executioner and his assistant did not, as was the usual practice, drag him but instead carried him courteously to the quartering block.

Only Henry Garnet, much shaken by his closest friend's execution, eluded them. Two years later Coke was examining in the Tower, shortly before his famous escape, the spirited John Gerard.

Coke: You say you have no wish to obstruct the government. Tell us then where Father Garnet is. He is the enemy of the state and you are bound to report on all such men.

Gerard: He isn't an enemy of the state. On the contrary I am certain that if he were given the opportunity to lay down his life for the Queen he would be glad of it. But I don't know where he lives and if I did I would not tell you.

Coke: Then we'll see to it that you tell us before you leave this place.

Gerard: Please God you won't.

'Then they pronounced a warrant for putting him to the rack.' But despite long hours of torture Gerard revealed nothing. That October he escaped from a window by rope, courteously leaving behind a note of explanation for the Lieutenant of the Tower. He was never recaptured. And astoundingly Henry Garnet, now Superior of the Jesuits in England, was never captured at all in the seventeen years he spent, constantly on the move, constantly in hiding and in disguise, in England in Queen Elizabeth's reign.

*   *   *

The old Queen died, 'easily, like a ripe apple from a tree', in the early hours of Thursday, March 14, 1603.

An era was over, a new era was about to begin. It began with a comparative calm and ease that surprised observers; and that did not last.

On the death of Elizabeth I the Council met at Richmond to proclaim James Stuart of Scotland King; but, estimating that there were 40,000 Catholics in London and fearing disturbances, called out the City's trained bands. The new King travelled slowly down from Scotland, pausing at York to confirm Robert Cecil in office as his chief minister, and at Burghley House to encounter the formidable Raleigh whose sneers at the Scots were only too well known. 'On my soul, mon,' he said, 'I have heard *rawly* of thee.' A fortnight later Raleigh was dismissed from his post as Captain of the Guard.

But there were no other disturbances of any sort. 'Great fears were but all are turned to greatest security; and a golden time we have of unexpected freedom abroad,' wrote Henry Garnet to Father Parsons. 'Great hope is of toleration and so general a consent of Catholics in the King's proclamation that it seemeth God will work much.'

From the first the Catholics in England expected great things from the son of Mary, Queen of Scots. What they wanted was an end to the Popham persecution, permission to practise their religion without being penalised and, in general, tolerance – if possible embodied in a Declaration. James, they knew, was a tolerant man. Had he not said, 'I acknowledge the Roman Church to be our Mother Church although defiled with some infirmities and corruptions'? The Catholic noblemen of the North had been in correspondence with him before his accession and believed they had his sympathy. The Pope in wise contrast to his predecessor had publicly declared that Catholics in England should be obedient to their kings. The Queen was unarguably a sympathiser. All over England the Catholic minority longed to hear that the new reign meant, in religious affairs, the start of a new policy.

'Truly the event proved contrary to all our hopes,' wrote John Gerard later. 'For first it was observed that after some weeks of being in England, he began to use far different speech of and against Catholics than was expected from the son of such a mother.' Disillusion set in as hope disappeared and the King's half-promises were abandoned. Among the most immediately disillusioned was a seminary priest, Father William Watson who had seen himself as the mouthpiece through which a Declaration of Tolerance would be announced. He devised a ludicrous plot to seize the King, detach him from Cecil and force from him the famous Declaration. Plots within plots were formed, involving among many others George Brooke, the dissolute brother of Raleigh's friend, Lord Cobham.

The Jesuits too became disastrously involved. They distrusted Father Watson who had earlier been an informer and, in order to give a solid proof of their loyalty to the authorities, arranged for information about the plot to be given to the Anglican Bishop of London. It was all a most unsavoury business. On July 12 two of George Brooke's fellow plotters were arrested. In understandable panic he appealed to his brother, at the time Lord Warden of the Cinque Ports, for a passport to enable him to flee to France, but on July 14 he was in his turn arrested.

A day or two later Sir Walter Raleigh went down to Windsor Castle to join the King and court for a hunting expedition. He was strolling on the Terrace when Robert Cecil took him aside. It was the King's wish, said Cecil, that Sir Walter should remain behind and answer certain questions that the Council wished to put to him.

Within a week Raleigh was in the Tower, charged with high treason in that 'he did conspire and go about to deprive the King of his government; to raise up sedition within the realm; to alter religion; to bring in the Romish Superstition and to procure foreign enemies to invade the kingdom.' Such were the charges against the leader of the war party, the man who had helped to singe the King of Spain's beard, Drake's friend, Cecil's enemy, a hero – as the people, with their traditional fickleness, soon began to feel – of the great epic just accomplished, the epic of Elizabeth of England.

That season, the plague drove the court down to Wilton House, the seat of the Herberts, for the summer and autumn, to indulge in hunting and in the equally exciting sport of treason trials. The great Raleigh was tried on November 17 at Wolvesey Castle in nearby Winchester before a tribunal presided over by the Lord Chief Justice, Sir John Popham.

John Popham

John Popham, Lord Chief Justice since June 2, 1592, 'a coarse

huge heavy ugly man' who in his youth had been 'as skilled a
man at sword and buckler as any in that age and wild in his
recreation' took his first major step towards his future position
at the age of forty by being elected to Parliament. He was the
sort of man around whom legends gathered. Born in Somerset,
he was educated at Balliol College, Oxford and from there went
on to a weird career in and around London, studying as an
apprentice of the law at the Middle Temple by day and mugging
passers-by, one of a large gang of highwaymen out on Shooters
Hill, by night. Marriage – or so the story continues – had been
his saving; at the age of thirty his wife persuaded him to reform.
Within ten years he had become not only M.P. for Bristol but,
successively, a special pleader under the Bar and a sergeant-at-
law with a profitable practice at the Court of Common Pleas – a
most successful lawyer. He used often to dine, even when he
became one of Queen Elizabeth's close advisers, with a slender,
delicate young man of no importance named Henry Garnet.
Garnet, a schoolmaster's son, worked at the time as 'corrector
of the press' for Tottel's, the greatest law printers of the day, at
Temple Bar.

It is infuriating that we do not know more about Popham's
character and true personality. There has never been, as far as I
know, any study of him published since Aubrey's *Brief Life*
which is very brief indeed. It is largely devoted to a very dubious
story about the manner in which Popham, as Lord Chief Justice,
acquired Littlecote House, a famous Elizabethan mansion near
Hungerford. He died there at the age of 72, drunken and in
debt, though he had £10,000 a year, the greatest income a judge
had yet acquired, and £6000 a year more from his wife, who
died shortly after him in much the same state. They were
childless. What could an apparent brute like Popham ever have
had in common with Garnet whose interests, outside religion
and the law, were music and mathematics?

'I well know this Popham is a cruel man of low extraction',
wrote in later years his old acquaintance Henry Garnet. 'The
felons he condemns to death tell him brazenly to his face that he
deserves the halter far more than they do, since he has been a
thief.' Popham became known as a hanging judge, very strict
about the 'neck verse' particularly in the case of highway
assaults and robberies as if to compensate for his own record.

Garnet was writing under the stress of emotion caused by the
Lord Chief Justice having condemned to death yet another
priest. But from the very first Popham was notorious for his
hatred of the Catholics. Shortly after his appointment one of

Walsingham's intelligence agents in Spain wrote to the Council: 'The recusants say they have but three enemies whom they fear: the Lord Chief Justice, Sir Robert Cecil and the Lord High Admiral.' To this list might well have been added the future Attorney General, a man who even more than Popham would merit the terms in which a Jesuit, shortly before being sentenced to death, described the Lord Chief Justice: 'a bloody man who lusts for the lives of Catholics.'

For the Attorney General, Edward Coke, was a monster. Domineering, bullying, utterly self-confident, the son of a Norfolk lawyer, he had shouldered his way up to the top of his profession by talent and hard work, by a particular legal triumph in Shelley's Case, and by his marriage to a great Norfolk heiress, Bridget Paston, who brought him no less than £30,000.

In the promotions that followed Popham's appointment as Lord Chief Justice Edward Coke became Solicitor General at almost exactly the same age as Popham had done, a little over forty and thereafter, like Popham, Speaker of the House of Commons. Two years later, in the spring of 1594, the post of Attorney General fell vacant. Francis Bacon, he of the 'delicate lively hazel eye . . . the eye of a viper', coveted the post. Though he was young – only thirty-three – he was brilliant, hard-working, smooth-tongued, a first cousin of the Cecils, and by nature obsequious. But it was Coke who was promoted to Attorney General. Bacon failed even to obtain the junior post, the Solicitorship. 'No man,' he wrote to his patron, Robert Devereux, Earl of Essex, 'ever had a more exquisite disgrace.' From this time onwards the lives of these two men, Coke and Bacon, were entangled, in professional, personal and political rivalry, almost to the grave.

Coke was not only a browbeating examiner and prosecutor but, in his personal life too, a ruthless man. Bacon, thanks to the publication of his *Essays* back in society's favour, was merely cold-blooded. He in 1598 was a bachelor; Coke a recent widower of middle age with a large family and a great fortune. They both put in a bid for the hand of a beautiful flighty capricious twenty-year-old, a very, very rich young widow, Lady Hatton. She was not only rich, she was well-connected – a granddaughter of old Cecil – and Coke broached the subject of marriage to young Cecil at the funeral of his father, less than a fortnight after he had buried his own wife, Bridget Paston. It was said that there were seven objections to Coke – his six children and himself. Bacon, as was his way, persuaded his patron Essex, the most popular man in England, to do his courting for him.

But perhaps Lady Hatton had read Bacon's cold-blooded *Essay of Love*. Perhaps she knew that this refined not-so-young man was, as Aubrey delicately puts it, a παιδεραστης (in plain English a pederast). Perhaps the brutal Coke wooed her more forcibly. Unfortunately we will never know precisely why but in the event she chose Coke, not Bacon. She married him clandestinely, without license or banns, in a private house on the evening of November 24.

A ludicrous episode followed. Coke was prosecuted in the ecclesiastical Court of the High Commission by Archbishop Whitgift, who had recently thundered against irregular marriages, and Coke had, ridiculously, to plead ignorance of the law and humbly submit before a dispensation was granted. Lady Hatton refused to call herself Mrs Coke (or Cook as she wrote it), too plebeian a name for her taste. What the marriage can have been like between this gay young widow, who enjoyed dancing, hawking, the company of poets and gallants, and the ageing ruthless energetic professional law officer, it is hard to imagine. They had a daughter, Frances, within the year – of whom more later.

The trial of Sir Walter Raleigh is one of the most notorious treason trials of England's history. It was presided over by the Lord Chief Justice, Sir John Popham, and a tribunal that included Raleigh's two greatest personal enemies, Robert Cecil and the venomous Henry Howard. The prosecution was conducted by the Attorney General, Edward Coke. It was Coke's brutality towards the accused, of which the following is a mere example, that has given the trial its notoriety.

Coke: Thou art a monster; thou hast an English face but a Spanish heart . . . thou art the most vile and execrate traitor that ever lived.

Raleigh: You speak indiscreetly, barbarously and uncivilly.

Coke: I want words sufficient to express thy viperous treasons.

Raleigh: I think you want words indeed, for you have spoken one thing half a dozen times.

Coke: Thou art an odious fellow; thy name is hateful to all the realm of England for thy pride.

Raleigh: It will go near to prove a measuring cast between you and me, Mr Attorney.

The 'thou'-ing of Sir Walter was an additional insult. 'All that he did was thy instigation, thou viper' hissed Coke at one point; 'for I *thou* thee, thou traitor.'

Yet for all this coarseness, Coke shook Raleigh only once. That was when he suddenly produced proof that Sir Walter had asked the Spanish Ambassador via his friend Lord Cobham for a yearly payment of £1500. 'Now, Raleigh,' cried Coke, 'if thou hast the grace, humble thyself to the King and confess thy treasons.' Raleigh could only answer that Cobham 'is a poor, silly, base, dishonourable soul.' The evidence was not utterly damning – even Sir John Hawkins had had a 'pension' from the Spaniards – but it was enough to turn the jury against him and to indicate his deviousness. Indeed there was probably more to the charge of treason than ever came out: for certainly Cobham had dreamt of placing on the throne, with Spanish help, Lady Arabella Stuart, daughter of Charles Darnley, the King's uncle.

There was no evidence, however, in any sense that we would understand it now, against Raleigh, merely gossip, hearsay evidence, the confession of confederates. As he himself pointed out, there should by law have been two witnesses to treason; there was only one, Cobham, and even then Raleigh was not allowed to be confronted with Cobham. He argued the point with the Lord Chief Justice.

Raleigh: Yet by your favour, my Lord, the trial of fact at the common law is by jury and witnesses.
Popham: No! The trial at the common law is by *examination*. If three conspire a treason and they all confess it, here is never a witness, and yet they may all be condemned of treason.
Raleigh: I know not, my Lord, how you conceive the law; but if you affirm it, it must be a law for all posterity.
Popham: Nay, we do not conceive the law. We know the law.

With this supreme example of judicial arrogance Sir Walter's trial drew towards its end. The jury were out only a quarter of an hour before returning with a verdict of guilty.

Lord Cobham and two fellow conspirators, Lord Grey and Sir Griffin Markham, were also tried and found guilty. On December 10, all three were led out to die, the first major executions of the reign. Sir Griffin was led out first: he mounted the scaffold and was praying before the axe descended, when suddenly the sheriff of Hampshire, Sir Benjamin Tichborne, stood him down, telling him that he had two hours' respite in which to meditate. He was taken back into Arthur's Hall in the

Castle. Lord Grey in his turn was led out, totally unaware of what had happened. He made an impassioned speech from the scaffold, claiming that he was no traitor. Before the axe descended, the sheriff again interrupted the proceedings to tell Lord Grey that it had been ordered that Lord Cobham should die first. Lord Grey joined Sir Griffin in Arthur's Hall. Lord Cobham was brought out. Then Tichborne sent for the other two prisoners to join him on the scaffold. The cat-and-mouse game lasted only a few moments before, to the delighted cheers of the crowd, the sheriff announced that their merciful Prince had granted the condemned men their lives.

It was entirely James' own doing. He had consulted nobody, informed nobody except the Scots page he had sent from Wilton to Winchester who had arrived almost too late to get through to Sir Benjamin. Raleigh had been watching this farce that might so easily have turned to tragedy from the window of his cell in the Castle. He too had his sentence commuted to imprisonment, though in less melodramatic a form, and joined Lords Grey and Cobham in the Tower for an indefinite imprisonment, consigned to a sort of limbo that was to last twelve long years. He was fifty-one. His much-loved estate of Sherborne Castle was forfeited. James presented it to his new Scots favourite, Robert Ker.

The plot that now loomed was real and deadly; its title was to become a synonym for treason long after the details were forgotten; had it succeeded, and it very nearly did, it would have been the most dramatic single incident in England's history. King, Prince, Commons, Bishops, Judges, the whole top echelon of the ruling class would have been eliminated. This, the climax of treason, is still remembered every Fifth of November as the Gunpowder Plot.

Its leading figure was not the man with whose name the Gunpowder Plot is always associated, Guy Fawkes, but Robert Catesby. He was aged thirty-one, a gentleman and a Papist, and a born leader. What everybody associated with him agreed on was his enormous charm. Sir Everard Digby, another exceptionally attractive and powerful young man, admitted afterwards that he had joined the plot for 'the friendship and love he bore to Catesby' for whose sake 'he was content to hazard himself and his estate.' These estates were not few: they extended over Rutland, Leicestershire and Lincolnshire. What made this devotion all the more extraordinary was that Sir Everard had no grievances at all.

The initial group were obscure men: John and Christopher Wright, soldierly brothers from York, Thomas Winter of Huddington, a relative of Catesby, and Thomas Percy, a distant kinsman of the greatest of the Catholic nobles of the North, the Percy Earl of Northumberland, who had certain connections at Court. It was the Wright brothers who brought in Guy Fawkes, a fellow Yorkshireman serving abroad as a soldier of fortune with a regiment of English recusant exiles under the command of Sir William Stanley. Christopher Wright crossed to Flanders and had Guy Fawkes commended to him as a most determined man.

It was the utter despair of the Catholics in England that threw up this little group of fanatics, determined to change the whole system at a blow. Popham had been reappointed to his position, Coke too. The existing penal laws against those refusing to attend the Anglican Communion Service, the 'recusants', were confirmed. There was nothing to be hoped for from the legal system; and still less to be expected, bar even more severe laws, more rigorously enforced, from Parliament.

While Parliament set about its work with a vengeance, Catesby summoned Thomas Percy and Guy Fawkes to a meeting in Clement's Inn. He first swore them to secrecy. Then he revealed the plot: to blow up Parliament when all assembled in the Painted Chamber, King, Lords and Commons alike, for the ceremonial meeting at the opening of the next session. Thomas Percy, as a courtier known in Westminster, was the key figure: he was to rent a house next door to the Palace of Westminster, a move which would be considered perfectly natural. Fawkes was to pose as Percy's servant, under the alias of Johnson. In fact he was to be, as it were, operational commander: to supervise the mining that would be necessary from the cellars of the rented house into the vaults of the Palace of Westminster.

In July, Parliament adjourned till the autumn of the year following. There was therefore plenty of time for the preparations to be made calmly and in slow stages. Percy hired a suitable house, and Fawkes installed himself. By December 11, 1604 the tools were all in, and 9000 pounds of gunpowder, in thirty-six barrels, was ready. Under Fawkes' direction the five conspirators started tunnelling. It was a more difficult job than they had expected, though; and it was with great relief that they learnt that a vault was available to rent directly under the Painted Chamber. That was in March 1605; by May all the gunpowder was in place, covered in iron bars, highly lethal at the moment of explosion, and hidden under piles of faggots. Not a rumour, not a breath of suspicion had leaked out. It seemed as if the plot could hardly fail. All that remained was to wait – five months of waiting.

Henry Garnet, the Superior of the Jesuits, had taken no notice of King James' early proclamation ordering all priests to leave the country. He was at the time, in the words of the warrant out for his arrest, 'of middling stature, full-faced, fat of body, of complexion fair, his forehead high on either side, with a little thin hair coming down upon the middest of the fore part of his head: the hair of his head and beard grisled. Of age between 50 and threescore. His beard on his cheeks cut close, and his gait upright and comely for a feeble man.' He lived as always a roving semi-clandestine life, usually based at White Webbs, outside London on the road to Ware, a house rented by Anne Vaux that could hide no less than fourteen priests.

That June 9 he saw Robert Catesby in London. In the course of their conversation Catesby started talking about the wars in Flanders and put a theoretical moral problem to the Jesuit: was it lawful to storm an enemy-held city even though innocent victims might be killed in an otherwise justified attack? Garnet took the question at its face value at first; but on thinking it over concluded that Catesby 'had some devise in his head'. Very worried, he wrote to the General of the Jesuits and received Claudio Aquaviva's reply, warning against 'any violent attempt whatsoever, especially at a time like this'. High-level negotiations were going on between Rome and London, diplomatic moves to ease the situation were afoot.

So far it seems that Father Garnet had no notion of what actually was in Catesby's mind, though he clearly knew that something was up, and, knowing Catesby, had guessed that it was bound to involve violence. On July 25, his ignorance was shattered. He was visited by another priest, Father Greenaway, who asked Father Garnet to hear his confession. This priest then told him all the details of the Gunpowder Plot which had been revealed to him, Father Greenaway, by Catesby, also under the Seal of Confession. The reason why Greenaway was confessing to Garnet was that he felt he had not done enough to hinder the plot – he had not been forcible enough in urging the young desperado to abandon it.

As Garnet declared later: 'Now I remained in the greatest perplexity that ever was in my life and could not sleep a-nights.' He knew the worst but there was little he could do. The Seal of Confession was absolutely inviolable – he could not even tax

Catesby with his knowledge. What he did do was to write urgently to Rome to ask the Pope to issue a Brief, in public, prohibiting any resort to violence by the Catholics in England, playing what John Gerard later described as 'the cooling card'. It was issued but it failed in its purpose; as it was bound to fail with such young fanatics.

The autumn was approaching. Catesby now had, inevitably, to widen the conspiracy, to plan the action to take once King, Lords and Commons – and the young Prince Henry, heir to the throne who would be with his father at the opening session of Parliament – had been blown to Kingdom Come. That summer he summoned three friends, three neighbouring landowners, to a meeting at White Webbs: Sir Everard Digby, Ambrose Rookwood and Francis Tresham. Sir Everard was to assemble the Catholic gentry of the Midlands at his seat, Dunchurch in Warwickshire, under pretext of a hunting expedition. The little Princess Elizabeth was living at Combe Abbey nearby, under Lord Harington's guardianship, and she – or her brother Prince Charles – was to be seized and proclaimed under a Regency. Sir William Stanley's regiment was to be brought over from Flanders, as the professional backbone of the *coup*. As with all conspiracies, though, the danger of betrayal grew enormously as soon as details began to be known or suspected outside the immediate nucleus of the original conspirators.

The young landowners at White Webbs had scruples only about their friends: the Members of the Commons whom they knew, and in particular the Catholic Lords. Could they not be warned? Catesby was forced to give way: they could *not* be warned directly but in the case of close friends or relatives obscure hints could be given. And so, on October 26, only ten days before the explosion was due, Francis Tresham wrote to his brother-in-law Lord Mounteagle. 'They shall receive,' the note said, 'a terrible blow this Parliament and yet they shall not see who hurts them. The danger is past as soon as you have burnt this letter.'

Mounteagle's true role is dubious; at any rate the letter was never burnt. That very evening it was in the Council's hands; and on November 3 it was shown to the alarmed and mystified King, a man after all whose own father had been blown up. On the evening of November 4 Thomas Howard, Earl of Suffolk, authorised a search of the whole complex of the Palace of Westminster, of all the buildings and vaults in that rabbit-warren.

The searchers noticed Guy Fawkes, an 'ill-favoured fellow'

guarding one of the vaults with a pile of faggots inside it. Fawkes left the vault to warn Thomas Percy that the plot appeared to be revealed and that the safe house should be evacuated. Then he came back to his post – a move which indicated a very determined man indeed.

Meanwhile, a stricter search was ordered, to be led by Sir Thomas Knyvett. He and his men were already in the vault, about to unearth the iron bars and the barrels, when Guy Fawkes returned. They arrested him at once, took him to the Council, they woke up the King, the Council met in the King's bedchamber at Whitehall – it was midnight, or thereabouts – and they all questioned him. But he would admit nothing. His name, he said, was Johnson. His purpose was to 'blow the Scots back again into Scotland'. He had no fellow conspirators. They seem to have been baffled by his composure, extraordinary in the circumstances in which he found himself. They called in the professional interrogators, Coke and Popham, and committed him to the Tower. 'The gentler tortures are to be first used unto him,' instructed King James, 'and so God speed your good work'. It was November 8 before he was broken on the Rack: even then he gave only the history of the plot, and named no names. He signed his confession with a trembling 'Guido Fawkes'.

Thanks to Fawkes' warning the conspirators knew by the morning of November 5 that they had failed. Catesby, Ambrose Rookwood, Thomas Percy, Thomas Winter and the Wright brothers rode via Dunchurch to the Catholic stronghold of Holbeach House on the Welsh border. There, on the night of Thursday, November 7, they were surrounded by the militia of Worcestershire. Ironically, an accidental explosion of their own gunpowder drove them out, wounded or maimed, and in a running fight Thomas Percy, the two Wright brothers and Catesby himself were killed. The others, and their servants were captured. So the moving figure behind the Gunpowder Plot was never brought to trial, and his name has almost been forgotten.

They did not hold the trials until Parliament, hastily prorogued on November 9, had reassembled, in January 1606. Understandably, the penal statutes were at once reinforced. Catholics were to be excluded absolutely from both London and Westminster, Oaths of Allegiance and Supremacy and attendance at Anglican church services were to be enforced, on pain of ruinous fines. On November 15 the Council issued an immediate proclamation ordering the arrest of all Jesuits; and on the

23rd, after nearly twenty years of clandestine living in England, Henry Garnet was at long last caught. It was Cecil's greatest *coup*. When Garnet was escorted into London, and taken to the gatehouse at Westminster, crowds poured out to see him being brought in: the arch-Catholic, the arch-Jesuit, the arch-traitor. Cecil's policy now was to prove that Garnet's was the directing brain behind the Gunpowder Plot and so discredit, for ever, not just the little group of plotters but the Jesuits as an order, and with the Jesuits, Rome and the Pope. Every effort of government propaganda and every means of pressure was to be exerted to this end. The chief governmental instrument in the confrontation with the Superior of the Jesuits in England was to be, inevitably, the Crown's Attorney General, Edward Coke.

Meanwhile the trial of the captured conspirators was to be held. There were eight of them. They were tried in Westminster Hall, by tribunal, on January 17. The facts alone would have been enough to damn the accused this time; instead, as always with Coke, it was ranting oratory. The prisoners had been 'most primarily seduced, abased, corrupted and Jesuited.' The Attorney General 'never yet knew a treason without a Romish priest'. Gunpowder itself had been invented by 'a friar – one of the Romish rabble'. It was an enormously lengthy speech.

While the jury for the seven who pleaded not guilty retired, Sir Everard Digby, who alone pleaded guilty, was brought in. He was strikingly dignified and clear; he admitted his crime, explained the motive, asked for pardon for his family, and beheading for himself.

To this Coke replied, 'that he must not look to the King to be honoured in the manner of his death . . . but that he was rather to admire the great moderation and mercy of the King in that, for so exorbitant a crime, no new torture answerable thereto was devised to be inflicted on him.' This paragon of English legal virtue then continued that, as for his wife and children, 'he should have his desire, as it is in the Psalms: Let his wife be a widow, and his children vagabonds; let his posterity be destroyed, and in the next generation let his name be quite put out.'

Digby and three others died first, executed at St Paul's churchyard on January 30. Sir Everard was cut down quickly, and was conscious during his castration and disembowelling. Next day, Friday, January 31, the remainder were executed in Palace Yard, at the entrance to the Palace of Westminster that they had so nearly blown up. Guy Fawkes, very weak and ill, was the last to die. By jumping forward at the last moment he broke his neck at once – unlike the man before him who had tried the same gesture. In his case, however, it had been the rope that had broken and the man, Keyes, totally alive, had been, as the justice of England prescribed, butchered.

On every Fifth of November thereafter the judges would close business at Westminster Hall and process to the Abbey to hear a Gunpowder sermon. Until the year 1859, a special prayer for the day was included in the Anglican Service. 'Lord, who didst this day discover the snares of death that were laid by Popish treachery', ran the thanksgiving, 'in a most barbarous and savage manner beyond the examples of former ages, scatter our enemies that delight in blood.'

Coke confronted Father Garnet. For six weeks, from February 13, date of the first examination before the Privy Council, to March 26 when the trial was held, the Attorney General tried to outwit and outmanoeuvre the Superior of the Jesuits. At first, it was all politeness and 'Mr Garnet'. Next it was the threat of no trial at all, merely an Attainder, an act of legislative murder which Parliament to its credit refused. Then it was trickery – eavesdroppers in the Tower to listen in to Garnet's conversations with Oldcorne, a fellow Jesuit; and finally, on March 7, torture and bluff. Told by Coke that Oldcorne had implicated him in the Gunpowder Plot, Garnet wrote an anguished letter to the Privy Council explaining the perplexities that the Seal of Confession had aroused. Between this 'confession' – which the King scrutinised, approved and refused to allow to be used – and the trial, Garnet was four times examined and five times made to write answers to sets of theological interrogations framed by the King. On March 24, the Lord Chief Justice, Popham, went to the Tower to threaten Garnet with the Rack the second time.

'What if I confessed nothing in my next torture, must I be tortured again? This was against the course of the common law. But they said no, not in the case of treason.'

Two days later, at Garnet's trial in the Guildhall, Coke masked the worries of the government with his habitual heavy-mouthed invective.

'He hath many gifts and endowments of nature, by art learned, a good linguist, and by profession a Jesuit and a Superior as indeed he is Superior to all his predecessors in devilish treason, a Doctor of Dissimulation, Deposing of Princes, Disposing of Kingdoms, daunting and deterring of subjects and Destruction.'

'I protest,' replied Garnet with accurate moderation, 'I am clear from approving and much more from fathering either this or any other treasonable attempts.'

The jury was out for fifteen minutes before returning a verdict of guilty. The King was dissatisfied both with the conduct and the result of the trial, and held up the execution for five weeks. It was not until May 3 that Garnet was hanged in St Paul's Churchyard. Spectators paid twelve pence each for standing room only. When the hangman slit open the trunk and, reaching out to grasp the beating heart, proclaimed: 'Behold the heart of a traitor', there was no applause. The bloody persecution of Catholics by the courts was – almost – over.

Part I
The Age of Upheaval 1607–1688

Sir Thomas Fleming
Sir Edward Coke
Sir Henry Montagu
Sir James Ley, Bt
Sir Ranulph Crewe
Sir Nicholas Hyde
Sir Thomas Richardson
Sir John Brampston
Sir Robert Heath
    Henry Rolle
    John Glynne
Sir Richard Newdigate
Sir Robert Foster
Sir Robert Hyde
Sir John Kelyng
Sir Matthew Hale
Sir Richard Raynsford
Sir William Scroggs
Sir Francis Pemberton
Sir Edmund Saunders
    George (Lord) Jeffreys
Sir Edward Herbert
Sir Robert Wright

The Tudor period had marked the stabilisation of the position of the Lord Chief Justices. Though theoretically the judges, including the Lord Chief Justice, could still be dismissed at the monarch's nod, in practice under the Tudors they had become more likely to remain in office until death. Dismissal was not, except in extraordinary circumstances, conventional or indeed acceptable.

By contrast the next eighty years saw almost as many Lord Chief Justices take office as the previous 150 years, and almost the same number – twenty-three – as have existed in the three centuries since, from the Glorious Revolution of 1688 up to the present day. Plots, trials, arrests, imprisonments, fortunes made, offices lost, families shattered, loyalties betrayed – the age of upheaval seems a mild enough title for the eighty years of struggle for power between the four Stuart Kings and their Parliaments.

In that struggle the Kings attempted to use the Lord Chief Justices, and the judicial system in general, as a potent instrument of political control. They were not always successful. The Lord Chief Justices too often came from precisely the same background, the class of the self-confident bourgeoisie and gentry, that was challenging the royal power. If they were too moderate or if indeed they veered towards the opposition, they were dismissed. Hence the high rate of dismissals – almost half – and the triumphant demand at the Glorious Revolution, that judges should be secure in office, that they should not be liable to be turned out at the whim of a King or a government. On the other hand if the King failed, then his loyal Lord Chief Justices came to a poor end: like Charles I's last Lord Chief Justice, Heath, who fled the country and died in impoverished exile, like James II's last Lord Chief Justice, Wright, who perished miserably in Newgate Gaol. Their consolation for these perils was, as always, power and riches; riches, which were usually won before or after their holding of office, clearly less than power. But Parliament on its side held a countermanding power: the Lord Chief Justices might on the King's instructions try and condemn to death. Parliament could on the instructions of its own members also try and condemn to death:

if not by impeachment then by attainder; and if by neither, then by such dubiously legal methods as setting up its own High Court of Justice to try the monarch himself. 'Justice' was by no means unevenly balanced in the Stuart period. Furthermore, even if the King normally controlled the judges, the opposition often controlled the juries.

In this fearsome power struggle where the penalties for failure were, legally, so often the loss of liberty, of possessions and of life, the Civil War itself seems to be merely an episode, and from one point of view a less melodramatic period than the final titanic ten years of the conflict, that saw six Lord Chief Justices follow one another in swift succession, including the most notorious of all time, Jeffreys. Rolle and Glynne, the two Chief Justices of the Commonwealth, were, by comparison to so many others, mild, reasonable and successful men, both retiring gracefully and wisely after several years in office, neither the object of much opprobrium, hatred or scorn. It is one of the paradoxes of this period that possibly the three most famous Lord Chief Justices of all time, Coke, Scroggs and Jeffreys each held that position for so short a time: for three years, three years and two years respectively. It is another of the paradoxes of the period, and the least easily explicable of all, that Coke, who by rights should have been the worst of the three and the greatest disgrace to the office of any judge in our legal history, should have, instead, donned the cap of the angels.

2

Coke Uneasy

Sir John Popham ended his term of office as Lord Chief Justice in the traditional way, by death. He died on June 10, 1607. He was not succeeded by Edward Coke. The fearsome pair who had worked so well in tandem against the Popish enemies of the Crown had already split up before Popham's death. There had been a vacancy at the head of the Court of Common Pleas and Coke, always greedy for money, had moved to that most lucrative court.

Thomas Fleming

The post went to Thomas Fleming, who shifted sideways from his position at the head of the third common-law court, the Exchequer. As Chief Baron he had sat in at the Gunpowder Trials where he 'looked wise and said nothing'. His talent was not great; the best they could say of him was that 'though slow, he was sure'. He had been considered 'too ungenteel' in his day to become Speaker of the House of Commons and had broken down in the one speech he delivered there. He was in fact a nonentity – and as such a welcome change after Popham. He stayed on as Lord Chief Justice for six uneventful years till he too died in office. In Westminster Hall he was completely overshadowed by his vigorous, forceful colleague. For as Chief Justice of Common Pleas Coke increased both his reputation and his already vast fortune. He devoted both his energy, which was formidable, and his legal erudition, which was immense, no longer to political prosecutions but to civil lawsuits.

Raleigh's imprisonment, meanwhile, was not harsh. He lived

in the upper storey of the Bloody Tower with his wife Bess and his son. He was befriended and often visited by the heir to the throne, the young Prince Henry. 'Who but my father,' said the Prince indignantly, 'would keep such a bird in the cage?' Sir Walter bought and borrowed books freely, he conducted his chemical experiments in a 'still house' in the Tower garden, he condensed fresh water from salt, he invented his Great Elixir and, encouraged by the Prince, he began his *History of the World*. His greatest anguish was caused by the forefeiture of his beautiful estate, Sherborne Castle, which the King had bestowed on his Scots favourite, Robert Ker. Prince Henry begged his father for it, intending to restore it to Sir Walter. But then in the autumn of 1612 Prince Henry fell ill suddenly and, despite frantic attempts to save him, despite the Great Elixir hastily administered, died. There were, inevitably, suspicions of poisoning. With the Prince's death all Raleigh's hopes of release and restoration to favour were dashed. But he had at least one consolation: that of being in a privileged position to observe the melodrama that followed, a conflict that pitted against each other two of his most detested enemies, Coke and Ker – and, indirectly, covered in ridicule the son of his dead rival, Essex. For the focus of that melodrama was the Tower.

The wretched Robert Devereux, third and last Earl of Essex, son and heir of Raleigh's rival and supplanter in the late Queen's favours, had been married, most unfortunately for him, at the age of fourteen to a little vixen two years his junior, a daughter of the Howard clan, Lady Frances Howard. He was a very different sort of man from his flamboyant father – punctilious, retiring and (according to his young wife) impotent. This was at least what Frances told her father and her great uncle, the most influential of the Howards, and this is what they, and other commissioners, by a majority of seven to five, publicly adjudged on September 25, 1613 when they pronounced the marriage void. Three months later Frances in great style, her hair flowing loose like a virgin's, celebrated by marrying none other than the King's arrogant favourite Robert Ker, long her lover.

One man, however, had, unwisely for himself, tried to prevent the wedding. This was Sir Thomas Overbury, poet and barrister, previously the favourite's chief friend and adviser in England. Six months before the annulment and remarriage he was shifted to the Tower. Probably Robert Ker merely wanted his embarrassingly forthright friend out of the way for a few months; but Frances Howard, displeased at being judged suitable for a mistress but not for a wife, wanted him out of the way for ever. She arranged with her great uncle, Thomas Howard, Earl of Suffolk, for the Governor of the Tower to be dismissed and replaced by a Howard nominee: Sir Gervase Helwys. Then she arranged for the Master of the Armoury, Sir Thomas Monson, to provide Overbury with an attendant, Weston. Then, very kindly, she sent in tarts and jellies to the prisoner and arranged for Weston to supply him with medicines from the apothecary. At 7 a.m. on September 15, ten days before the annulment hearings, Sir Thomas Overbury fell ill and died. An inquest was at once held by the Governor in the Tower, and at 3 p.m. the same day death from natural causes was diagnosed, and the corpse buried in the Tower precinct. Not a whisper of suspicion clouded the wedding festivities that followed so soon after. The King and the Queen graced the wedding with their presence, and all went merrily for the nineteen-year-old murderess.

Edward Coke

Thomas Fleming had died before the annulment. After various intrigues by Bacon, who had now fawned his agreeable way into James' favour, on October 25, 1613 – two months before the wedding – Coke was appointed Lord Chief Justice. Bacon became his right-hand man as Attorney General; not a combination that was destined to be anything like as smooth or successful as the combination of Popham and Coke had been.

Coke first came, indirectly, into conflict with the Governor of the Tower, Sir Gervase Helwys, in the case of the Reverend Edward Peacham, a Somerset clergyman of radical views who had dared to libel the bishops and criticise the King. James was furious: early in 1615 he issued a warrant for the torture treatment of the manacles to be used and for Peacham to be examined in the Tower 'before torture, in torture, between tortures, after torture'. Sir Gervase Helwys applied the torture willingly. The Lord Chief Justice and the Attorney General disputed not only the value of evidence under torture but the whole question of whether notes for sermons or pamphlets could in themselves be treason – a very different tune from the one Coke had sung when he had himself been Attorney General and was prosecuting Papists.

In the summer of that same year, 1615, whisperings began at long last to be voiced in public about the curious circumstances of Sir Thomas Overbury's death. This was largely because Robert Ker's star was fading. The previous November an extraordinarily attractive young page had put in his appearance at Court; and, as cupbearer, had caught the eye of the ageing King. James was eager enough to get rid of his previous favourite when that summer the truth started coming out. Warrants for the arrest of seven concerned, including the Governor and the two principals, were issued.

> The King had a loathsome way of lolling his arms about his favourites' necks and kissing them, and in this posture the messenger found the King with Somerset [Ker], saying *When shall I see thee again?* When he was arrested by Sir Edward's warrant, Ker exclaimed that never such an affront was offered to a peer of England in the presence of the King. *Nay, Man!* said the King, *If Coke sends for me, I must go*; and when he was gone, *Now the Devil go with thee*, said the King, *for I will never see thy face more.*
>
> About three in the afternoon the Chief Justice came to Royston, and so soon as he had seen the King, the King told him that he was acquainted with the most wicked murder by Somerset and his wife that was ever perpetrated upon Sir Thomas Overbury, and that they made him a pimp to carry on their bawdry and murder: and therefore commanded the Chief Justice with all the scrutiny possible to search into the bottom of the conspiracy and to spare no man, how great soever, concluding: *God's curse be upon you and yours if you spare any of them; and God's curse be upon me and mine if I pardon any one of them.*

Coke was in his element. He presided at the Guildhall over the five trials of the commoners involved, and he personally examined over three hundred witnesses, mainly before the actual trials. For ten months the trials dominated all else in London. 'I desire God,' said Coke, 'that this precedent of Overbury might be an example and a terror against this horrible crime and therefore it might be called *The Great Oyer of Poisoning*.' It was. At Gervase Helwys' trial the Lord Chief Justice confronted the deposed Governor of the Tower with a letter he had wrung from Franklin, the apothecary, that morning. Helwys was hanged. Franklin was hanged. Mistress Ann Turner, the go-between, was treated to a memorable summing-up – 'Thou hast the seven deadly sins, for thou art a whore, a bawd, a sorcerer, a witch, a papist, a felon and a murderer' – and hanged. But Sir Thomas Monson's trial was halted after Coke had made an unguarded remark, implying publicly what had only been whispered privately, foul play and even poisoning close to the Throne: 'God knows what became of that sweet babe, Prince Henry, but I know somewhat.' And when it came, in May 1616, to the trials of the two principals before their peers in Westminster Hall, the Attorney General, Bacon, did not press too hard. Frances Howard pleaded guilty and was sentenced to death; Robert Ker stood undaunted but was found guilty and also sentenced to death. The King had been at Greenwich all day, refusing dinner and supper, sending messengers to meet every boat that came from Westminster to Tower Wharf. Despite his bold words to Coke he pardoned them both. Coke had, unlike the more tactful Attorney General, antagonised powerful interests. But it was not merely the Lord Chief Justice's actions that displeased the King; it was the Lord Chief Justice's character.

For Coke was a cantankerous man. King James could not stand it, nor could his son King Charles, nor could Coke's great rival Francis Bacon, nor indeed could his wife, Lady Hatton. All through the memoirs, the diaries, the correspondence of the period runs that same note: Coke's cantankerousness. Yet all his enemies, all perhaps except for his wife, seem to have had a certain grudging respect for him: for his immense energy and learning, for his earnestness, for what one commentator has well called his 'grim pedantry'. It was not that he was a particularly great or even just judge, it was not that he could not be cowed, it was not that his personality was appealing. But he stood – and everybody recognised it – in a very special way for the common law of England. 'The monarch is the law, *Rex est lex loquens*, the King is the law speaking,' said Lord Chancellor Ellesmere. In a more profound sense Coke was the common law speaking: crabbed, inaccurate, often unjust, but free from flabbiness, and as embroidered by Coke's tongue, animated by Coke's emotion, passionately stirring. 'No man may be punished for his thoughts,' ruled Coke, 'for it hath been said in the Proverb, THOUGHT IS FREE.' 'When an Act of Parliament is against common right and reason,' ruled Coke even more controversially, 'the common law will control it and adjudge such Act to be void.' 'No appeal from the King's Bench,' ruled Coke recklessly, challenging the Lord Chancellor and the

Courts of Chancery, 'to any court except the High Court of Parliament.' 'The common law of England,' declared Bacon, 'is an old servant of the crown. The twelve judges of the land may be compared to the twelve lions supporting Solomon's throne.' Coke was having none of that. 'The King is under God and the law,' he ruled. This was hardly likely to appeal to a King who had declared that: 'The state of monarchy is the supremest thing upon earth. For Kings are not only God's lieutenants upon earth and sit upon God's throne, but even by God himself they are called Gods.' 'The common law,' Coke told James in Star Chamber, 'protecteth the King.' 'A traitorous speech,' cried James, 'the King protecteth the law, and not the law the King! The King maketh judges and bishops. If the judges interpret the law themselves and suffer none else to interpret, they may easily make, of the laws, shipmen's hose.'

Coke wrote afterwards in his *Report*:

> Then the King said that he thought the Law was founded upon Reason and that he and others had Reason as well as the Judges. To which it was answered by me, that true it was that God had endowed his Majesty with excellent science and great endowments of Nature. But his Majesty was not learned in the Laws of his Realm of England; and Causes . . . are not to be decided by Natural Reason but by the artificial Reason and Judgement of Law which requires long study and experience before that a man can attain to cognizance of it.

That was Coke's position, that was always Coke's position, and that was the position of the common lawyers, as opposed to chancery lawyers and the 'civilians': the law of England is fixed, detailed, definite, the product of tradition and precedent, has nothing to do with the concept of an overriding 'Natural Justice' and can only be interpreted by the judges; or, in the ultimate resort, by Parliament acting as a High Court. Kings and commoners alike are subject to it. 'With which,' adds the *Report* 'the King was greatly offended, and said then he should be under the Law, which was treason to affirm (as he said).'

What Coke does not go on to report, but what a letter-writer of the time does, is how their confrontation ended: 'After which his Majesty fell in to the high indignation as the like was never known in him, looking and speaking fiercely with bended fist, offering to strike him, & c. which the Lord Coke perceiving fell flat on all fours, humbly beseeching his Majesty to take compassion on him and to pardon him if he thought zeal had gone beyond his duty and allegiance.'

How different from the picture of James telling his erstwhile favourite that if Coke sends for the King, even the King must go. The truth seems to be that James got on very well with Coke when they were tête-a-tête but could not bear his contradicting him in public, particularly when it was a question – as it almost invariably was – of the opposing Scots and English views of the King's powers: the prerogative absolute, in the lawyer's jargon of the time, versus the prerogative ordinary. Coke was continually on the offensive: against the encroachments of other courts, especially the ecclesiastical Court of High Commission – his altercations with the Archbishops were even more ferocious than his confrontations with the King – against Ellesmere, the greatest enemy of the common law that century, against the royal desire to create new offences by proclamation, against in a word anything that might leave the common law in a lower position than that which he thought it merited: the position of supremacy in the state. He did not win all his battles: far from it. But even Bacon, who had a totally different concept of the law, who was much more polished and elegant both as a writer and as a person, could not wholeheartedly oppose him. 'He felt towards Coke,' wrote Macaulay, 'as much malevolence as it was in his nature to feel towards anybody.' Yet Bacon's attitude towards the older man was more complex than Macaulay suggests: to his face he seems to have been silkily courteous or silkily discourteous, as the occasion demanded and as indeed is inevitable when an Attorney General has to work with a Lord Chief Justice despite a long history of personal antagonism. But behind Coke's back Bacon never seems to have sneered. Rather the contrary. 'Never a man's person and his place,' said Bacon generously, 'were better met in a business than my Lord Coke and my Lord Chief Justice on the cause of Overbury.'

Because Coke's private papers have almost all been lost or deliberately destroyed, we know more of Bacon's reaction to Coke than vice versa. At the age of thirty-six Bacon had won a fame that still endures with his short, pithy Essays. Ten years later, in 1607, a great speech in favour of the Union with Scotland had won him James' favour and set him on a glittering path of political and legal success. He married a rich City merchant's daughter and escaped – at last – from debt. His books, popular and learned, appeared at intervals. He had the quickest and most flexible brain in England, if not in Europe: all learning was his province. When in 1613 the then Lord Chief Justice died he had at first aspired to the post himself. On the evening of Fleming's death Bacon, at the time Solicitor General, the junior law officer of the Crown, sent his letter off.

'It may please your excellent Majesty. Having understood of the death of the Lord Chief Justice, I do grant in all humbleness on assured hope that your Majesty will not think of any other but your poor servants, your attorney (Hobart) and your solicitor (Bacon) for that place. Else we shall be like Noah's dove, not knowing where to rest our foot.'

But within hours he had hit on a better plan. The post of Attorney General 'worth honestly £6000 a year' for himself, and the post of the Lord Chief Justice for Coke. He penned an epistle to the King headed: 'Reasons why it should be exceeding much for his Majesty's service to remove the Lord Coke from the place he now holdeth to be Chief Justice of England, and the Attorney (Hobart) to succeed him and the Solicitor (Bacon) to succeed the Attorney.'

It was a skilful and long memorandum. It worked – though according to another letter-writer 'the Lord Coke doth so stickle and fence by all the means he can make, not to remove, as being loth, he says, to be brought out of a court of law, which is his element, and out of his profit.' In other words Coke knew that he would make far more money if allowed to continue as Chief Justice of Common Pleas; and at the same time feared that, as Bacon had planned, he might be forced to 'turn obsequious' in his new post as Lord Chief Justice of King's Bench. After the appointments were made, he met Bacon in Westminster Hall.

'Mr Attorney,' said Coke angrily, 'this is all your doing. It is you that have made this great stir!'

'Ah my Lord,' replied Bacon, unruffled, 'your Lordship all this while hath grown in breadth. You must now grow in height, or else you would be a monster!'

Like so many of Bacon's intrigues, this move did not work out as well as he had hoped. Coke's promotion to Lord Chief Justice was all his doing; Coke's removal three years later was almost all his doing. The other eleven judges of the common-law courts usually – though not invariably – 'turned obsequious' when pressed. Coke would not. In June 1616, after the Overbury trials, matters came to a head with the Case of Commendams and James' unprecedented appearance as a royal judge on the long vacant throne in Star Chamber. 'Kings are proper judges,' declared James, 'and judgement properly belongs to them from God, for Kings sit on the throne of God, and thence all judgement is derived.' This was too much for

Coke, and his colleagues. 'I was a little plain with my Lord Coke in these matters,' wrote Bacon to James, 'I said he could never profit too much in knowing himself and his duty.' Despite Bacon's 'plainness' all twelve judges drafted a letter of protest to the King. They were summoned to face Lord Chancellor Ellesmere, Mr Attorney Bacon, and the King himself in Whitehall. James tore their letter to pieces. All twelve judges fell on their knees and asked pardon. But from his knees Coke, and Coke alone, declared *That when the case should be, he would do that which should be fit for a judge to do.*

On June 30 Coke was suspended from his place on the Privy Council and from the public exercise of his duties as Lord Chief Justice. The alleged reasons were frivolous. 'Amongst other things the King is not well pleased with the title of the book wherein he entitled himself Lord Chief Justice of England whereas he could challenge no more than Lord Chief Justice of the King's Bench.' More seriously, he was given the summer vacation, 'while he hath time to live privately and dispose himself at home,' to review his *Reports* 'wherein, as his Majesty is informed, be many extravagant and exorbitant opinions set down and published for good and positive law.'

His Majesty was by no means misinformed. Coke's *Reports*, eleven volumes of them, had been published over the previous fifteen years. They covered the forty years of Coke's legal life, setting out (in law French, with the pleadings of counsel on both sides in Latin) virtually all the cases with which he had been concerned, or at which he had sat in. They were not *Reports* in the strictly factual sense, but educational models: taking each case as the basis for a mini-treatise on the points of law involved. They were not always accurate; the authorities cited did not necessarily bear out the decisions given, *obiter dicta* were taken as judicial maxims, and even the judgments themselves were sometimes wrongly reported. As late as Blackstone's time, all the same, it was considered that the *Reports* had an 'intrinsic authority in the courts of justice', so vast was Coke's legal reputation. Their great merit, despite all the pedantry, despite the weaving of Coke's own opinions into what were superficially objective studies, was that they existed, that they brought the practice and theory of case-law together in a way none of the previous dry law-books had ever done. 'To every man his due,' as Bacon told the King, 'had it not been for Sir Edward Coke's *Reports* . . . the law by this time had been almost like a ship without ballast.' To give Bacon his due, that was a generous comment.

Yet it was Coke's failure to find anything wrong with his own writings bar trivialities that was at least the pretext for his definite dismissal. At the beginning of October he reappeared from Stoke Pogis and, as Bacon put it, 'offered his Majesty only five animadversions, being rather a scorn that a satisfaction to his Majesty; 'whereof one was that in the Prince's case he had found out the French status which was *filz aisne*, whereas the Latin was *primogenitus*; and so the Prince is Duke of Cornwall in French, and not Duke of Cornwall in Latin . . . and such other stuff; not falling upon any of those things which he could not but know were offensive.'

On November 10 James announced Lord Chief Justice Coke's removal from the bench for his 'perpetual turbulent carriage', and three days later Bacon with feelings of triumph that we can only imagine sent this note to the King:

'May it please your excellent Majesty. I send your Majesty a form of discharge for my Lord Coke from his place of Chief Justice of your Bench.

'I send also a warrant to the Lord Chancellor for making forth a writ for a new Chief Justice, leaving a blank for the name to be subscribed by your Majesty.'

On November 15 Coke was formally removed, receiving the news, it was said, with dejection and tears.

Yet before the end of the year an anonymous open letter to Coke appeared, candidly critical but helpful, almost certainly written by Bacon. In discourse Coke delighted to speak too much, and did not listen enough to other men. He conversed with books and not with his fellow men, who are the best books. His bitter tongue bred him many enemies. He was too much given to vain glory, to making the law lean to his own opinion, and to love of money. In the Overbury trials and in the dispute with the Courts of Chancery his intentions were good but he had shown a want of discretion. The letter-writer, having closely observed and commented, fairly enough, upon Coke's faults, proceeded to give him some not unfriendly advice. Let him bend to those in power, 'make friends of the unrighteous mammon', so that he might be enabled to carry on more vigorously his war against injustice – and against the papists. That counsel certainly has the Bacon touch and, in its final point, the Bacon subtlety about it. But it is the letter of a student of human nature, not of a malevolent enemy of Coke's. A complicated relationship, indeed.

Henry Montagu

Upon Coke's dismissal Sergeant Montagu, Bacon's right-hand man at the *Great Oyer of Poisoning,* 'a perfectful gentleman', good-looking, idle, the grandson of a former Lord Justice, was installed in his place. On the day of his installation he rode out from London to Westminster escorted by fifty cavaliers, 'besides the whole fry of the Middle Temple'. The ageing, ill Lord Chancellor Ellesmere administered the oath of office. 'Remember also,' he said with spite, 'the removing and putting down of your late predecessor and by whom: the great King of Great Britain.'

Sir Walter Raleigh, meanwhile, had been quietly released from the Bloody Tower during the *Great Oyer.* Frances Howard, who had grown hysterical when threatened with being locked in Sir Thomas Overbury's cell, was given his rooms instead. The old adventurer was now sixty-four; for years he had been intriguing for his release, luring James with Elizabethan visions of the mountain of gold he had once discovered up the Orinoco. Cecil, the little hunchback, had damped down any enthusiasm the King might have felt; but Cecil was dead, and the swiftly rising favourite George Villiers was almost as impressed by Raleigh as that 'sweet babe' the dead Prince of Wales had been. Raleigh set sail from Plymouth with a squadron of fourteen ships on June 12, 1617.

He was back a year later. It had been a disastrous expedition. His elder son, young Walter, had been killed. His chief captain Kemys had committed suicide. No gold had been found. The ships had been lost. Worst of all, against express instructions from the King, and express though insincere guarantees from himself, Spaniards had been killed. The Spanish minister to the Court of St James, Gondomar, demanded that James keep his promise; that Raleigh and his followers should be surrendered to Spain and hanged in the public square of Madrid.

James, to his credit, angrily denied the promise and refused the gesture. But he appointed a commission of five under Bacon, now Lord Chancellor, to investigate the whole affair. Coke was brought out of retirement to assist in that commission. Repeatedly they examined Raleigh till, 'exasperated by the audacity of his lying, they came to the conclusion that there was not a single word of truth in his assertions; that his belief in the very existence of the mine was a mere fiction invented for the purpose of imposing upon his too credulous colleagues.'

James ordered Raleigh to be brought to trial. But there was a legal obstacle; a man attainted and already under sentence of death, as Raleigh had been since 1603, could not be legally condemned to death for a subsequent offence. On October 28, 1617 therefore he was brought up before the Lord Chief Justice. He argued that the Winchester sentence was discharged by his commission for the late voyage. He was told that 'unless he could produce an express pardon from the King, no argument he could use would be admissible.' This was Montagu's one major 'trial'. He conducted it fairly. But the only memorable words were those uttered by the Attorney General, Sir Henry Yelverton; a greater contrast to the phrases of the Attorney General in Sir Walter's previous trial could hardly be imagined.

'Sir Walter hath been a statesman,' he said, 'and a man who in regard of his parts and quality is to be pitied. He hath been a star at which the world hath gazed. But stars may fall, nay they must fall, when they trouble the sphere wherein they abide.'

Many came up from the West Country to see their old hero die. He made a quiet farewell speech on the scaffold. The King had ordered the penalty to be changed from hanging, drawing and quartering to a nobleman's death: beheading only. He had a long journey to take, he said, and must bid the company farewell. He felt the axe edge, saying, 'A sharp medicine but one to cure all diseases.' When it was suggested that he should face east in memory of Christ's rising he replied with the famous words that symbolised the *panache* of his whole life: 'So the heart be right it matters not how the head lie.' The headsman hesitated. 'Strike, man, strike,' were his last words. Bess Throckmorton, Lady Raleigh, took his head away in a red velvet bag and embalmed it. She cherished it for the remaining twenty-nine years of her life: a macabre touch but somehow suited to the life and death of this most extraordinary man.

James Ley, Ranulph Crewe, Nicholas Hyde

Henry Montagu bored with his post, and no doubt disgusted with the notion that he would only be remembered as Lord Chief Justice for dredging up a death sentence on a famous man passed fifteen years previously, made an offer for the post of Lord Treasurer. He went to Newmarket, paid £20,000 for the white wand of office – 'wood is very dear this year at Newmarket,' Bacon warned him – , bought Kimbolton Castle, and founded the ducal house of Manchester, himself progressing up the honours ladder first to Baron Kimbolton, then to Viscount Mandeville, finally to Earl of Manchester. His successor, Sir James Ley, a mediocre Devonian, had already bought for another £20,000, one of the first baronetcies – by private arrangement with the favourite George Villiers. In a sense he made a better bargain than Montagu: for Montagu only held the Lord Treasurer's post for a year, till he quarrelled with Villiers and was dismissed. At least Ley had bought a title that lasted a lifetime and descended to his son. He later added the Earldom of Marlborough to his baronetcy; by that time he had followed in his predecessor's footsteps and bought the Treasurership, which he held for four years, till James I died and Charles I came to the throne. Montagu had been promoted Lord Treasurer from Lord Chief Justice at the end of 1620; Ley, already 'a decrepit old man' when he had become Lord Chief Justice, was promoted at the end of 1624. Montagu had distinguished himself by sentencing Raleigh to death; Ley distinguished himself by sitting in judgment on both Bacon and Coke, far more illustrious lawyers than he would ever be. Understandably there was pressure after this pair for a lawyer's lawyer to be appointed. So on January 16, 1625 Sir Ranulph Crewe, a competent, thoroughly honest, failed politician (who had once tickled James' fancy by tracing his descent back to Cerdic, founder of Wessex, on the English side and almost to Noah on the Scots side) was appointed. This proved to have been a paternal mistake from the point of view of James' eldest son who succeeded three months later. Crewe opposed as illegal the forced loan of 1626 and so, on November 10 of that year, was dismissed. His fame, such as it is, rests on a memorable sonorous passage in his one great case, the Oxford Peerage suit between Robert de Vere, Heir Male to the Earldom, and Lord Willoughby de Eresby, Heir General.

'I suppose,' said the Lord Chief Justice, 'there is no man that hath any apprehension of gentry or nobleness but his affection stands to the continuance of a house so illustrious . . . And yet time hath his revolutions: there must be a period and an end to all temporal things – *finis rerum* – an end of names and dignities and whatsoever is terrene. And why not of De Vere? For where is Bohun? Where is Mowbray? Where is Mortimer? Nay, which is more and most of all, where is Plantagenet? They are entombed in the urns and sepulchres of mortality!'

Sir Ranulph's successor-designate, Sir John Davies, died within the month, and a cold creature of Villiers', a man 'of mean aspect', Sir Nicholas Hyde was, on February 6, 1626, appointed in his place. There was general indignation among lawyers at the appointment:

> Learned Coke, Court Montagu.
> The aged Lea, and honest Crew,
> Two prepared, two set aside,
> And then up starts Sir Nicholas Hyde.

And there was general satisfaction when he died in office, of gaol fever, on August 25, 1631. All his four predecessors survived him, Montagu indeed not dying till a few months after the outbreak of the Civil War. All four were undistinguished men. The real protagonist, even when out of office, of this whole period was undoubtedly Edward Coke.

3

Coke Triumphant

As Coke sank, at the age of sixty-five, into retirement and obscurity, Bacon's star rose ever higher. Within months of the Lord Chief Justice's dismissal, the ailing Ellesmere had died, and Bacon had become (on March 7, 1617) Lord Keeper, nine months later Lord Chancellor, and six months later still, Baron Verulam, a prelude to the title of Viscount St Albans. In town he occupied York House, his father's mansion on the bank of the Thames. In the country outside St Albans he lived in two near-palaces, a mile apart: Gorhambury and Verulam. A gentleman, he said, should have seats for summer and winter, as well as clothes. Verulam House, his own creation, decorated with tall figures of Jupiter and Apollo, was for summer use, the vast Gorhambury reserved for winter.

Not that Coke was by any means impoverished, either. From 1576 to 1616 he had been buying up property: beginning with his first few acres at Tittleshall Austens for £5 from Robert Austen, a yeoman: continuing with the estate of Pitsey from the Earl of Arundel for £1,260, the estate of Chippenham from Lord Burghley for £4,200, the estate of Elmham from Lord Cromwell for £6,200, the estate of Stoke Pogis from the Countess of Huntingdon for £4,000, the estate of Minster Lovell from the Earl of Bedford for £5,000, the estate of Wood Ditton from the Earl of Suffolk for £2,350, the estate of Huntingfield Hall from Lord Hunsdon for £4,500, and the estate of Donyatt in Somerset from the Earl of Pembroke for £4,200. And that is only the list of the major estates he bought from noblemen. According to a famous but probably apocry-phal anecdote when James desired his Lord Chief Justice to buy no more land, Coke petitioned – it was 1616 – to buy 'one more acre', and proceeded to add to his vast if scattered possessions his largest purchase yet, Castleacre bought for £8,000 from Thomas Cecil, Earl of Exeter.

He had of course, five surviving sons and two daughters by

his first marriage to Bridget Paston to provide for. He made a list of 'Precepts for the use of my children and their posterity'. Precept No. 16 read: 'Keep yourself within your circle and out of debt, for old Divines said that Debt went before deadly sin.' It was preaching to the wind, as far as his five sons went: Sir Robert, the eldest, his heir, had two 'great lists' of debts for his father's executors to pay, amounting to no less than £27,975 – and this despite the fact that he had married a great heiress and, to Coke's delight, a thorough aristocrat, Lady Theophila Berkeley of Berkeley Castle. The only one of his sons who was any use at all was the youngest of them all, 'Fighting Clem', born at Huntingfield in 1594, an M.P. in 1614, in 1620, and from 1625; who died in 1629, before his father, with debts of only £1,656.15.2.

His daughters turned out rather better. When Coke was dismissed he went rather than to his own home of Stoke Pogis, to stay with his eldest daughter, Anne Sadleir, at the great mansion of Standon Lordship in Hertfordshire. Certainly there was no question at the time of his going to stay with his wife at Hatton House. Lady Hatton – she still refused to call herself Elizabeth Coke – had stood by her husband when his career was in the balance, though they had long lived separate lives. But the collapse of his career brought about, as so often in marriage, the collapse of any remnants of affection that may have kept them together. Squabbles about property became acute. Coke had settled Stoke Pogis upon his wife and her issue in the event of his death, and she raided his house, 'embezzling all his silver plate and vessels', he complained to the Privy Council, and also giving him 'to his face or by letter these unfit words of false treacherous villain'. That was certainly paying the ex-Lord Chief Justice back in his own coin. Bacon, the distinguished Lord Chancellor, must have smiled at these antics of his discredited rival and been only too glad that Lady Hatton had resisted his own wooing so long ago. As for her Ladyship, she had a fine tale to tell the Privy Council on her side, about Sir Edward having 'broken into Hatton House and secured her coach and coach horses and even her apparel'. He 'and his fighting son Clement', she said, 'had threatened her servants so grievously that the men ran away to hide themselves.' It was a splendid performance. 'Divers said,' wrote Chamberlain the letter-writer, 'Burbage could not have acted better.'

After three months' wrangling their quarrel was settled; and Coke left Hertfordshire for London – and one daughter for another. He actually came to live at Hatton House, with the beautiful Frances, his daughter by Lady Hatton, and, incidentally, with Lady Hatton herself. Frances was almost fifteen, very affectionate, very charming, and very marriageable. George Villiers the generous still sweet-tempered favourite, Earl (soon to be Duke) of Buckingham, was in the full flush of his twenty-four-year-old beauty but not yet in the marrying game himself. However he was keen to please his strong-willed mother; he had a weak-minded elder brother, Sir John; and his mother thought young Frances Coke would be an ideal match – with £10,000 dowry, and £1,000 a year.

Coke objected, not apparently, because Frances might be miserable but because he thought the dowry too large and the annual payment unnecessary. As Coke sourly put it in the negotiations over his daughter's dowry, he 'would not buy the King's favour too dear, being so uncertain and valuable'.

This very remark, though, indicates that Coke appreciated the point of the whole manoeuvre: by marrying off Frances to John Villiers he would win not only George Villiers' favour but, far more important, gain the goodwill of the King again. In March 1617 the King set out for Scotland; he was to be away till September. By June Coke had come round, and agreed to the dowry. His old friend Sir Ralph Winwood, a Secretary of State, acted as a mediator with Buckingham. Coke, he wrote, longed to be restored to the royal favour 'without which he could no longer breathe'. As Lord Chancellor and virtual ruler of England in the King's absence across the Border, Bacon was alarmed. But what could he do? Nothing.

Lady Hatton, though, could and did. She suddenly conceived a hitherto unsuspected concern for her daughter's welfare. Coke had always had the habit of going to bed early at nine in the evening, and rising at three in the morning. Coke rose to find both his wife and daughter had flown to Oatlands, a house near Hampton Court, that Lady Hatton's cousins, Sir Edmund and Lady Withipole, had rented for the summer. He immediately applied to Secretary Winwood for a warrant to search Sir Edmund's house. Armed with the warrant and 'weaponed in violent manner', accompanied by his sixth son, fighting Clem, and about a dozen retainers, the ex-Lord Chief Justice galloped off to Oatlands and after a certain amount of shouting and parlaying announced that he was going to break in. If anyone resisted him and was killed, it would be justifiable homicide – there spoke the true common lawyer – for he had a legal warrant. But if any of his own retainers were killed, 'it would be Murder!' With a makeshift battering ram his men broke down the main entrance door to Oatlands, and tore mother and daughter apart. Coke sternly ordered Frances home to Stoke with him, and Clem set her up behind him, riding pillion, and galloped off into the night.

Lady Hatton was not the sort of wife to take all this calmly. She summoned her own kinsmen and retainers, harnessed her horses, and set off in pursuit, as in some Border ballad. But her coach stuck in a ditch, and the chase was abandoned. What next? Why, to the Lord Keeper's of course! Bacon had not been feeling well; he had gone early to bed in York House in the Strand, and his doorkeeper had strict orders not to allow him to be disturbed. But it would have taken more than a doorkeeper to keep an infuriated Cecil out. She 'rose up and bounced against my Lord Keeper's door, and waked him and affrighted him,' – poor Bacon, – only pacifying him by explaining that she was like a cow who had lost her calf.

The Privy Council heard all about it on Sunday, July 13, heard her 'complaining in somewhat a passionate and tragical manner'. On the Tuesday Coke was summoned up to the Council Chamber to answer a charge of 'riot and force'. So far from defending himself he passed at once over to the attack, bringing counter-charges against his wife 'for conveying away her daughter *clam et secrete*' and 'for plotting to surprise her daughter and take her away by force and for that purpose assembling a body of desperate fellows, whereof the consequences might have been dangerous'. The Lords of the Privy Council, fairly reasonably, considered this a case of the pot calling the kettle black: though perhaps they did not quite believe that Lady Hatton had already set out with an armed posse to attack Stoke Pogis. 'Some tall fellows' she later described them as, but in fact, it was a band of sixty horsemen armed with pistols. Actually Frances at that moment was also on the road, being escorted to her future mother-in-law's. Fortunately the two bands did not meet. 'If they had,' wrote a Londoner, 'there had been a notable skirmish, for there was Clem Coke, my Lord's fighting son, and they all swore they would die in the place before they would part with her.' What had begun as a somewhat ridiculous family quarrel now began to take on the aspects of a political *cause célèbre*, with Bacon seeing in it an opportunity to scotch, once and for all, Coke's chance of a comeback. Even before the Privy Council hearing, on the Saturday, he had written to Buckingham, who was with James in Scotland, advising against the whole marriage: against, that is, a marriage 'into a disgraced house' and 'into a troubled house of man and wife'. But once more Bacon had wrongly gauged the political winds. Coke also wrote to Buckingham, and James wrote to Winwood approving the marriage. The last blow in this battle by long-distance correspondence fell on Bacon.

Buckingham wrote back to him at the beginning of August,

My Lord

In this business of my brother's that you overtrouble yourself with, I understand from London by some of my friends that you have carried yourself with much scorn and neglect both towards myself and friends; which if it prove true I blame not you but myself, who ever was

Your Lordship's assured friend,
G. BUCKINGHAM

In Macaulay's words: 'Bacon's eyes were at once opened to his error and to all its possible consequences. He apologised submissively for his interference. He directed the Attorney General to stop the proceedings against Coke. He sent to tell Lady Coke that he could do nothing for her. He announced to both the families that he was desirous to promote the connection.' Having given these proofs of contrition he ventured to present himself before Buckingham. It is said that on two successive days Bacon repaired to Buckingham's house – that on two successive days he was suffered to remain in an antechamber among footboys, seated on an old wooden box, with the Great Seal of England at his side; that when at length he was admitted, he flung himself on the floor, kissed the favourite's feet and 'vowed never to rise again until he was forgiven.'

As for the principal parties in this affair, Sir John Villiers who had actually seen his future bride, was so struck that he vowed that he would take her penniless, even 'in her smock'. He did not have to: Lady Hatton doubled the dowry, to spite her husband. Frances, from under her father's roof, wrote a rather sweet and dutiful letter to her mother, 'hoping that conscience and the natural affection parents bear to children will let you do nothing but for my good, and that you may receive comfort, I being a mere child and not understanding the world or what is good for myself.'

'So I hardly take my leave,' she ended after a few words of faint praise for Sir John Villiers, 'praying that all things may be to everyone's contentment.

Your Ladyship's most obedient & humble daughter for ever,
Frances Coke
Dear Mother, believe there has been no violent means used to
me by word or deed.'

The wedding day was set for September 29, at Hampton
Court. King James gave Frances away. He sent for her mother
to attend all the same; but Lady Hatton sent back word that she
was sick. All the same, Coke did not trust his wife. He went to
Bacon, asked for a warrant for her arrest, which Bacon made
out at once, and had her comfortably confined in the City house
of Alderman Bennett.

Thus Coke was restored to favour. The day before the
wedding, on September 28, he took his seat at the Privy Council
again. There were rumours that he was going to be made a peer
but they came to nothing. He was morose, attending the
Council Chamber in his night-cap, exhausted by the quarrel
with his wife which continued long after the wedding, 'more
ambulant than current' in his own words, 'tossed up and down
like a tennis ball' in those of an observer. What was more
significant were the words with which, on September 28, James
greeted Coke on his return to the Council.

'I am neither a god nor an angel,' said the King rather
touchingly, 'but a man like any other, and confess to loving
those dear to me more than other men. You may be sure that I
love the Earl of Buckingham more than anyone else. Christ had
his John, and I have my George.'

Three years passed, years during which the ageing, gloomy
and underemployed Coke tried, with moderate enthusiasm, and
success, to make friends of the unrighteous mammon, as that
'anonymous' letter-writer had advised him. Then the Privy
Council advised the King to call a Parliament – the first for
many years. As a Privy Councillor Coke was returned, in
January 1621, for Liskeard in Cornwall 'by the King's com-
mandment'. Fighting Clem was elected for Dunwich. Coke
could hardly have guessed, at the time that the next eight years
of his life would be the most distinguished of all his career: that
he, the careerist lawyer, would in his seventies become the
champion of Parliament's rights against the Crown, the Parliament Man *par excellence*.

In January 1621 Lord Chancellor Bacon published the
Novum Organum. 'Every part of the book,' wrote Macaulay,
'blazes with wit but with wit which is employed only to
illustrate and decorate truth. No book ever made so great a
revolution in the mode of thinking, overthrew so many pre-

judices, introduced so many new opinions.' Coke would not have agreed with Macaulay. Bacon sent him a presentation copy as a courtesy. On the title page Coke wrote:
'It deserveth not to be read in Schooles.
But to be freighted in the ship of Fooles.'
'Perverse and testy' was how Macaulay described Coke, and without 'dignity of character'. Bacon's reputation and success, throughout England and Europe were at their height.

On January 30 Parliament met. 'I have piped to you, but you have not danced. I have often mourned but you have not lamented,' said James in his speech from the Throne. 'It may be it pleased God, seeing some vanity in me, to send back my words as spit in my face.' Coke as Chairman of the Committee of Grievances, as an M.P. of extraordinary prestige, who had first sat in the Elizabethan Parliament of the year following the Armada, swiftly became a leading figure, back in the limelight again, using that weapon whose public use had so long been denied him: his tongue. 'He that questions whether this House is a Court of Record' – that is, a Court with power to fine and imprison – 'I would his tongue might cleave to the roof of his mouth,' he declaimed.

The Lord Chancellor Bacon sat on the woolsack in the Lords, only slightly disturbed by the ever-growing attacks on patents of monopoly that had been granted to Buckingham's family and friends. Two of these, Sir Giles Mompesson and Sir Francis Michell, were impeached. Then on March 15, Sir Robert Philips, M.P. for Bath, rose to report that great abuses had been discovered. 'The person against whom these things are alleged is no less than the Lord Chancellor, a man so endowed with all parts, both of nature and art, as that I will say no more of him, being not able to say enough.' Very swiftly the charges of corruption, from a trickle, became a flood. Bacon took to his bed on Sunday March 18, and refused to see anybody. The charges increased from two to twenty-five. A special commission was set up to examine witnesses during the Easter Vacation. James refused to dissolve Parliament and save his Chancellor. On April 17 Parliament reassembled, and by April 30, after various pathetic attempts at evasion, Bacon pleaded guilty, by letter, to twenty-eight charges of corruption, 'and do renounce all defence, and put myself upon the grace and mercy of your Lordships'. 'My Lords,' he said to a deputation who came to make sure this unexpected, unlikely confession was genuine, 'it is my art, my hand, my heart. I beseech your Lordships to be merciful to a broken reed.'

'So strong was the contagion of good feeling,' wrote Macaulay, 'that even Sir Edward Coke for the first time in his life behaved like a gentleman.' The truth of the matter seems to have been that Bacon was extraordinarily careless about money; he had accepted presents of money, of gold, of plate, sometimes from both plaintiff and defendant in the same case, almost absent-mindedly.

At Gorhambury a visitor had seen one of his servants come into his study where he was writing, open a chest of drawers, stuff his pockets with money, and leave the room without saying a word. 'Sir,' said Bacon to his astonished and indignant guest who reported the incident, 'I cannot help myself.'

On May 3 the members of the House of Commons crowded into the Lords. Their speaker demanded in their name judgment against 'a corrupt Lord Chancellor'.

'I speak not because the Chancellor is in a cloud,' said Coke while judgment was pending, 'but according to the liberty of the subject. A corrupt judge is the grievance of grievances.' The Lord Chief Justice rose to pronounce sentence.

'The Lord Viscount St Albans,' said Ley, 'to pay a fine of £40,000. To be imprisoned in the Tower during the King's pleasure. To be for ever incapable to holding any public offices, place or employment in the common wealth. Never to sit in Parliament nor come within the verge of court.'

On May 9 Fighting Clem was also sent to the Tower by Parliament – for striking the M.P. for Hertfordshire, Charles Morrison, in Westminster Hall. 'God made bees and bees made honey,' – Charles Morrison was quoting an old rhyme – 'God made men and men made money . . .' How did it go on? 'The King makes judges – somewhat of asses and glasses – judges riding upon asses.' Clem took umbrage. Coke pleaded for his son, 'but cannot for weeping'. Clem was released from the Tower, as Bacon had been – after only one day.

But on December 27, 1621, just before Parliament was dissolved by an angry King, Coke himself was sent to the Tower; and unlike his rival, or his son, he was kept there, as he himself recorded it, for 'twenty-six weekes and five dayes'. Coke had mortally offended the King's sense of his own importance once again, and even more drastically than before. When the eight guards took him to the Tower, he found scrawled on the door of his cell, which had once been a kitchen, 'This room wants a Cook'. Grim humour, but no grimmer than he had exercised in his day upon his own victims. He was kept in close confinement, allowed no visitors or exercise.

The Earl Marshal, the Earl of Arundel, examined Coke in the Tower and threatened him with a charge of treason and with losing his head. It looked as if Coke was doomed at last. But his papers were searched in vain for any sign of disloyalty (though to his annoyance he lost many manuscripts of importance). There was a last attempt, in July to keep him in the Tower, despite the general pardon granted to all members of the last Parliament. Under it, the Attorney General Yelverton, also impeached, also sentenced by the Lord Chief Justice, had been pardoned. But no pardon could be granted to a man who had a lawsuit pending against him, so they drudged up an hoary affair: a Hatton heritage suit under which, it was alleged Coke owed the Crown £50,000. Yelverton demanded that not a sixpence be abated. Lord Chief Justice Ley sat in judgment in the Court of Wards, with his two senior colleagues, Chief Justice Hobard of Common Pleas and the Chief Baron of the Exchequer. But, to their credit, they cleared Coke. When he was released in August, James was half furious, half impressed.

'Throw this man where you will,' he said, 'and he falls upon his feet.'

'*Heu, fuge crudelem turrim, fuge litus amarum*
Omnia deterrent, horridus ille locus'
the old man had written with a coal in his Tower cell,
'*Det mihi nosse deus quae sint statu tempora turris*
Ut me habeat Godwick, parvula, villa Dei.'

But, though he was out of the 'Cruel Tower, that horrid place', he really had not the slightest intention of retiring to his godly little villa at Godwick, his first modest home. An untypical but understandable burst of sentimentality and bad verse, this. He soon pulled himself together. He scotched a proposal to ship him off to Ireland on a commission of enquiry by announcing, ominously, that 'he hoped to discover and rectify many abuses' there.

Before James' death he had see-sawed his way back into favour again by praising Buckingham's drastic plans for war with Spain. That was a proposal after his own heart. It was the 1624 Parliament, he was M.P. for Coventry, and he and Buckingham were working hand in glove – not only for war on the Spaniards whom Coke had always hated and who had just humiliated the favourite, but in launching a successful impeach-ment against the Lord Treasurer, Lionel Cranfield, a deeply unpopular City merchant, who had been one of Coke's bitterest enemies during his disgrace. Coke had his revenge, scathless. But James did not like it. 'By God,' he told the favourite, 'you are a fool. You are making a rod with which you will be scourged.' But Buckingham boasted that he was Parliament-proof. To his own son and heir James was even more explicit: Charles, he warned, would 'live to have his bellyful of impeachments'.

At Christmas the foolish-wise King James fell seriously ill, though he was only fifty-seven. He died on March 27 the following year, 1625. The new King, Charles I, was a year younger than the century. Buckingham, as much a favourite with the son as with the father, continued to direct policy.

For the next three years Buckingham as Lord High Admiral to all intents and purposes ruled England. The fleeting popularity that his own personal generosity and his defeat of Spain had aroused soon disappeared. Like many a would-be statesman before and after him, he was ruined by his attempts to impose a war-policy that he had not the skill to conduct nor the money to fight.

Coke was there, leading the Commons, in two of the three Parliaments whose criticisms the all-powerful Lord High Admiral had to face. In the first Parliament, at Oxford, in the summer of 1626, his attack was veiled.

'The office of Lord Admiral is the place of greatest trust and experience. The wisdom of Ancient times' – always Coke's favourite theme – 'was to put great men into places of great title but men of parts into such places as require experience.' A totally inaccurate, yet obviously pointed, aside misinformed the House that there had been no dukes in England between the Conquest and Edward III's time. Then and only then did Coke produce one of his unforgettably pithy phrases: 'It was never heard that Queen Elizabeth's navy did dance a pavane.'

Stung by the implication that his navy was basically ornamental, Buckingham attempted to re-singe the King of Spain's beard at Cadiz, and failed. In Charles' second Parliament, the following year, Buckingham was impeached – but saved by a dissolution before the Lords had time to pass a verdict on his guilt or innocence. Coke had been appointed High Sheriff of Buckinghamshire, a manoeuvre that effectively kept him out of that Parliament. But he was back again in the third Parliament of the reign, aged seventy-six, elected for both Suffolk and Buckinghamshire and taking his seat for the former in March 1628. Pym was there too, Hampden, and his cousin Oliver Cromwell. In the meantime Buckingham had master-minded yet another naval fiasco, this time off the French coast at the Ile de Re. Far more ominous than any naval defeat, however, was the attempt by the authorities to subvert one of the traditional freedoms of Englishmen. In the Case of the Five Knights, the Refusers (so-called because they had refused to pay the King's forced loan), the Lord Chief Justice, Sir Nicholas Hyde, and all eleven of his common-law colleagues had ruled that the King had the power to arrest and detain whomever he liked virtually at will, for no crime known to the law. All that was needed was a special mandate – a royal warrant.

'Shall I be made a tenant-of-will for my liberties, having property in my own house but not liberty in my person? There is no such tenure in all Littleton!' exclaimed Coke, rising in his own fashion to the occasion. 'I leave it as bare as Aesop's crow. It is a maxim, *The common law hath admeasured the King's prerogative*, that in no case can it prejudice the inheritance of the subjects. It is against law that men should be committed and no cause shown. I would not speak this but that I hope my gracious King will hear of it. Yet it is not I, Edward Coke, that speaks it, but the records that speak it.'

So that Parliament went on, one of the most memorable Parliaments England has ever seen, with its Propositions, its Declarations, its Remonstrances, its confrontations between Lords and Commons, with all Coke's great and increasingly outspoken speeches, with its first climax, his own brainchild, the Petition of Rights. Charles refused to pronounce the necessary formula, *Soit droit fait comme il est desiré*. He announced dissolution within the week and forbade the Commons to discuss or criticise the government.

'That black and doleful Thursday' there were, a newswriter reports, 'above an hundred weeping eyes' when the foiled Commons reassembled, uncertain if another Parliament would ever again be called. On June 8, Coke rose to make his last great speech.

'Now when there is such a downfall of the state, shall we hold our tongues? How shall we answer to God and man? Why may we not name those that are the cause of all our evils?' he proclaimed. 'Nothing grows to abuse but this House hath power to treat of it. What shall we do? Let us palliate no longer! If we do, God will not prosper us. Thus therefore, not knowing if I shall ever speak in this House again, I shall now speak freely. I think the Duke of Buckingham is the cause of our evils. And till the King be informed thereof, we shall never go out with honour or sit with honour here. That man is the grievance of grievances!'

'The Duke! The Duke! Tis he! Tis he!' cried the Commons;

'as when one good hound recovers the scent, the rest come in with a full cry, so they pursued it, and every one came on home, and laid the blame where they thought the fault was.'

On the Saturday the King with great charm pronounced the desired formula as if it had all been a mere misunderstanding. Bells rang and bonfires were lit. But most of the country was under a misapprehension: they imagined the Duke of Buckingham, now the most hated man in England, either had been, or was about to be, sent to the Tower and the scaffold. He had not; he was not. Charles himself forbade Buckingham's bold attempt to answer the Commons' remonstrance in person and placed him once more in charge of a proposed naval expedition, to relieve the Huguenot fortress of La Rochelle. But he never set out. He was stabbed to death in Portsmouth on August 23 by John Felton, a lone assassin intent on ridding his country of a tyrant and inspired by the charges in the Commons. So it can be said that Coke's last and most effective denunciation inspired murder: an extraordinary end to an ex-Lord Chief Justice's career, though there is a certain consistency in the fact that Coke went out as he had so long lived, on a death-dealing speech.

Parliament reassembled in January 1629. The King abruptly dissolved it and all understood that Parliament was never to meet again. Sir Nicholas Hyde, the Lord Chief Justice, played his part as required. Once Parliament was dissolved, offences committed in Parliament could be punished – provided Parliament was not, as Coke had argued, primarily a Court itself. Six M.P.s came before him, charged with seditious speeches. They all refused to plead, claiming parliamentary privilege. Hyde rejected their arguments and, servile instrument of a new supreme and absolutist monarch, sent them to the Tower.

But Coke was not one of those six M.P.s. He never took his seat in the January 1629 session, though he was summoned. His public career was over. He retired to Stoke, to the country but not to idleness. He had his *Institutes* to write, a vast schema in four parts covering the whole of English law: property law (*Coke on Littleton*: the only part published in his lifetime), statute law, criminal law and the system of courts. 'A work arduous,' Coke called it, 'and full of such difficulties as none can either feel or believe but he only which maketh trial of it.'(Students both in England and America, who for centuries had to wrestle with the convoluted pedantry of *Coke on Littleton* agreed.) 'And albeit it did often terrify me, yet it could not in the end make me desist from my purpose; so far hath the love and honour of my country, to pass through all labours, doubts and difficulties, prevailed with me.'

It terrified the King too, particularly reports of Coke's *Second Institute* and Coke's commentaries on *Magna Carta*. When Coke at long last was dying, the Privy Council sent men to ransack his study and library. They confiscated the manuscripts of all the *Institutes* and of the last two *Reports*, and it was not till Parliament controlled the capital in 1642 and 1644, that by order of Parliament these were published. For the non-specialist the *Third Institute*, on the criminal law, is the most fascinating of the four. On 'Brothel Houses and Bordelloes' (Chapter 98) – just to quote one eye-catching example – we are first informed that: 'The keeping of them is against the law of God, on which the common law of England in that case is grounded' and later – for all the chapters are little essays on the offences named – that 'before the reign of H.7 there were eighteen of these infamous houses, and H.7 for a time forbade them: but afterwards twelve only were permitted, and had figures painted on their walls, as a Boars Head, the Cross Keys, the Gun, the Castle, the Crane, the Cardinals Hat, the Bell, the Swan etc.' If Coke is right here, what a curious conclusion must be drawn by all who frequent the Bells, the Cross Keys or the Boar's Heads that still litter the country.

He dedicated all four Parts of his *Institute*, rather movingly, 'To my much honoured and beloved allies and friends of the country of Norfolk, my dear and native country; and to Suffolk, where I passed my middle age; and of Buckinghamshire, where in my old age I live.' Stoke House in Buckinghamshire was only twenty miles from London, a fine Elizabethan mansion set in a thousand acres.

'The 3 May, 1632,' the old man noted, 'riding in the morning at Stoke, between eight and nine o'clock to take the air, my horse under me had a strange tumble backwards and fell upon me (being above eighty years old) where my head lighted near to sharp stubbles, and the heavy horse upon me. And yet by the providence of Almighty God, though I was in the greatest danger, yet I had not the least hurt, nay, no hurts at all.'

It is probable, though not sure, that his daughter Frances looked after him in his old age. Her marriage to Sir John Villiers had been as unsuccessful as her mother's was to Coke. She had separated, had a bastard son by a Howard, been condemned for adultery, fined and condemned to do public penance. His wife

Lady Hatton certainly did not look after him. Age had not mellowed her. A year after his fall a rumour reached London that Coke was dead. She set out to take possession of Stoke House but much to her disappointment crossed one of his doctors at Colebrook with news that it was all a false alarm. Coke did not believe much in doctors. He had a disease, he told kind friends, that all the drugs of Asia, the gold of Africa, the silver of America, all the doctors of Europe could not cure: old age. In the margin of one of his books he scribbled another of his bad rhymes:

> If physic fail,
> For thy avail,
> Three Doctors you shall find,
> Doctor due diet,
> And Doctor quiet,
> And Doctor merry-mind.

By August 1634 it was clear he was dying. On September 1 Sir Francis Windeband came to Stoke with that Order of the Council already referred to to search for 'Seditious and dangerous Papers'. His chambers in the Temple were also searched and yielded *inter alia* 'a black buckram bag of the Powder Treason'. What a life it had been. On September 4, the then Master of the Rolls made the following entry in his diary:

'Died at his house at Stoke mine old friend and fellow Bencher, Sir Edward Coke, Knt., being Wednesday between eleven and twelve of the clock at night, in his bed quietly, like a lamb, without any groans or outward signs of sickness, but only spent by age.'

'We will never see his like again' was another, later comment, – 'Praise be to God.'

4

King's Men

For over ten years from 1629 to 1640 Charles I ruled England without calling a Parliament. These were his happiest years, his golden thirties, though in the legal struggles of that time were contained the seeds of the Civil War that was to follow. But Charles himself, at least by comparison to his father, was uninterested in the law. James I had been fascinated, technically, argumentatively, by both the principles involved and the details of cases. He had, as much by dogged tenacity as by the use of royal power, struggled against Coke's plan for the judges to become the ruling element in the State and finally scotched an idea that in any case had never had much appeal to the English people. He had reduced the judges, after Coke, to insignificance, though never to the extreme degree of subservience that had marked them in Elizabethan times. But, Charles' personal interest being more slight, his control was more sporadic and the results more confused. Probably it would be fair to describe six of the more famous legal figures of that decade as King's men: Bankes, Brampston, Finch, Heath, Noy and Richardson. As supporters of the King's policies, however, they wavered, never entirely reliable, though never outspokenly independent.

Of the six, Sir Robert Heath, Attorney General from 1625 to 1631, is the only one whose official career spanned the entire length of Charles I's reign, and beyond. There is a portrait of him in St John's College, Cambridge. It shows a stern, regular face marked out by penetrating eyes. He was a stern man. He and the Speaker for the 1629 Parliament, John Finch, a younger, vainer lawyer, violent in prejudice, worked together on the official investigation of Buckingham's murder. Felton, inevitably suspected of being the instrument of a plot though in fact he was a lone assassin, awaited with dread his official 'examination'.

It never came. The judges met at Sergeant's Inn – it was by this time becoming a recognised practice for the judges to meet, all twelve together, outside the courts to give a ruling on a point of law – and they laid it down that torture itself was illegal: 'The prisoner ought not to be tortured on the Rack, for no such punishment is known or allowed by our law.' Felton was of course executed but to the credit of the judges he was spared the savage examination the Attorney General and the Speaker wished. Since that ruling torture has never been used, legally at least, in England. One judge dominated his colleagues and forced that ruling through, the then Chief Justice of the Common Pleas, Sir Thomas Richardson. Though Buckingham's own nominee he was universally recognised as a decent man.

Thomas Richardson

Sir Nicholas Hyde, the Lord Chief Justice, died unlamented on August 25, 1631. Heath was the natural choice to succeed him. But Heath had a grave disadvantage. He was suspected of puritanism and had therefore incurred the mistrust of the man who became for the next ten years virtually the King's minister of the interior, Laud. Thomas Richardson may have been too slack for Laud's taste but he was at least an honest Anglican; and so, after months of official hesitation, Richardson was, on October 24, appointed Lord Chief Justice. Attorney General Heath moved up to Richardson's post as Chief Justice of Common Pleas; but his own post to the general surprise went not to ex-Speaker Finch but to a meritorious barrister who in the 1629 Parliament had taken the popular side, William Noy. It looked very much as if the moderates of the legal world had displaced the hard-liners.

All that was eventually changed by Laud, though it took him some time to achieve his aims. For a clergyman Laud understood better than most lawyers how to manipulate the legal system. Possibly he missed his vocation, he would have made a fearsome Lord Chief Justice himself. Laud was the son of a Reading clothier, a man of great natural energy, sharp and authoritarian, utterly fearless, determined to impose uniformity of worship on a divided realm and in this sure of the support of the King. To achieve this aim he made use of a 'prerogative' court that was not the preserve of the professional lawyers but where *inter alios* he himself could sit in judgment: the Star Chamber.

Up to this period Star Chamber had not been seen as an oppressive but, on the contrary, as an eminently sensible court. Compared to the dreadful intricacy, the enormous delays and expense and the totally unpredictable judgments of the common-law courts, Star Chamber was a haven of speed and light. The judges there were not professional judges but the ordinary members of the Privy Council – strengthened admittedly by the presence of the two Chief Justices, whose advice, though important, was not necessarily decisive. Even so great a lover of the common law as Coke had only words of praise for the Court of the Star Chamber: 'It is the most honourable court (our Parliament excepted) that is in the Christian world, both in respect of the judges of the court and of their honourable proceeding.' He wrote this at the end of his life, in the reign of Charles I; and if even Coke, even at that stage, could find no way in which this 'prerogative' court had infringed the liberties of the subject, we may be fairly sure there were none.

The procedure was that the Attorney General drew up a charge; for the Court of Star Chamber was a criminal court, dealing with offences against the Crown and in particular against the King's peace. So in February 1632 Attorney General Noy drew up a charge against a fellow barrister, Henry Sherfield, in a case that rapidly became celebrated. Henry Sherfield, a bencher of Lincoln's Inn, had broken a glass window in St Edmund's Church, Salisbury, a city of which he was himself at the time Recorder. The window was in the Recorder's view heretical, not a true picture of the Creation 'for that' – among many other inaccuracies – 'it contained divers forms of little old men in blue and red coats, and naked in the head, feet and hands.' The indignant Sherfield demolished these unjustified addenda to Genesis with his pikestaff, thereby arousing the wrath of the Anglican clergy who had no desire at all to see self-righteous Puritan laymen rampaging through their churches as Christ had cleansed the Temple. But though Bishop Laud was all in favour of a harsh deterrent sentence, in this particular case the professional lawyers – Noy as prosecutor, Richardson and Heath as judges – carried the day. Sherfield was only fined – although the fine, at £500, was twice as heavy as the sympathetic Heath had proposed.

Very different was the savage punishment inflicted on the next member of Lincoln's Inn to be hailed before Star Chamber.

'The Cato of his Age' they called William Prynne, the great Puritan pamphleteer. Not that one could describe *Histriomastrix*, which he published in November 1632, as a pamphlet: it was 1000 pages long. What Coke had been to the common law, Prynne, an Oriel man, was to the moral law: he listed offences and he described them in vivid and unflattering detail. Drinking healths was sinful, long hair in men was 'unseemly and unlawful for Christians', music and dancing and hunting were sinful, but most sinful of all were plays and sinfullest of the most sinful, female actresses. By way of counterblast the Inns of Court promoted the following January a splendid pageant stage-managed by ex-Speaker Finch, that danced its way from Chancery Lane to Whitehall, where the Queen, the enchanting Frenchwoman Henrietta Maria, herself acted a role in the performance of a masque, *Shepherd's Paradise*. Fresh thunderbolts from Prynne. Attorney General Noy indicted him before Star Chamber.

Laud was by this time Archbishop of Canterbury, and hence more powerful and even more determined to use that power to stem the rising Puritan tide that had now dared to attack the Royal Family. Noy, supported by Finch, showed far greater zeal in the prosecution. Prynne was first sent to the Tower for a year; then on February 17, 1634, he came back to Star Chamber for sentencing. In Star Chamber (unlike at treason trials) the accused were allowed counsel; and on Prynne's behalf one of his counsel made a formal apology. 'For the manner of his writing he is heartily sorry, that his style is so bitter, and his imputations so unlimited and general.' It did him no good. He was sentenced to be imprisoned during life, to be fined £5000, to be disbarred, to be deprived of his degree by Oxford University, and even worse. The procedure for giving judgment in Star Chamber was that each of the many judges was asked in turn for his opinion. 'I would have him branded in the forehead, slit in the nose, and his ears cropt too,' proposed the Royalist Lord Dorset. The Court did not go quite as far as that but they did condemn Prynne to be pilloried and to lose both his ears in the pillory. This time, to their shame, both Chief Justices acquiesced.

As for Noy, the Attorney General had gone to extremes that even the Archbishop disapproved of, in his demands for Prynne's punishment. When Noy died that August, Puritans everywhere felt it to be God's punishment. A more obvious earthly casualty was Heath. Though he had concurred in the savage sentence against Prynne, he was suspected of half-heartedness and removed from office. But Finch as a reward for his role in the prosecution was appointed Chief Justice of Common Pleas in Heath's place. That left the post of Attorney General vacant. A brilliant, grave lawyer Sir John Bankes was appointed in Noy's place. Though only forty-six, Bankes was rich enough next year to buy Corfe Castle and a vast tract of Dorset from Coke's widow, Lady Hatton. He 'exceeds Bacon in eloquence, Ellesmere in judgment, and Noy in law', it was said. Sir John Bankes was to prove almost the most faithful of all the King's legal men.

As for the Lord Chief Justice, even the mild Richardson had had his back put up by the Archbishop's constant encroachments. He was scolded by Laud before the Privy Council for interfering with the Somerset wakes. On leaving the Chamber the Lord Chief Justice declared that he had been 'almost choked by a pair of lawn sleeves'. It was his last noteworthy remark. He died in office on February 4, 1635.

In view of Noy's death, of the recent promotions of Bankes and Finch, and of Heath's dismissal, there was a certain difficulty in finding a suitable successor. Noy's best pupil Matthew Hale, a future Lord Chief Justice, known at the time as 'young Noy' and considered far more brilliant than his master, was too young. At this stage King Charles needed a man who was both subservient and yet respected. He picked a fifty-two-year-old Essex lawyer, half a Noy protégé, half a Parliament man.

John Brampston

'Now the judges interpret the law and what judges can be made to do we all know,' wrote the parliamentary lawyer, John Selden who had suffered at their hands. At first for Charles, desperate for money at this stage, all went, judicially speaking, very well. The new Lord Chief Justice and the other eleven common-law judges met at Sergeant's Inn, Chief Justice Finch of Common Pleas dominated their debates. Under his influence they all answered – and signed – 'yes' to the two following, famous questions:

'1. Whether, in cases of danger to the good and safety of the

Kingdom, the King may not impose ship-money for its defence and safeguard, and by law compel payment from those who refuse?

2. Whether the King be not the sole judge both of the danger and when and how it can be prevented?'

That was in February 1637. John Hampden, a rich Buckinghamshire landowner and a Parliament man, refused however to pay what would in fact have become a new and general land tax levied by the King without consent of Parliament, and took the case to the courts. It was heard by the Court of Exchequer, as all taxation cases inevitably were. But, recognising the importance of this test case, the Chief Baron and his three colleagues called in the eight other common-law judges to help them decide. Attorney General Bankes argued for three days in favour of the King's prerogative; and in a rambling judgment Chief Justice Finch of Common Pleas supported this view and carried the majority of the judges – seven out of the twelve – with him. But three totally disagreed; and two disagreed on technical grounds, these two being, most significantly, the Chief Baron and the Lord Chief Justice, Brampston himself. The King should have seen this divided judgment as a warning; instead, and foolishly, he treated it as a triumph.

The judgment in Hampden's case was given on June 12, 1637. Two days later Prynne was up for sentencing before Star Chamber again. Even from the Tower he had continued to pour forth some of the 200-odd books and pamphlets which he produced in his lifetime, attacking the bishops both in general and in particular, and citing his persecutor Noy's sudden death as a kind of warning in *God's Judgment upon Sabbath-breakers*. They sentenced him once more, Lord Chief Justice Brampston concurring, to imprisonment for life, and to a fine of £5000. But Chief Justice Finch of Common Pleas went further in savagery. He pointed out that some stumps of Prynne's ears were left and proposed to his colleagues that these should be cut off and also that Prynne should be branded on the cheeks with the letters S.L. signifying 'Seditious Libeller'. It was done; but the reaction in the country to this judge-inspired cruelty and indeed to the judge-granted economic triumph of the King can be imagined.

Shortly after Prynne's trial a young man of twenty-three, an apprentice clothier named John Lilburne, was brought before Star Chamber on a charge of printing and circulating Prynne's *News from Ipswich*. On April 18, 1638 he was whipped from the Fleet to Palace Yard, pilloried, and, as he refused to remain silent, gagged; then imprisoned and treated with great barbarity.

But legal and judicial injustice, however oppressive, would never have provoked Englishmen to civil war. It needed the collapse of the government's prestige and the threat of a military dictatorship to do so. 'Black Tom Tyrant' – Thomas Wentworth, Viscount Strafford – became the man all decent men hated and feared, even more than Archbishop Laud with whom he worked closely. He was ruthless enough to have used the common law – always a flexible instrument in the hands of the ruthless – as the means of imposing on the English an absolutist monarchy. When the reaction came it came swiftly, and the parliamentarians proved as shockingly ruthless in their use of the legal system as the King's men had previously been.

The Long Parliament met on November 3, 1640; and the storm broke. One of its very first acts was to order the release of John Lilburne – and indeed of William Prynne. The sentences against Prynne were voted to be illegal, his degree and his membership of Lincoln's Inn were restored, and on November 28 he rode triumphantly through the City. This was Parliament acting in the role Coke had claimed for it, that of the highest court in the land, able to overrule all other courts. At the same time it was acting in Coke's phrase as a 'court of record' – a court with the right to sentence and punish. Three days earlier Strafford had been impeached.

The charge against him was vague: that he had endeavoured 'to subvert the fundamental laws and government . . . and to introduce an arbitary and tyrannical government against law'. But Strafford was only the first of many. Finch, Lord Keeper since the preceding January, was impeached mainly on charges connected with his role in Hampden's Case, appeared before the Bar of the Lords to deliver an impassioned plea in his own defence, but then fled out of the country. The Secretary of State, Sir Francis Windebank, fled before appearing. Then the Lord Chief Justice himself, Brampston, was impeached with five of the other judges – though charged only with 'high crimes and misdemeanours' and allowed to continue in office. He and his colleagues were however effectively muzzled – bound over for £10,000 each to attend Parliament from day to day until such time as the dates for their trials might be fixed. Then on December 18 Archbishop Laud himself was impeached, like Strafford on a charge of treason for 'endeavouring to subvert the fundamental laws . . . and alter religion by law established'.

Like Strafford, the Archbishop was removed to the Tower. Thus within weeks of Parliament meeting the King was deprived of all his most experienced and loyal ministers, the two most eminent imprisoned, others fled abroad, others – the judges – skilfully terrorised. It left Charles politically naked and legally rudderless.

Strafford's trial opened in Westminster Hall, specially cleared for the occasion, on March 22 the following year. It swiftly became clear – for he defended himself vigorously – that the case against him was legally feeble and that there was a probability of his being acquitted by the Lords. So the parliamentary ultras – against the advice of both Pym and Hampden – determined to abandon even the pretence of a fair trial and switched to the procedure for legislative murder. On April 21 a Bill of Attainder against Strafford was given its third reading in the Commons by 204 votes to 59. Under the pressure of mob violence the wretched Charles signed what then became the Act of Attainder; and on May 12, 1641 'Black Tom' was beheaded on Tower Hill before the largest crowd ever gathered to watch a public execution, estimated at 200,000. Archbishop Laud, who was to remain in prison for three years and then suffer exactly the same form of murder after the same abandonment of the process of impeachment, tried to bless the victim from his window in the Tower but, uncharacteristically, fainted.

Legal civil war was now being waged to an extent never previously known in England since the days of the Lords Ordainer. By the opening of the year 1642 matters had come to a crisis. It was feared that Parliament would impeach the Queen; and Charles decided on a pre-emptive strike. He attempted to turn their own weapons against his parliamentary enemies. On January 3 he sent the Attorney General Sir Edward Herbert to the House of Lords to impeach five members of the Commons including Pym and Hampden and one member of the Lords, on the same vague charges of subverting the fundamental laws. At the same time he sent his sergeant-at-arms to the Commons to arrest the members charged. That failed. Next day the King rode down with a large escort of swordsmen to arrest the five members in person only to find in his own words that 'all the birds are flown'. That second ignominious failure ruined what was left of the royal prestige. A few days later Charles I left London, with a handful of followers only, riding north to York.

Sir John Bankes had, a year before the crisis in the capital, been appointed Chief Justice of Common Pleas in Finch's place;

and Sir Robert Heath at the same time had been restored, mildly, to favour as a puisne judge of King's Bench. The King found Mr Justice Heath already at York, on circuit, a loyalist despite his puritanism. Bankes eventually followed his royal master north but Brampston did not. When the King raised the royal standard at Nottingham on August 12, 1642 and the Civil War officially began, the Lord Chief Justice stayed on at Westminster as his parliamentary masters had ordered. Clearly it was an impossible position. By a writ of *Supersedeas* the King dismissed Brampston on October 10; but in order to show that this was no reflection upon a judge who was generally considered both solid and grave, shortly afterwards sent him a patent appointing him a sergeant-at-law. From Parliament's point of view they could not but admit the legal right of the King to dismiss his Lord Chief Justice. They even proposed in the failed peace negotiations of the following February that he should be reappointed Lord Chief Justice but on new terms – not during the King's pleasure but during good behaviour *(quamdiu se bene gesserit)*. Brampston turned down all approaches, as he turned down a later approach by Cromwell. It is not a comfortable position to be a judge in a country at civil war. He lived quietly in Essex and died there in 1659, just before the Restoration, aged seventy-eight. The King appointed in his place Sir Robert Heath who thereby at last reached the position which a decade earlier he had expected. The new Lord Chief Justice moved with the King and with his colleague Chief Justice Bankes of Common Pleas down to the Royalist war head-quarters at Oxford.

Robert Heath

The new Lord Chief Justice, sixty-seven when appointed and a man set in stern ways, was by no means overawed by the difficulties of his position. The country might be at war but the King's government must go on and the rebels be crushed by legal as well as by military means.

Unfortunately for the strict legalists it was not as simple as that. John Lilburne, now a Captain in Lord Brooke's parliamentary regiment of foot, was taken prisoner by the Royalists in the

fight at Brentford on November 10. Four weeks later he and
three other parliamentary officers were on trial for their lives at
the Guildhall in Oxford, faced with charges of high treason for
levying war against the King. He was of course guilty; but so
were all Parliament's leaders, Parliament's officers, Parliament's
men. In a state of civil war it is impossible to apply the strict
rules of Edward III's Statute of Treason; and in practice the
status quo ante obtained: that is to say, the unspoken convention prevalent in England's previous great ideological civil war,
Earl Simon de Montfort's, when it was accepted that levying
war against the King was merely a form of political protest,
whereas compassing – plotting – his actual death would be
high treason. In the case of Lilburne and his brother officers
Parliament threatened immediate reprisals if sentence of death
was pronounced. After six months in prison in Oxford Lilburne
was eventually exchanged for a Royalist officer.

The Royalists however would have been extraordinarily and
unprecedently enlightened if they had abandoned their legal
weapons totally. There was one that they were in fact enlightened enough never even to attempt to use: that was the Lord
Chief Justice's power as Chief Coroner of England to declare an
attainder on rebels killed in battle. This would have resulted
automatically in the forfeiture to the Crown of dead rebels'
lands and goods. It must have been very tempting to try it out; it
was indeed rumoured that King Charles had it in mind; but
Heath, it seems, scotched that idea. Less wisely, he did try,
sitting with Bankes and two other Royalist judges at Salisbury a
year later, to indict the absent living for high treason. Bills of
Indictment were prepared against the Earls of Northumberland,
Pembroke and Salisbury – a Percy, a Herbert, and a Cecil – and
against various members of the House of Commons. But despite
the city of Salisbury's almost fanatical loyalty its Grand Jury
threw these Bills out, with the traditional formula of *Ignoramus*
and with more good sense than the King's judges. All the same
Parliament was naturally enough infuriated by the attempt and
retaliated by impeaching the Lord Chief Justice and his three
colleagues – an equally idle gesture as the judges were of course,
fortunately for themselves, outside Parliament's grasp.

This continued, futile, legal manoeuvring merely served,
apart from exacerbating feelings of vengeance and suspicion on
both sides, to show how inadequate both the common law and
the statute law of England are in time of civil war. The only
sensible legal principle to apply seems to be that of the great
international lawyer Grotius: when there is a civil war, he and

the 'civilian' lawyers of his school laid down, the opposite parties must treat each other as if they were belligerents belonging to two independent nations.

Unless this principle is adopted in practice, viciousness follows. The Civil War in England, unlike so many other civil wars elsewhere, was barely marred by atrocities. But the Turpin affair shows how inadequate law breeds, in a civil war, vicious reprisals. In that same Western Circuit Heath and Bankes and the other Royalist judges sentenced to death for high treason Captain Turpin, a parliamentary naval officer. He was reprieved but kept in prison in Exeter. There next year Sir John Berkeley, the ruthless commander-in-chief of all Royalist forces in Devon, hanged him. The pretext was this: that Parliament had executed a Royalist officer, Captain Howard. But there was far more excuse, legally speaking, for Parliament: Captain Howard was a deserter from their own forces whom they had recaptured, and he had suffered the usual deserters' penalty.

As a result of Turpin's semi-judicial murder Heath and his fellow judges were again impeached by Parliament but this time the follow-up was more bitter and, inevitably at this stage in the war, more effective. They were all voted guilty of high treason in the Lords, and placed on the list of those to be condemned before the passing of the Act of Oblivion. All Bankes' property was declared forfeited, but his wife, Lady Mary, defended Corfe Castle in a famous siege that lasted for three years – till it was finally captured by the Bankes' turncoat ex-Royalist neighbour of Wimborne St Giles, Anthony Ashley Cooper. Bankes himself escaped punishment and avoided the sour taste of defeat by dying at Christ Church in December 1644.

In June 1646 Oxford, the only remaining Royalist stronghold, at last surrendered and the Civil War was at an end. Lord Chief Justice Heath had been exempted from pardon. His estates were sequestered, his place declared vacant as if he were dead. He fled to France and there, more loyal but less fortunate than his predecessor Lord Chief Justice Fortescue in the Wars of the Roses, died in exile on August 30, 1649 – seven months to the day after the execution of his royal master.

5

Commonwealth Men

In the enormous turmoil of the parliamentary and Puritan triumph all men, of good will and bad will alike, agreed on one thing: that the whole legal system needed to be reformed, from top to bottom. The delays and costs had become quite intolerable. Exorbitant fees had to be paid not only to lawyers and law-court officials, but to the judges. 20,000 cases were waiting in Chancery, some indeed had been waiting for up to thirty years. But what is extraordinary is how little, in the end and despite all the talk and theorising, was changed. The obvious abuses were swept aside, and the obvious administrative improvements made. But the general system of the laws and the courts was in the end left almost exactly as it had been. To take one trivial but striking example, the Commission for Law Reform ordered that the two Courts of Chancery and Upper Bench (as King's Bench had for obvious reasons been rechristened) should be moved from the end of Westminster Hall to the north side, thus having all three courts in a row, leaving the south side for shops and booths and the west side unoccupied. This was sensible – as was the ruling that all laws should be in English, that all the judges should be paid £1,000 a year and circuit money, that a court of appeal should be established – but it could hardly be described as revolutionary. As regards the laws themselves, only ten days after the King's execution the House of Commons passed a Declaration, to be read aloud in every court in the land, that the fundamental laws should remain in force. And the laws that were eventually added – a Statute against Duelling, an Act against Adultery, an Act against Cursing and Swearing (noblemen to be fined 30/-, gentlemen 6/8, all others 3/4) – were not exactly unprecedented.

It was the same with the judges. During the Civil War itself no judges had ridden out on formal circuit. But once the war was over and the first turmoil of reform had died down, the old system was re-established. On November 15, 1648 both Houses of Parliament voted in a Lord Chief Justice, a Chief Justice of Common Pleas, and a Chief Baron of the Exchequer, plus their puisnes. It was not quite business as before, however, for five of the judges voted in refused to serve. Those who did – and they included the three principal judges – were given, for obvious reasons, a new title after the execution of the King. They became the Judges of the Commonwealth of England, and such they, and their successors, remained till the Restoration eleven years later. But, for all the change in title, the keynote was continuity, not revolution.

Henry Rolle

Henry Rolle was about sixty when he was appointed Lord Chief Justice of the Upper Bench – a Devonshire man, educated at Exeter College, Oxford, a barrister of the Inner Temple, a sergeant-at-law, Recorder of Dorchester, three times M.P. for Callington in Cornwall, three times M.P. for Truro, married to Margaret, daughter of Sir Thomas Foot – of the still well-known, still radical, still West Country Foot family. He was, more importantly, a thoroughly decent man, a good, hard-working, respected lawyer and a plain, unornamental advocate.

He did *not* preside at the King's trial.

The judges and the laws of England had remained almost unchanged. Not so the courts – the more hated of the prerogative courts, in particular the Court of Star Chamber and the ecclesiastical Court of High Commission, were immediately swept away. Yet no sooner had the new authorities disposed of the legal instruments of tyranny than they found, almost inevitably, that they had to replace what had gone with an equally tyrannous court system of their own. It seems to be the sad experience of all revolutions. The House of Commons – the House of Lords refused to have anything to do with the proposal – set up a High Court of Justice. Originally it was established for one month only, to try the King. Rolle was invited to preside over it; he refused. So did his two far more bitterly anti-monarchist fellow judges, the Chief Justice of

Common Pleas and the Chief Baron of the Exchequer. The
Attorney General refused to prosecute. In the end Cromwell
had to choose as presiding judge – Lord President – the obscure
Chief Justice of Chester, a man called Bradshaw; and the
prosecution was undertaken mainly by a Dutchman, Isaac
Dorislaus, Professor of Ancient History at Cambridge.

Despite its high-sounding title the High Court of Justice was
basically a one-man tribunal, a court-martial, with, as a gesture
towards the idea of a 'popular court', 135 nominated members,
a sort of mass jury. Even crop-eared Prynne denounced the
'trial' that followed, even 'Free-born John' Lilburne considered
that Charles should have been tried, as was any English man's
right, by a normal jury. The trial itself, held in a cleared
Westminster Hall, was in one sense the most famous trial in
English history; but in the legal and actual sense, it was a non-
event, a fiasco. The King, quite rightly and with great dignity,
denied that the court had any jurisdiction to try him, and
refused to plead. There was a certain irony, admittedly, in
hearing Charles of all men appeal to the common law of
England. Between January 20 and January 27 there were four
brief confrontations between the King and the steel-helmeted
Lord President. On the final day Charles was sentenced to
death. He was refused leave to speak after sentence. Bradshaw
was the first to sign the death warrant, followed by Lord Grey,
Oliver Cromwell and fifty-six others. Forty-seven of the nominated members never attended the trial at all, the rest, despite
intense pressures refused to sign. The legal profession, for once
representing the feelings of the vast majority of the country,
looked on the whole affair with intense disfavour. It was a clear
case of judicial murder and, justified or not, seemed to have the
exact flavour of those royal excesses from which the Commonwealth was intended to deliver the people of England. Nevertheless Cromwell saw his new High Court as a most useful
instrument of vengeance and prolonged its life, his object being
to mete out in all the fairness of severity, the same justice to the
King's associates as had been meted out to the King himself.
Between February 9 and March 6 James Hamilton, Duke of
Hamilton, was tried by Lord President Bradshaw. He was
executed on March 9. Lords Holland, Norwich and Capel
followed him; as did various others, including the Reverend
Christopher Love, involved in a Presbyterian plot; and Gerard,
Vowell and Fox, three would-be assassins of Cromwell. Bradshaw became a member of the Council of State. He died in
1659. At the Restoration his carcass, like Cromwell's, was dug

up and hanged at Tyburn. His head, and Cromwell's, were exposed on poles at the top of Westminster Hall. It was a gruesome epilogue to a gruesome episode, and no Lord Chief Justice has ever suffered precisely the indignity that Lord President Bradshaw posthumously incurred.

In March 1649 the Lord Chief Justice of the Upper Bench, and the other judges, set out to ride the circuits as Commissioners of Assize. Their progress throughout the counties and shires was marked by enormous pomp and in itself signified the re-establishment of ordered local government throughout England after the years of turmoil. Constables and church-wardens had to be re-appointed, the gaols re-established, the Poor Law administered, high sheriffs reproved or encouraged, rates, assessments and a thousand and one financial problems settled, criminals punished, civil suits heard, and everywhere complaints and petitions arising from the years of turmoil noted and, if possible, dealt with. They were as much ombudsmen as judges, and more administrators than either.

Henry Rolle himself rode out on the Western circuit. All seemed quiet and in order; but in fact, following the King's execution on January 30, Royalists, of whom there were many in this part of England, were stunned rather than totally cowed. All around England's coasts islands were still held for the new King, the exiled King, Charles Stuart's and Henrietta Maria's son, the future Charles II. The Channel Isles and, even nearer, the Scilly Isles were still Royalist strongholds. It took a year for the Royalists of the West Country to begin to re-organise; but a year after the Lord Chief Justice's tour the first of the great Royalist resistance movements was formed: the Western Association. It held its inaugural meeting in Salisbury. Emissaries flitted to and fro between Jersey, Portsmouth, Weymouth and Henrietta Maria's exiled court in the Louvre. Henry Seymour, Lord Beauchamp, son of the Marquess of Hertford, whose prestige was unsurpassed in the West Country, took its head. A year later the whole conspiracy had been betrayed and Beauchamp was in the Tower. 'It seems,' wrote his only moderately sympathetic father, the Marquess, 'it is a place entailed upon our familie, for wee have now helde it five generations.' The Scillies surrendered, young Charles Stuart marched south with the Scots only to be defeated at Worcester, the Isle of Man fell, Lord Derby, its Royalist proprietor, was executed, Jersey and Guernsey were reduced. It looked as if all Royalist pretensions were at an end. Secretary of State

Thurloe's intelligence service had been, from the Royalist point of view, only too efficient.

Yet only two years later another Royalist conspiracy was formed in the West Country, by Sir Robert Phelips of Montacute who had helped Charles escape after Worcester, and was himself a former member of the Western Association. He was arrested, questioned by Cromwell and by that pillar of the parliamentary establishment in Dorset, Anthony Ashley Cooper. The planned uprising was still-born but Phelips escaped. A lesson had been learnt. The next rising planned was, in theory, far more carefully co-ordinated. It took place two years later still, in early 1655. The plan was for simultaneous regional uprisings of Action Party Royalists throughout England, and not only of Royalists, either. The growing opposition to Cromwell had brought them strange bedfellows. Sir Robert Phelips' son and namesake, young Colonel Robert, was approached in Antwerp by an Anabaptist and 'agitator', Colonel Edward Sexby, who called Cromwell a 'false, perjured rogue' and promised nation-wide co-operation. Sexby was by no means a negligible quantity; he had served in Cromwell's Horse and been on foreign missions for a leader to whom he had once been devoted. Wilmot, Prince Charles' reckless, cheerful companion, was sent across from France as overall co-ordinator, with special responsibility for Yorkshire and the North-East. Local leaders were appointed in every county and region. The day for the uprising was set as March 8. Sir Joseph Wagstaffe, a professional soldier with great experience in the European wars, had crossed from Dunkirk with Wilmot. Salisbury again was to be the centre of the uprising in the West Country. A group of judges, including Lord Chief Justice Rolle, were sitting in assize at Winchester, and the plan was to descend on Winchester and strike a spectacular *coup* by seizing the Lord Chief Justice there. Unfortunately a strong troop of Commonwealth horses appeared first at Winchester. However the Lord Chief Justice was due to move to Salisbury on the Sunday, and preside over assizes the following morning, on Monday, March 12. Sir Joseph Wagstaffe was hiding out with a fervent young Royalist, Sir John Penruddock of Compton Chamberlayne. There was a small detachment of parliamentary troops at Marlborough – they could be kept occupied by a diversionary attack led by Sir Henry Moore of Fawley. The only substantial garrison in the whole of the West Country was at Bristol. Rightly calculating that initial success is vital in any uprising, Wagstaffe decided to ignore what was happening in the rest of the country and to postpone his *coup de main*, of which the Lord Chief Justice would be the prize, till the small hours of Monday morning.

In the small hours of Monday morning Henry Rolle and his fellow judge, Nicholas J., were roughly tumbled out of their beds and placed under arrest by the Royalist rebels. The city of Salisbury awoke to find itself occupied by 400 horsemen and to hear King Charles II proclaimed, though not by the High Sheriff of Wiltshire, the judges' host, who had refused and had been very roughly handled. Wagstaffe, used to the more violent ways of the Continent, wanted to string up Rolle, the Sheriff and the other judge out of hand. They were, understandably half-dead with fright already. But the more knightly Penruddock released the trembling Rolle and his companions, reminding them only 'to remember on another occasion to whom they owed their lives'. From the King's Arms – their aptly chosen headquarters in Salisbury – Penruddock and Wagstaffe and their men rode south to Blandford, in Dorset, to proclaim the King. But the country did not rise behind them. Further west Smyths, Wyndhams and Grenvilles had already been arrested on suspicion weeks earlier. Worst of all, the Marquess of Hertford, from whom great things had been expected, failed to make a move, demoralised – on a charitable assumption – by his son Henry, Lord Beauchamp's recent and unexpected death.

That evening news of the Penruddock Rising reached the Lord Protector, as Cromwell had now become, in London. He reacted with his usual vigour. The military forces from Bristol were ordered to occupy Exeter and Taunton. The dwindling band of rebel horsemen headed towards central Devon, to join up with the leader of the Devon uprising (which had not, in fact, taken place), Sir Hugh Pollard of King's Nympton. There on a Wednesday night, in a desultory fight ranging through the streets of South Molton, Penruddock and sixty of his men surrendered, the rest escaping.

It had all been something of a fiasco. But it had frightened not only the Lord Chief Justice but the Lord Protector. A general repression followed; the hated regime of the Major Generals, and the imposition of strict military discipline on a restless army by decimation trials followed. At first Rolle refused to try Penruddock, and his men declaring that 'he much doubted whether they had done anything which amounted to treason; and that at any rate he was unfit to give judgment in a case wherein he might be considered a party concerned.' But both he and his equally terrified fellow judge Nicholas had sufficiently

overcome their honest and honourable scruples to sit as commissioners on the tribunal that eventually tried Penruddock in
April at Exeter. The tribunal was presided over by a much more
whole-hearted Cromwellian Sergeant Glynne who, in Penruddock's own words, 'after a most bitter and nonsensical speech,
gave sentence against me, viz to be drawn, hanged and quartered'. This can hardly have been unexpected despite Penruddock's two powerful arguments: a) that what he had done was
not high treason for 'The "Protector" is unknown to common
law'; and b) that he had surrendered on terms, having been
promised security of life. This was denied by his captor, Captain
Unton Croke.

Penruddock was not hanged, drawn and quartered but he
was beheaded at Exeter on March 16, as were thirteen of his
companions. On June 15 Sergeant Glynne had his reward: he
became the second Lord Chief Justice of the Upper Bench.

John Glynne

It was not exactly that Rolle was dismissed. But he was old,
tired, and had been badly frightened by the Salisbury affair.
Requested to ride North and try the equally incompetent
'rebels' there, he refused. He wanted to die peacefully, and he
did die peacefully a year after his resignation, a judge much
admired for his rulings and in particular by his judgment in the
case of the Portuguese Ambassador's brother, Dom Pantaleone
Sa.

Glynne was a much younger, more vigorous man, born and
bred in Caernarvon, and M.P. for Caernarvon in the Long
Parliament, who had won his laurels for the Presbyterian party
as one of the managers of Strafford's impeachment. He had
had, as every active politician had had in those up-and-down
times, his own rise, fall and rise again on the wheel of fortune.
He was accused by contemporaries of two-facedness and political dishonesty. No doubt he was unscrupulous; but he was
admired for his lucid, methodical judgments and for his persis-
tent loyalty to Presbyterian principles which paralleled in its
way Brampston's loyalty to the royal prerogative. He seems to
have believed in the monarchical principle – a belief that came

in handy at the Restoration – and certainly supported Alderman Packe's 'petition and advice' to the Lord Protector that he, Cromwell, should assume the Crown as Oliver I.

Sexby, the 'agitator', had been chased out of England back to Flanders in February 1655, with the Protector's men hard on his heels, just in time to scotch his proposed part in the Penruddock Rising that spring. Disillusioned with his Royalist allies, and with the prospects of open revolt, he laid plans to assassinate Cromwell at the opening of Parliament the following year, on September 17, 1656. As his assassin he selected a certain Miles Sindercombe, previously a leveller, a cashiered trooper of General Monck's. But Secretary of State Thurloe's secret police service was, as always, efficient. Cromwell learned of the plot, and reached Parliament safely, describing Sexby in his speech there as 'a wretched creature, an apostate from religion and all honesty'.

Miles Sindercombe did not give up. On January 8, 1657 he made a bungled attempt to burn Whitehall. Next day Thurloe's men arrested him and his accomplices, after a hard fight in which Sindercombe was badly wounded. He came up before the Lord Chief Justice, charged with high treason, on February 9. He 'carried himself insolently to the Court', was found guilty and condemned. Four nights later he was discovered dead in the Tower. Was it murder or, as the Governor of the Tower, Colonel Barksted, asserted, suicide from poison after the visit of Sindercombe's two sisters? At any rate the wretched corpse was adjudged guilty of self-murder, the dead body dragged through the streets on a hurdle at a horse's tail, and buried at the foot of the gallows erected for his execution. A stake was then driven through his body. The top end, cased in iron, was left in place, visible, as a warning to all others who might try by such means to cheat the Lord Protector's justice.

There seems little doubt that the Sindercombe assassination attempt was one of the reasons that induced the Lord Protector to decide against assuming the Crown. The fanaticism of his erstwhile supporters frightened even a man of such iron strength as Cromwell; and the plot's sequel rendered the last year and a half of his life miserable. In May, from Antwerp, Sexby the 'agitator' published a pamphlet, which he ironically dedicated to Cromwell, entitled *Killing No Murder*. It called for the assassination of the Protector and caused Cromwell 'many an hour of unspeakable trouble'. Thereafter England's ruler made sure he was escorted by a body of Life Guards whenever he ventured out, carried his own pistol and constantly shifted his sleeping quarters. Death must almost have come as a relief to that great, disappointed man.

It came unexpectedly, on September 3, 1658. Prideaux, the Attorney General throughout the Commonwealth period, was at once summoned by the Council and advised the immediate proclamation of Oliver's son, Richard, as the new Lord Protector. To the agonised frustration of the Royalists overseas the transition went incredibly smoothly. The country had never seemed so calm. Sir Henry Vane soon emerged as the chief figure of the new regime. 'Oh, Sir Henry Vane, Sir Henry Vane,' Cromwell had exclaimed five years earlier, 'the Lord deliver me from Sir Henry Vane!' Nevertheless before their quarrel over the dissolution of the Long Parliament, they had been great friends and allies: both Puritans, both parliamentarians, 'Brother Heron' and 'Brother Fountain' in their vigorous and frequent letters to each other. Sir Henry had lived quietly and fairly uneventfully since the quarrel. He was in his late forties, talented, totally incorruptible but crafty and not much loved.

The following year, 1659, was marked by yet another failed Royalist uprising – Sir George Booth's in Lancashire and Cheshire. General Lambert, Cromwell's chief-of-staff, crushed it easily; but this time there was no serious attempt at legal repression. Glynne saw which way the wind was blowing, and wisely enough before the end of the year he resigned. General Monck was slowly moving down from Scotland with a large army to fill the void left by Richard Cromwell's disappearance. But in January 1660, though Monck was approaching London, the Rump Parliament resolved that a new Lord Chief Justice must be created and issued an Ordinance filling the post in the name of 'the Keepers of the Liberties of England'. The man they chose was a puisne judge of the Upper Bench who had that summer wisely acquitted various Royalists at York Assizes on the paradoxical charge of 'levying war against the King'.

Richard Newdigate

The last of the three Lord Chief Justices of the Commonwealth was destined to hold office for a mere four months, from January 17, 1660 to May 29 when he retired to the country and obscurity. He, and various fellow lawyers of his, had been dubious about becoming judges at all under the questionable legal auspices of the Lord Protector. They had been summoned into Oliver's formidable presence.

'If you gentlemen of the red robe,' said Cromwell, 'will not execute the law, my red coats shall.'

'Make us Judges,' the suitably cowed lawyers had cried, 'we will with pleasure be Judges!'

Newdigate's pleasure was little and brief. Monck reached London in February, dissolved the Rump Parliament, dismissed Sir Henry Vane, and let it be known, somewhat to the general surprise, that he favoured a Restoration rather than a military government. Elections were then held to what was called the Convention Parliament, which met on April 25, 1660. Ex-Lord Chief Justice Glynne was back as M.P. for Caernarvon, Matthew Hale, another of Oliver Cromwell's judges but one who had refused to serve under his son Richard, was back too as M.P. for Gloucestershire, William Prynne as M.P. for Bath and Anthony Ashley Cooper – 'no man is so difficult to manage as the little man with three names,' Cromwell had said of him,was back not only as M.P. for Poole but as one of the twelve Parliamentary Commissioners who were sent over to Breda in Flanders to treat with Charles I's son and heir. On May 1 Parliament voted the decisive, traditionalist motion that set the seal on the Restoration: 'the Constitution resides in King, Lords and Commons'. And on Tuesday, May 29, amidst scenes of delirious joy, King Charles II rode into a flower-bedecked London, straight to St Paul's Cathedral, where he was welcomed by twelve Presbyterian ministers in Geneva gowns and Puritan hats who presented him with a Bible, which he kissed. The same day Sir Richard Newdigate resigned; and the Court of Upper Bench retransformed itself without more ado into the Court of King's Bench, as it had always been before and has always been since. An interlude of just a little more than a decade, a comparatively painless interlude, legally speaking, was painlessly over.

6

Lord Chief Justices of the Restoration

Whatever the country, whatever the century, after any civil war or rebellion has been settled one question invariably arises: how to punish the losers. Fortunately both Charles II and his chief adviser Edward Hyde were forgiving men: the young King by natural temperament, the elder statesman and Lord Chancellor as a matter of policy. The House of Commons too was in favour of clemency all around: naturally enough, since so many of its elected members had been involved in the Cromwellian regime. As early as May 9, 1660, they were listening to a proposed Bill of General Pardon, Indemnity and Oblivion.

The Bill did not become an Act of Parliament till August 29. In the meantime its terms had been more and more bitterly debated. The restored King was known to be willing to pardon all his father's enemies and his own except for one category: those who had actually been responsible for his father's execution. At first only seven 'regicides' were excepted from the Act of Indemnity by name. They included such men as Colonel Thomas Harrison, an extremist who had signed Charles' death warrant and was much hated by all Royalists for his activities in the Civil War and after. These seven were immediately arrested. No M.P. was more venomous against the regicides and their supporters in the Commons than, surprisingly, Prynne. As for the restored Lords, they proposed that all the 'regicide' judges should be executed, whether they had signed the death warrant or not. In the end thirty living persons together with the two (unknown) executioners were exempted from the Act of Indemnity.

The next problem was judges. At the Restoration all twelve judges were dismissed. They were not impeached or punished in any way. Indeed Glynne, who had resigned so wisely from the post of Lord Chief Justice, was created a King's sergeant and knighted – he was to have a bad tumble in the Coronation procession the following year; Pepys, who thought him a rogue, saw the hand of God in this and only regretted that he had not been killed. But there seems to have been no question of any of them, ever, being reappointed. Edward Hyde's problem as Lord Chancellor was where to find decent Royalist lawyers to fill the vacant places; inevitably he was thrown back to the pre-revolutionary generation, and the field there was thin. Indeed he was forced to leave two of the three chief posts vacant and to appoint an ageing loyalist, Sir Orlando Bridgman, as Lord Chief Baron of the Exchequer. The 'regicide' trials began on October 6, under these curious circumstances. Sir Orlando defined the essence of treason as 'wicked imagination', and sure enough sentenced twenty-nine to death. Charles II spared the lives of nineteen of them, but ten were duly executed, including Harrison and Colonel Hacker, who had commanded the Halberdier guard at Charles I's trial, been present on the scaffold, supervised the execution, and signed the order to the executioner. 'A bloody week,' Pepys noted in his diary on October 20. The very next day, as if dismayed by the irregularity of the position, the King appointed a Lord Chief Justice for King's Bench.

Robert Foster

The new appointee had been made a judge over twenty years earlier by the King's father, had been loyal to Charles I, was dismissed by the Commonwealth, and lived quietly ever since. Reappointed a puisne judge, he had sat with Sir Orlando on the regicide trials and proved his loyalty, hence his promotion. The question now arose of the trials of two great upholders of the Commonwealth who were certainly not in any except a strictly legalistic sense 'regicides' – General Lambert and Sir Henry Vane.

These two were in a very special class: the House of Commons had voted for their exclusion from the Act of Indemnity, but had petitioned that their lives be spared. Charles II had not only granted that petition, but in his Declaration of Breda, before the Restoration, had gone out of his way to assure that there would be no vengeance taken on Sir Henry Vane, for Sir Henry had taken no part in his father's trial; indeed he had refused the oath approving Charles I's execution and the abolition of the monarchy. All the same, by mid-1662, two years after the Restoration he was on trial before the Lord Chief Justice accused of high treason. He was, it seems, judged too dangerous a man to leave alive, and a permanent focus of possible rebellion.

It was impossible to allege that Sir Henry Vane had conspired against the life of Charles I. So the Crown's lawyers, led by the turncoat ex-Lord Chief Justice, Glynne, with as a colleague another King's sergeant and future Lord Chief Justice, Kelyng, put together an extraordinary charge: that Sir Henry had 'compassed the death' of Charles II. How? By subverting the ancient form of government, keeping the King out of his realm, and 'taking upon him the government of the forces of this nation by sea and land, and appointing colonels, captains and officers'. In other words Vane's 'treason' had consisted in the double offence of administering the country under Protector Richard Cromwell and of doing nothing to aid the Restoration.

The accused came up for trial before Lord Chief Justice Foster on June 6, 1662. He put up a very bold defence against a browbeating judge. He pointed out the bad faith of the proceedings in view of the promises of pardon – fair enough, but Penruddock had had the same treatment, in roughly similar circumstances. He then went on to argue that in the King's absence from the realm and from government Parliament was supreme and treason to a monarch outside the realm and without actual power was therefore impossible. It was the boldness of the argument that sealed his fate. (Lambert, tried at the same time, was submissive and ended his life in comfortable confinement in Guernsey.) On the day following Vane's trial, King Charles wrote as follows to his Lord Chancellor, Edward Hyde:

'Sir Henry Vane's carriage yesterday was so insolent as to justify all he had done; acknowledging no supreme power in England but a Parliament, and many things to that purpose. If he has given new occasion to be hanged, certainly he is too dangerous a man to let live, if we can honestly put him out of the way.'

He was executed on Tower Hill a week later. He died very bravely, though he was known to be a physically timid man. Pepys thought the King had lost more by Sir Henry's death than he had gained. To us too it can hardly seem other than a grave stain on a comparatively bloodless king. There is a sinister modern ring to that phrase 'if we can honestly put him out of the way' that chills the blood.

What must never be forgotten is that Charles (and his younger brother and successor James) saw their judges as royal servants, almost as a branch of the government's bureaucracy. They took (as the Domestic State Papers show) great interest in their appointments and indeed in the dismissals of 'their' judges. At first, indeed, in this opening period, there was no question of dismissals: the Lord Chief Justice's warrant was made out 'during good behaviour' – *quamdiu se bene gesserit* – rather than 'at the King's pleasure' – *durante bene placito*. Indeed it was not till his fifth Lord Chief Justice, when the crisis of his reign was looming, that Charles dared use the weapon of dismissal. Thereafter the remaining six Lord Chief Justices of these last two Stuart Kings knew that they had to temper their behaviour to their monarch's wishes if they desired to keep their positions: these last six were, inevitably, lawyer-politicians, who had built their careers on devotion to the royal power and knew that if they wavered they would be dismissed. In fact, however, royal power was by no means absolute: three of them did waver, and were dismissed. Two did not waver; they were not dismissed, but, as it happens, both died in prison. There was a lot to be said therefore for wavering. It was not until after the 'Glorious Revolution' that the problem was solved for ever, and judges were given what so many of them had, rightly, longed for: security of tenure, though that too was to bring its own problems, as later episodes in this book will show.

However, during this first period of Charles II's reign, when the government was virtually conducted by Edward Hyde as Lord Chancellor, there were three Lord Chief Justices, all of them loyalists and Royalists to their core, none young men, and all three dying in office. None of the three were particularly talented lawyers, and none particularly tolerant or pleasant men. Yet they did not have an easy time of it, dealing with the hangover of the Puritan period, as the following exchange shows:

Lord Chief Justice Foster: John Crook, when did you take the oath of allegiance?
Crook [a Quaker]:   Answering this question in the negative is to accuse myself which you ought not to put me upon. *Nemo debet seipsum prodere.* I am an Englishman, and I ought not to be taken nor imprisoned nor called in question nor put upon answer but according to the law of the land.
Lord Chief Justice: You are here required to take the oath of allegiance, and when you have done that you shall be heard.

Crook: You that are Judges on the bench ought to be my counsel, not my accusers.

Lord Chief Justice: We are here to do justice, and are upon our oaths: and we are to tell you what is law, not you us. Therefore, sirrah, you are too bold!

Crook: 'Sirrah' is not a word becoming a judge. If I speak loud, it is my zeal for truth, and for the name of the Lord. Mine innocency makes me bold!

In this exchange it is difficult not to have a certain sympathy for the Lord Chief Justice – whose patience, however, wore out a few minutes later:

Crook: I owe dutiful allegiance to the King but cannot *swear* without breaking my allegiance to the King of Kings. We dare not break Christ's commandments, who hath said SWEAR NOT AT ALL; and the apostle James says 'Above all things, my brethren, *swear not*!'

'The Chief Justice thereupon interrupting,' goes Crook's own account, 'called upon the executioner to stop my mouth, which he did accordingly with a dirty cloth and a gag.' Lord Chief Justices of course always have and always will have the last word in their own courts.

Foster died on October 4, 1663. The Lord Chancellor, Edward Hyde (now Lord Clarendon) cast around and hit upon an aged kinsman of his own for the post.

Robert Hyde

Edward and Robert were first cousins, both being grandsons of Lawrence Hyde of West Hatch, Wiltshire, and nephews of Sir Nicholas Hyde, Charles I's first Lord Chief Justice. But in this distinguished legal family Robert was a nonentity. He had been, since the Restoration, a puisne judge to Sir Orlando Bridgman. He held office for only a year and a half, dropping dead on the bench on May 1, 1665. He sentenced a group of booksellers to several hours in the pillory and imprisonment for life for publishing a factual account of the trial of the regicides.

'*Dying men's words*, indeed!' he said as he pronounced

sentence. 'If men are as villainous at their death as in their lives, may what they say be published as the words of dying men? God forbid! It is the King's great mercy that the charge is not for high treason.'

The King showed no such great mercy in the case of a printer who was indeed arraigned for high treason. The following appalling exchange occurred before the printer, John Troyn, was sentenced to be hanged, drawn and quartered.

Lord Chief Justice Hyde: There is here as much villainy and slander as is possible for devil or man to invent. To rob the King of the love of his subjects is to destroy him in his person. You are here in the presence of almighty God, as you desired; and the best you can now do towards amends for your wickedness is by discovering the author of this villainous book. If not, you must not expect, and indeed God forbid! there should be any mercy shown to you.

Prisoner: I never knew the author of it.

Lord Chief Justice: Then we must not trouble ourselves. You of the jury, there can be no doubt that publishing such a book as this is as high treason as can be committed, and my brothers will declare the same if you doubt.

So it was back to 'high treason' not by any overt act, but by words alone – even the rabid pro-Royalist reactions sweeping the country could hardly excuse such judges as Sir Robert Hyde or, indeed, his successor.

John Kelyng

Two things can be said in mitigation of Kelyng's brutality. The first is that he spent almost two decades of the prime of his life imprisoned at Windsor Castle, for the sole crime of supporting the King – from the outbreak of the Civil War in 1642 till the Restoration. That was not designed to improve any man's temper. The second is his conduct in the notorious Bury St Edmunds witchcraft trial of March 1661. It was the last occasion on which two 'witches' were sentenced to death in this country, and Sergeant Kelyng, as he then was, came out of the whole episode far better than the judge presiding over the Commission, the reputed Sir Matthew Hale.

Two old women, Amy Duny and Rose Cullender, were accused of laying spells on children, on three children in particular. They had caused them, mothers and neighbours witnessed, to vomit pins and twopenny nails, to see mysterious mice, ducks and flies invisible to others; in the case of Amy Duny to produce a great toad which exploded like gunpowder and then disappeared; in the case of Rose Cullender to have a secret teat lately sucked. Kelyng, who seems to have been on the tribunal, roundly and rightly declared himself 'much unsatisfied with this evidence and thought it not sufficient to convict the prisoners; for admitting that the children were in truth bewitched, yet, said he, it can never be applied to the prisoners upon the imagination only of the parties afflicted.' Hale played far safer: he told the jury, correctly, that it was for them to decide on the evidence whether a) the children were bewitched b) if so, whether the prisoners were guilty of it. But for sole guidance he added: 'That there are such creatures as witches I make no doubt at all.' The jury were out for half an hour. The two old women died protesting their innocence even though pressed – literally – to confess.

Seven months elapsed between the death of Sir Robert Hyde and the promotion of Mr Sergeant Kelyng to fill the vacant place, proof enough that the Lord Chancellor was in a quandary. Sir Matthew Hale, at the time Lord Chief Baron of the Exchequer, was a far more learned and, despite the witches' shameful trial, a far more judicial judge. But he had been embroiled with the Commonwealth; he was a reputed Puritan. So Kelyng was chosen instead. There were rumours that Barbara Villiers, Charles' mistress, had influenced the choice: but they were almost certainly idle rumours. For Kelyng was very much in the line of Foster and Hyde – only worse. He carried the 'high treason' approach to minor incidents to ludicrous lengths, even directing that some apprentices who had set out to raid brothels in Moorfields should be indicted on the charge of 'levying war against the King'.

'By levying war,' said Kelyng, 'is not only meant when a body is gathered together as an army but if a company of people will go about any public reformation, this is high treason.'

This extraordinary definition was concurred with by all the other judges, except Sir Matthew Hale, who treated the offence as a misdemeanour. How could such a judgment be possible?

Reason of state is the answer; the judges saw themselves as a branch of the royal administration, and the royal administration was very wary, even eight years after the Restoration, of any attempt at armed demonstration.

'There is reason we should be very cautious,' as Kelyng put it a little further on in the same judgment. 'We are but newly delivered from rebellion, and we know that that rebellion first began under the pretence of religion and the law.'

Yet even this loyal servant of the Crown went too far when he imprisoned or fined jurymen for giving verdicts of which he disapproved; and on one occasion, when the famous clause, the cornerstone of our liberties, was cited to him: 'No freeman shall be imprisoned except by the judgments of his peers or the laws of the land,' retorted only, 'Magna Carta – Magna Farta!!'

The House of Commons set about impeaching the Lord Chief Justice, accusing him of 'innovations in the trial of men for their lives and liberties', of 'tending to the introducing of an arbitrary government', of having 'undervalued, vilified and condemned Magna Carta'. Times were changing, old Edward Hyde had been dismissed and retired in dudgeon to the Continent, the rabid Royalism of the early Restoration was wearing out and impeachments of the King's servants were in the air once more. Kelyng was brought to the House, was heard in his own defence and dismissed with a warning. Not long afterwards, he had to make a public withdrawal and apology to the House of Lords for libelling one of its members. And not long after that, on May 9, 1671, he died. Sir Matthew Hale, who had been Lord Chief Baron of the Exchequer for eleven years, was appointed in his place.

Matthew Hale

When John Bunyan had come up, in July 1661, before Lord Chief Baron Hale on a charge of preaching without authorisation, 'a tinker and a poor man', as his wife Elizabeth said in his defence, Hale sent the accused to prison with obvious regret: 'I am truly sorry,' he said, 'we can do you no good sitting here, we can only act as the law gives us warrant; and we have no power to reverse the sentence, although it may be erroneous . . . I am truly sorry for your pitiable case, I wish I could serve you, but I fear I can do you no good.'

Literature, as so often, profited immensely from an oppressive imprisonment. But was Roger North right when he wrote this about Sir Matthew Hale?

> He was an upright Judge if taken within himself; and when he appeared, as he often did and really was, partial, his inclination or prejudice, insensibly to himself, drew his judgment aside. His bias lay strangely for and against characters and denominations, and sometimes the very habits of persons. If one party was courtier and well-dressed, and the other a sort of Puritan with a black cap and plain clothes, he insensibly thought the justice of the cause with the latter.

This certainly seems to be true in the Bunyan case where Twisden J., Hale's colleague, was far more snappish with Elizabeth Bunyan and her 'four small children, one of them blind, with nothing to live on while their father is in prison'. But the difficulty is that Roger North was a prejudiced writer: so good and vivid a writer, however, that he will often be quoted in the pages to come. He and his elder brother Francis, whose biography he wrote, had, like Hale, been bred among the Puritans; but, unlike Hale, they had switched to High Church Anglicanism and ultra-Royalist attitudes – both lawyers, Francis rising to be Attorney General and (as Lord Guilford) eventually Lord Keeper. So Roger's accounts of other lawyers are not necessarily to be taken at face value, whether commenting on a high-minded Puritan like Matthew Hale or a low-minded High Anglican like George Jeffreys (who eventually displaced his brother).

> Yet [added Roger North of Matthew Hale], when he knew the law was for the King (as well he might, being acquainted with all the records of the Court to which men of the law are commonly strangers) he failed not to judge accordingly – I have known the Court of King's Bench sitting every day from eight to twelve, and the Lord Chief Justice Hale managing matters of law to all imaginable advantage to the students, and in which he took a pleasure, or rather a pride. He encouraged inquiry when it was to the purpose, and used to debate with the counsel, so as the court might have been taken for an academy of sciences, as well as the seat of justice.

This is an appealing picture, and one echoed by all other writers of the time, particularly by Bishop Burnet, the author of the famous *History of My Own Time*. Yet there is no denying that the man was something of a prig. His *Letters of Advice to the Sons and Grandchildren*, in Victorian times the most popular of all his writings, are, (as his great admirer and biographer Lord Campbell noted) 'regarded as a *great bore* by the rising generation'. And what is one to say of a Lincoln's Inn law student who was so greatly impressed by Cornelius Nepos' *Life of Pomponius Atticus* that he resolved to take Pomponius Atticus as his model throughout life? Indeed, when he went up to Oxford at the age of fifteen in 1626, Hale had been planning to take holy orders. All through his life he regularly attended church morning and evening, on Sundays expounded the sermon to his children, and gave up some time every day to prayer and meditation. He sounds more the Victorian *beau ideal* than the Victorians themselves. There was always a Puritan side to his character, however. He dressed so plainly that even his admirers complained of it to him. After a brief period of *lapsus* at Oxford, he vowed that he would never see a stage-play or drink a health again. His recreations were the study of mathematics, philosophy, history, medicine, theology and learned conversations upon the same subjects. He signed the solemn League and Covenant, as a leading member of Cromwell's Commission for Law Reform, and agreed to become one of Cromwell's judges – a puisne judge in Common Pleas.

Yet there was another side to his character, or at least to his politics. It was Hale who, before he became a judge, defended almost all the accused in Cromwell's state trials – usually unsuccessfully. It was Hale who refused to continue to serve under Richard Cromwell, or even to attend Oliver's funeral. It was Hale who married Anne, daughter of Sir Henry Moore of Fawley, the Royalist squire whose task it had been in the Penruddock Rising to keep Marlborough's garrison occupied. (He had ten children by her – hence, no doubt the *Letters*. When she died he married a maidservant, also from Fawley, excusing himself with the incredibly pompous remark, *per* Roger North: 'There is no wisdom beneath the girdle.') On the other hand it was Hale, too, who just before the Restoration, in the Convention Parliament, wished to impose conditions on Charles II as a form of guarantee. It would be unfair to call him a trimmer; he was a moderate, who wished to reconcile both sides, who acted according to his lights, and yet who invariably managed, whichever side was in power, to find himself in office.

He was tall, strong and active, a paragon in settling difficult legal questions after the Great Fire of London, totally uncorrupt and incorruptible, but hard on the more frail of his colleagues at the Bar, especially on the lackadaisical Saunders and on the debauched Sergeant Scroggs.

He wrote a vast number of treatises (mainly – and fortunately – in manuscript) edificatory, scientific, and religious as well as legal. Among those essays of his that did appear were twelve long *Reasons why I desire to be spared from any place of public employment*, composed shortly before he accepted the position of Lord Chief Baron, and also *Things necessary to be continually had in remembrance*, eighteen short rules for himself as a judge. These are admirable; they ought, as Lord Campbell observed, 'to be inscribed in letters of gold', on the walls of the courts of law; and they end with a point that judges of our own day might do well to meditate:

18. To be short and sparing at meals, that I may be the fitter for business.

In the autumn of 1675 Hale fell ill. In his usual way he wrote a long and extraordinarily pompous *Meditation* on whether he should or should not resign, comparing his profession to 'something of religious duty' and comforting himself with 'the conscience of my own industry, fidelity and integrity'. Yet early the following year he had decided that he must go.

This drew upon him [wrote Bishop Burnet], the importunities of all his friends, and the clamour of the whole town, to divert him from it; but all was to no purpose. So he made applications to his Majesty for his *writ of ease*, which the King was very unwilling to .grant him ... Such was the general satisfaction which all the kingdom received by his excellent administration of justice that the King, though he could not well *deny* his request, yet he deferred the granting of it as long as was possible.

The main reason that Charles II was so eager to keep on a Lord Chief Justice with whom he could hardly have felt less temperamental sympathy was the extraordinary turbulence of the lawyers and of Parliament in that autumn of 1675. Hale was a rock of respectability in a sea of troubles that had set Lords against Commons, embroiled the whole nation, and almost led to a renewed outbreak of civil war. But by suddenly proroguing Parliament for fifteen months Charles won a respite. Sir Matthew was no longer so necessary; he was allowed his writ of ease; he retired to the house where he had been born at Alderley in Gloucestershire and died there, the Christmas Day following, spared the knowledge of the judicial upheavals that were about to follow.

7

Foam and Threat

When Parliament met on February 4, 1673, the Lord Chancellor, following the Speech from the Throne, addressed both Houses:

'My Lords,' he said, 'and you the knights, citizens and burgesses of the House of Commons, the King hath spoken so fully, so excellently well, and so like himself, that you are not to expect much of me.' Nevertheless he spoke so well, and so racily, that Charles, much satisfied, declared: 'My Chancellor knows more law than all my judges and more divinity than all my Bishops.' Who was this so eminently satisfactory Lord Chancellor? None other than the 'little man with three names' whom Cromwell had found so difficult to manage, Anthony Ashley Cooper.

This was the heyday of the *rapport* between the King and the man whom he was soon to find quite remarkably unmanageable. To describe Ashley Cooper as a Dorset squire is to give entirely the wrong impression. He had estates in Hampshire, Wiltshire and Somerset, with an unearned income of never less than £7,000 a year. He was more of a magnifico than a rustic. He had entertained the King sumptuously in London at Durham House in the Strand. One of his three wives had been a Cecil. He behaved courteously to them all, but rivalled Charles II for 'merriness'.

'Shaftesbury,' said the King – he had created Ashley Cooper an Earl shortly before raising him to the Lord Chancellorship – 'you are the most profligate man in my dominions.'

'Of a subject sir', replied Ashley Cooper, 'I believe I am.'

He was energetic, subtle, vivid, adventurous – he had organising ability and, clearly, charm. But his most unmistakable characteristic was ambition. He was, in his way, a mixture of a Francis Bacon and a Sir Henry Vane – but far more dangerous to the Stuarts than the executed Sir Henry had ever been, and, by contrast to Bacon, veering from time-serving sycophancy to vivid, cunning opposition to the Crown. Was he ambitious for himself, or for England? Royalist Dryden has so damned Ashley Cooper in the eyes of posterity that it is difficult to drive out of one's mind that picture of an Achitophel – a name to all succeeding ages curst.

> A fiery soul which working out its way
> Fretted the pigmy body to decay
> And o'er informed the tenement of clay.

Within weeks of that opening of Parliament Ashley Cooper had turned against his royal master, and began that ten-year-long role as leader of the opposition, the Country Party, the Whigs as they later came to be called, which ended only with his death.

As the fervour of the Restoration when virtually the whole country was Royalist changed, inevitably, to a certain disillusion, no one forgot, neither the royal brothers Charles II and the future James II, nor their opponents, how King Charles I's reign had ended. The government always feared, and the opposition always envisaged, a second armed struggle, a second uprising, a second civil war between King and Parliament. The fear and dread of Roman Catholicism reasserted itself after a long period of quiescence – largely because of the threatening presence of His Most Catholic Majesty Louis XIV across the waters. All these varied fears and apprehensions came boiling to a head when it became clear that Charles II, the most philoprogenitive of England's monarchs, would, paradoxically, never produce a legitimate son and heir; the Crown therefore would go to his brother, a Catholic and a feared absolutist, James Duke of York.

'What a rogue you have as a Lord Chancellor,' whispered James Duke of York, enraged, to his brother during that same 1673 Parliament (it led to James' open acknowledgement that he had been converted a Catholic and therefore to his resignation from the post of Lord High Admiral). 'Codsfish, what a fool you have for a Lord Treasurer,' retorted the King. All the same, in November, after proroguing Parliament, Charles decided to dismiss his Lord Chancellor. 'Sir,' said Ashley Cooper who had held the post for only a year, 'I know you intend to give the Seals to the Attorney General but I am sure your Majesty never designed to dismiss me with contempt.' 'Codsfish, my Lord,' replied the cynical good-humoured King, 'I will not do it with any circumstance as may look like an affront.'

When the Great Seal was discreetly sent for from Ashley

Cooper's mansion that evening, he gave it up cheerfully enough. 'It is only laying down my gown and putting on my sword,' he said, and at once he did so.

At the height of the Civil War young Francis Pemberton, of the Pembertons of Pemberton in Lancashire was admitted to the Honourable Society of the Inner Temple, came of age, wasted his fortune on clothes, wine, horses, borrowed a large sum of money to pay a gaming debt, was unable to pay and was shut up, like so many other debtors, in the civil prison of the Fleet. He stayed there probably no less than five years. In Roger North's words: 'having been one of the fiercest town rakes, and spent more than he had of his own, his case forced upon him that expedient for a lodging; and there he made so good use of his leisure, and busied himself with the cases of his fellow collegiates whom he informed and advised so skilfully that he was reputed the most notable fellow within those walls; and at length came out a sharper at the law.' He pointed out to his creditors that he would never be able to pay them back if he remained in gaol but would do if he came out. Perhaps he showed them the huge Commonplace Book of law and law reports which he had compiled in the Fleet. Wisely, they agreed to the discharge of this extraordinary young law student. He was called to the Bar on November 27, 1654 and by the time of the Restoration had discharged all his debts, compound interest included. He must be our only Lord Chief Justice to have studied law (and Shakespeare, for he was no pedant) in prison before being called. It never seems to have been held against him.

After the Restoration he rose rapidly, becoming a Bencher and, on April 21, 1675, a sergeant-at-law. Parliament was at the time sitting again, and appeals were brought to the House of Lords from the Court of Chancery in three lawsuits in which members of the House of Commons were involved. The House of Commons, on Ashley Cooper's secret advice, resolved that it would be a breach of privilege for any lawyer to act in these appeals. Sergeant Pemberton took no notice; he and three other barristers appeared in the Lords and argued the cases. Thereupon the Commons voted them into the Tower and ordered their sergeant-of-arms to see to it.

Ashley Cooper was delighted. He had made a long and inflammatory speech in the Lords, describing the imprisonment of the four barristers as an insupportable outrage on the rights of the peers. He demanded from the Lords a writ of Habeas

Corpus addressed to the Lieutenant of the Tower. The Commons retorted with a bellicose declaration against 'the House of Peers'; and, as tempers mounted, the King was forced to prorogue Parliament. This was the precise objective, brilliantly achieved, of Ashley Cooper's tactical manoeuvres, of which the wretched again-imprisoned Pemberton was at this point the stooge. Pemberton always afterwards considered Ashley Cooper the most unprincipled statesman of the age.

Parliament was prorogued for fifteen months and Sir Matthew Hale was replaced by a puisne judge of King's Bench who had also been Hale's colleague in the Court of Exchequer Chamber, an inoffensive, decent lawyer, Richard Raynsford, descended from the Raynsfords of Raynsford, also, like the Pembertons of Pemberton, from Lancashire.

Richard Raynsford

Parliament met again, in February 1677. This was the fifteenth session of the Restoration/Cavalier Parliament, and there was a strong desire throughout the country for a new Parliament to be elected. Ashley Cooper argued, reasonably enough, that Parliament must be taken to be dissolved under the Statutes of Edward III, on the legal grounds that a prorogation of Parliament for more than a year was tantamount to a dissolution. This was a tactical mistake. M.P.s used to what must by then have seemed a lifelong tenure, had no wish to face an election; the Lords voted that Ashley Cooper should retract and apologise. When he refused, he was sent to the Tower 'for high contempts committed against this House'. He applied to King's Bench for a writ of Habeas Corpus on the grounds that the warrant contained no precise charge. The Lord Chief Justice heard the case.

'It is true,' said the ex-Lord Chancellor in reply to a taunt from his prosecutor, the Attorney General, 'that I am a Peer, and no man hath a greater reverence or esteem for the Lords than myself. But I hope my being a Peer shall not lose my being an Englishman, or make me to have less title to Magna Carta and the other laws of English liberty.'

But the Lord Chief Justice ruled otherwise.

'The consequences would be very mischievous,' Raynsford declared, 'if this Court should deliver a member of the House of Peers or Commons committed for contempt, for thereby the public business may be retarded, for it may be the commitment was for evil behaviour or indecent reflections on other members, to the disturbance of the affairs of Parliament.' A bad, silly, submissive reasoning, though the conclusion was defensible. 'This Court has no jurisdiction, and therefore the prisoner must be remanded.'

Anthony Ashley Cooper was now in his late fifties, an apparent failure, disowned by the factions, scorned by the King, and obliged after a year in the Tower to procure his release ignominiously by apologising to the Lords on his knees:

'I Anthony, Earl of Shaftesbury . . . do also acknowledge that my bringing of a *habeas corpus* in King's Bench was a high violation of your Lordships' privileges, and a great aggravation of my former offence, for which I likewise most humbly beg the pardon of this House.'

It is the one case for which Lord Chief Justice Raynsford is remembered.

Sergeant Pemberton meanwhile was in high favour, as was a colleague of his, Sergeant Scroggs. In later life a rumour, quite untrue, had it that William Scroggs was a butcher's son. In fact he was the son of an Oxfordshire squire, well-educated, good-looking, bold and quick. But unlike Pemberton, he carried on with his dissipations even when he had been called to the Bar.

'He was,' wrote Roger North, 'a great voluptuary, his debaucheries egregious and his life loose; which made the Lord Chief Justice Hale detest him.' One result was that, when he was imprisoned for debt – arrested by a creditor when he was just leaving Westminster Hall – Sir Matthew refused to release him, and Scroggs, though a sergeant-at-law, spent a spell in the debtors' prison of Fleet that Pemberton had known as a student – another 'first' for a future Lord Chief Justice. He was a brilliant talker, a witty vivid raconteur, and Charles enjoyed his company. He had as a young man commanded a troop of Royalist horses in the Civil War, which did him no harm. In October 1676 he was knighted and made a judge of Common Pleas; and, when on February 27, 1678 Ashley Cooper was released from the Tower and re-entered public life, Charles' retinue advised him that only a man like Sir William Scroggs, nimble-minded and devoted, could as head of King's Bench deal with the renewed manoeuvres that might now be expected.

Charles II had never removed a Lord Chief Justice yet, and he was reluctant to do so, even though Ashley Cooper was already launching a movement to edge out his brother James from the succession in favour of his illegitimate son Monmouth. Raynsford did not want to retire in the least, but he was told it was for the King's good, and he quietly gave way. He 'resigned' in May 1678 and died eighteen months later. Scroggs took office on the last day of that month, at the age of fifty-five, delighted at having been invited to fill the place of a Lord Chief Justice at whose abilities he had frequently, and indeed justifiably, sneered.

William Scroggs

In the summer of 1678, a few months after Scroggs was appointed, the King was taking his usual early morning stroll in St James' Park when he was stopped by a man he knew slightly who warned that he was in danger of being killed. How? 'By shot.' That evening Charles gave twenty minutes to the go-between and his informant, a half-crazed, left-wing clergyman, Israel Tonge. They landed at the Privy Stairs on the river, and were shown into the Red Room at the top of Whitehall's Privy Gardens. They told the King that a Benedictine monk, Thomas Pickering, and a Jesuit lay brother, John Grove, had vowed to shoot him; failing which Sir George Wakeman, his wife's physician, was to poison him. The puzzled King was also given a long document in forty-nine parts, setting out the full details of the plot. That document listed the names and functions of scores of Jesuits of the English Province, reported their movements, their letters, their finances and their conversations. It appeared that Thomas Whitbread, the Provincial of the English Province, had had twelve of his colleagues sign a letter that they would murder James as well as Charles 'if he should not answer to their expectations'. It appeared that the Jesuits of the Spanish Province had offered £10,000 towards the good work, and that Père La Chaise, Louis XIV's confessor, had chipped in with another £10,000. It transpired that their Benedictine allies in the form of Thomas Pickering had already tried to shoot the King in St James' Park, only to be frustrated by a loose flint in his pistol. The composer of this detailed and fascinating narrative was a young man who had himself attended a Jesuit seminary, and been expelled: Titus Oates.

It appeared that the details of the assassination had been settled at a Jesuit Consult, a meeting of forty Jesuits held on April 24 at the White Horse Tavern in the Strand. Almost a year later when the panic produced by the Popish Plot was still at its height, Salvetti the Modenese Resident wrote as follows:

'Whether these insane tales are true or false I do not presume to decide, but so many persons of quality, moderation and intelligence affirm them to be true that I am confounded in my thoughts.' That was the trouble: the details were so factual and were so constantly being embroidered by the informers who sprang up in Oates' footsteps – Bedloe, Dugdale and the rest – that even honest men, at first sceptical, ended by believing that there must be something in it all. But it was all smoke without fire. There was nothing in it, nothing in what soon became a nation-wide conspiracy with, as sub-plots, armed risings in Staffordshire, South Wales and elsewhere. Nothing in the rumours of night-riders galloping across the whole country. Nothing in the expected French invasion of the Isle of Purbeck. Nothing. Nothing at all, except certain indiscreet letters from the Duchess of York's secretary, a rabid Catholic convert, to the French court; and a still-mysterious murder, that of Sir Edmund Berry Godfrey, a London magistrate who had taken Titus Oates' deposition.

'And it is surprising,' continued Salvetti, '(considering the temper of this nation) that they have not risen and massacred all those suspected of such crimes, and I have heard it said by several people that all the Catholics deserve to be killed.'

Only old men in their eighties could have personally remembered the last wave of Catholic-inspired terror, at the time of the Gunpowder Plot. But the fact was unforgettable: there had certainly been a plot then, and in the folk-memory of the people as of the lawyers the Jesuits had been behind it. They had suffered of course: there had only been a handful then, and they had been legally liquidated. But it was common knowledge that there were roughly 500 priests in England now, and of those roughly a quarter were Jesuits. Well over a hundred dangerous, indeed murderous. foreign agents at large! With the potential support of about one Englishman in every twenty, with bastions scattered across the countryside, a nest of Benedictines openly in the Strand, and foreign embassies and royal chapels celebrating that odious ceremonial, the Mass, in the heart of the capital.

Well might young Lord Russell tell the House of Commons: 'I despise such a ridiculous and nonsensical religion. A piece of wafer, broken betwixt a priest's fingers to be our Saviour! And what becomes of it when eaten and taken down, you know.'

Scroggs' name has gone down in legal history as that of one of the worst and most brutal of our judges ever; but I cannot help feeling that he has been unjustly lambasted. True, his tirades against priests and popery are of almost ridiculous vehemence; but when even a young incorruptible of the ilk of William Russell could make the sort of comment quoted above, the brutal and, it must be admitted, often pithy remarks of the Lord Chief Justice are less difficult to accept. Furthermore, there is no indication that these tirades ever convicted priests or Catholic laymen whom the juries would otherwise have acquitted. I have gone rapidly through most of the treason trials over which Scroggs presided [rapidly because they occupy three volumes – 2000 closely printed pages – of the State Trials] and my distinct impression is that, for all his bellowing, he did his best to do justice. He pressed hard on the accused but he pressed almost equally hard on the prosecution, and on the prosecution witnesses. In the chaotic state of the law of evidence he stuck firmly to the guiding principle that one witness alone, however plausible, was not sufficient to convict on a charge of treason. If he was duped by Oates and the rest of the informers, as seems to have been the case, then he shared that misfortune with the rest of the English nation. Gradually, however, he came to believe that he *had* been duped; unfortunately for himself, a belief that anticipated the nation's. The result was that, when he veered towards the defence and towards acquittals, he became as detested by the Whigs – and by their historians – as he had previously been by the Papists. Damned by both sides, he was ignominiously discarded by the government when his services were no longer of use.

What Scroggs would not do, and did not do, is succumb to mob pressure, and this was all the harder because mob pressure was enormous, during the two and a half years when the Popish Plot and the trials that followed kept the kingdom in a state of perpetual turmoil. For much of that period Anthony Ashley Cooper was virtually tribune of the people, a popular dictator, whose writ ran in the streets and indeed in Parliament, though not entirely in the government or the administration. Ashley Cooper almost certainly was not the brains behind the Plot, but once panic had broken out, he seized the rudder and steered the rickety ship of state into waters more and more turgid. But

Scroggs stood up to him. Even at social events like the Lord Mayor's dinner when rival toasts were proposed, the Duke of Monmouth's health and the Duke of York's too, Scroggs declared that 'the Duke might be a papist, but he could not conceive how he might be popery'. At which 'all the lords in a great scuffle rose from the table and went into another room, whither the Lord Chief Justice singly of all the judges followed them.'

Ashley Cooper had his revenge on Scroggs a year later, arranging for the House of Commons to vote eight Articles of Impeachment against the Lord Chief Justice for 'high treason and other high crimes and misdemeanours' of which one read as follows: that the Lord Chief Justice 'did know best and curb Dr Titus Oates and Captain Bedloe, two of the principal witnesses for the King . . . and that the said Chief Justice, to manifest his slighting opinion of the evidence of the said Titus Oates and Captain Bedloe . . . did dare to say that Dr Titus Oates and Captain Bedloe always had an accusation ready against any body.' What could be, with hindsight, better evidence of Scroggs' worthiness and Ashley Cooper's unscrupulousness than that Article? For good measure it was added in another Article 'That the said Lord Chief Justice is very much addicted to swearing and cursing in his common discourse, and to drink to excess, to the great disparagement of the dignity and gravity of his office'. Unfortunately one of the people with whom it was proved that he had drunk to excess was Ashley Cooper himself. Not that that would have saved him; though it is hard to see where the 'high treason' lay in this or in any other of the Articles of Impeachment. He was saved in the end by the abrupt dissolution of Parliament – only to be dismissed by a Writ of *Supersedeas* soon afterwards, to retire to Essex and to die, in the Whig historian Lord Campbell's phrase, 'still a solitary, selfish bachelor'.

Sir Edmund Berry Godfrey, the magistrate, had last been seen alive on the afternoon of October 12, 1678. Five days later his body was found in a ditch at the foot of Primrose Hill, run through with his own sword. But it soon became clear that he had been strangled several days before. Parliament met within nine days, to hear the plausible Oates explain that the General of the Society of Jesus, on the authority of the Pope, had set up, on paper, a popish government, headed by Lord Arundell of Wardour as Lord Chancellor. From that moment on it was pure panic. The Lord Chief Justice was sent for, the doors were barred, no one was allowed to leave the chamber though it was late at night, and Scroggs issued a warrant to arrest Lord Arundell and four other aged and innocuous Catholic peers. After that it was trial upon trial.

First to suffer was William Staley, son of a Catholic banker who had been heard to say: 'The King is a great heretic. I would kill him myself.' He was tried on November 20, and sentenced in King's Bench. 'Excuse me, gentlemen,' said Scroggs in his summing-up, 'if I am a little warm when perils are so many, murders so secret, that we cannot discover the murderer of that gentleman whom we knew so well . . . It is better to be warm here than in Smithfield.' But this was a mere opening.

The next trial was held on November 27 in Westminster Hall before a full panoply of five judges, including that brilliant young advocate, Sir George Jeffreys, who had just been elected Recorder of London. Sir Edward Coleman, the accused, the Duchess of York's secretary, was the only man who perhaps deserved to die. His third letter to Père La Chaise condemned him, not Oates and Bedloe, whose testimony Scroggs half dismissed.

'We have a mighty work upon our hand, no less that the conversion of three Kingdoms, and the utter subduing of a pestilent heresy,' Coleman had written; and of course these words added fuel to the notion of a plot.

Before the year was out, at the Old Bailey, Scroggs, with Recorder Jeffreys' assistance, tried Thomas Pickering, the Benedictine, and John Grove, the Jesuit lay brother – the two presumed potential assassins plus the Provincial of the English Provinces, Thomas Wentworth, and two more Jesuits. The defendants attacked both Oates' testimony and Oates' character. This was in a sense the key trial of the whole plot. Scroggs pointed out, again and again, what every English Protestant believed, that any priest could obtain a dispensation to lie. He culminated his accusation with the ringing, ranting words: 'They eat their God, they kill the King, and saint the murderer.' For all that the King was unconvinced, and reluctant to sign the death-warrant for his 'murderers'. When they were, eventually, executed, the drawing and quartering were perfunctory gestures only; on the government's instructions they were hanged by the neck long enough to be almost certainly dead. And so it was with all the rest of the priests who were to be executed.

On February 10, 1679, two laymen were tried and convicted for murder, the murder of the magistrate. But on the following day Samuel Atkins was acquitted on the Lord Chief Justice's instructions. Scroggs had found Bedloe's evidence too thin, and told Atkins it was 'nothing to the purpose . . . you need not labour your defence as to anything he says.'

In April Sergeant Pemberton was promoted to be a puisne judge of King's Bench and sit by the Lord Chief Justice's side.

On June 13 four more priests were tried before a panel of judges. The youngest, a Jesuit, John Gavan aged forty, dominated the trial: but a new informer, a respectable man unlike Oates or Bedloe, a certain Stephen Dugdale, land steward of the Catholic Lord Aston, outfaced them all. The defence brought forward sixteen witnesses from St Omer's to prove that Oates had never left that seminary in the first six months of 1678. 'Take great heed of what they say,' Scroggs told the jury, 'and be governed by it according to the credibility of the person and the matter.' But, unlike the confused governnment witnesses, they had clearly all been prepared and rehearsed, which destroyed their credibility. Next day the Catholic lawyer Richard Langhorn (future Attorney General in the papist government, *per* Oates) was tried, amidst an increasingly abusive crowd. 'Here is a gentleman,' summed up Scroggs, 'that stands at the bar upon his life on the one hand; but if Mr Oates says true, all our lives and liberties, our King and our religion, are at stake on the other hand. God defend that innocent blood should be shed, and God defend us also from popery, and from all popish plots and from all the bloody principles of papists.' The jury brought in the usual verdict; and as Recorder in his own Court of Old Bailey Judge Jeffreys, pronounced the death sentence on priests and laymen alike with energy and elegance, to much applause.

Then on Friday, July 18, 1679 came the trial of two priests, a Benedictine lay brother and the Queen's physician Sir George Wakeman. This trial marked the legal turning point of the whole affair. By this time Oates and Bedloe were almost discredited. They tied themselves up into knots. The Lord Chief Justice was as hard and impatient with one side as he was with the other. His final directions to the jury now varied in emphasis. 'We would not,' he said, 'to prevent all their plots (let them be as big as they can make them) shed one drop of innocent blood: therefore I would have you in all these gentlemen's cases, consider seriously and weigh truly the circumstances and the probability of things charged upon them . . . These men's bloods are at stake, and your soul and mine, and our oaths and consciences are at stake; and therefore care never what the world says, follow your conscience.' It was a courageous, decent summing-up – and all four accused were acquitted.

The mob went wild with frustrated rage. A dead dog was thrown at the Lord Chief Justice's coach. Wherever he went, he was greeted with cries of 'A Wakeman! A Wakeman!' One popular lampoon went:

> The judge is a butcher's son
> Yet hates to shed innocent blood
> But for ten thousand pounds he has done
> The Pope a great deal of good.
>
> He that villain Wakeman cleared
> Who was to have poisoned our King
> As it most plainly appeared
> For which he deserves to swing.

But Scroggs cared nothing. He declared 'that he had condemned Coleman against the will of the Court, that he had acquitted Wakeman against the will of the City and he would keep his office against the will of the Devil'. He set out, that summer, on a circuit that took in Assizes at Monmouth, at Hereford, at Stafford and at Worcester, ordering the immediate execution of several priests and Jesuits already tried locally and condemned, and in his own trials acquitting one secular priest, admittedly, but condemning brutally a seventy-eight-year-old Jesuit to immediate execution.

On January 17, 1680, seven more priests, a very mixed bag, appeared before Scroggs at King's Bench charged with high treason under Elizabeth's statute of 1585 for simply being priests and in England. All except one were found guilty and condemned to death, but in fact none were executed.

In February Mr Justice Pemberton was dismissed, apparently for being overly-keen in his Protestant zeal, and returned to the Bar, to practise at Common Pleas.

On June 11 the Lord Chief Justice tried a Catholic lady, Mrs Cellier, who had been accused of contriving the 'Meal Tub Plot' to discredit the Whigs. But the informer in this case, Dangerfield, was even more notoriously perjured than Oates or Bedloe. 'I wonder at your impudence,' Scroggs told him, 'that you dare look a court of Justice in the face.' Mrs Cellier was acquitted, unwisely boasted about in her case in a pamphlet entitled *Malice Defeated*, was hauled back before King's Bench and sentenced to a spell in the pillory. At least Scroggs appears to have been even-handed in his severity.

On June 23, came the trial of Lord Castlemaine (at King's

Bench, for he was an Irish peer) on charges of treason for being involved in the plot. He was acquitted.

Finally, on November 29, the only member of the House of Lords to face trial, William Howard, Lord Stafford, was tried by his peers, the Lord Chancellor as Lord High Steward presiding, the Lord Chief Justice advising. He was a man much disliked, and he was found guilty by a majority of fifty-five to thirty-one (nine other Howard peers voting for his death). By then Scroggs was facing impeachment, James Duke of York was facing exclusion from the succession; and the Whigs, as they were now beginning to be called, were in the ascendant, led by England's first party manager, Anthony Ashley Cooper, Earl of Shaftesbury, in the Lords and by his young disciple William Lord Russell, 'the patriot', M.P. for Tavistock and heir to the Earldom of Bedford in the Commons.

Charles II's fourth and last Parliament was summoned to Royalist Oxford on March 21, 1681. The King was escorted by his Horse Guards. Ashley Cooper's Londoners, also armed, wore on their hats blue silk ribbons, proclaiming 'No Popery! No Slavery!' The Whigs were testing their strength, but went too far. They rejected out-of-hand a proposed compromise on the succession, and in their high-handedness they tried to impeach before the Lords an ordinary commoner, a wretched informer called Fitzharris, whom both sides had been hoping to use. The House of Commons voted 'that it amounted to a denial of justice, a violation of the constitution of Parliament, and an obstruction to the further discovery of the Popish Plot' if Fitzharris should be tried by any inferior court. But the Lords voted the other way, and this time the quarrel between the two Houses was fatal to Ashley Cooper. The King by a bold and unexpected stroke dissolved Parliament a week after it had met, returned to London, dismissed a Lord Chief Justice who could not be entirely relied on, and reappointed to the Bench in Scroggs' place the man who had for a few brief months sat by his side, the poacher-turned-gamekeeper, Francis Pemberton.

Like Scroggs, Pemberton was a youngish man to become Lord Chief Justice, in his energetic mid-fifties; unlike Scroggs, thought to be a fitting instrument for royal revenge. For with the sudden dissolution of the Oxford Parliament the Whig power-base had collapsed. They did not realise it at the time; they were cowed, and fled from dangerous Oxford back to the safety of London. But they confidently expected another Parliament. From his secure base, his mansion in Aldersgate, Ashley

Cooper started planning for the next elections – which were never to be held.

Francis Pemberton

It was to a very dangerous position, then, that the new Lord Chief Justice stepped up on April 11, 1681. One of the most popular themes in the Whig pamphlets of the times was that unjust judges must be punished. The fates of Lord Chief Justices Tresilian and Belknap during the reign of Richard II, were often cited; and one pamphlet, wildly unhistorical, repeated how King Alfred had had a brisk way with his judges, hanging no fewer than thirty in one year.

On the other hand the Whigs themselves were totally unscrupulous in their use of witnesses. Their excesses, when they started mobilising Irish witnesses for the Irish end of the Popish Plot, played into the hands of the Tories and ruined their credit with even their own moderate supporters. Ever since the Irish Rebellion of forty years earlier and the massacre of Protestants in Ireland, almost any atrocities could be believed of these native savages. But when the witnesses to the Irish Plot were themselves bog-Irish Papists, how, sneered the Tories, could such men be trusted? These Irish witnesses, whose evidence was totally manufactured, soon proved themselves as unreliable as they were despicable.

In the long nave of Downside Abbey is an ornate baroque tomb at which we schoolboys used to gaze and, occasionally, to pray. It contained, we were told, the body (but not the head) of the Blessed Oliver Plunket, martyr. The martyr's head was in Ireland, in Drogheda, partly because he was, it seemed, an Irishman, an Archbishop of Armagh and Primate of all Ireland. What his body was doing in a Benedictine abbey in Somerset, and how and why he had been martyred, we were perhaps told but paid very little attention to. In the summer of 1981 St Oliver Plunket, as he had since become, had his head and body briefly reunited, by helicopter, in a rather macabre but moving ceremony on Clapham Common, presided over by the Duke of Norfolk and Cardinal Basil Hume. It marked of course the

300th anniversary of his execution: he was hanged, drawn and quartered at Tyburn on July 1, 1681.

Plunket's was an extraordinarily unnecessary execution. He had been Primate of Ireland since 1670, on good terms with the Anglican Viceroys, 'in due submission to the government, without engaging into intrigues of state', as Bishop Burnet wrote, arrested in the panic months after the outbreak of the Popish Plot but in very little danger till orders came a year later that he should be brought over for trial in London. He lay in Newgate from November 1680, one of his fellow prisoners being Anthony Corker, the English Benedictine monk, sentenced to death by Scroggs but later reprieved (hence the final resting place of Plunket's body). The charge against him was high treason: that he had conspired to bring a large French army into Ireland and to raise 60,000 men of his own. It was ridiculous, economically, psychologically, financially and geographically. But the Archbishop had to face his trial without witnesses on his side – bad roads had delayed them, and the Lord Chief Justice, appealed to, refused to delay the trial beyond June 8.

There is nothing admirable in the way Pemberton conducted the trial. He was reasonably moderate in his strictures against the Papists, and at one stage he stopped Jeffreys who, for the prosecution, was going too far. But Pemberton did not dare push the contemptible prosecution witnesses, as Scroggs might have done. The jury were out for only a quarter of an hour. 'God almighty bless your Lordship!' said the Archbishop, after sentence had been pronounced. 'And now, my Lord, as I am a dead man to this world, and as I hope for mercy in the next, I was never guilty of any of the treasons laid to my charge, as you will know in due time.'

The King was even more cowardly on this occasion than his Lord Chief Justice. When a former Viceroy of Ireland, Arthur Capel, Earl of Essex, assured him that the charges could not be true, he replied that he dared not pardon the Archbishop. Plunket was executed with all the traditional barbarities that the English priests had, generally, been spared. He was the last, and the noblest, of the sacrificial victims of the Popish Plot; his trial and execution caused a revulsion against the Whigs, and it seems quite possible that Charles, as cynical and skilled a manoeuvrer in his own way as Ashley Cooper, failed to pardon him not because he was afraid of popular reaction, as he implied, but precisely in order to show that the Whigs were inhuman in their bloodlust.

The Royalist reaction, what came to be known as the 'Tory Revenge' had begun.

On the very same day that Archbishop Plunket was executed, the villainous informer Fitzharris, also tried by Lord Chief Justice Pemberton at King's Bench, was executed – an open blow at the Whigs. Next day, July 2, Ashley Cooper was arrested in Aldersgate on a charge of high treason. His papers were seized, he was examined by the Council (and indeed by the King himself, who had come up specially from Windsor for the pleasure) and committed to the Tower.

Charles was now determined to have Ashley Cooper's head. The man was sixty, his popularity had waned, his party was in disarray, his personal enemies were innumerable, his attempts to impeach both James, Duke of York, and, more unforgivable still, the Queen herself, could not be forgotten. For forty years he had been an active intriguer, true to his principles but false to his friends and at last it seemed he had been given more than enough rope with which to hang himself. He was charged with planning an open insurrection if he should be worsted at the Oxford Parliament, that is to say with the *intention* of 'levying war against the King'.

Charles may have believed it, and indeed Ashley Cooper may have planned it. But the extraordinary thing in the long, long conflict between those two men is that it never in fact came to a trial of armed strength, though it had so often seemed to be verging on civil war. Their battlefields, their only battlefields, were Parliament and the law courts. So it was to be in this, final fluctuating round of what was a struggle not merely between personalities and parties, but between principles and indeed philosophies.

As Earl of Shaftesbury, Anthony Ashley Cooper would have to be tried by his peers, by (in the absence of a sitting Parliament) the Lord High Steward's court, a tribunal of selected peers. The problem did not lie there; there were peers enough, even among his former supporters, who hated or despised Ashley Cooper, and Charles had made up his mind to give no pardon. The legal problem was that the accused would first have to appear before a Grand Jury, whose role it would be to decide whether there was sufficient evidence or not to allow the charges to be brought. If they believed the evidence sufficient, they would bring in a 'true bill' – *Billa Vera* – and the prosecution would proceed.

On November 24, 1681, after four months in the Tower, Ashley Cooper was brought to the Old Bailey to face the Grand

Jury and the Lord Chief Justice. Witnesses were called to prove that he had said 'that the King was a man of no faith and deserved to be deposed like Richard II' and 'that he, the Earl of Shaftesbury, would make England into a Commonwealth like Holland.' They were bad witnesses, unreliable, contradicting each other despite Pemberton's efforts to hold them to a coherent story; but they were certainly better witnesses than in the Plunket trial. At the end of the evidence the Lord Chief Justice sent the Grand Jury out with the instruction, 'You are to enquire whether it be fitting for the King to call my Lord Shaftesbury to question upon this account of treasonable words.' The period of waiting was extraordinarily tense. When the Grand Jury returned their foreman handed their copy of the indictment to a court official. He turned it over and read aloud the one word on the back: '*Ignoramus*' – no case to answer. The shouting and cheering lasted over an hour, there were bonfires and illuminations in every street in the City. The accused was playing a game of piquet with his wife in the Tower; the story goes that he calmly continued. He was not released till several months later. When he was released he took up his residence in Thanet House in Aldersgate, and took special care not to go beyond the limits of the City of London and County of Middlesex.

'It is a hard case,' said the King mildly, 'that I am the last man to have law and justice in the whole nation.' Charles' point was this: that however good the evidence might have been against Ashley Cooper, the Grand Jury would still have returned a verdict of '*Ignoramus*', because the Grand Jury was selected – packed – by the two Sheriffs of London and Middlesex, and the Sheriffs were selected under the City Charter by the burghers of London, that bastion of Whig sentiment and Whig power. They were elected once a year, at a midsummer election held at the Guildhall.

The power of the City of London in Stuart times lay not only in its wealth, but also in the fact that approximately one Englishman in ten was living inside (or just outside) the City walls, a pullulating, throbbing mass of excited humanity that has, three centuries later, disappeared: the importance of the City was not just a matter of money. There lay concentrated political power; independent of the monarchy and the government, ruled by its own rules, electing all its own officials, with, in the Common Council, a body that when Parliament was not sitting could and did claim to speak for the nation.

The King was determined to break the power of London with

the help of his lawyers and judges. For some time the government had been using the services of an extraordinarily skilled
'special pleader', an unambitious, jovial, talented lawyer of
very humble origins named Saunders, who lodged with a
tailor's family in Butcher Row near Temple Lane. He was
instructed to find a pretext for accusing the City of having
overstepped its legal prerogatives and thus to justify a *Quo
Warranto* suit: a challenge by the Crown against the City
Charter. Saunders set to work with a will. Though he was not
particularly interested in money or politics, he was fascinated
by legal subtleties.

> His great dexterity [wrote Roger North] was in the art of
> special pleading, and he would lay snares that often caught
> his superiors, who were not aware of his traps. And he was so
> fond of success for his clients that, rather than fail, he would
> set the Court hard with a trick; for which he met sometimes
> with a reprimand, which he would wittily ward off, so that
> no one was much offended with him. But Hale could not bear
> his irregularity of life; and for that, and suspicion of his
> tricks, used to bear hard upon him in the court. But no ill
> usage from the bench was too hard for his hold of business,
> being such as scarce any could do but himself.

Even with the 'hold of business' of a barrister such as Saunders,
however, the *Quo Warranto* suit would inevitably be long,
complex and uncertain. Meanwhile the King was determined, if
possible, to have Ashley Cooper brought to trial by ousting the
Whig Sheriffs of the City of London. Once Tory Sheriffs were
elected they would empanel a Tory Grand Jury that would find
a True Bill for high treason against the man the government so
loathed and feared, the poison-sucking Tapski, as the courtiers
had nicknamed the pale Whig leader.

So, inevitably, the midsummer election of the two Sheriffs in
1682 became the focus for violent and farcical manoeuvres.
Finally after annulments, riots, lawsuits and postponements the
two Tory candidates were declared elected – though not till
September 19. The night following the declaration of the result
Ashley Cooper left his house and thereafter shifted his lodgings
nightly. Warrants for his arrest were out again, and this time he
knew that his opponents would have the whip hand.

It was a desperate moment for the Whigs. Ashley Cooper,
with all the despair of a man virtually condemned to death,
determined on a desperate gamble – an uprising. Its success
would depend on the young man whom he had groomed and

dominated, James, Duke of Monmouth, 'the Protestant Duke'. Two years earlier he had sent Monmouth on a triumphal tour of the West Country. He had been based at Longleat, staying with his crony Tom Thynne, the richest landowner in the West. His greatest welcome then had been at Nonconformist Taunton. At this moment Monmouth was on a semi-royal 'progress' through the North-West. The plan was for John Trenchard, M.P. for Taunton in the last, Oxford, Parliament, to raise the West Country and divert Charles' standing army from London; for Ashley Cooper, then, to seize the City and Westminster with his 'ten thousand brisk boys' from Wapping, and for Monmouth to raise his standard in the North-West. But Trenchard cried off; the other Whig grandees stood at least half aside; and, evading arrest by a few hours, Ashley Cooper slipped off in disguise to Harwich and to Holland.

That was on November 18. Five days later the Whig grandees gathered publicly, to show as it were their undaunted unity, at the trial of one of their number, Lord Grey de Werke. It was not a political trial as such. Lord Grey, a rabid Exclusionist, was up at King's Bench, charged before Lord Chief Justice Pemberton with conspiring to seduce his own sister-in-law Lady Harriet Berkeley. His real offence had been his interference in the Sheriff's election at the Guildhall in the summer. Pemberton had not been overawed by the Wapping mob that Ashley Cooper had brought with him to the Old Bailey a year earlier; but he seemed to be overawed by the presence of the Whig lords and their retainers. He conducted an extremely fair trial, no doubt too fair for the government. When, despite Lady Harriet's protests, the jury brought in a verdict of guilty, Lord Berkeley called on all his Whig friends present to help him seize his daughter. Swords were drawn, blows exchanged, and bloodshed in King's Bench itself was only avoided by Pemberton's stern warnings: 'a scene unparalleled in our legal history', Macaulay has called it.

In public the Whig grandees might be defiant but in private they were despondent. Their leader had been driven overseas, his papers had been found and were being examined, their figurehead Monmouth was being trailed by police spies, they themselves had been completely outmanoeuvred by the government. Each party had in the last years been trying to destroy the other by the use of the courts, and the Whigs had just been given a foretaste of how the battles there would go now: against them, even with reasonably impartial judges. Not that there was any reason to assume that reasonably impartial judges would be allowed to continue in office. Furthermore, the *Quo Warranto* action was proceeding and it seemed as if the last bastion of their independent power, London, would be permanently subjected to direct royal authority. That piercing-eyed ambitious lawyer, Sergeant Jeffreys, voted out of his position as Recorder of London, was serving his royal master nobly by preparing both that attack and legal attacks on the rights of other corporations. The Whigs could hardly rest inactive in the face of threats not only to their political power bases and indeed their lives and property but to the principles for which they undoubtedly stood. They met at John Hampden's London house and formed, formally or informally, a Council of Six. The Six were the Duke of Monmouth himself, Arthur Capel, Earl of Essex, the former Viceroy of Ireland, William Lord Russell, heir to the Bedford estates, Algernon Sidney of Penshurst Place, Lord Howard of Escrick and John Hampden, grandson of the famous Hampden.

That a Council of Six was formed seems incontrovertible. What they planned, or plotted, is much more arguable. At any rate their plots and plans were temporarily thrown into confusion by the death of a man whom, had he lived, would have been impossible for them to ignore. On January 21, 1683 Anthony Ashley Cooper, who had been living splendidly in exile in Amsterdam, died of gout in the arms of an old companion. It must have seemed to him in his dying moments that his life had ended in total ignominious failure. So it did. But if he had lived six years longer, he would have seen the triumph of all he stood for; the end of the Stuart monarchy, the end of an absolutist government, the beginnings of modern England. Without his turbulence, above all without his organisation of a political party that survived his death, none of this would necessarily have followed. But perhaps the most extraordinary thing of all about the life of this pale, lean, detested little man was that it did not end, as his King and his enemies had so understandably desired on the block at Tower Hill.

8

Judge Jeffreys

One week before Ashley Cooper's death Saunders to his astonishment received a letter from the Lord Keeper announcing that it was his Majesty's pleasure that he should become Lord Chief Justice.

'As to his person, he was very corpulent and beastly,' wrote Roger North of the new Lord Chief Justice, 'a mere lump of morbid flesh.' It would be a sin, as my predecessor Lord Campbell put it, to abridge or alter North's extraordinarily vivid description.

He used to say '*by his troggs* (such an humourous way of talking he affected) *none could say he wanted issue of his body, for he had nine in his back.*' He was a fetid mass that offended his neighbours at the Bar in the sharpest degree. Those whose ill-fortune it was to stand near him were confessors, and in summer-time almost martyrs. This hateful decay of his carcase came upon him by continued sottishness; for, to say nothing of brandy, he was seldom without a pot of ale at his nose, or near him. That exercise was all he used; the rest of his life was sitting at his desk or piping at home; and that *home* was a tailor's house, in Butcher Row, called his lodging, and the man's wife was his nurse or worse; but by virtue of his money, of which he made little account, though he got a great deal, he soon became master of the family; and, being no changeling, he never removed, but was true to his friends and they to him to the last hour of his life. With all this, he had a goodness of nature and disposition in so great a degree that he may be deservedly styled a *philanthrope*. He was a very *Silenus* to the boys, as in this place I may term the students of the law, to make them merry when ever they had a mind to it. He had nothing of rigid or austere in him. If any near him at the Bar grumbled at his stench, he ever converted the complaint into content and laughing with the abundance of his wit. As to his ordinary dealing he was as honest as the driven snow was white; and why not, having no regard to money or desire to be rich? And for good nature and condescension there was not his fellow. I have seen him for hours and half hours together before the Court sat, stand at the Bar, with an audience of students over against him, putting of cases, and debating so as suited their capacities and encouraged their industries. And so in the Temple, he seldom moved without a parcel of youths hanging about him, and he merry and jesting with them. Once, after he was in the King's business, he dined with the Lord Keeper, and there he showed another qualification he had acquired, and that was to play jigs upon an harpsichord, having taught himself with the opportunity of an old virginal of his landlady's; but in such a manner, not for defect but figure, as to see him was a jest.

To his extraordinarily well-contrived character sketch Roger North could have added one thing: that Saunders' Law Reports of cases at King's Bench were so sharply written and so entertaining (even in the law French which Charles II had restored) that his reputation as a shrewd writer was as great and as well-deserved as his reputation for jovial conviviality.

Edmund Saunders

Francis Pemberton was not exactly disgraced. He was shifted sideways, to the office of Lord Chief Justice of the Common Pleas on January 13, 1683, the day on which his successor was appointed. The Lord Keeper told Saunders that this was at Pemberton's own desire 'for that it is a place (though not so honourable) yet of more ease and plenty'. Possibly it was indeed Pemberton's wish, though as he had on at least one notorious occasion been bested by Saunders in the matter of the legal effects of an impeachment, he can hardly have been delighted at the choice of his malodorous successor.

One reason for the choice of Saunders and one reason for the dismissal of Pemberton became almost immediately apparent.

The first was the opening of the *Quo Warranto* case on February 7: *the King* versus *the Mayor and Commonalty of the*

City of London. The lawyer who had prepared the Crown's case was now, as Lord Chief Justice, to preside over its hearing. The second was another trial, on February 16, of the man to whom Pemberton had been so overly fair: Lord Grey de Werke. This time he was charged with the real 'offence' for which the government wanted him sent down: 'rioting' at the previous midsummer's Sheriffs' election at the Guildhall. The double-barrelled legal assault on the Whigs was at last therefore properly launched: almost simultaneously on their power base and on their persons.

The new Lord Chief Justice was not excessive. He heard the *Quo Warranto* proceedings argued twice, in two different terms, the second time by the Attorney General for the Crown and by the Whig lawyer Pollexfen for the City. 'We shall take time to be advised of our opinion,' he said (announcing he would give judgment the term following after looking into the precedents) 'but I cannot help now saying what a grievous thing it would be if a corporation cannot be forfeited or dissolved for any crime whatsoever.'

He was not excessive either, in the far more rowdy trial of Lord Grey de Werke, plus, indicted with him, various Whig former Sheriffs of London and Middlesex. The energetic clear-minded Sergeant Jeffreys, who had already opposed Lord Grey de Werke in the Lady Harriet Berkeley abduction case, weighed in with his by-now usual trademark: the apposite use of familiar quotations: 'Here's a tale of a tub indeed,' said Jeffreys in reply to the defence's challenge against the jury. 'Aye,' said the Lord Chief Justice, 'it is nothing else, and I wonder that lawyers should put such a thing upon me.' 'Robin Hood on Greendale stood!' added Sergeant Jeffreys more obscurely, 'I pray for the King it may be overruled.' By the end of the exchange he was telling the nominal master of the court precisely what to do.

Jeffreys: This discourse is only for discourse' sake. Swear the jury.
Lord Chief Justice Saunders: Aye, swear the jury.

Saunders' summing-up was more pathetic than truculent. 'Pray, gentlemen, forebear,' he said when interrupted by the gallery, 'such demeanour does not become a court of justice. When things were topsy turvey I can't tell what was done, and I would be loth to have it raked up now.' He may not have known that he was a dying man but he was clearly ill and easily upset. 'Gentlemen, it hath been a long trial, and it may be that I have not taken it well; my memory is bad, and I am but weak: I don't question but your memories are better than mine. Consider your verdict and find as many guilty as you think fit.'

The jury of course found all guilty; but sentences were only imposed on June 15, and were comparatively mild, mere fines (1000 marks for Lord Grey de Werke: he failed to pay up and his goods were seized). Two days earlier judgment had been given on the *Quo Warranto*. It went of course in favour of the Crown. The City Charter was abolished and a new one eventually granted, which gave the King virtually complete control over the appointments of Lord Mayor, Sheriffs, Recorder and Town Clerk of London. Saunders had done his work – though only just in time. On June 23 he died, in a house in respectable Parson's Green to which he had, much against his wishes, removed on his respectable appointment. His will rather touchingly appointed Nathaniel Earle and Jane, his wife, the tailors of Butcher Row, his executors and residuary legatees 'as some recompense for their care of him and attendance upon him for many years'.

Edmund Saunders has now been totally forgotten, though he was perhaps the most extraordinary and eccentric Lord Chief Justice of all time. His successor has not been forgotten, and never will be. Indeed his is probably the only Lord Chief Justice whose name means anything at all to the ordinary man or woman. For his successor was that legendary monster of legal iniquity known to posterity neither as Lord Chief Justice nor as Lord Chancellor (both of which positions he held) but simply, and strikingly, as 'Judge': Judge Jeffreys.

Before I began this book I had my own mental picture of Judge Jeffreys, which I am sure is shared by almost everyone who visualises the typical hanging judge of popular imagination: thin-lipped, beak-nosed, hideous and, above all, old and wicked. George Jeffreys may have been wicked – that is something that will have to be discussed in the pages that follow – but he was certainly not hideous. His portraits, of which there are many, show an elegant, extremely well-dressed and undeniably handsome man – indeed almost effeminately good-looking in his thirties. As he ages, his jowl becomes heavier, his rosebud lips more ordinary, his black eyebrows blacker and thicker, while his long, shapely nose and large, fascinating eyes remain much the same. He is certainly putting on weight; his contemporaries alleged that he drank, and was often drunk on the Bench. If so, he was no better and no worse than his predecessors of whom they said exactly the same thing. In his last years he suffered dreadfully from the stone, and almost certainly died of an inflammation caused by this. The most extraordinary misconception, however, is that Judge Jeffreys was old. He was never old. He died at the age of forty-five. He became Lord Chief Justice of England at the age of thirty-nine, the youngest Lord Chief Justice, that we ever have had, at least in post-medieval times (for there is no telling their ages before); and indeed one of our youngest judges ever. In judicial terms George Jeffreys so far from being an aged monster was an infant prodigy.

And that, no doubt, was why he was *not* appointed Lord Chief Justice on Saunders' sudden death. He was far too young. Also, though he was one of the governmental 'team' of prosecuting lawyers, there were two men senior to him with, theoretically, far better claims: the Attorney General, Sawyer, and the Solicitor General, Finch. Also he had never been an M.P. Also he had written nothing; he had no legal learning. Also there is a story (nowadays strongly queried) that the King disliked him. Charles had commented that Sergeant Jeffreys had 'no learning, no sense, no manners and more impudence than ten carted street-walkers'. Charles may have said it, in a fit of pique, but it most certainly did not represent his usual attitude. In August 1678 the King and his current reigning mistress, Louise de Kerouailles, had driven from Windsor across the Thames to young Jeffrey's newly acquired country house, Bulstrode Park, near Gerard's Cross. At that dinner, gossip-writers recorded, Charles drank to his host no less than seven times. As well he might. George Jeffreys came of solidly Royalist gentry family, sixth son of John Jeffreys of Aston Park on the Welsh border, and only the year before the King had knighted him on the occasion of his becoming Solicitor General to James Duke of York, the King's brother and potential successor. He was a most promising advocate, a brilliant, energetic cross-examiner, and an excellent, irrepressible conversationalist in ordinary, social life. James of course was even closer to his own Solicitor General, and, however wicked Jeffreys may be judged to have become, he cannot be criticised for disloyalty. He was loyal to James all his life, even when everyone else was abandoning him. And my view is that he too could have successfully abandoned James in the end: as James' daughters did, as his favourite politicians did, as his military commanders did, and as even (possibly a more comparable case) the notorious Kirke of 'Kirke's Lambs', the bloodstained Tangiers regiment, did. Jeffreys may have been tarnished but he was not more tarnished, in the eyes of his contemporaries at least, than many of those whom William of Orange found acceptable. And above all Jeffreys was, in 1688, the most powerful man in the kingdom and totally untainted by what would have been totally unacceptable, his royal master's Catholicism. Yet he remained loyal to the Stuart cause at a time when the rats were scampering on all sides. It is worth emphasising.

It is also worth mentioning that Jeffreys' private life was never criticised, even by his most bitter enemies. He married his first wife, Sarah Neesham, in 1667, a year before he was called to the Bar. He kept her pregnant during the rest of her short life and had six children by her, four sons and two daughters. He did not marry again till he was well up on the ladder of success. Then he chose a widow, Ann Bladworth, daughter of a Lord Mayor and formerly married to a knight. She bore him another brood of children (all but a daughter dying young) and lived on long after her husband had died. It is remarkably like Coke's story, but without the family dramas, without the excesses. The same is true of Jeffreys' rise in the social scale. He acquired estates in several counties – Shropshire, Buckinghamshire and Leicestershire – and he married off his son and heir John at the age of fifteen to a great heiress of a noble family: Lady Charlotte Herbert, daughter of the Earl of Pembroke and Montgomery. But he never acquired a tenth of the number of estates that Coke had done; and though he too settled in Buckinghamshire and he too bought and added to an estate that eventually amounted to 2000 acres and he too rebuilt the original house, Bulstrode was never comparable to Coke's Stoke Pogis, still less to Francis Bacon's Gorhambury or Verulam.

As for his legal attainments, he may well, as the stories go, have been boisterous and dissipated in his days as a law student and as a young (though married) barrister. But he was never imprisoned for debt, like his predecessors Scroggs and Pemberton, never as sottish as Saunders and according to Roger North, he had even made great friends with that puritanic holder of the office of Lord Chief Justice, Sir Matthew Hale, 'by little accommodations administered to him in his own house after his own humour, as a small dinner, it may be a partridge or two upon a plate, and a pipe after, and in the meantime diverting him with satirical tales and reflections upon those who bore a name and figure about town.'

Roger North, though a High Anglican like Jeffreys, was inevitably biased against the man. Jeffreys in the end displaced his own brother Francis North, Lord Guilford, the Lord Keeper. Therefore, though their religious and political sympathies were identical, what Roger North writes about Jeffreys must always be viewed with a certain suspicion. The same unfortunately is even more true of the other vivid contemporary historian, Bishop Gilbert Burnet. He is almost as attractive a writer as Roger North, but, though his religious sympathies were similar, his political sympathies were absolutely opposed. Burnet's *History of My Own Time* was not published till after his death. He was a man fascinated by the law and lawyers; in 1682 the year of which we have just been treating he had published a biography of Sir Matthew Hale. He was an out-and-out Whig, in the closest of contact with William of Orange and Mary. So Jeffreys, James' most energetic and able supporter, inevitably became his particular *bête noir*. Unfortunately Burnet is one of the main sources for the two Whig historians of Victorian times who have done most to create the monstrous impression of Jeffreys that still dominates our minds – Lord Macaulay and Lord Campbell.

'I am sorry to say,' writes Lord Campbell in the opening paragraphs of his biography of Jeffreys 'that, in my matured opinion, although he appears to have been a man of high talents, of singularly agreeable manners, and entirely free from hypocrisy, his cruelty and his political profligacy have not been sufficiently exposed or reprobated; and that he was not re-deemed from his vices by one single solid virtue.'

This of course is as nothing to Macaulay's rolling rhetoric. 'The depravity of this man has passed into a proverb,' is how he puts it in his *History of England*.

> Both the great English parties have attacked his memory with emulous violence: for the Whigs considered him as their most barbarous enemy; and the Tories found it convenient to throw on him the blame of all the crimes which had sullied their triumph. A diligent and candid enquiry will show that some frightful stories which have been told concerning him are false or exaggerated. Yet the dispassionate historian will be able to make very little deduction from the mass of infamy with which the memory of the wicked judge has been loaded.
>
> Impudence and ferocity, [continues Macaulay] sat on his brow . . . There was a fiendish exultation in the way in which he pronounced sentence on offenders. Their weeping and imploring seemed to titillate him voluptuously . . . Even in civil causes his malevolent and despotic temper perpetually

disordered his judgment. To enter his court was to enter the den of a wild beast, which none could tame, and which was as likely to be roused to rage by caresses as by attacks ... Even when he was sober, his violence was sufficiently frightful. But in general his reason was overclouded and his evil passions stimulated by the fumes of intoxication.

Heady stuff, this. But Hugh Trevor Roper, who, while Regius Professor of Modern History at Oxford, edited and abridged Macaulay's *History*, points out that Macaulay illustrates the character of Jeffreys from the Whig tirades, and adds that 'although attempts to whitewash Jeffreys are doomed to fail, it should be observed that Macaulay's portrait is a caricature, based on partial sources.' Campbell, who published three years before Macaulay, was not that 'dispassionate historian' that Macaulay mentioned; nor indeed was Macaulay himself. Inevitably, therefore in modern times (but in fact before Trevor Roper added those comments) a 'whitewash' attempt has appeared: an extremely detailed and carefully researched biography of Jeffreys: *Lord Chancellor Jeffreys and the Stuart Cause*, by George Keeton. But Keeton, though in intention impartial, in fact only redresses the balance: he omits almost all the events or quotations that tend to show Jeffreys in an evil, monstrous light. The 'dispassionate historian' must waver somewhere between the two. All he can hope, particularly in a brief sketch such as this, is neither excessively to whitewash nor outrageously to blacken but to give a flavour of both extremes, with perhaps a touch or two of indifferent grey.

Sergeant Jeffreys, then, was not appointed Lord Chief Justice on Saunders' death. No one was appointed. Saunders had died at the worst possible moment, when a new plot had just been discovered. On the day he died the Privy Council issued warrants for the arrest of seven ex-Cromwellian soldiers who had planned to assassinate the King and his brother on their way back from Newmarket races, dangerous but obscure men. The arrests sparked new informers. Richard West, a barrister of the Middle Temple, surrendered himself to Sergeant Jeffreys and implicated the Whig leaders. On June 26, three days after Saunders' death, there was a house-by-house search of the City for arms; by June 30 all the members of the Council of Six were under arrest and in the Tower, except James, Duke of Monmouth, who went precipitously into hiding.

From the professional point of view it was a blessing that fell into Pemberton's lap. Only a few months had passed since he had been eased out of his position as Lord Chief Justice of King's Bench. Now he had an obvious chance to ease himself back in again. But the authorities hesitated, they did not quite trust Pemberton. They wanted to test him out before reappointing him. Fortunately, as Lord Chief Justice of Common Pleas, he was, in the absence of an appointed head of King's Bench, the senior common-law judge and as such entitled to preside over treason trials. So they gave him two batches of treason trials to preside over – on July 12 and July 13.

On July 12 Pemberton, from the government's point of view, acquitted himself well. The three men tried, Walcot, Hone and Johnnie Rous, were condemned to death. They could hardly complain: the evidence was clear that they had planned to shoot Charles and James at Hoddesdon, where the London to Newmarket road narrows, from the shelter of Rye House, a house that belonged to one of their number, the malster Rumbold. These plotters were hard men, London-based, in many cases fanatical (Hone was a Fifth Monarchy man); and what is absolutely clear is that the plot did exist. The Rye House Plot was not, like the Popish Plot, a mere tissue of informers' fabrications. In both cases informers had alleged that there was a plot to assassinate the King. But the vital all-important difference was that in one case the information was true, in the other it was false.

Yet whether the Whig lords were implicated in the assassination plot is much more open to question. They were certainly plotting armed insurrection, both in England and Scotland, and it seems that two of them had been in close contact with the would-be assassins, Lord Howard of Esrick and Algernon Sidney. They were both men in their early sixties. Both had fought in the Civil War on the parliamentary side. Lord Howard indeed had been an Anabaptist, and a member of Cromwell's Lifeguards. Sidney, a convinced republican, had been a Captain of Horse, and a Commissioner for the trial of Charles I (though in fact he took no part in it, and had quarrelled with Cromwell). It would be wrong to describe them as a pair of ageing desperadoes. Sidney had 'a huge deal of wit and much sweetness of nature' according to his friends. But according to his enemies he was, though courageous, a cold, pedantic and overbearing man. He was certainly a convinced Republican.

The government however decided to put neither of these men on trial, not Sidney because the evidence linking him with the assassination plot was too sketchy, not Howard because, to save his skin, he had decided to turn King's evidence. Monmouth had not been found; and whatever Monmouth's faults everyone knew that he would never have countenanced the murder of his own father. John Hampden was too young to be taken very seriously. That left two out of the Council of Six: William Lord Russell, and Arthur Capel, Earl of Essex. On the evening of July 12 Arthur Capel committed suicide in the Tower: equivalent, popular opinion felt, to an admission of guilt; for foul play, for once, could not reasonably be suspected. On July 13, therefore, William Lord Russell went on trial for his life at the Old Bailey before a tribunal of nine judges, presided over by Lord Chief Justice Pemberton of Common Pleas. The trial lasted all day. The prosecution team was headed by the Attorney General, the Solicitor General, Sergeant Jeffreys and Roger North. The accused was advised by Pollexfen and a young Whig lawyer, Holt, though of course on points of law only.

William Russell has been held up by historians of succeeding generations as a model of integrity and virtue. Witness after witness at the trial testified to his high character. But he was the first of the Whigs to be hoist by his own petard. Three years earlier the Whig lords had been ruthless in manipulating tales of murder and plots to down their own enemies, and none had been more ruthless, for all his integrity, than William Russell. Indeed he had even argued, unsuccessfully, that the wretched Lord Stafford, the aged (and, as it happens, innocent) Catholic peer should be hanged, drawn and quartered rather than simply beheaded. The Whigs had exploited the legal system without mercy; now the tables were turned and it was being used against them. It is difficult to feel much sympathy for their plight, particularly as, whatever the degree of their guilt (and that is arguable), they were certainly all guilty men as compared to the innocent victims of the Popish Plot.

Lord Howard's evidence damned Russell, though it was the evidence only of one man, and only of a plot to raise rebellion, not to assassinate the King. But there was other evidence, again that of a plotter whose life was to be spared, a man named Ramsey, to show that Russell at least knew of the Rye House Plot. Russell tried to argue that there must be two witnesses to the same overt act at the same time. But the prosecution pointed out, fairly enough, that in Lord Stafford's case one witness for the treasonable act in England, another for another treasonable act in France, had been enough. Sergeant Jeffreys summed up for the prosecution.

'Gentlemen,' he said, 'I would not labour in this case, far be it from any man to take away the life of the innocent.' On the other hand: 'Let not the greatness of any man corrupt you, but discharge your consciences both to God and the King, and your posterity.'

This moderation of tone was typical, if not of Jeffreys, at least of this particular trial. Russell's wife, Rachel Wriothesley, a great heiress, owner of Southampton House in Bloomsbury Square where the Whig Lords had so often met, was at the trial.

Lord Russell: My lord, may I not have the use of pen, ink and paper?

Lord Chief Justice Pemberton: Yes, my lord.

Lord Russell: My lord, may I not make use of any papers I have?

Lord Chief Justice Pemberton: Yes, by all means.

Lord Russell: May I have somebody write to help my memory?

Attorney General (interrupting): Yes, a servant.

Lord Russell (ignoring him): My wife is here, my Lord, to do it.

Lord Chief Justice Pemberton (also ignoring the Attorney General): If my Lady please to give herself the trouble.

Despite these courtesies Russell was found guilty by the jury, and sentenced to the usual penalty. Immense pressure was put on the King to spare Russell's life; but he would only commute the sentence to beheading. Burnet (not yet a Bishop) attended Russell to the scaffold, where Ketch barbarously bungled the execution. Lord Grey de Werke, arrested in the next few days, escaped – Jeffreys was sure he had bribed his captor, and so he probably had. It was what all the Whigs who were still at liberty to do so were doing. For the Whigs, lords and lesser men alike, were in a mood of understandable panic. The execution of such a respected and loved figure as Russell, despite all the petitions flooding in to save him, even despite a rumoured offer of £50,000 for his life from his father, the Earl of Bedford, seemed to portend a bloody purge of the Whigs.

In fact, however, no bloodbath occurred. The day Russell was condemned, Captain Blague was acquitted. Admittedly the accusation was ridiculous: a plan to bombard the Tower from a small boat on the Thames; but even further-fetched accusations had been believed, and men sent to their death for them, in the recent days of the Popish Plot. Any acquittal was a hopeful sign of real justice in the air. There was a long summer pause. Then, as if to show that they were about to rage, the government not only failed to promote Pemberton to his old post, they dismissed him. He had undoubtedly been too courteous at Russell's trial for their taste. He reverted, for the second time in his life, from being a judge to practising as a barrister once again: Sergeant Pemberton. That was on September 7. On September 29 the vacant post of Lord Chief Justice of King's Bench was filled at last, and by the man whom the Whigs rightly feared far more than the Attorney General or Solicitor General. There would be no question of civilised courtesies to be expected, they knew, from Sergeant Jeffreys. 'All people were apprehensive of very black designs,' wrote Gilbert Burnet, 'when they saw Jefferies made Lord Chief Justice, who was scandalously vicious and was drunk every day, besides a drunkenness of fury in his temper that looked like enthusiasm.'

George Jeffreys

In fact what the Whigs feared, and rightly feared, was not Jeffreys' drunken fury or viciousness but his energy, his fearsome ability as a cross-examiner, and his desire, already proved as a judge (both in London where he had been Recorder and in Chester where he had been, like Lord President Bradshaw, Chief Justice) to go straight to the point and cut through irrelevant arguments.

Furthermore, in the first important trial over which he presided, that of Algernon Sidney, the new Lord Chief Justice behaved with a moderation almost equal to Pemberton's. Sidney came up before King's Bench on November 7, and the Lord Chief Justice, unusually, allowed Sidney a fortnight in which to prepare his defence. The trial was held therefore on November 21, before Jeffreys and six other judges.

There has been a great deal of argument about Sidney's trial, for he was as much condemned for writing an (unpublished) Republican treatise as for his actual conspiracies. It was a long, heated trial, with Sidney arguing his own case strongly. When he objected to a general account of the Rye House Plot, on the grounds that he personally had not been involved, the Lord Chief Justice had a very pertinent reply to him.

'Mr Sidney,' he said, 'you remember in all the trials about the late Popish Plot how there was first a general account given of the plot given in Coleman's trial, and so in Plunket's, and others. I do not doubt that you remember.'

The jury were out for half an hour only before coming back with the inevitable verdict. Jeffreys pronounced sentence. At this stage, it was usual for the accused to accept verdict and sentence, and reserve his most vehement protestations of innocence for the scaffold. But not this accused, a man who after the far more popular Russell's condemnation could hardly have expected mercy.

Sidney: Then, O God, O God! I beseech thee to sanctify these suffereings unto me, and impute not my blood to the country; let no inquisition be made for it, but if any, and the shedding of blood that is innocent must be revenged, let the weight of it fall only upon those that mailiciously persecute me for righteousness' sake.

Lord Chief Justice Jeffreys: I pray God work in you a temper fit to go unto the other world, for I see you are not fit for this.

Charles detested Algernon Sidney, and there was no question of a pardon. Jeffreys was criticised (by Evelyn in his *Diary*) for having the bad taste to go to a grand City wedding, with much merry-making, two days before the execution. Sidney was executed on Tower Hill on December 7. He made no further speech. 'He died stoutly,' noted James, Duke of York, 'and like a true Republican.' James' own nephew, Monmouth, had meanwhile given himself up and been pardoned by his ever-indulgent father, which did not please the future James II nearly so much. Of the original 'Council of Six' therefore, only young John Hampden, remained in prison. Hampden was tried before Jeffreys on February 6, 1684. He was charged with the lesser crime of sedition, found guilty, condemned to pay £40,000, was inevitably unable to pay this enormous sum, and was therefore imprisoned.

And that was almost that. Two more alleged plotters, a Bristol merchant James Holloway, and a close associate of Monmouth's, Sir James Armstrong, were tried for treason in King's Bench; both were sentenced to death and executed. But there was no general judicial slaughter of the Whigs, and far fewer executions than there had been in the case of the Popish Plot. Admittedly Jeffreys' temper and behaviour in court was gradually getting worse. He had always prided himself on giving opponents 'a rough lick' of his tongue, and he certainly treated the accused as opponents. It was not that he was an unjust judge by the standards of the time: but he phrased his insults and ironies so forcefully that they stood out in men's memories. He was merciless to Sir Thomas Armstrong at the end.

Armstrong: I ought to have the benefit of the law, and I demand no more.
Lord Chief Justice Jeffreys: That you shall have by the grace of God. See the execution be done on Friday next, according to law. You shall have the full benefit of the law!!

This meant that Armstrong was hanged, drawn and quartered rather than merely beheaded. According to Burnet, when the Lord Chief Justice went to Windsor shortly after the trial, 'the King took a ring of good value and gave it to him for these services. The ring upon that was called his *blood stone.*' The King accompanied the gift with a piece of advice somewhat extraordinary from a king to a judge: 'My Lord, as it is a hot summer, and you are going the circuit, I desire you will not drink too much.' It is absolutely clear from Jeffreys' comments and asides at all the other criminal trials of this time that his health was going due to drink, probably, but also, certainly, to intrigue, overwork, and illness. He was intriguing to oust the Lord Keeper whose place he coveted. He had become not only a member of the Privy Council but of its much-preoccupied inner circle. He had agonising attacks of the stone, and it seems probable that he took acid: it was believed at the time that quantities of acid dissolved the stone. For all that in civil cases his judgments were extraordinarily good – Lady Ivy's Case and the great Monopolies Case of the East India Company v Sandys are two examples, famous in their day. And in criminal cases his greatest severity fell on a man even more unscrupulous and indeed even more bloodstained than himself: Titus Oates.

It was a curious twist of events that set face-to-face two of the folk-villains of English history, the cruel judge and the lying informer. Oates had been overheard in a coffee-house conversation referring to the Duke of York as a traitor. Fortunately for him that was in the spring of 1684. Had it been a year later, he would have been arrested for high treason. As it was, James could only bring an action for *scandalum magnatum* against his libeller. Oates offered no defence, the jury awarded the Duke of York £100,000, and Oates of course went to prison by default. But that was only the first, and most minor, of his legal difficulties. A year later, on May 8 and May 9, 1685, Oates was tried on two separate charges of perjury before the Lord Chief Justice. He was of course ultra-guilty on both counts, and it was only justice that he should be found guilty. He tried to argue that judges and juries in the trials of the Popish Plot were as guilty – or as innocent – as he. To this Jeffreys retorted, quite rightly, that 'a judge's opinion is of value in points of law but is no evidence of the fact ... Therefore what my Lord Chief Justice Scroggs said at any of those trials, or what I said, or any other person, that either was of counsel or a judge upon the bench, was said in our opinions on the fact as it occurred to our present apprehensions, but is no evidence nor binding to this jury. I must tell you, there is no doubt but that those juries did every one of them believe the evidence you gave, or they would not have convicted the prisoners.'

This is a classic, and correct, statement of the legal facts, restrained in tone and as true now as then. Whether, though, Jeffreys and the other judges, lawyers and indeed juries were as pure as driven snow in the circumstances of the time is quite another question. But, whatever their blame for connivance, Oates' guilt was far greater. 'He has deserved much more punishment,' Jeffreys summed up, 'than the law of this land can inflict.' The punishment for perjury had been death or mutilation. It was so no longer. That omission, however, the Lord Chief Justice proceeded to attempt to fill nine days later when it came to the sentencing. He sentenced Oates to fines, to perpetual imprisonment, and to stand in the pillory for an hour every year as long as he lived, at Tyburn, Westminster Hall, Charing Cross, Temple Gate and the Royal Exchange in turn. Worse than that, he sentenced Oates to be whipped on the Wednesday following from Aldgate to Newgate (about a mile and a half), and then on Friday from Newgate to Tyburn. He was whipped by the executioner Ketch. James refused a petition to cancel the Friday's punishment. Titus Oates was not expected to survive the second day of whipping but he did survive it, though he was dragged most of the way to Tyburn unconscious on a hurdle. The new King, James II, created Jeffreys a peer that same week, the first Lord Chief Justice since early mediaeval times to be made a member of the House of Lords.

If Baron Jeffreys of Wem, as he now was, had succeeded in his plan to oust the Lord Keeper just a few months earlier, he would have appeared in history, and indeed in this book, as a judge of considerable abilities but a short-term Lord Chief Justice, certainly more respectable than his two immediate predecessors, no more harsh than the Restoration Lord Chief

Justices, memorable only for the extraordinarily young age at which he had been appointed and for being the instrument of vengeance upon Titus Oates. Unfortunately for Jeffreys, however, and – more immediately – for many hundred others, James Duke of Monmouth landed less than a month later at Lyme Regis to claim the throne. With him landed that other surviving Whig grandee, Lord Grey of Werke.

Charles II had died on February 6, 1685. His eldest illegitimate son landed in the West Country on June 11. Parliament immediately brought in a Bill of Attainder for high treason against Monmouth. The battle of Sedgemoor was fought on July 6. On July 7 Lord Grey de Werke, his Captain of Horse, whose inefficiency had largely been responsible for the rout at Sedgemoor, was captured; so, almost simultaneously, was Monmouth himself. On their own request James saw them. 'The Duke of Monmouth,' he wrote to his son-in-law William of Orange, 'seemed more concerned and desirous to live and did not behave himself so well as I expected nor as one ought to have expected from one who had taken upon him to be King. I have signed the warrant for his execution tomorrow. For Lord Grey, he appeared more resolute and ingenious and never so much as once asked for his life: his execution cannot be so soon by reason of some forms which have to be complied with.'

Monmouth, condemned to death by Attainder, did not need to be tried. The 'some forms' to which James referred were presumably the trial for high treason of Lord Grey de Werke by his peers. In fact Lord Grey did not have to face a court or his old legal enemy, Jeffreys, again. He compounded for his life by forfeiting his estates and promising to reveal all he knew about Monmouth's rebellion.

On July 8, meanwhile, the Lord Chief Justice had been appointed head of the commission that was to ride the Western circuit and judge the captured rebels at assizes. The judges who were to sit with the Lord Chief Justice were four in number, including Lord Chief Baron Montagu, and another judge of his court, Wright, plus Levinz of King's Bench and Wythens of Common Pleas. On Wednesday, August 24, the five judges, escorted by cavalry, attended by throngs of lawyers and clerks, rode into Winchester where they were welcomed by the mayor and corporation and lodged in the castle. On the Thursday the whole tribunal sat in judgment at the trial that opened the 'Bloody Assizes', the only trial at Winchester, the most notorious single trial of the whole circuit, that of Alice Lisle.

There is enormous controversy about the 'Bloody Assizes', and in particular about the number of victims and the responsibilities of James and Jeffreys respectively. One important point is that it was all over in a month. By September 28 Jeffreys was back at Windsor Castle to report to the King and, the Lord Keeper having died, was appointed Lord Chancellor as a reward for his services. The best evidence shows that the King and the Lord Chief Justice were equally responsible and, more surprisingly, that nobody at the time considered the punishment of the rebels particularly outrageous. At Winchester there was only one trial for high treason, that of Alice Lisle. At Royalist Salisbury six persons were convicted of seditious words, and pilloried. It was not till the tribunal reached Dorset in the first days of September that the pace hotted up. Jeffreys almost immediately introduced a form of plea bargaining. Those who pleaded guilty were sentenced to death but could hope for their sentences to be commuted. If commuted, they were normally sentenced to be transported to the West Indies. Those who pleaded not guilty had a very faint chance of being acquitted – at Dorchester Assizes three were acquitted. But if not, they were hanged, drawn and quartered. The prisoners were tried in batches. Hundreds were tried at three places: at Dorchester in Dorset, at Wells in Somerset, and at the centre of Nonconformity in the West Country, Taunton in Somerset, a town which awaited the arrival of the tribunal 'paralysed with fear'. At Bristol and Exeter only a handful were indicted. Those tried were by no means all peasants or cloth-workers. There were many members of the middle classes and indeed of the gentry. According to the gaol-books, probably the most reliable sources, 1,388 people were indicted for high treason, seven were acquitted, probably 800-odd were transported and possibly not more than 150 were executed. Macaulay admittedly calculates that at least twice this number were executed – and neither count allows for the massacre of the defeated army by the victors after the battle. Whichever figure is taken, the number of executions is far less than those inflicted on the defeated rebels in the uprisings against Henry VIII and his daughter Elizabeth.

The peculiar horror of the Bloody Assizes lies therefore not so much in the numbers sentenced, the methods of execution or the general injustice (indeed the injustice was very little, since almost all those sentenced were clearly guilty of 'levying war against the King') but in the manner in which the trials were conducted. It is paradoxical that judges in England are pardoned for condemning people to death, provided they do so politely. What outrages public opinion is when they deprive their victims of dignity as well as of life. It is Jeffreys' blustering and browbeating rather than his black-cappery that has caused him to be regarded with such horror. Jeffreys certainly had no sense of fair play. At best he can be credited with a certain gallows humour.

'Villain, rebel,' said Jeffreys to the constable of Churdstock, 'me-thinks I see thee already with a halter about thy neck.' And as a constable was meant to be an officer of law and order, the Lord Chief Justice ordered him to be hanged first, declaring, 'that if any with a knowledge of the law came in his way, he would take care to *prefer* them'. 'You deserve a double death,' he told a certain Hucher who had passed information to Monmouth's commander, 'one for rebelling against your Sovereign, and the other for betraying your friends.' After the jury had been out and back three times he condemned Alice Lisle to death with the entirely believable preliminary comment: 'Gentlemen, I think in my conscience the evidence was as full and plain as it could be, and if I had been among you and she had been my own mother I would have found her guilty.'

The evidence against Alice Lisle, however, was by no means full or plain. She had sheltered a fugitive from Sedgemoor – *She knowing of his treason* said the indictment, which she totally denied. Her denial was probably false; but in any case she was a woman, an old woman and a lady at that, and the offence was morally of a different category from actually bearing arms against the King. The point however was not so much what she had done, as who she was. She was a widow, living at Moyle's Court near Ellingham in Hampshire. Her husband, John Lisle, had been a Cromwellian judge, indeed at one time, Bradshaw's successor as President of the High Court of Justice. She (and the fugitive) were arrested by her neighbour, the Royalist Penruddock's son. She was highly respected locally. If Alice Lisle were to be found guilty and executed, then from the point of view of the rebels awaiting trial, no one was safe. Jeffreys was determined to secure a conviction. He took over the cross-examination from the half-hearted Whig prosecutor Pollexfen, conducted it with his usual ruthless efficiency, and in the end condemned her to be burnt – the only punishment prescribed by law for a woman not being a noblewoman, convicted of high treason. The trial took place in the Great Hall at Winchester Castle. James commuted the sentence but only to beheading, and the execution was carried out at Winchester on September 2, two days before the assizes opened at Dorchester. This judicial murder had in every way the desired effect. Apart from the terror it spread, it benefited Jeffreys directly. Edmund Prideaux, son of Cromwell's Attorney General, was implicated in the uprising. He owned Forde Abbey near Axminster, not far from the scene of Monmouth's landing. Jeffreys extracted £14,500 from him as a semi-official bribe, a 'reward' for not indicting him of high treason. He was satisfied with that one massive stroke, though. He took no part in the selling of prisoners for transportation (at £10–£15 a head). He resisted pressure and bribes from other courtiers eager to save, for instance, the lives of Alice Lisle's two brothers. They were executed at Taunton. He even hanged Jenkyn, a protégé of his own patron Sunderland.

'As for news,' wrote James II to his nephew William of Orange on September 24, 'there is little stirring but that the Lord Chief Justice has almost done his campaign. He has already condemned several hundreds, some of which are already executed, some are to be, and others sent to the plantations.' It is typical of the general indifference of the time to a decimation that now seems so appalling. But in the West Country they did not forget. In the short term the memory of the Bloody Assizes acted in the way the government had intended it should act, as a deterrent. Hardly any West Country men joined William of Orange when three years later he too landed in the West and raised the standard of revolt against King James.

In the long term of course it has been a very different story. 'And now Jeffreys had done his work and returned to claim his reward,' wrote Macaulay. 'He arrived at Windsor from the West, leaving carnage, mourning and terror behind him. The hatred with which he was regarded by the people of Somersetshire has no parallel in our history. It was not to be quenched by time or by political changes, was long transmitted from generation to generation, and raged fiercely against his innocent progeny.' When Jeffreys surrendered his position on September 28, 1683 he had been Lord Chief Justice for two years less a day. What is absolutely undeniable is that his brief period as holder of the office of Lord Chief Justice had become unforgettable.

9

The Last Days of Four Lord Chief Justices

Three short and crowded years remained, to James II of rule and to George Jeffreys of life. As Lord Chancellor he was to become the most powerful man in England after the King, and virtual Regent in the capital during those last few weeks of hesitation and last few days of chaos. For all his energy and comparative youth, though – and for all his loyalty too – he failed. He failed to divert the last of the Stuart monarchs from any of those iniquitous actions or merely silly mistakes that cost the King his throne. He could have been a statesman; he remained a manager. Possibly, surprising though it seems, it was because he simply did not care enough.

> I dined with the Lord Chancellor, [wrote the courtier Sir John Reresbey], where the Lord Mayor of London was a guest, and some other gentlemen. His Lordship having, according to custom, drank deep at dinner, called for one Mountfort, a gentleman of his, who had been a comedian, an excellent mimic; and to divert the company, as he was pleased to term it, he made him plead before him in a feigned cause, during which he aped the Judges and all the great lawyers of the age in their tone of voice and in their action and gesture of body, to the very great ridicule, not only of the lawyers, but of the law itself, which to me did not seem altogether so prudent in a man in his lofty station in the law: diverting it certainly was, but prudent in the Lord Chancellor I shall never believe.

Jeffreys seems to have had two totally different personalities: the almost lunatic ranter, and the reasonable, indeed moderate judge. 'Come, come,' he raved to the Grand Jury at Bristol:

> 'I find you stink for want of rubbing. It seems the dissenters and fanatics fare well amongst you, by reason of the favour of the magistrates, for example if a dissenter who is a notorious and obstinate offender comes before them, one alderman or

another stands up and says *He is a good man* (though three parts a rebel) . . . Well, for Mr Alderman's sake, he shall be fined but half-a-crown, so *manus manum fricat.* You play the knave for me, and I will play the knave for you by-and-by. I am ashamed of these things but, by God's grace, I will mend them; for, as I have told you, I have brought a brush in my pocket, and I shall be sure to stick the dirt wherever it is or on whomsoever it sticks.'

This is vigorous stuff no doubt but is bewildering to read even now. It must have sounded even more bewildering in court at the time. The Mayor of Bristol was thereupon, Roger North writes, sent to the Bar like a common rogue or thief, bawled out, rated and stamped at.

Yet this very same man could preside, as he did preside, with fairness and moderation over the treason trial of an old personal enemy of his, Henry Booth. In 1680 Booth, a leading Cheshire Whig, had told the House of Commons that the then Chief Justice of Chester, Sir George Jeffreys, 'behaved himself more like a jack-pudding than with that gravity which becomes a judge'. Six years later Booth, now Lord Delamere, was accused of having received a messenger of Monmouth's in London and of having left the capital hurriedly using a false name to raise Cheshire for the rebels. As a peer he was tried by a tribunal of his fellow peers with the Lord Chancellor presiding as Lord High Steward. The 'jack-pudding' remark was not one that a man like Jeffreys would have forgotten. The King badly wanted a verdict of guilty. The evidence was moderately damning though it now seems that Booth was probably hurrying to Cheshire to warn the Whigs there to have nothing to do with Monmouth's rebellion. The trial was conducted with an almost twentieth-century impartiality.

'Your Lordships are judges,' Jeffreys summed up, 'and if you do not believe the testimony of Saxon, whose testimony hath been so positively contradicted by diverse witnesses of quality, the prisoner ought to be acquitted of this indictment. If your Lordships please, you may go together, and consider it.' The Lords withdrew for half an hour; and unanimously found Delamere innocent.

Despite James' annoyance at this acquittal, these years marked Jeffreys' high tide period. His elder brother was knighted. His favourite nephew was knighted and made High Sheriff of Denbigh. He himself was extraordinarily popular personally. His portraits were frequently copied, engravings of him were eagerly bought up, addresses were showered on him. Perhaps he had even mellowed, in a briefly mellow period.

Jeffreys' successor as Lord Chief Justice was certainly – which indeed would not have been difficult – a far more relaxed man.

Edward Herbert

The new Lord Chief Justice had been, like his predecessor, Chief Justice of Chester and Attorney General to James as Duke of York. He had been born in exile to an ardently Royalist family, and educated, after the Restoration, at Winchester and New College. Unlike his more talented and ambitious brothers, who had planned their lives respectively in the Army and the Navy, he had been pushed into a career at the Bar. He was decent, cultured, somewhat ineffectual and apparently totally surprised at his appointment. Or, as Gilbert Burnet put it, 'He was a well-bred, virtuous man, generous and good-natured, though an indifferent lawyer. He unhappily got into a set of very high notions with relation to the King's prerogative. His gravity and virtues gave him great advantages: chiefly succeeding such a monster.'

Burnet was not entirely accurate about Herbert's 'very high notions with regard to the prerogative'. Herbert's notions were certainly high but they were not high enough for James. That was why Herbert was dismissed on April 21, 1687 after exactly a year and a half in office. There had already been a major crisis in the judiciary the year before which had resulted in the King dismissing both of Herbert's senior colleagues, the Lord Chief Justice of Common Pleas and the Lord Chief Baron, plus the two law officers of the Crown, the hitherto totally reliable Sawyer and Finch, respectively Attorney General and Solicitor General. It was all to do technically with the Dispensing and Suspending powers of the King, and in practice with the appointment of Roman Catholics to official posts. Even the most Tory of judges, such as Montagu of Common Pleas, one of Jeffreys' colleagues on the Bloody Assizes, could not stomach this last move. But Herbert could. He clearly was a man of more strength of character than he had at first seemed to be; for in 1686 he withstood against what must have been considerable pressure from his senior colleagues, and in 1687 he held out against what was certainly very great pressure from both the King and the Lord Chancellor.

What is paradoxical is that the issue which led to Herbert's dismissal was an issue, unlike the constitutional question, on which common sense and reason seemed to be totally on the side of the Crown. The King wanted what did not then exist, the creation of a military code, an Army Law, to regulate the conduct of his troops. In time of peace, however, no special code applied to relations between officers and men. If a soldier struck an officer, he could only be charged with assault and battery in the normal way. If a Life Guardsman deserted, he could only be sued for breach of contract. It was an impossible way to keep discipline, and nowadays any military man, whether officer, N.C.O. or simple soldier of our large standing army, would consider with incredulity the very idea that such a system ever functioned. The Crown first brought a test case at the Old Bailey; Sir John Holt the Whiggish Recorder of London rejected it. Encouraged by his Lord Chancellor, James appealed to his reliable Lord Chief Justice. But to the consternation of both of them Herbert ruled 'that a statute altering the common law might be suspended by the King, who is really the lawgiver . . . but that the common law cannot be altered by the King's sole authority . . . as the common law must be considered coeval with the monarch.'

The attempt by the hitherto amenable Lord Chief Justice Herbert to follow in the footsteps of the illustrious Coke as the defender of the common law did not end there. The Attorney General prosecuted a soldier for deserting the colours and the judges at Reading Assizes agreed to a death sentence. The Lord Chief Justice and his puisne, Wythens J. (a colleague of the Lord Chancellor's on the Bloody Assizes) peremptorily ruled that the court had no jurisdiction. Next morning, predictably, they were both removed from office. But Herbert was too well-liked a man to be dismissed ignominiously, as Scroggs had been. Instead, like Pemberton, he was transferred sideways, to the office of Lord Chief Justice of Common Pleas.

Pemberton, at this time was only sixty-two, and despite his eventful career, still going strong; as Mr Sergeant Pemberton he practised extensively in both courts over which he had once presided, King's Bench and Common Pleas. But he was not really in the running for appointment to the post of Lord Chief Justice again. The man who at the time was Lord Chief Justice of Common Pleas was a creature of the Lord Chancellor. It was he who exchanged posts with Herbert to become the last Stuart Lord Chief Justice of King's Bench.

Robert Wright

The new Lord Chief Justice appears to have been a man in the physical mould of Jeffreys, 'of a comely person, airy and flourishing in his habits and manner of living'. He was probably five years older than Jeffreys, since he had come down from Peterhouse, Cambridge in 1661. He too was of a gentry family, and uxorious. Indeed his third wife was Elizabeth Scroggs, daughter of his disgraced predecessor. But, unlike Jeffreys, he had almost no talent at all as a lawyer, and, like Pemberton and Saunders, he had got into debt as a debauched young law student and barrister, though Jeffreys had at the last moment saved him from the Fleet. Jeffreys was amused by his mimicking and almost contemptuously had him appointed a judge in Exchequer Chamber. 'As you seem to be unfit for the bar or for any other honest calling,' Jeffreys had told him, 'I see nothing for it but that you should become a judge yourself.' 'My Lord,' said Charles II to Roger North's brother, 'what think you of Mr Wright? Why may not he be the man?' 'Because, Sir,' the Lord Keeper replied, 'I know him too well and he is the most unfit person in England to be a judge.' Jeffreys, nothing dismayed, seems to have replied to this challenge in his usual combative style. What had perhaps begun as half a joke became a point of honour in the then Lord Chief Justice's battle against the Lord Keeper. When Charles next saw Francis North the following exchange (if Roger North is to be believed) took place:

King: Why may not Wright be a Judge? He is strongly recommended to me; but I would have a due respect paid to you, and I would not make him without your concurrence. It is impossible, my Lord?

Lord Keeper: Sir, the making of a Judge is your Majesty's choice and not my pleasure. I am bound to put the Seal as I am commanded, whatever the person may be. It is for your Majesty to determine, and me, your servant, to obey. But I must do my duty by informing your Majesty of the truth respecting this man, whom I personally know to be a dunce and no lawyer; who is not worth a groat, having spent his estate by debauched living, who is without honesty, having been guilty of wilful perjury to gain the borrowing of a sum of money. (Personal pique played a role here; Robert Wright had borrowed £1500 from Francis North himself on the strength of his estate and then gone on to remortgage the deeds for £500 to another 'friend'.) 'And now, Sir, I have done my duty to your Majesty, and am ready to obey your Majesty's commands in case it may be your pleasure that this man shall be a Judge.

King: My Lord, I thank you.

Next day 'our right trusty and right well beloved Sir Robert Wright' was appointed one of the twelve judges of England. He was confirmed in office on the accession of James and made Recorder of Cambridge. He was one of the four judges who went with Jeffreys on the Bloody Assizes, and on the death of the Lord Chief Justice of Common Pleas on April 16, 1687, he was rewarded with that office – which he held for only five days till the exchange with Herbert took place. He immediately gave proof of his malleability. 'Be it so,' he said to the Attorney General's renewed plea in the case of the army deserter, and the man was executed.

But even Wright did not live up to the expectations his patron had had of him. He played his allotted part well enough to satisfy the Lord Chancellor in the great attacks on the privileges of the Universities that set the Anglican and Royalist Establishments at odds in the remainder of the year 1687. But when it came in June 1688 to the trial of the Seven Bishops, he failed. They were acquitted. That autumn when William of Orange had landed far away in the West, Hyde's son, the second Earl of Clarendon, took a note in his diary on an official visit to Jeffreys at Bulstrode Park.

'I went in his calash with him,' he wrote. 'He talked very freely to me of all affairs; called the Judges a thousand fools and knaves; that Chief Justice Wright was a beast.' What the Lord Chief Justice called the Lord Chancellor is nowhere, alas, recorded.

The trial of the Seven Bishops is one of those dramatic turning points in English history of which most people have some vague recollection, with however little or no notion as to the precise details. It turned on an utterly trivial matter: a charge that in presenting a petition to the King at Whitehall the

Seven Bishops had been guilty of having 'written or published in the County of Middlesex a false, malicious and seditious libel'. Its importance was totally out of proportion to its subject matter. It brought to a head all the grievances that had been festering since the start of James II's reign, it united against a reigning monarch for the first time since the Middle Ages the hierarchy of the Church and the people, and it opened the way to the final overthrow of the Stuart regime. A Lord Chief Justice presided over the trial, a former Lord Chief Justice instigated the trial, and another former Lord Chief Justice appeared for the defence.

The story began on April 28, 1688 and ended eight weeks later on June 30. During that time the whole country was on tenterhooks and London in ferment. On April 28 James issued a Declaration of Indulgence permitting religious toleration. That may not have been a wise move, but it was a decent move. The King's great mistake, though, was to issue an Order in Council as Head of the Church of England, commanding his Declaration to be read out publicly at the time of divine service on successive Sundays, first in all the City churches, then in all the churches in England. The clergy were given a fortnight in which to prepare themselves. Late on the Friday evening before the first reading was due, six Bishops (the famous Seven less Sancroft, the Archbishop of Canterbury) went to Whitehall to present the King with a Petition respectfully stating that they could not be a party to this public reading to their dioceses. James received them jovially. His frown darkened as he read the Petition, written out in Sancroft's handwriting and signed by them all. 'This is a standard of rebellion,' he declared. 'Rebellion,' cried Bishop Trelawney of Bristol, 'For God's sake, Sir, do not say so hard a thing of us. No Trelawney can be a rebel. Remember that my family has fought for the Crown. Remember how I served your Majesty when Monmouth was in the West.' But for all their protestations of loyalty, an obstinate, foolhardy King dismissed them with threats, telling them that they were 'trumpeters of sedition'. Yet for all his threats that evening thousands of copies of the Petition were circulating in London; and that Sunday the Declaration was read in only four out of the hundred-odd City churches.

James was now in an impossible position. The authority of the government had been successfully defied. Sunderland, the Lord President of his Council, advised appeasement. Jeffreys, the Lord Chancellor, was all for severity, and pressed for a charge of seditious libel to be brought before the subservient Lord Chief Justice Wright in King's Bench. And so it was agreed. Next Sunday, June 3, the parishes of England followed London's example. On the Friday following 'Black Friday', the Seven Bishops were examined by the Privy Council. They had taken the best legal advice. They refused – which must have been as infuriating to the Council as it was pettifogging in practice – to acknowledge that the Petition or the signatures were in their own handwriting. They were told that they would appear before King's Bench a week later: who would stand bail for them? They argued that as peers they were not obliged to seek bail in a case of libel. 'You believe everybody rather than me,' said James, with that petulant readiness to take any opposition as a personal affront from which his more cynical brother Charles had never suffered. All around Whitehall on that long summer evening anxious crowds were gathering. When they saw the Bishops being sent by barge to the Tower, the emotion reached its height. Thousands of boats were out on the Thames, from all of which rose the cry: 'God bless your Lordships.' Even the soldiers guarding Traitor's Gate asked the incarcerated Bishops for a blessing.

Two days later, on the Sunday, occurred an event that was almost as fatal in its way to the Stuarts as the Bishops' trial. A child was born, prematurely, to the Queen – a son. The Papist succession was assured. The Lord Chancellor, and many others of the Privy Council were there to witness the birth, but not Princess Anne, away in Bath, nor of course the Archbishop of Canterbury, imprisoned in the Tower. Stories of Jesuits and warming-pans began to circulate, no one present had the authority there successfully to deny them. On Friday, June 15, the Seven Bishops were hailed before King's Bench, pleaded Not Guilty, were released on their own recognisances, and given two weeks to prepare for the trial.

When the day for the trial, June 29, came, Westminster Hall and its surroundings were packed with at least 10,000 spectators. Thirty-four peers of the realm were in the Hall itself. Lord Chief Justice Wright sat with three fellow judges of King's Bench, his puisnes, Allibone J., a Catholic, appointed to the Bench under the dispensing power, Holloway, J., a tool, and Powell J., a judge of some independence of mind. Excitement was intense all over the country. As far away as Cornwall they were singing (admittedly with exaggerated fears) the famous ballad:

And shall Trelawney die,
And shall Trelawney die?

Then thirty thousand Cornish boys
Will know the reason why.

In the court all the best legal talent of the day appeared on the side of the defendants, including James' former Attorney and Solicitor General, Sawyer and Finch. The legal arguments put forward were full of chicanery. The Bishops' advocates denied the handwriting was theirs. When that was proved, they denied that the libel had been published in Middlesex. When that was proved, they denied that it had been *written* in Middlesex. Then Finch by a *faux pas* nearly ruined the defence. But the day was saved for the Bishops by Pemberton and Pollexfen. Mr Sergeant Pemberton stood up to a worried and uncertain Lord Chief Justice with all the authority of one who had occupied his seat on the occasion of great political trials, long before him. 'Record what you will, Mr Solicitor,' he exclaimed at one dramatic moment. 'I am not afraid of you.' Jeffreys would probably have ordered the question to be recorded, and Pemberton to be committed for contempt. Wright did not dare. In his summing-up he was studiously moderate. But Holloway J. summed up in favour of an acquittal, and Powell J. openly declared the Declaration of Indulgence illegal. Allibone J. only did the cause of Catholic toleration harm by calling fiercely for a verdict of guilty.

The jury were out all night, without meat or drink, fire or candle, debating their verdict. When the court reassembled at ten next morning the verdict was announced: Not Guilty. Cheering and hurrahs spread from Westminster to the City. James was visiting his military commander on Hounslow Heath when the news reached him. Next day he issued writs of *Supersedeas*, dismissing Holloway and Powell. He nearly dismissed Wright too but Allibone, the possible successor, died soon after and for lack of a possible substitute Wright continued in office.

That night several ornate effigies of the Pope, attended by a train of devils and cardinals and Jesuits, were paraded through the streets and, amid great rejoicing, burnt. But on the day the Seven Bishops were acquitted, a far more serious, though far more secret, event occurred. A group of seven magnates, including a Russell and a Sidney, four peers and a Bishop, wrote to William of Orange, inviting him to invade England and assume the direction of the realm. At the foot of the document they signed their names in code. The invitation was taken over to Holland by Arthur Herbert, Edward Herbert's elder brother. All this was of course, by any standards, high treason.

Treason doth never prosper, [goes a famous, later rhyme],
Here's the reason,
For if it prosper,
None dare call it treason.

None of the initial traitors or the more illustrious ones who
later joined them were ever tried. If they had been, there is no
doubt that they would have been legally and, according to the
laws of England, justly condemned. However, this treason
prospered to the point where it became known to history not as
another plot or as another uprising but as the Glorious Revolution. Arthur Herbert commanded the invading fleet for the
Prince of Orange under the unusual but fascinating title of Lord
Admiral General. It initially set sail from Holland on October
19. On October 26 Lord Chancellor Jeffreys called his friends
together at his house in Duke Street, Westminster, resettled his
property on his wife and sons and sent his family out of London
to his brother-in-law's house at Leatherhead. On November 5
William landed at Torbay in Devon with an army largely of
foreigners, 15,000 strong.

Thereupon a curious lull of about two weeks occurred. The
invading army marched around Devon unopposed; but no
important landowners or peers rallied to the Prince of Orange.
As for the ordinary people, they remembered only too well the
gibbets and quarters seen all over the West Country after the
last unsuccessful uprising so savagely repressed.

At this stage therefore the aces still seemed to lie in the
government's hands. Jeffreys wisely insisted that a 'free Parliament' should be called.

On November 17 James executed his will (probably drafted
for him by Jeffreys) and set out for Salisbury, that perennial
bastion of loyal support in the West, where his armed forces
were concentrating. Jeffreys, like a Justiciar of old, was left to
preside at Westminster over a Committee of State. Nine days
later the King was back at his capital. 'God help me,' he said
miserably, 'my own children have forsaken me.' Churchill, his
best commander had defected, the soldierly Duke of Grafton,
his brother's bastard, had defected, Prince George of Denmark
had disappeared and by the time James was back in London
Prince George's wife, Princess Anne, and her boon companion
Sarah Churchill had left to join the invaders. The Lord Chancellor began to dismantle his house in Duke Street and send the
furniture down to Bulstrode. All the same, even at this moment
of near-débâcle, Jeffreys did not panic. He took up, as James

had ordered, residence in Whitehall. On November 28 he announced that the new Parliament would be summoned on January 15, 1689, and issued writs to the Sheriffs of the counties and boroughs for the election. Two days later his youngest daughter Anne Jeffreys died at Leatherhead. Yet despite even this blow Jeffreys' willpower did not crumble. He told young Hyde that 'the King and Queen were to dine with him on Thursday next; that he had still great hopes the King would be moderate when Parliament met. When we came to Dr Hickman's my Lord was inclined to be merry: saying he had papists and spies among his own servants, and therefore must be cautious at home.' It is impossible not to admire the man in this emergency. Even when news reached London that the Prince of Orange had caused two impeachments for high treason to be printed and published in Exeter against the Lord Chancellor and the Lord Chief Justice, Jeffreys (and, to do him justice, as far as we know Wright) did not waver.

The end came, however, suddenly and dramatically on the morning of Tuesday, December 11. The night before the King had retired to his bedroom, burnt the election writs, and written to his military commander Feversham ordering him to disband his Army. The Prince of Orange was at Abingdon. In the early hours of the morning James secretly rode out of Whitehall, in disguise, and, while crossing the Thames, threw the Great Seal of England into the river. Jeffreys awoke in Whitehall on the Tuesday morning to find the King gone, the King's friends abandoned, the symbol and instrument of his own office gone, and the government therefore dissolved. He and the Lord Chief Justice, went into hiding. A day of chaos and confusion was followed by a night of anarchy. In Macaulay's words:

> The morning of the twelfth of December rose on a ghastly sight. The capital in many places presented the aspect of a city taken by storm . . . The agitation grew hourly more formidable. It was heightened by an event which, even at this distance of time, can hardly be related without a feeling of vindictive pleasure.

Jeffreys had panicked at last. No one knows where he spent the Tuesday night. But on the Wednesday a man in seaman's clothes, with his heavy eyebrows shaved off, was seen drinking a pot of ale in 'The Red Cow' at Wapping, in Anchor and Hope Alley near King Edward's Stairs. A hue and cry had been raised for the missing Lord Chancellor, and the ships on the Thames had been searched. Jeffreys had planned to board a collier ostensibly bound for Newcastle, but in fact for Hamburg; and, to avoid the search, he had landed again. Unfortunately for him he was recognised by a scrivener of Wapping, who had once appeared before him in court applying for relief on a bummery bond. When he had left Jeffreys' court, his friends had asked him how he had come off. 'Come off?' he replied. 'I am escaped from the terror of that man's face, which I would scarcely undergo again to save my life; and I shall certainly have the frightful impression of it as long as I live.'

Jeffreys saw the scrivener eyeing him. He coughed and turned towards the wall, pot in hand, trying desperately to avoid recognition. He was too well known in the City, robes or no robes, eyebrows or no eyebrows. The scrivener rushed out, the mob rushed in, and Jeffreys' life was only saved by the arrival of the trained bands who took him to the bewildered Lord Mayor, Sir John Chapman. There Jeffreys, according to a contemporary letter, 'cowardly knelt down to kiss his hand, which struck such amazement into the Lord Mayor that he fell into a swoon and continues very ill'. At the Mansion House he was, on his own request, given a strong guard and taken to the Tower amid cries of 'Vengeance! Justice! Vengeance!' from the mob and of 'For the Lord's sake keep them off! For the Lord's sake keep them off,' from himself.

As for the Lord Chief Justice, he had apparently disappeared off the face of the earth. One popular rhyme of 1688 went:

> Farewell Brent, Farewell William,
> Farewell Wright, worse than Tresilian,
> Farewell Chancellor, Farewell mace,
> Farewell prince, Farewell race.

In fact, an astonishing two months later, the Lord Chief Justice was discovered by Sir William Waller hiding in his own bailiwick, the Old Bailey itself. He was taken to Newgate.

There is little more to add. Both Jeffreys and Wright were charged with high treason and exempted from the Act of Indemnity but neither man came to trial. Jeffreys died of fever in the Tower on April 19, 1689, at four thirty-five in the afternoon. A satiric 'Last Will and Testament' was printed and circulated.

'In the name of Ambition,' it began, 'the only God of our setting up and worshipping, together with cruelty, Perjury, Pride, Insolence, etc. I George Jeffreys being in sound and perfect memory, of high commissions, *quo warrantos*, dispensations, pillorisations, floggations, gibilations, barbarity, butchery etc. do make my last will.' '*Item,*' it concluded 'I order an ell and a half of fine cambric to be cut into hankerchiefs for drying up all the wet eyes at my funeral; together with half a pint of burnt claret for all the mourners in the kingdom.'

Wright died of fever in Newgate, a month later, on May 18. His body was thrown into a pit with those of other common criminals.

Of the two surviving ex-Lord Chief Justices, a year later Pemberton was imprisoned in the Tower for eight months as a measure of revenge and on a trivial trumped-up charge of 'long past breach of the Commons' privileges'. He was 'deficient in moral fervour', Lord Campbell noted pompously, and 'however meritorious his services may have been, he well deserved the punishment inflicted on him.' Though the oldest of the trio, he did not oblige by dying. He returned to practice and as late as 1696 was one of the counsel for Sir John Fenwick in the disgraceful Attainder case of which more will be heard in the next part. He died, aged seventy-four, on June 10, 1699 and was buried in Highgate.

Edward Herbert had died a little earlier, and it is a pleasure to end this grim catalogue on a note of some nobility. He had followed his King into exile, as in his day his father had done. And, like his father, he became a Stuart Lord Chancellor in exile, dying unmarried, at St Germains in November 1698. His elder brother Arthur, the Lord Admiral General, had, in the meanwhile, acquired Edward's English estates as a reward for his treachery. The millenium, whatever Lords Campbell and Macaulay may have thought, did not begin with the 'Glorious Revolution' – not even, as readers will soon learn, the judicial millenium.

Part II
The Age of Politics 1689–1900

Sir John Holt
   Thomas Parker (Lord Macclesfield)
Sir John Pratt
   Robert (Lord) Raymond
   Philip Yorke (Lord Hardwicke)
Sir William Lee
Sir Dudley Ryder
   William Murray (Lord Mansfield)
   Lloyd (Lord) Kenyon
   Edward Law (Lord Ellenborough)
   Charles Abbott (Lord Tenterden)
   Thomas (Lord) Denman
   John (Lord) Campbell
Sir Alexander Cockburn, Bart.
   John (Lord) Coleridge
   Charles Russell (Lord Russell of Killowen)

After the squalls, the calm. Over the next two centuries and eleven years, that is to say until the beginning of our own century, there were a mere sixteen Lord Chief Justices, as opposed to twenty-three in the brief eighty years of the Age of Upheaval. Of these sixteen, ten died if not peaceably in their beds at least in workmanlike manner, on the bench. Three resigned – or were forced to resign – because of ill-health. Three became, with extraordinarily varying results, Lord Chancellor. None were executed, assassinated, officially dismissed or removed – at least *qua* Lord Chief Justice – to the Tower. It might seem rather a dull period by contrast to its predecessor. So, in one sense, it was. There was less high adventure. On the other hand, as modern times approach, the personalities of the various Lord Chief Justices become much more marked, and almost inevitably much more interesting.

Almost all of the Lord Chief Justices – thirteen out of sixteen – were, before achieving that eminence, Whig M.P.s. Not that this implied that they were all cast in the same mould; far from it. But they did all support the prevalent system of government and society: there were no revolutionaries among them: indeed, liberal principles or no, there were several fairly rabid reactionaries. The name of Edward Law (Lord Ellenborough) springs at once to mind. The nearest to an out-and-out reformer was Charles Russell (Lord Russell of Killowen), the first Irishman to become Lord Chief Justice; but that was only on Irish affairs. The first Welshman, Lloyd Kenyon, was a petit-bourgeois diehard. The two Scotsmen, William Murray and John Campbell, were essentially careerists and very successful ones. Indeed, it is William Murray (Lord Mansfield) who will inevitably dominate the pages that follow: a politician who could have been Prime Minister, a judge who held the office of Lord Chief Justice for no less than thirty-two years, a name still remembered outside the legal world when all the rest have, justly or unjustly, sunk into oblivion. That of course may – ironically enough – be more thanks to 'Junius' than to Murray's own abilities: of which more in its due place and time.

10

Knavish Tricks

One of the main and most necessary glories of the Glorious Revolution of 1688 was the clean sweep it made not only of the Lord Chief Justice but of the whole pack of Stuart judges. Only one, Atkyns J., was reappointed. Purges of course give enormous opportunities for promotion but purges as drastic as this present problems. John Holt, a King's Sergeant, chosen as assessor to the peers who had formed the Provisional Government and had summoned William and Mary over, distinguished himself in the constitutional debates of the Convention Parliament, both in the Lords and the Commons. When each Privy Councillor was asked to produce a list of twelve potential judges, his name was found on every list.

John Holt

John Holt was therefore appointed Lord Chief Justice on April 17, 1689. He remained in office for twenty-two years, twice refused promotion to the post of Lord Chancellor, won golden opinions even in treason trials, and conducted himself as a moderate, learned and upright judge. But his period in office is chiefly noticeable for the change in status accorded to all the judges. In effect, under the Act of Settlement of 1701, the judges were made virtually irremovable: to be precise, judges could – and can – only be removed following a joint petition by both Houses of Parliament. This was a vast improvement on the Stuart system under which the Lord Chief Justices, and their colleagues, had been promoted and dismissed at the King's pleasure. But it was to lead to its own abuses: twice at least

Prime Ministers – the younger Pitt and Churchill, as it happens – had to bring enormous pressure to bear to remove Lord Chief Justices who were clearly incapable of continuing in office but who obstinately refused to go. Never, however, as far as I am aware, has there been any serious attempt to remove any judge, still less a Lord Chief Justice, by the formal parliamentary process.

It is ironic that the liberal Act under which those accused of high treason should not be condemned unless the charge was supported by two witnesses should have become law on January 21, 1696, just as the first serious conspiracy against King William was about to take effect. This Jacobite 'Assassination Plot' under which forty armed men were to attack the royal coach at Turnham Green, en route from the King's new residence at Kensington Palace to his weekly hunt out at Richmond, could easily have succeeded if it had not been revealed by a Catholic gentleman with a conscience, a certain Pendergrass. On February 21 most of the would-be assassins were arrested, Habeas Corpus suspended, the fleet mobilised against invasion, and a Loyal Association formed. All twelve of the judges, including the Lord Chief Justice, presided over the treason trials that followed. The first was held on March 11; the new Act was not due to become operative until March 25. Six conspirators, including two knights, were executed under the old law, Sir William Parkyns on April 13 being the last Englishman so to suffer. Three were then tried under the new law; two witnesses, both informers, were found; and so Ambrose Rookwood became the first to suffer under the new law.

That summer, a bigger fish was netted: Sir John Fenwick, brother-in-law of the Howard Earl of Carlisle, a former general of James II. His case was much more debatable. Imprisoned and pressed to confess, he very adroitly produced a confession, false in the details but true enough in general, that implicated most of William's Whig supporters and ministers in Jacobite conspiracies. Then one of the two witnesses on whom the government had been counting to secure Fenwick's condemnation disappeared to France. The fury of the Whigs was understandable; was this dangerous traitor and plotter to escape simply because his friends had bribed and threatened one of the two vital witnesses? Brushing aside the law they themselves had just passed, the government instructed the Attorney General and the Solicitor General to draw up a Bill of Attainder against Fenwick. All that autumn, as the Bill was debated in both Houses, political passions ran higher than at any time since the Glorious Revolution itself. 'One witness', argued the government, 'is enough to convict a murderer, a burglar, a highwayman, an incendiary, a ravisher.' But was it right, all the same, for the legislature to interfere with the process of law? In the end, just before Christmas, the Lords passed the Bill on its third reading by the very close vote of sixty-eight to sixty-one. William refused the desperate petition for mercy of Lady Mary Fenwick, and on January 28, 1697, with all the honours due to a peer, Sir John was executed on Tower Hill, the last Englishman in our history to die attainted.

Attainder might thereafter be out; impeachment however was very much still in, and it was used rather ludicrously twelve years later, during the reign of Queen Anne, in the case of 'the Doctor' – Sacheverell – a high-church Tory and Fellow of Magdalen College, Oxford, who had preached and had printed two extremely violent sermons that attacked dissenters, low churchmen, broad churchmen and, much to their annoyance and his own danger, Whig ministers – 'wily Volpones'. The House of Commons voted these attacks to be 'malicious, scandalous and seditious libels, highly reflecting upon her Majesty and her government, the late happy revolution and the Protestant sucession'. Seditious libel was to become, indeed, in the eighteenth century the crime against the State that high treason had been in the seventeenth. On December 14, 1709, the Doctor was impeached by the House of Commons, to the delight of Sarah, Duchess of Marlborough, who described him as 'an ignorant and impudent incendiary'. On February 27, 1710 he was driven to Westminster Hall, where the Lords were assembling to hear the trial. Queen Anne, who went as she occasionally did in a private manner to hear the proceedings, was greeted by the crowds lining Sacheverell's route with cries of 'God bless your Majesty and the Church. We hope your Majesty is for Dr Sacheverell.' She was, of course, not.

The Lord Chief Justice had been summoned, as was usual, to attend the impeachment as an assessor, or legal adviser. His death passed almost unnoticed in the excitement of the trial – which had become less of a trial of the Doctor than a trial of strength between Whigs and Tories. The Attorney General, Sir James Montagu, the chief 'manager' of the prosecution, did not distinguish himself; the Solicitor General, Robert Eyre, was equally lukewarm. Only Sergeant Parker, a self-made attorney and Whig M.P. for Derby, really lashed Sacheverell, quoting the

Psalms to devastating effect: 'Their throats are open sepulchres and their words are smoother than oil, yet be they very swords. Like Joab, they pretend to speak peaceably and smite us mortally under the fifth rib.'

On March 23, their Lordships by sixty-nine votes to fifty-two (including seven Bishops to six) voted the Doctor guilty but merely condemned his sermons to be burnt by the common hangman. Extraordinary rejoicings followed this virtual acquittal: bonfires, escorts, mass meetings of up to 50,000 people. But Sacheverell's triumph was short-lived; Sergeant Parker's was the more impressive. Ten days before the verdict was announced, and over the heads of the Attorney General and Solicitor General, his fellow Whig M.P.s, he was appointed Lord Chief Justice.

Thomas Parker

It was not merely his pugnacity that had brought Thomas Parker so rapidly to great office. Attorneys (solicitors as we would now say) turned barristers are usually unsuccessful: but Parker was not only an extraordinarily hard worker who made himself a good jurist but an excellent advocate. 'Silver-tongued Parker' they called him, and he won more cases than any of his fellow barristers on the Midland circuit even before he had first distinguished himself, in 1704, in Westminster Hall. His manners were rough and ready and; writes Campbell, he 'had no relish for literary society and was never admitted of the Kit-Cat' – for in the eighteenth century a culture that would not have been expected from a Scroggs or a Jeffreys was part of the normal equipment of every gentleman in office. Parker, though, was no gentleman; he was a grammar school boy from Leeke in Staffordshire.

From almost exactly the same background – an attorney's son who might normally have hoped to rise only to the dignity of local town clerk – came Parker's protégé, young Philip Yorke. The Lord Chief Justice was looking for a law tutor for his sons: Philip Yorke was recommended. His manners were good, his capacity for hard work impressive; he moved into the Lord Chief Justice's house in Lincoln's Inn Fields, polished himself up, submitted a paper under the pseudonym of 'Philip Homebred' to Addison's *Spectator*, was called to the Bar at Easter 1715, aged twenty-three, and began to practise in the Court of King's Bench under the ever-favourable eye of the new Lord Chief Justice. Yorke was an extremely smooth young man, extremely ambitious, extremely handsome. He married a dashing widow, the niece of Lord Somers, despite her father's concern at hearing that all young Mr Yorke's estate consisted of was 'a perch of ground in Westminster Hall'. When after only eight years as Lord Chief Justice, Parker was promoted to Lord Chancellor and given a peerage – he had, like Sir Robert Walpole, won the favour of the new King, George I, by talking to him in bad Latin – Yorke followed his patron into the Court of Chancery, and into Parliament. In Chancery, he continued to be favoured – 'what Mr Yorke said has not been answered,' the Lord Chancellor used continually to observe to the annoyance of the older pleaders; in Parliament his opportunity came when in the great financial scandal following the bursting of the South Sea Bubble the Solicitor General accused the Attorney General of corruption. An unwise move. By 1720, Philip Yorke was Solicitor General and a knight – after only four years at the Bar. Naturally the resentment against Thomas Parker for the blatant favouritism shown to his sons' tutor, and against Philip Yorke himself for his almost immodest talent, only increased.

John Pratt

Meanwhile, Parker, on his promotion to Lord Chancellor, had decided that an inoffensive colleague of his should succeed to his former post. On May 15, 1718, John Pratt took his seat as Lord Chief Justice, a position he was to hold until his death almost seven years later.

The new Attorney General, Robert Raymond, had been a high Tory, one of the barristers who had defended 'the Doctor', and had been rewarded with a knighthood when the Tories came in. But Walpole had softened him up, and Raymond, much to the disgust of the Tories, turned his coat, accepted office, and worked hand-in-hand with his junior partner, Philip Yorke. Their great opportunity to shine came in October 1722, when they jointly conducted the prosecution for high treason of Christopher Layer, accused of conspiring to bring in the Old Pretender. Layer, himself a barrister of the Middle Temple, had entrusted the papers of his ridiculous conspiracy (written in the house of one of his many mistresses) to a brothel-keeper named Elizabeth Mason. He was betrayed by two women, arrested, escaped, recaptured, confined in the Tower, and brought to court in chains – much to the general scandal of this comparatively refined age. He asked to have them taken off.

Attorney General (Robert Raymond):   I am sure nothing is intended but that he should have a fair trial; but to complain here of chains carries with it a reflection of cruelty, and we know what effect these things may have abroad.

Lord Chief Justice (John Pratt):   Alas! If there had been an attempt to escape, then there can be no pretence to complain of hardship: he that hath attempted an escape once, ought to be secured in such a manner as to prevent his escaping a second time.

Solicitor General (Philip Yorke):   It is well known that when this gentleman was in the custody of a messenger, he not only made an attempt to escape but actually escaped out of a window, two pair of stairs high. It does not become the candour of a person in the prisoner's circumstances to aggravate and make such misrepresentation of the usage he has received.

Gentleman Gaoler of the Tower: My Lord, he never has attempted to escape since he was in my custody.

The chains were left on. Robert Raymond made an unctuous speech full of reference to 'His Majesty's Sacred Person'. Philip Yorke made a much-praised 'hanging-speech', quiet, dispassionate and totally effective. Layer was hanged, drawn and quartered at Tyburn. Raymond then astonished the legal world by accepting the junior judgeship of the Court of King's Bench – never before had there been an instance of an Attorney General sinking into such low obscurity. Philip Yorke succeeded him as Attorney General.

Thomas Parker, meanwhile, was at the height of his success – recognised as a great equity judge, assured of the King's favour (he had supported His Majesty in the first of those family quarrels that were to become so familiar a part of the political scene under the Hanoverians), Lord Lieutenant of Oxfordshire and Warwickshire, Earl of Macclesfield, proprietor of splendid

Shirbourn Castle, the friend and colleague of Walpole, now undisputed Prime Minister.

Suddenly, almost out of the blue, a scandal blew up. As in the case of so many self-made men, Parker's one great fault was avarice. Rumours spread that great frauds had been committed in Chancery, with the Lord Chancellor's connivance. Parker was suspended from office and, in January 1725, by a majority vote of 273 to 164 in the House of Commons, impeached. Philip Yorke, his protégé, made a fairly feeble stand for him in the impeachment debate, though it could be said – and was said – that it was Parker's favouritism towards Yorke that had caused the bitter hostility of such Chancery lawyers as Sergeant Pengelly, the moving force behind the impeachment.

The trial of the Lord Chancellor began on May 6 amidst intense excitement and lasted for thirteen days; the peers – the jury – wore their robes; the managers for the Commons – the prosecutors – were led by Sir Clement Weary, the Solicitor General. They much resented Parker's attitude. 'The managers,' as one of them put it, 'cannot but observe the indecent behaviour of this Lord, and his unworthy manner of treating us. We do not think the Lord at the bar should be directing the managers as if he sat in his place as Judge. We are here advocates for all the Commons of Great Britain, to demand justice against him.' Parker gave not an inch; he conducted himself like the sharp country attorney he basically was and questioned in minute detail all the evidence. But how could he win against such obviously ingenuous witnesses as Master Elde, who had bought a Mastership in Chancery off Parker's main agent in wheeling and dealing, a certain Cottingham?

'I spoke to Mr Cottingham, meeting him in Westminster Hall, and told him "I had been at my Lord's, and my Lord was pleased to speak very kindly to me," and I proposed to give him £5,000. Mr Cottingham answered, "Guineas are handsomer!!"'

On May 25, ninety-three Peers unanimously found the Lord Chancellor guilty. He was dismissed and disgraced, fined £30,000, imprisoned in the Tower for six weeks till the money was raised (easily done), retired to a small house near Derby, languished there for seven years, and died on April 28, 1732, aged only sixty-six – yet another hopelessly corrupt judge, as so many of our Lord Chief Justices have been.

Robert Raymond

It was Lord Chief Justice King of the Court of Common Pleas who had presided as Lord High Steward over the Lord Chancellor's trial. For John Pratt died as it was being prepared and, after a suitable gap, his place was taken by Robert Raymond, thus rescued from obscurity. King went on to become Lord Chancellor and Philip Yorke remained as Attorney General, having carefully abstained from taking any part in the Parker trial and adopting as his new patron the Duke of Newcastle. Though he sat in the House of Commons for fifteen years, he made few speeches and little impression: he was too didactic and logical in style, a common fault of professional barristers in the House. Even as public prosecutor he was not always successful in his attacks on *The Craftsman*, the main scurrilous journal of the time. Its editor, Pulteney, wrote after one triumphant acquittal for libel:

> For Sir Philip well knows
> That his innuendoes
> Will serve him no longer
> In verse or in prose:
> For twelve honest men have decided the cause
> Who are judges alike of the facts and the laws.

Philip Yorke

Lord Chancellor King was growing ill and old; it was expected that he would resign and that Philip Yorke would take his place on the Woolsack and in the Cabinet. However, Robert Raymond, though only sixty-one, died first – in Red Lion Square, on April 15, 1733. After several months of intrigues, Philip Yorke, the Attorney General, was made Lord Chief Justice and created a peer while the Solicitor General, Talbot, a man of more open character, generally better liked, was raised to the post of Lord Chancellor. As a member of the House of Lords, Philip Yorke did much better. His speaking improved, his confidence improved, his usefulness to the government improved. But it was the sudden and totally unexpected death of Lord Chancellor Talbot on February 1, 1737, that gave

Philip Yorke his opportunity to pass from the role of a decent but highly forgettable Lord Chief Justice, as Robert Raymond had been, to that of a great Lord Chancellor and a great, if unappealing, politician.

In the spring of 1736, William Murray, unhappily in love, retired disconsolately to a small cottage on the banks of the Thames near Twickenham. His friend Alexander Pope sent him a poem of comfort:

> Shall one whom native learning, birth conspired
> To form, not to admire, but be admired,
> Sigh while his Chloe, blind to wit and worth,
> Weds the rich dulness of some son of earth?

Sure enough within two years the youngish barrister had forgotten the wretched squire-wed Chloe, and won fame by defending a certain Colonel Sloper on a charge of 'criminal conversation' (adultery) with the famous actress Mrs Cibber – the husband who brought the charge was proved to have put a pillow under the heads of the infamous couple when they were in bed together, so his moral standing was not high. Patronised by an extremely tiresome and selfish client, Sarah, Duchess of Marlborough – 'I could not make out, Sir, who she was, for she would not give her name,' his clerk told Murray, 'but she swore so dreadfully that she must be a lady of quality' – he eventually married on November 20, 1738, Lady Elizabeth Finch, daughter of the Earl of Winchelsea, with whom he lived happily though childlessly for nearly half a century.

William Murray was a Scotsman who had been sent to seek his fortune in far richer England. Though coming of a poverty-stricken family – he was the eleventh of fourteen children – he was anything but a peasant. He was born on March 2, 1705 in the ruined but splendidly picturesque castle of Scone; his father was the fifth Viscount Stormont; his relatives a pack of Jacobites. Educated first at Perth School, he was then sent, by Highland pony, to London, entered at Westminster School, elected a scholar of Christ Church, won the prize there for a Latin poem on the death of George I much to the disgust of William Pitt who had submitted a rival but rejected entry, as a student at Lincoln's Inn 'drank champagne with the wits', and was called to the Bar at Lincoln's Inn Hall on November 23, 1730. After which he remained for two years without a brief.

But by the time of his marriage his fortunes had changed

dramatically. He was the leading barrister of the day, making well over £3000 a year, wooed by both Whigs and Tories, yet carefully noncommittal – a brilliant and happy contrast to self-seeking, low-born, money-grabbing lawyers like Thomas Parker and Philip Yorke (who was just as avaricious as his patron, though far more careful) and to the dull plodders who succeeded them.

William Lee

Philip Yorke had during the chancellorship of Lord Talbot been eclipsed in the House of Lords by that talented and popular man. He arranged for one of his 'puisne' judges at King's Bench, a man of no pretensions to a peerage or indeed to anything except decent competence, to succeed him as Lord Chief Justice. In the words of the *London Magazine*, 'he was resolved to *rule the roast*.' So on June 13, 1737, much to his own surprise, William Lee became Lord Chief Justice. He is famed chiefly for the single joke that he loved to make. Having been born in the year of the Glorious Revolution, he would declare that 'as he *came in with King William*, he was bound to be a good Whig.' He had a villa at Totteridge where he 'kept an orderly table', and used to entertain members of the Bar and the Bench. He might lay a claim to being our first feminist judge. 'I am clearly of the opinion,' he laid it down in an *obiter dictum*, 'that a woman may be sexton of a parish.'

As Lord Chancellor, Philip Yorke had been a brilliant equity judge, affable in manner, rarely reversed in judgment. As a politician, he had been much less successful: blusteringly eager for war with Spain in the matter of Jenkin's Ear, vehemently attacking both the liberty of the press and opposition peers, defending indefensible war manoeuvres, and finally unpleasantly enmeshed in Walpole's fall, which occurred in February 1742. Yorke was very much afraid that his official career was over, and greatly regretted having abandoned his safe position as Lord Chief Justice. Instead, within a year, he found himself not only still Lord Chancellor but the backbone of the new Pelham administration, the virtual ruler of England. 'When Yorke had left none but his friends in the Ministry,' wrote

Horace Walpole, brother of the former Prime Minister, 'he was easily the most eminent for abilities.'

In the new government led by Pelham, the Earl of Winchelsea, William Murray's father-in-law, was First Lord of the Admiralty; and by November 1742 William Murray found himself in politics with a vengeance: installed, by courtesy of the Duke of Newcastle, as M.P. for Boroughbridge, appointed Solicitor General and a Bencher of Lincoln's Inn.

> We ply the memory, we load the brain [wrote Pope].
> Bind rebel wit and double chain on chain
> How sweet an Ovid, Murray, was our boast!
> How many Martials were in Pulteney lost!

Yet for all Pope's regrets over his lost vocation as a poet, Murray made an excellent politician. He had studied oratory; he now, to the delight of the House of Commons, practised it. His official superior, Sir Dudley Ryder, the Attorney General, was a decent enough lawyer but of little or no interest. Mr Solicitor General Murray very soon became virtually government leader in the House of Commons. He was elegant, lucid and polished. By contrast, his chief antagonist William Pitt, three years his younger though he had become Member for Old Sarum two years before Murray entered Parliament, was savagely emotional. But Pitt's great days had not yet come.

In 1744 the Young Pretender, Prince Charles Edward, was reported at Dunkirk. Ryder, the Attorney General, introduced a bill to suspend Habeas Corpus in the Commons. Philip Yorke as virtual head of the government caused another Bill to be introduced attainting the sons of the Pretender, King James III, if they should attempt to land in Great Britain; and when the Bill came up to the Lords, added clauses making it high treason to correspond with the sons of the Pretender and retaining until their death the iniquitous punishment for high treason of 'corruption of blood'. 'The execution of a traitor is a fleeting example,' Ryder told the House of Commons, 'but the poverty of his posterity is a permanent lesson of obedience to our laws.' So much for the liberal principles of Whig lawyers. William Murray's elder brother had been for twenty years with the Pretender, who had created him Earl of Dunbar. His mother, whom he loved dearly, was a fervent Jacobite. Nevertheless, he supported the government of which as Solicitor General he was now a leading member.

The King, as usual, was abroad when Bonnie Prince Charlie

landed at Moidart. Philip Yorke as a Lord Justice was virtually regent and in the position of a Justiciar of old – at least until, much to the Lord Chancellor's relief, George II returned from Hanover on August 31, 1745. It was just as well that he returned when he did, for the apathy that legalistic leaders instil in times of peril was totally prevalent. 'I apprehend,' wrote Horace Walpole, 'that the people may perhaps look on and cry *Fight, dog. Fight, bear!* if they do no worse.' Lawyers, as is always the case, proved incapable of managing a war: Yorke and his coterie tended at first to treat it as a triviality until, with the crossing of the Border, they gave way to near panic, succeeded when Bonnie Prince Charlie turned back at Derby by a cold desire for blood.

As Lord High Steward, Philip Yorke presided over the trials for high treason of three Scots peers, Lords Kilmarnock, Cromarty and Balmerino, that were held in the Great Hall at Westminster nine months after the Battle of Culloden had ended the '45'. He did not distinguish himself. 'Though a most comely personage with a fine voice, his behaviour was mean,' wrote Horace Walpole. 'To the prisoners he was peevish; and instead of keeping up to the humane dignity of the law of England, whose character it is to point out favour to the criminal, he crossed them and almost scolded at any offer they made towards defence.' Murray fared little better.

> While the Lords were withdrawn, the Solicitor General Murray (brother of the Pretender's minister) officiously and insolently went up to Lord Balmerino and asked him how he could give the Lords so much trouble. Balmerino asked the bystanders who this person was, and being told, he said 'Oh, Mr Murray, I am extremely glad to see you; I have been with several of your relations; the good lady, your mother, was of great use to us at Perth.'

Kilmarnock and Balmerino were beheaded; Cromarty pardoned out of respect for his wife. Meanwhile, the commoners who had also been captured at the siege of Carlisle were being tried by Lord Chief Justice Lee and his eleven brother judges at a special tribunal in Southwark. Various defences – in Colonel Townley's case that he held a commission from the King of France and was therefore a prisoner of war, not a traitor; in the case of Alexander McGrowther that he was a feudal vassal of the Duke of Perth; in the case of the Kinloch brothers that they were native-born Scotsmen and so under the Articles of Union ought to be tried by the Court of Justiciary in Scotland; in the case of Sir John Wedderburn that he had merely collected money for the rebels – were all thrown out, and the accused found guilty.

The final and most extraordinary of these Jacobite trials was that of the wily, treacherous but appealing eighty-year-old, Simon Fraser, twelfth Lord Lovat. He had committed no overt act of rebellion and so could only be proceeded against by way of impeachment. William Murray acted as the main 'manager' for the House of Commons in conducting this prosecution at the bar of the House of Lords. The evidence was tricky; even Murray regretted that the old Lord was by law denied any expert legal help. Not that Lovat allowed himself to be over-awed. 'I beg your Lordships' pardon,' he said at the end of his own defence, 'for this long and rude discourse. I had great need of my cousin Murray's eloquence for half an hour, and then it would have been more agreeable.' As for Philip Yorke, he dealt with him equally urbanely when the Lord High Steward asked him, after the inevitable verdict of guilty, whether he wished to say anything further.

'Nothing,' said Lovat, 'except to thank your Lordship for your goodness to me. God bless you all, and I wish you an eternal farewell. We shall not all meet again in the same place, I am sure of that.'

He was beheaded at the Tower on April 9, 1747. An extraordinary crowd was there to see the extraordinary old reprobate die. A scaffold fell, killing several of them. 'The more mischief,' commented Lord Lovat, 'the better sport.' He died with quotations from Horace and Ovid on his lips.

Thereafter Philip Yorke introduced the disgraceful Coercion Bill that forbade the tartan and the plaid and put Highlanders into breeches; following which, his career relapsed for some time into comparative obscurity. Whereas William Murray was faced with the first scandal of a so-far successful career, and one that was to plague him, on and off, throughout the rest of his life.

It all began with a triviality as scandals so often do: rumours that over twenty years before at 'love feasts' with old school friends, Murray had drunk the health of the Pretender. A petition to the King was got up by the government's opponents and the Privy Council was forced to hold an enquiry. Behind the charge was a feeling that the Solicitor General had been too courteous in his prosecution of the Jacobites. That he answered very firmly and well: 'If I had been counsel for the Crown against Sir Walter Raleigh, and that unfortunate man had been as clearly guilty of high treason as the rebel Lords, I would not have made Sir Edward Coke's speech against him to gain all Sir Edward Coke's estate and all his reputation.' George II sensibly commented: 'It is of very little importance to me what the parties accused may have said or done or thought while they were little more than boys,' and there, it might be thought, the matter should have ended. It did not. Murray's opponents, Pitt especially, saw that he had a weak point; and for years afterwards proceeded to exploit it. One result was that Murray became far more timid in debate. On one occasion, when Pitt referred obliquely to the incident in the House, 'Colours, much less words, could not paint the confusion and agitation that worked in Murray's face during this almost apostrophe.'

In 1752, the Lord Chief Justice, Lee, presided over a trial from which he emerged covered with ridicule. The Attorney General, Sir Dudley Ryder, had filed a criminal information for libel against William Owen, a bookseller who had published a bold pamphlet censuring the House of Commons. Lee instructed the jury to bring in a verdict of guilty. They withdrew, to troop back into the Guildhall two hours later.

Clerk of the Court: Gentlemen of the jury, are you agreed on your verdict? Is the defendant guilty or not guilty?
Foreman: Guilty!
Some Members of the Jury: No! No! My Lord! It is all a mistake – we say Not Guilty.
Foreman: Yes, My Lord, it was a mistake; I meant to say Not Guilty.
Bystanders: Huzza! Huzza!! Huzza!!!
Attorney General (Ryder): My Lord, this must not be; I insist on the jury being called back and asked their opinion upon the only question submitted to them.
Lord Chief Justice (Lee): Gentlemen of the jury, do you think the evidence laid before you of Owen's publishing the book by selling it is not sufficient to convince you that the said Owen did sell this book?
Foreman: Not guilty! My Lord! Not guilty!
Juryman: Yes, my Lord, that is our verdict, and so we say all.
Rest of the Jury: So we say all, so we say all.

There were bonfires in the City that night to celebrate Owen's acquittal. Ryder was forced on his way home to drink a health to the jury and hear a ballad addressed to himself that proclaimed: 'Mr Attorney's grim wig, though awfully big. No more shall frighten the nation.' The wretched Lee went into a decline, and eventually died of apoplexy on April 8, 1754. There was no doubt about his successor: the Attorney General, with a sigh of relief, stepped into his shoes.

Dudley Ryder

In March 1754, a month before the Lord Chief Justice's apoplexy Pelham, the Prime Minister, had died suddenly. This was William Murray's great opportunity. There seems little doubt that he could have become Prime Minister and First Lord of the Treasury if he had boldly struck out for that position. But his boldness seems to have been sapped by that one scandal of the Jacobite toast that hung over him. Pelham's brother, the Duke of Newcastle, whom George III had described as fit only to be 'master of the ceremonies at a small German court', became Prime Minister. William Murray became Attorney General and government leader in the House of Commons – a post he would probably never have taken if he had known that Pitt, who for eight long years had lived in obscurity and comparative silence, was about to resign his post as Paymaster and set out upon a wild anti-government rampage. Philip Yorke, who had successfuly piloted his Jew Bill (that allowed Jews to become citizens) and his Marriage Bill (that set the formalities for marriage as we know them today) through both Houses, remained as Lord Chancellor and was promoted to the rank of Earl. The new Lord Chief Justice was furious, as were all his fellow common-law judges, that Yorke should be the only law lord, and apparently determined to remain so. He pressed for a peerage for himself and indeed, on May 24, 1756, the King signed the warrant appointing him 'Lord Ryder, Baron Ryder of Harrowby in the county of Lincoln'. His family and his beloved wife were overjoyed. But within twelve hours, still officially a commoner, before the next day dawned he had had a seizure and was dead.

Lord Campbell, the amiable Sir Dudley's previous biographer, quoted two of his early letters to his wife – an example I intend to follow, a rather fetching sidelight on the life of a lawyer in the first half of the eighteenth century.

Lincoln's Inn Hall, Nov. 3, 1742.

My Dear,

I have received your letter and must answer it now or not at all tonight. I have been to pay my compliments at the Prince's Court. Miss Fazackerley appeared there for the first time, and kissed hands. Mrs. Campbell inquired there after your health. She looks like a ghost – not at all improved by Tonbridge. I to-day dined, by invitation, at the Chancellor of the Exchequer's . . .

I would have you make haste to town and keep me out of bad hands, for I am in great danger òf growing a rake whilst left to myself, for I have been no less than twice at the play in a week's time. It's true the immediate temptation was to see Garrick, but how soon I may recover my youthful taste for *diversion* I can't say. I'm glad the Bishop is coming to town.

Adieu, my dearest.

D.R.

The next day, the Bishop had come; in time to console a hung-over Attorney General.

Nov. 4, 1742.

My Dear,

The Bishop is come very well, after a pleasant journey. I wish I had seen you come in at the same time; but I must wait . . .

You bid me tell you every post how my health stands, which is of more moment to me as you are interested in it. I am obliged therefore to let you know that I have had the headache all day. You'll expect, I know, an account how it came. I believe it was owing to my quitting my full-bottom and gown, without an equivalent, at the Chancellor of the Exchequer's. I am sorry to give you the trouble of hearing this but I am bound to be ingenuous and make a full confession. I fear I shall not be completely careful of myself till you come and give that cheerfulness to my spirits which makes me think it worthwhile to be well, as I hardly do while you are absent.

Adieu, thou best of women,

D.R.

As the Bishop – by then Archbishop, also a Ryder – wrote to the Lord Chief Justice's widow:

A greater loss could not be to his family or his friends. Few were ever so great a blessing to all that had the honour to be related to him. His kindness to me and to my nephews has been boundless: what his Majesty and the public have lost by his death will be testified by the universal lamentation of it.

One voice however was noticeably not lamenting. For William Murray, Ryder's sudden death offered the chance of escape from a position that had become quite impossible.

11

William Murray

Your fate depends upon your success as a speaker; [wrote Lord Chesterfield to his son], and take my word for it, that success depends more upon manner than matter. Mr Pitt, and Mr Murray the Attorney General, are beyond comparison the best speakers. Why? Only because they are the best orators. They alone can inflame or quiet the House; they alone are attended to in that numerous and noisy assembly, that you might hear a pin fall while either of them is speaking. Is it that their matter is better, or their arguments stronger, than other peoples'? Does the House expect extraordinary information from them? Not in the least; but the House expects pleasure from them, and therefore attends; finds it, and therefore approves.

Unfortunately for the Attorney General, the House found its greatest pleasure in Pitt's savage and witty attacks on Murray.

Having for some time tortured his victim by general invective, he suddenly stopped, threw his eyes around, then fixing their whole power on Murray, uttered these words in a low, solemn tone, which caused a breathless silence: 'I must now address a few words to Mr Attorney: they shall be few but they shall be daggers.' Murray was agitated; the look was continued; the agitation increased. 'Judge Festus trembles!' exclaimed Pitt; 'he shall hear me some other day.' He sat down. Murray made no reply, and a languid debate provoked the paralysis of the House.

Parliament adjourned in early May 1756; the French attacked Minorca, and war was declared on May 18. Murray, already regretting his position as a leading member of a disastrous and clumsy government, looked forward with horror to the prospects of renewed and far more vicious and justified attacks when Parliament reassembled. All he wanted to know of politics, he used often to say, could be found in a weekly newspaper taken in by a village club. Then, a week later, as if in answer to his prayers, Ryder died and an avenue of escape immediately opened. As Attorney General, Murray quite legiti-- mately claimed the succession; he also, equally legitimately, claimed a peerage and a seat in the Lords. But the Duke of Newcastle resisted his attempts, declaring, acutely enough, that 'the writ for creating Murray Chief Justice would be the death-warrant of his own administration'. Murray was his only protection in the House of Commons against his doubtful supporter Fox and his open enemy Pitt. He offered Murray the chancellorship of the Duchy of Lancaster for life at £2,000 a year, plus a reversion of one of the golden Tellerships of the Exchequer to his nephew Stormont, if only he would stay on as leader of the House of Commons. This in addition to the £7,000 a year that Murray received officially as Attorney General. Murray declined. On July 14 news reached London of the surrender of Minorca. 'To the block with Newcastle and to the yard-arm with Byng!' cried the mobs. Desperately the Duke upped his offer by another £6,000 a year. Still Murray refused. 'He knew,' wrote Horace Walpole, 'that it was safer to expound laws than to be exposed to them: and exclaiming, "Good God! what merit have I, that you should load this country, for which so little is done with spirit, with the additional burden of £6,000 a year?" at last peremptorily declared that if he was not to be Chief Justice, neither would he be any longer Attorney General.'

Even so, it was not until November 8, 1756, after months of intrigue, that William Murray was sworn in by the Lord Chancellor, Philip Yorke, as Lord Chief Justice of the King's Bench and created a peer – Baron Mansfield of Mansfield in Nottinghamshire. Next day, Newcastle, as he had predicted, fell; and ten days later Philip Yorke finally resigned the Great Seal, but not before he had been praised by Murray in what amounted to a farewell panegyric at Lincoln's Inn:

'It is the peculiar felicity,' said Murray, 'of the great man I am speaking of to have presided very near twenty years, and to have shone with a splendour that has risen superior to faction, and that has subdued envy.'

Philip Yorke lived on for seven years more, always an influence in the Lords and in politics, famed as a lawyer for having reconciled equity with the common law. He died in 1763 it was said worth a million. A perhaps more just estimate of his long career is given by Lord Chesterfield:

He presided in the Court of Chancery above twenty years, and in all that time none of his decrees were ever reversed, or the justness of them questioned. Though avarice was his ruling passion, he was never in the least suspected of any kind of corruption – a rare and meritorious instance of virtue and self-denial under the influence of such a craving, insatiable and increasing passion. He was an agreeable, eloquent speaker in Parliament, but not without some little tincture of the pleader. He was a cheerful, instructive companion, humane in his nature, decent in his manners, unstained by any vice (avarice excepted) – a very great magistrate but by no means a great minister.

Horace Walpole was pithier than the somewhat pompous Earl.

He was a creature of the Duke of Newcastle, and by him introduced to Sir Robert Walpole, who contributed to his grandeur and baseness, in giving him the opportunity of displaying the extent of the latter by raising him to the height of the former. He had good parts, which he laid out so entirely upon the law in the first part of his life, that they were of little use to him afterwards, when he would have applied them to more general views.

A complete contrast, here, to the next Lord Chief Justice, William Murray, whose narrowing career at the age of fifty-one was to lead to far greater a reputation; but as a lawyer not as a politician.

William Murray

No sooner was William Murray appointed Lord Chief Justice than he was offerd not once but twice the Lord Chancellorship. Wisely, both then and thereafter, he refused this apparent promotion – preferring the security of lifelong tenure on the Bench to political pre-eminence. Certainly as a member of the House of Lords he did not abandon politics; indeed, he was often a member of the Cabinet in that period when, for all their internal faction-fighting, the Whigs held power. He remained Lord Chief Justice for thirty-two years, though his term of office might have come to a sharp end on the death of George II and the accession of his son and rival George III in October 1760. For, theoretically at least, all judges had to resign on the demise of the Crown. This would have been particularly dangerous for Murray as the young King was a Tory. But George III abolished this rule; and Murray, despite his political principles, soon found that he could work hand-in-hand with his fellow Scotsman, soon to be Prime Minister in succession to the victorious Pitt, Lord Bute.

There can be little argument now about Murray's greatness as a judge, though at the time he was accused of disregarding the rules of the common law in favour of Roman or civil law, and equity. One of the difficulties was that his Scots training automatically inclined him to look for the principle upon which to judge a case, not for the exact precedent in the limited English style. More generally, and with hindsight, it becomes clear that what he was doing was simply adapting the law to the needs of a great and increasingly prosperous commercial trading nation. Already as Solicitor General, he had arranged for the brilliant Blackstone to set up in Oxford – a move which led eventually to the creation of a Professorship of Common Law, and the publication of 2,000 pages of Blackstone's *Commentaries*, an elegant and up-to-date compendium of the laws of England, written in a style as remote as possible from the discouraging pedantry of Coke's *Institutes* and *Reports*. In the criminal law, Acts of Parliament were modernising the archaic processes – the 1730 Act, bitterly opposed by the then Lord Chief Justice, Raymond, substituting English for Latin in indictments, the 1736 Act abolishing witchcraft as a crime, the 1747 (post-Lovat trial) Act allowing counsel to those impeached of high treason. Admittedly by the end of the reign of George III there were over 160 capital offences; a man could be hanged, for instance, for stealing in a shop to the value of five shillings. As a criminal judge, Murray constantly ruled, however, in the face of all the evidence that valuable articles were worth less than five shillings. He did not, as it happens, preside over the trial of the last peer to be hanged in England. Earl Ferrers, who had shot his steward, was tried by all his peers in April 1760; and on May 5, wearing a specially embroidered silver suit, drove from the Tower to Tyburn in his own landau, drawn by six of his own horses – the first man to be hanged by a clean drop rather than by cart, ladder and gibbet. The Lord Chief Justice of course assisted Lord Keeper Henley, who presided as Lord High Steward over the trial in Westminster Hall.

It was as a commercial judge, though, that he was the greatest innovator. He practically created the law of insurance; shipping law, bills of exchange, colonial law were all brilliantly analysed and expounded in his judgments. He ruled on the law of evidence, on the rights of authors, and on slavery. 'The air of England,' he adjudged with elegance, in the case of James Somersett of Jamaica, 'has long been too pure for a slave and every man is free who breathes it. Every man who comes into England is entitled to the protection of English law, whatever oppression he may heretofore have suffered and whatever may be the colour of his skin.

Quamvis ille niger, quamvis tu candidus esses
Let the negro be discharged.'

He ruled on wagers (which nowadays have no force in law). Mr Codrington and Mr Pigott, young racing men and great heirs, decided to 'run their fathers'; that is to say, to bet on which of the two Mr Codrington Senior or Mr Pigott Senior would survive the longer. Unfortunately, at the time of the wager, Pigott Senior was, unknown to either of them, dead. Did the wager stand? The Lord Chief Justice, without moralising, ruled that it did. The most famous case ever in this category was the case of the Chevalier d'Eon, a duellist, but a very effeminate foreigner. Mr Jones waged Mr Dacosta a large sum that the Chevalier was a woman. Many witnesses were heard. For once Murray was indignantly moralistic: 'The trial of this case,' he commented without exaggeration, 'made a great noise all over Europe . . . Here is a person who represents himself to the world as a man, is stated on the record to be *Monsieur le Chevalier d'Eon*, has acted in that character in various capacities, and has his reasons and advantages in so appearing. Shall two indifferent people, by a wager between themselves, try whether he is a cheat and imposter, and be allowed to subpoena all his intimate friends and confidential attendants to give evidence that will expose him all over Europe? Such an inquiry is a disgrace to the judicature.' Much to the disappointment of polite society, the sex of the Chevalier d'Eon was therefore never legally established.

John Wilkes, M.P. for Aylesbury, member of the Sublime Society of the Beef Steaks, and of the Hellfire Club, roué, son of a City merchant, friend of the notorious Sir Francis Dashwood, political supporter of Pitt's, hated Pitt's successor as Prime Minister, the despicable Lord Bute. His journal, ironically entitled *The North Briton* – a jibe at Scots influence on the

Court – first appeared on June 5, 1762. Despite the ailing Pitt's fierce opposition, Lord Bute steered the peace treaty, the Treaty of Paris, through Parliament. On April 8, 1763, the King in his speech from the throne described the peace as 'honourable to my Crown and beneficial to my people'. Just over a fortnight later, there appeared the notorious Issue No. 45 of *The North Briton*. This, by way of contrast, described the speech from the throne as 'the most abandoned instance of ministerial effrontery ever attempted to be imposed on mankind'. The article was of course anonymous. The government, in a fury of rage inspired largely by the King, issued a general warrant for the arrest of the authors, printers and publishers of this allegedly seditious libel.

Wilkes was arrested and sent to the Tower. His friends moved a writ of Habeas Corpus. He was sent for trial in the Court of Common Pleas; and on May 6, the Lord Chief Justice of that court, Sir Charles Pratt, won the greatest popularity that any Lord Chief Justice has ever enjoyed by ruling that parliamentary privilege covers even seditious libel. Wilkes was discharged amidst wild rejoicings, the popular hero of the day.

There, it might have been thought, the government ought to have been content to let the matter rest. Unwisely, they did not. Bute had been forced out of office but George III and his new Prime Minister, George Grenville, determined to prosecute Wilkes in the Court of King's Bench under the more reliable Lord Chief Justice, William Murray. On November 15, in the autumn session of Parliament, it was moved that No. 45 of *The North Briton* was a 'false, scandalous and seditious libel' likely to excite the people to 'treacherous insurrections against his Majesty's Government'. The Ayes had it, by 237 votes to 111. Wilkes, wounded in a duel, harmed by government-inspired sexual blackmail, slipped away to France and exile and friendship with the Chevalier d'Eon to avoid being expelled from the House and thereby become liable to prosecution. The following February he was convicted *in absentia* by Murray of seditious libel, and a few months later formally outlawed.

There again the matter would have rested, a mere footnote in history, if Wilkes, driven by poverty and pride alike, had not taken the great risk of returning to London two years later, outlaw or no outlaw, and standing for election. On March 28, 1768, he was elected by a vast majority M.P. for Middlesex. Two nights of tumultuous rejoicing followed; and then Wilkes voluntarily surrendered to the Court of King's Bench. He was an ugly creature physically, with a leering squint, but a man of wit, and fine manners, a dilettante, a man of fashion rather than a demagogue, whose company was enjoyed even by those who, like Dr Johnson, mistrusted him.

From the moment when, on April 27, William Murray as Lord Chief Justice formally committed Wilkes to prison, his life became for four years a hellish affair. It became even more hellish for the then Prime Minister, the Duke of Grafton, hag-ridden by the Wilkes affair, and for the Attorney General, Charles Yorke, who cut his own throat in anguish, just at the time when he could have followed in his father's footsteps and accepted the post of Lord Chancellor. Clearly the Wilkes agitation, though supported by Horne Tooke, the radical parson of Brentford, and Sergeant Glynn, a legal antiquarian who had fallen foul of the Lord Chief Justice, would have died down if it had not been based on genuine upheavals in society. The weavers of Spitalfields, the Thames watermen, the tailors, the glass-grinders, the coal-heavers, the Southwark joiners and hat-dyers were all striking against reduced wages and economic distress. Four thousand sailors left their ships to claim higher pay and roamed about London cheering for Wilkes. In prison Wilkes became a martyr and a symbol. On May 5, Lord Weymouth, a Secretary of State, ordered out the troops to suppress a pro-Wilkes riot at St George's Fields, unwisely choosing the Scots Guards. Several people were killed and the inquest jury found Private Maclane guilty of murder. Wilkes accused the ministry, with apparent justification, of using Scottish butchers to intimidate free Englishmen.

Such was the general atmosphere when on June 8 the Lord Chief Justice pronounced judgment in Westminster Hall. 'It is fit,' said Murray,

> to take some notice of the various terrors being held out; the numerous crowds which have attended and now attend in and about the Hall, out of all reach of hearing what passes in court; and the tumults which, in other places, have shamefully insulted all order and government . . . I pass over many anonymous letters I have received. Those in print are public; and some of them have been brought judicially before the court. Whoever the writers are, they take the wrong way. I will do my duty unawed. What am I to fear? That *mendax infamia* from the press, which daily coins false facts and false motives? The lies of calumny carry no terror to me.

Not an entirely accurate statement of fact, as 'Junius' was later to prove. 'The threats,' continued Murray, 'go further than abuse: personal violence is denounced. I do not believe it; it is not the genius of the worst of men of this country, in the worst of times.' That was certainly true (at any rate for the moment and even twelve years later), particularly when the Lord Chief Justice on a technical point reversed Wilkes' outlawry, though sentencing him to fines and a brief spell of imprisonment for seditious libel and obscene publications.

Nonetheless, and once again, the government decided that Wilkes must be crushed. Time and again, he was expelled from Parliament and re-elected by the electors of Middlesex. Pitt, now Lord Chatham, reappeared in the House of Lords with all his traditional biting verve apparently intact, to inveigh against his old enemy Murray. Murray quailed, though the government won. Meanwhile, on January 21, 1769, the cause of Wilkes gained a new supporter; the first letter of the still mysterious 'Junius' appeared, savaging the authorities, with, as Burke later said, more strength, wit and judgment than *The North Briton* had ever done, but also with more rancour and venom. 'Junius' was evidently a member of the inner circle of the fashionable, political world; he mixed private gossip with political attacks, populist propaganda with reactionary views. Nothing so devastating has ever been written in English political life. His Letters dominated men's minds and shaped their emotions.

As Lord Chief Justice, Murray was inevitably involved in the government's attempt to suppress 'Junius' when after a year of libelling the ministry he at last, on December 19, 1769, turned his pen against the King. In the next six months, trials at King's Bench of printers and publishers followed, one after another, culminating on July 18, 1770, despite Murray's directions, in an acquittal at the Guildhall that sent cheers reverberating outside the City walls, right to Bloomsbury Square where many thousands had gathered outside the Lord Chief Justice's private home. He had, wrote Horace Walpole, 'endeavoured by the most arbitrary construction to mislead the jury, telling them that they had nothing to do with the *intention*, nor with the words in the indictment – *malicious, seditious*, etc. The despotic and Jesuitical judge went further . . . It did the jury honour that they preferred liberty to the voice of the Inquisition. What criminal could be more heinously guilty than such a judge?'

But it was not Horace Walpole whose pen the Lord Chief Justice had now to fear. It was that of 'Junius' himself. On November 14, 'Junius' published his first Letter to Murray. 'Our language has no term of reproach,' 'Junius' began, 'The mind has no idea of detestation, which has not already been applied to you, and exhausted. Ample Justice has been done by abler pens than mine to the separate merits of your life and character. Let it be *my* humble office to collect the scattered sweets till their united virtue tortures the senses.'

He proceeded to do so. Murray had exposed himself, unwisely, to charges of avarice by agreeing to act as Lord Chancellor after young Yorke's suicide until a successor was appointed.

'You secretly engross the power while you decline the title of minister; and though you dare not be Chancellor, you know how to secure the emoluments of the office. Are the seals to be for ever in commission that you may enjoy five thousand pounds a year?'

Much, much more followed: including, inevitably, an attack on Murray's early Jacobite sympathies and his subsequent turning of coats. 'Permit me,' wrote 'Junius', 'to begin with paying a tribute to Scotch sincerity wherever I find it . . . I see through your whole life one uniform plan to enlarge the power of the Crown at the expense of the liberty of the subject.'

The Attorney General urged Murray to prosecute for libel the *Daily Advertiser* in which 'Junius'' letters were published. But the Lord Chief Justice was wary of stirring up the sleeping dogs of his past. He declared, pretentiously, that he 'would confide in the good sense of the public and the internal evidence of his own conscience,' and, as if to prove 'Junius' justified, surrendered the seals of the Chancellorship to Mr Justice Bathurst. All the same, 'Junius' continued his attacks until the Lord Chief Justice, it was said, did not dare open the *Daily Advertiser* at his breakfast table, for fear of finding in it some fresh onslaught upon himself under his official title of Lord Mansfield.

When the guards are called forth to murder their fellow-subjects is it not by the ostensible advice of Lord Mansfield? Who attacks the liberty of the Press? Lord Mansfield! Who invades the constitutional powers of the juries? Lord Mansfield! Who was that judge who, to save the King's brother, affirmed that a man of the first rank and quality, who obtains a verdict in a suit for criminal conversation, is entitled to no greater damages than the meanest mechanic? Lord Mansfield! Who is it makes Commissioners for the Great Seal? Lord Mansfield! Who is it frames a decree for these Commissioners deciding against Lord Chatham? Lord Mansfield! Compared to these enormities, his original attachment to the Pretender (to whom his dearest brother was confidential secretary) is a virtue of the first magnitude. But the hour of impeachment *will* come, and neither he nor Grafton shall escape me!!

It did not come. In the spring of 1772, to the enormous relief of the governing class and no doubt of Murray in particular – unlike Grafton, he had not been forced out of office – the Letters of 'Junius' ceased as suddenly as they had begun.

It must, all the same, have been a considerable relief for the Lord Chief Justice to turn, in 1775 and 1776, to the trial of the Duchess of Kingston – alias the Countess of Bristol – for bigamy. Miss Elizabeth Chudleigh was renowned for her sex-appeal even in that age of great beauties; she had once appeared at a masked ball, wrote Horace Walpole, whose letters were full of her, 'so naked that you would have taken her for Andromeda'. The Duke of Hamilton had been in love with her, but married Miss Elizabeth Gunning. George II flirted with her, to the point of presenting her with a watch which cost thirty-five guineas. Frederick the Great gave a ball for her at which she emptied two bottles of wine and staggered around the floor as she danced. She was, alas, all of fifty-five by the time she came before the Lord Chief Justice at King's Bench. He indicted her for bigamy, and assisted next year at her full trial by the House of Lords in Westminster Hall – where she was found guilty by all, only the Duke of Newcastle adding 'but not intentionally'. The Attorney General most ungallantly urged that she be punished by being branded in the hand, bigamy being a clergyable offence; but she pleaded privilege of peerage, and retired first to St Petersburg where she got on famously with the Empress Catherine, and then to Paris where she died.

The Lord Chief Justice also enjoyed a visit to Paris, where he was presented to the young Louis XVI and Marie-Antoinette and where his noble appearance and excellent manners made a great impression. These were his halcyon years. He lived at Caen Wood – Kenwood – on Hampstead Heath, allowed his wife £7,000 a year for housekeeping (and his rat-catcher £7.7.4. a year for his wages), held a *levée* every Sunday night in the winter season; was easy and polished in society, and had a Scottish taste for claret.

As for his professional conduct, from the very first it had been said of him that 'Mr Murray's *statement* is of itself worth the argument of any other man.' He was a quick worker as a judge, polite to timid barristers, firm with the long-winded or the insolent. When a friend of his, a general, came to him for advice on being appointed governor of a West Indian island where he would have, he learnt to his horror, also to sit as supreme judge: 'Be of good cheer,' Murray said, 'take my advice, and you will be reckoned a great judge as well as a great commander-in-chief. Nothing is more easy; only hear both sides patiently – then consider what you think justice requires, and decide accordingly. But never give your reasons; – for your judgment will probably be right but your reasons will certainly be wrong.'

This of course was the relaxed attitude that had made 'Junius' thunder against him:

In contempt or ignorance of the common law of England, you have made it your study to introduce into the court where you preside measures of jurisprudence unknown to Englishmen. The Roman code, the law of nations, and the opinion of foreign civilians, are your pepetual theme; but who ever heard you mention Magna Carta or the Bill of Rights with approbation and respect? By such treacherous arts the noble simplicity and free spirit of our Saxon laws were first corrupted!

But 'Junius' had in 1772 silenced himself or been silenced; and even such a dyed-in-the-wool reactionary as Dr Johnson was forced to admit that the Lord Chief Justice was as good a man, in his way, as any of his military friends.

Johnson: Every man thinks meanly of himself for not having been a soldier, or not having been at sea.
Boswell: Lord Mansfield does not.
Johnson: Sir, if Lord Mansfield were in a company of general officers and admirals who had been in service, he would shrink; he'd wish to creep under the table.
Boswell: No, he'd think he could *try* them all.
Johnson: Yes, if he could catch them.

This was praise indeed, coming from the Doctor for a Scotsman – though, strangely enough, he and Murray never met.

The one occasion when Murray's customary good manners deserted him was at that most famous scene in the House of Lords when the aged Pitt, supported under each arm by his relatives, rose to speak in favour of negotiations with the American rebels.

He fell back on his seat, [wrote Lord Camden, Pitt's great

supporter, to the absent Duke of Grafton] and was to all appearance in the agonies of death. This threw the whole House into confusion; every person was upon his legs in a moment, hurrying from one place to another, some sending for assistance, others producing salts and others reviving spirits. Many crowding about the Earl to observe his countenance, all affected, most part really concerned; and even those who might have felt a secret pleasure at the accident, yet put on the appearance of distress, except only the Earl of M, who sat still, almost as much unmoved as the senseless body itself.

Admittedly the Lord Chief Justice was, on the American question, a hard-liner; and Pitt had been his life-long enemy and rival. But whatever his virtues there was a coldness in William Murray's nature, a lack of warmth and friendship in his life, what his biographer and fellow-Scot Campbell called 'a refined calculating selfishness' that is unappealing. Though such perhaps is the essence of a great judge.

That is not to suggest that he was inhuman or illiberal. On the contrary when a Catholic priest was brought up before him, charged with celebrating mass, Murray virtually directed the jury to acquit despite the evidence. 'Why do they not call someone who was present at this ordination?' he asked, ridiculously. 'You must not infer that he is a priest because he said mass, or that he said mass because he is a priest . . . Take notice that if you bring him in guilty the punishment is very severe, a dreadful punishment indeed! Nothing less than perpetual imprisonment!'

The priest was acquitted: an example of judge-made law overriding acts of Parliament and their clear intention, for which it is worth giving the Lord Chief Justice's reasoning, if only by way of contrast to the rantings of his predecessors on the same subject. He put it to the jury,

At the Reformation, they thought it in some measure necessary to pass these penal laws, for then the Pope had great power and the Jesuits were then a very formidable body. Now the Pope has little power, and it seems to grow less every day. As for the Jesuits, they are now banished from almost every state in Europe. These penal laws were not meant to be enforced except at proper seasons, when there is a necessity for it; or, more properly speaking, they were not meant to be enforced at all, but were merely made *in terrorem.*

The opinion of enlightened jurymen and eminent judges, however, was not shared by the mob.

Historians are still baffled by the last lurid flare-up of 'No Popery' in London known as the Gordon Riots. On June 2, 1780 no less than sixty thousand supporters of 'the General Protestant Association' gathered in St George's Fields with blue cockades in their hats to cross the Thames and accompany their President Lord George Gordon through the City and to Westminster where he was to present their monster petition against the recent Catholic Toleration Act to both Houses of Parliament. That day the Lord Chief Justice, because of the illness of the Lord Chancellor, was due to preside as Speaker of the House of Lords. In Parliament Street the mob recognised Murray, cursed him as a notorious Papist and broke the windows of his carriage. He was seventy-five years old. Wig askew, robe torn, he calmly took his seat on the Woolsack. Rather in the spirit of the Roman senators at the invasion of the Huns, the Lords proceeded with their debates, though the Archbishop of York had had his lawn-sleeves torn off, the Duke of Northumberland was robbed of his watch and his purse, Lords Hillsborough, Townsend and Stormont had been mildly beaten up and Lord Boston was dragged out of his carriage. Meanwhile the mob shouted, hooted and booed in Palace Yard until, at 9 p.m. the House adjourned, the peers disappeared, and the Lord Chief Justice was left alone, with only his own servants, to drink tea for two hours in his private room and to await the imminent bursting-in of the rioters.

Revolutions blow up in the most extraordinary way and this might well have been the beginning of an English revolution, preceding the French by a mere nine years, with Parliament stormed and a Lord Chief Justice torn to bits or strung up like his 'brother Cavendish' in the good old days, in place of the Governor of the Bastille. It did not turn out that way. The mob dispersed as night fell, to burn the Sardinian Ambassador's chapel in Lincoln's Inn Fields but not to interfere with the Lord Chief Justice's coach ride home to Bloomsbury Square.

A lull followed the *journée* of June 2. But the government, and the authorities, were seized with that sort of inexplicable lassitude, which is so often the prelude in other countries to a complete overthrow of the social system. On Tuesday, June 6, the House of Commons adjourned for a fortnight. The mob began to take control, ignoring the appeals for calm launched by the leaders of the Protestant Association. Gin distilleries in

Holborn belonging to Catholics were looted and set on fire; the Inns of Court were besieged; Newgate prison on the City walls was broken open, and two thousand criminals joined the rioters. A few red coats appeared here and there; their appearance only inflamed passions and provoked the mob. The cry went up that the Lord Chief Justice's house in Bloomsbury Square should be burnt to the ground: that Papist-lover, that oppressor. As night fell, a vast multitude carrying torches and faggots marched down Holborn and into the north-east corner of the square.

Whatever criticisms there might be of William Murray, no one ever suggested that he was a physical coward. He and his wife waited until the front door of their house was being battered down before escaping through a back passage. By the following morning the house in Bloomsbury Square was a blackened shell; and Murray's vast library had been destroyed. The poet Cowper wrote:

> So then – the Vandals of our isle,
> Sworn foes to sense and law,
> Have burnt to dust a nobler pile
> Than ever Roman saw!
>
> And Murray sighs o'er Pope and Swift
> And many a treasure more,
> The well-judged purchase and the gift,
> That grace his letter'ed store.

For all that it must be noted that 'the Vandals' strictly forbade plundering; even gold and silver plate was tossed into the fire. In this case at least there was true revolutionary fervour abroad, not mere mindless destruction. And in the end, it was not the ruling classes who lost their lives but, as invariably happens in England, the revolutionary mob. When on the Friday the Bank of England was threatened and the troops at last were called in, over 300 rioters were killed. Next day Lord George Gordon was arrested and sent to the Tower. In the repression that followed fifty-nine rioters were sentenced to death and twenty-one executed. On February 3 next year Murray himself presided over the trial for high treason at King's Bench of Lord George Gordon.

Lord George was defended (as was allowed under the new treason laws) by two lawyers: a dull Welsh barrister named Kenyon, who had become a favourite of the talented but lazy Lord Chancellor, Thurlow, (Kenyon did most of his hard work for him) and the brilliant young junior, Erskine. Following Mr Kenyon's wretchedly lame summing-up for the defence, Lord George afterwards declared that 'he gave himself up for lost'. Erskine redeemed his 'leader' by a first-class summing-up of the law and history of high treason, which resulted in Lord George's acquittal – for he had neither 'imagined the King's death' nor 'levied war against the King' within the meaning of the Statute. As a result the Lord Chancellor rewarded Mr Lloyd Kenyon, Whig M.P. for Hendon in Wiltshire, with – on March 8, 1782 – the post of Attorney General.

As for the Lord Chief Justice, everybody agreed that he presided with admirable impartiality over a trial which affected him so closely; that in his summing-up he pointed out to the jury the circumstances favourable to the prisoner as well as those against; and that he fairly stated, and left the jury to decide, the two questions on which the case technically hinged. All the same, Lord George Gordon ended in Newgate, convicted, five years later, of – of all things – libelling Marie-Antoinette; and dying on November 1, 1793, with the song '*ça ira*' on his lips.

The Lord Chief Justice was getting old, very old. Young Mr Pitt, his great antagonist's son, became First Lord and Prime Minister on January 12, 1784 aged only twenty-four, a cold and efficient administrator. That spring, Kenyon was reappointed Attorney General and Master of the Rolls.

The Prime Minister now found himself confronted with a problem. The separation of powers, the principle of judicial independence, had been so successfully achieved that it appeared impossible to remove an unwilling judge, except by death. The Lord Chief Justice had hardly missed a day in Westminster Hall, except when he was on circuit, since being first appointed. Now, at the age of eighty-one, he found his joints stiffening, though his brain was as agile as ever. He could not sit at King's Bench; he would not retire. He took the waters at Tunbridge Wells and did ornamental gardening at Kenwood. His favourite and puisne, Mr Justice Buller, 'the Prince of Pleaders', an extremely popular and hospitable judge, presided *de facto* in Westminster Hall. But Mr Pitt did not favour Buller J.; there was the matter of a certain election in a Cornish borough and *Quo Warranto* proceedings which Mr Pitt held against him. He favoured the Master of the Rolls, Kenyon, who was a very precise and hard-working Chancery judge. On the other hand, the said Master of the Rolls had, the aged Lord

Chief Justice learnt, dared to sneer at some of his own past decisions favouring a fusion of law and equity. For two years the Lord Chief Justice tended his garden, and made no appearance in court. At long last, Mr Pitt threatened that it might be necessary to appeal to both Houses of Parliament for an address to the Crown to remove him, both on the grounds of incapacity as well as criminality. And so, finally, on June 4, 1788, at the age of eighty-three, William Murray signed his resignation.

The ex-Lord Chief Justice lived on, in retirement at Kenwood, perfectly sound mentally, laughing at his successor's notoriously bad Latin quips, for five years more. He was extremely rich. He invested all his wealth in mortgages that were said to bring him in the enormous sum of £30,000 a year. He did not think much of the French Revolution. 'Well, my Lord,' said his apothecary, 'the troubles in France are now over.' 'Over, sir, do you say?' he replied, 'my dear sir, they are not yet begun!' His last words were 'Let me sleep! Let me sleep!' He died on the night of Wednesday, March 20, 1793, left his property to his nephew, Lord Stormont, and was buried quietly in Westminster Abbey by the side of his rival the elder Pitt.

12

Two Whig Reactionaries: Kenyon and Law

Shortly before the aged Lord Chief Justice's official retirement perhaps the most stupendous and unexpected brief ever to land in a struggling barrister's lap was delivered to the chambers of a certain Edward Law. It was a general retainer, marked with a fee of 500 guineas. Law's instructions were to settle the answer to the articles of impeachment against the former Governor-General of India, Warren Hastings. Law immediately realised that his fortune, and his reputation, were made.

'Struggling barrister' is perhaps a little too much of a cliché. Law was in his mid-thirties, earning a handsome income, acknowledged leader of the Northern circuit; but he was not a K.C. and he seemed to have reached a dead end in his profession. This was partly for personal and partly for political reasons. In person, though smoothly educated at Charterhouse and Peterhouse, he was clumsy and awkward, with shaggy eyebrows, an ungainly rolling walk, and a marked Cumbrian accent. In politics he was, like his father the Bishop of Carlisle, a decided Whig, at a bad period for Whigs. He had hardly had in seven long years at the Bar a single case of interest in London, despite his undoubted intellect and forceful character. In London the leading barrister of the day was now Erskine, famous for his successful defence of Lord George Gordon. It was Erskine, naturally enough, whom Warren Hastings first decided to brief; but here politics, that had so far worked to Edward Law's disadvantage, now worked to Erskine's. Eager though Erskine was to take up the case and to cross swords with Burke, Warren Hastings' main opponent, he decided he could not go against his own personal friends in the House of Commons, Fox and Sheridan, who were also pressing the impeachment. Why Law then? Simply because Sir Thomas Rumbold, who had served under Warren Hastings in India, was married to Joanna Law and suggested his brother-in-law: fame and fortune, as so often in England, depending on the right word in the right ear at the right time.

The trial began on February 13, 1788 and ended on April 23, 1795. At its centre, at the Bar in Westminster Hall, stood the tiny figure of the man who for over thirteen years had governed the Company's possessions in India from its headquarters, Calcutta, capital of Bengal: a man aged fifty-six when the trial began, but sixty-three when it ended, five foot six inches in height, under ten stone in weight, dressed in a plain red suit, a nabob worth only £80,000; utterly confident of his own virtues, megalomaniac, uncorrupt, unEnglish. Burke's opening denunciation of Warren Hastings lasted four days; his description of the cruelties of Rajah Debi Singh had ladies of fashion in Westminster Hall shrieking aloud and fainting away. Sheridan excelled himself in his picturesque description of the sufferings of the Begums of Oudh. Should the Brahmin money-lender Nanda Kumar have been hanged? Had Hastings been justified in treating Rajah Chait Singh, *zamindar* of Benares, as a treacherous feudatory? Though the trial went on year after year until it became, even for the fashionable political world, a bore, it did not in fact cover many days each year: partly because of the ruling that *all* the judges had to be present as assessors. It was not until February 14, 1792, four years after Burke's opening phillipic and on the seventy-fifth day of the trial that Law rose to open the defence. 'Mr Law was terrified exceedingly,' wrote Fanny Burney, who was there in the Royal Box, 'he looked pale and alarmed and his voice trembled.' On the second day however he apparently did much better; he 'was far more animated and less frightened, and acquitted himself so as almost to merit as much commendation as, in my opinion, he had merited censure at the opening.' Indeed by the end of the third day, the end of his opening speech for the defence, he had made his reputation. 'The finer passages have rarely been surpassed by any effort of forensic power,' wrote the great lawyer Lord Brougham, 'and would have ranked with the most successful exhibition of the oratorical art had they been delivered in the early stage of the trial.' Indeed even before opening the defence, years before in fact, the ugly Law, boosted by the brief alone, had wooed and won, after three refusals, the incredibly beautiful Miss Towry: such a sight for sore eyes that Londoners used to gather outside her husband's house, like Murray's in Bloomsbury Square, for the sheer pleasure of seeing her water the flowers on the balcony. By the time the trial had ended with Hastings' acquittal on its 145th day, the beautiful Miss Towry had produced several of the vast batch of children whom her Caliban was to spawn (five sons and five daughters survived Law). By the time it was all over, Law was £3,000 the richer, and Warren Hastings over £70,000 the poorer.

Lloyd Kenyon

Not that Law's fees were particularly high, though of course fame, not money, was what he sought and won in the impeachment. An idea of what successful lawyers could earn in the eighteenth century is given by Kenyon's fee-books before he became Lord Chief Justice. He had been badly educated in Cheshire, articled to a solicitor there, switched to the Middle Temple as a student at the age of eighteen, and was called to the Bar six years later in 1756. For many years he lived as a note-taker and 'devil', on his farming father's allowance of £80 a year. Until 1764 he made nothing. In 1764 he made £80. Then, six years later, came the breakthrough. In 1770 he made £1,124; in 1771 £2,487; in 1772 £3,134; in 1780, when he became a K.C., £6,359, and in 1782 when he became Attorney General, £11,038. However, when Kenyon became Lord Chief Justice, his income sank to £6,500; he refused to add to this by selling offices in his gifts, as had been the custom, though he did obtain two valuable sinecures for his two eldest sons when they were old enough to accept them: one became, splendid title alas no longer in existence, Filazer of the King's Bench.

Kenyon's appointment was not popular. He was too much of a contrast to Murray's favourite, the urbane Buller. 'Little conversant with the manners of polite society, he retained all the original coarse homeliness of his early habits. Irascible, destitute of all refinement, parsimonious', he was notorious for his stinginess. At his large gloomy house in Lincoln's Inn Fields he gave dinner parties for himself, his wife, and now and then an aged attorney. It was rumoured that he had wine in his cellar but he was never known to offer it to anyone. In his early days as a student he used to dine with Horne Tooke at a small eating-house in Chancery Lane for 7½ pence a head. 'Dunning and myself,' Tooke used to say, 'were generous, for we gave the girl who waited on us a penny-a-piece but Kenyon, who always knew the value of money, rewarded her with a half-penny.' He hated Edward Law, his eventual successor, who mocked his bad

Latin mercilessly. In his will Kenyon directed that a short Latin inscription should be put over the door of his house: it was painted wrongly – without a hyphen. 'Mistake?' said Law, 'it is not a mistake. The considerate testator left particular directions in his will that the estate should not be burdened with the expense of a diphthong.' He left at least a quarter of a million pounds.

In addition to being a miser he was a moralist – always a mistake for a judge. 'My endeavours, I confess, to deter men from the enormous crime of adultery have hitherto proved ineffectual,' he once, engagingly, confessed. He wanted to treat gaming dens as a public nuisance, and threatened the guilty with the pillory 'whatever may be their rank and station in the country, though they may be the first ladies of the land'. The Earl of Carlisle retorted that the Lord Chief Justice was a 'legal monk'. That stung: Kenyon often brought the phrase up bitterly. 'A great discovery has been made,' he would say, 'that the judges of the land, who are constantly conversant with business, who see much more of actual life on their circuits and in Westminster Hall than if they were shut up in gaming-houses and brothels, are only *legal monks*.'

Kenyon had a point; but in a more important sense the Earl was right. The great divide between judges and ordinary human beings began with men like Kenyon: out of touch with everyday life, moralistic, hating the world of entertainment, humourless in private life and in politics, interested only in the law, just but severe on the bench, impatient of contradiction, bullying towards subordinates, notably bad-tempered ('My Lord Chief Justice,' George III once said to him, 'I hear that you have lost your temper and from my great regard for you I am glad to hear it, for I hope you will find a better one.') a caricature of a Victorian judge and in almost every way a complete contrast to the man of the world, the true Georgian, who had been his predecessor. This is not to suggest that all Lord Chief Justices since Kenyon have been cast in this narrow mould; but certainly there are obvious resemblances between him and the most famous Lord Chief Justice of our century, Goddard. Even the lately-dead Widgery, though much less in the public eye, was much of the same muchness. That is how, unfortunately, the ordinary person expects a judge to be, and to this model far too many judges still think it almost their duty to conform. Kenyon has a lot to answer for.

For it is not every honest citizen who has the nerve to treat a judge as Horne Tooke treated the Lord Chief Justice, admittedly a man whose personal foibles he knew. Admittedly, too, Parson Tooke, one of those fine old pugnacious English radicals, had had considerable experience of the Court of King's Bench before he came up against Kenyon. As early as 1770 he had come up before Murray for libel, had been condemned but then – a great feather in his cap – had managed to get the Lord Chief Justice's judgment reversed in the Court of Common Pleas. Seven years later, he was up before Murray again on a charge of seditious libel for having written of 'our beloved American fellow subjects' that they had been 'inhumanely murdered by the King's troops'. That cost him a fine of £200, and a year in prison. Eleven years later he was once more before the Lord Chief Justice, pleading his own case on an election expense issue against Erskine as counsel for Mr Fox.

Lord Chief Justice (Kenyon, in a sharp, contemptuous tone):   Is there any defence?

Horne Tooke (taking a pinch of snuff and looking round the Court for a minute or two):   There are three efficient parties engaged in this trial – you, gentlemen of the Jury, Mr Fox and myself, and I make no doubt that we shall bring it to a satisfactory conclusion. As for the Judge and the Crier, they are here to preserve order; we pay them handsomely for their attendance, and, in their proper sphere, they are of some use; but they are hired as assistants only; they are not, and never were intended to be, controllers of our conduct. Gentlemen, I tell you there is a defence, and a very good defence to this action, and it will be your duty to give effect to it.

So it went on; Parson Tooke, in between relaxed pinches of snuff, informing his Lordship that he expected to meet no further interruption from him, criticising common-law judges for accepting peerages, unlike Coke or Hale, reducing Kenyon to a blabbering wreck – 'I want no defence, Sir; I want no defence' – and in the end, despite the Lord Chief Justice's instructions to the jury, winning his case.

A few years later, in November 1794, Horne Tooke had to face a much more serious charge of high treason, but before Lord Chief Justice Eyre of the Court of Common Pleas, not before Kenyon. This time he took the precaution of briefing Erskine to defend him, and once again won his case. But, all the same, he was lucky. As the Revolution across the Channel veered from a movement for constitutional reform to the violent overthrow of the French ruling class, politics in England became embittered rather than sporting. Mr Pitt, in the interests as always of efficient administration, led the forces of reaction; and the lawyers, for the most part, followed. War was declared on France, Habeas Corpus suspended, leaders of the Corresponding Societies and their like arrested on charges of high treason, the 'Committee of Secrecy' instituted in Parliament as an instrument of government, the so-called 'Gagging Acts' against Seditious Meetings and Treasonable Practices passed, which effectively stifled political life. Working-class reformers were imprisoned without trial, the nascent trade unions suppressed by the Combination Acts, the Great Rebellion of 1798 ferociously put down in Ireland. Kenyon sentenced the publisher of Paine's *Age of Reason* to a year's imprisonment with hard labour. Law, like many nominal Whigs, joined the Pittites and was accused of 'renegade rancour' against his former friends. When Pitt resigned at the conclusion of the brief peace with France in 1801, Law, now recognised as a sincere Tory, was at last offered promotion. 'Rise, Sir Edward,' said George III. 'Sir Edward, Sir Edward, have you ever been in Parliament? No? Right, Sir Edward; quite right, Sir Edward; for now when you become my Attorney General, Sir Edward, you will not eat your own words, Sir Edward, as so many of your predecessors have been obliged to do.' His Majesty was not perhaps as deranged as he has sometimes been made out to be.

The Parliament that Law joined was the first Parliament of the whole United Kingdom, with for the first time Irish members, no less than a hundred of them, a new factor which was, however, only to become vitally important seventy or eighty years later when the suffrage was extended. The new Attorney General would have made an ideal public prosecutor. His maiden speech in the Commons was in favour of continuing martial law in Ireland, thus giving military courts the right of life or death over all offences there. He then argued that Habeas Corpus should once again be suspended in England and that Horne Tooke, elected as M.P. for Chelmsford, was ineligible to sit, being a priest in Holy Orders. In both these arguments he failed. He succeeded, however, in his one great case as prosecutor, in having Governor Wall of Goree in West Africa hanged on a gibbet in front of Newgate, for an execution ordered twenty years earlier, amid the screams of the most numerous mob ever gathered to witness a public execution in England.

Campbell, his future biographer, 'happened to be sitting in the students' box in the Court of King's Bench, on April 5, 1802, when a note announcing Kenyon's death was put into the

Attorney General's hand.' Kenyon had been ailing since the autumn of the previous year when his eldest son had died, and for several weeks had been lying in bed with black jaundice. Law was determined to have the post, wrote Campbell, not because he did not want to continue as public prosecutor but because he could not bear the idea of any other barrister, particularly his rival Erskine, being promoted over his head. Have it he did. On April 12, he was sworn in as Lord Chief Justice and at the same time promoted to the House of Lords as Lord Ellenborough.

Edward Law

'I remember being told by a learned Sergeant,' wrote Lord Brougham, 'that at the table of Sergeant's Inn, where the judges met their brethren of the coif to dine, the etiquette was in those days never to say a word after the Chief Justice nor ever to begin any topic of conversation. He was treated with more than the obsequious deference shown at court to the Sovereign himself.' Certainly the new Lord Chief Justice was a formidable figure. On the bench, he was authoritarian, severe, as bad-tempered as his predecessor, browbeating the juries, but unlike Kenyon, bitingly sarcastic and successfully domineering. He spoke loudly, solemnly and energetically. On going into court, he would swell his cheeks out by blowing and compressing his lips, looking like a warhorse about to snort. When a famous actor, Charles Mathews, took him off in the theatre, Law wrote to the Lord Chamberlain to complain that not since *The Clouds* of Aristophanes had there been such an outrage on public decency. The terrified Mathews agreed never to repeat the performance – but was summoned by Prinny to do so in private. 'The Prince was in raptures,' wrote Mrs Mathews, 'and declared himself astonished at the closeness of the imitation shutting his eyes while he listened to it with excessive enjoyment and many exclamations of wonder and delight, such as Excellent! Perfect! It is he himself!!' Like so many people in authority, the Lord Chief Justice was perfectly prepared to make a fool of others, though he would not tolerate being mocked himself. 'The unfortunate client who appears by me,' said a nervous young barrister, 'the unfortunate client who appears by me – my Lord, the unfortunate client . . .' 'You may go on, sir,' interrupted Edward Law, softly and almost encouragingly, 'so far the court is quite with you.' Often, of course, his sarcasms were justified. 'An estate in fee simple, my Lords,' said a famous Chancery conveyancer who assumed that the judges knew nothing of the law of real property, 'is the highest estate known to the law in England.' 'Stay, stay,' said the Lord Chief Justice solemnly, 'let me take that down.' He dictated it slowly to himself: 'An estate – in fee simple – is – the highest estate – known to – the law in England.' Then he looked up. 'Sir, the court is much indebted to you for the information.'

Law was, in his way, an excellent Lord Chief Justice, famed for his decisions in commercial and maritime law, hard-working, learned – he had been a senior wrangler at Cambridge and was, unlike his predecessor, a classical scholar – puncturing the pretensions of the pompous, dominating both his own court and the profession, till gout and ill-temper ruined him. In the enticingly named Case of the Hottentot Venus no one could fault his judgment or even his tact. He ruled, in a most twentieth-century manner, that fox-hunting could be trespass: 'Can it be supposed that these gentlemen hunted for the purpose of killing vermin and not for their own diversion?' – that cock-fighting was illegal: 'I believe that cruelty to these animals forms part of the dehortatory charge of judges to grand juries' – that literary criticism should be free: 'The critic does a great service to society who exposes vapid as well as mischievous publications' – that trial by battle was still legal: the defendant, brought before King's Bench, cried 'Not guilty and I am ready to defend the same by my body,' hurling a gauntlet on to the floor of the court (his opponent cried 'craven', though, and soon after the right was abolished by law, though the defendant won his case); and, most fortunately, that 'an aeronaut is not liable to an action of trespass at the suit of the occupier of every house and inch of ground over which his balloon passes in the course of his voyage.'

Kindness to animals was, however, in Edward Law's make-up balanced by a complete lack of kindness to his fellow men. He opposed, successfully, the Pillory Abolition Act, condemned indeed Admiral Lord Cochrane for a fraud offence to a year's imprisonment and an hour in the stocks, which caused an immense uproar, held that the criminal law could not be too severe, and in 1803 pushed through Parliament Lord Ellenborough's Act creating ten new capital offences (for injuries, let it however be said, to the person, not to property). Five years later he utterly opposed Sir Samuel Romilly's great efforts to have the total number of offences for which the punishment was death reduced to reasonable proportions, arguing that the removal of the death penalty for stealing privately had increased thefts 'to a serious and alarming degree'. He opposed all attempts at lightening the laws against Catholics or Aliens. His manners in the House of Lords were too coarse and brutal to appeal; and he was amazed at the hostility to his appointment as a Cabinet Minister in the 'Ministry of All the Talents' – as it happened, an extremely short-lived government. The most notorious state trial over which he presided was that of Colonel Despard who planned to massacre the King, plus the Royal Family and most of the Lords and Commons and establish a Republic. 'At two in the morning,' wrote Campbell – the date was February 7, 1803 – 'I saw the Chief Justice put on the black cap to pronounce the awful sentence of the law on Colonel Despard and his associates' – six of whom, with the Colonel, were executed. The most curious case was probably that of a libel action brought by the First Consul of France, Napoleon Bonaparte, against a French emigré in London: the resumption of war prevented, however, the future Emperor from winning the only battle – a legal one – that he attempted to fight on this side of the Channel.

In both these cases the prosecutor had been the then Attorney General Spencer Perceval. Within a few years Perceval was himself conducting, rather courageously, the war against Napoleon as Prime Minister. On Monday, May 11, 1812, a bankrupt with an imagined grievance, John Bellingham, waited for the Prime Minister in the lobby of the House of Commons and, as he came in, placed a pistol at his breast and fired. 'Oh I am murdered,' exclaimed Perceval with accuracy, as he staggered a pace or two before falling – the first and so far the last, Prime Minister ever to be assassinated. The trial took place not before the Lord Chief Justice but at Assizes, in the Old Bailey before three minor judges, with what was later agreed to be indecent haste, on the Friday. A week after firing the pistol, Bellingham, coherent though clearly slightly mad, was executed.

Years later, in June 1817, the Lord Chief Justice presided over another great treason trial. The war against Napoleon was over, but victory had been followed by terrible popular sufferings. Corn was taxed, food short, the new industrial system oppressive, and the governing class harsh and unresponsive. On

November 15, 1816, a great working-class meeting was held at Spa Fields in Islington. The cry of 'four million in distress!' was raised. Three weeks later Dr James Watson, a surgeon of Bloomsbury, addressed a mass meeting. 'Ever since the Norman conquest, kings and lords have been deluding you,' he cried. A tricolour was produced, brief rioting followed, the leaders were arrested probably thanks to a government *agent provocateur* named Castle who 'found' plans for blowing up the cavalry barracks in Portman Square, barricading the streets and seizing the Tower and the Bank. The trial of Dr Watson, the first on a long list, lasted a whole week. The Lord Chief Justice did all he could to secure a conviction; but he had been ill, the Cochrane case had destroyed his spirit, and the defence was energetically conducted by Sergeant Copley, a future Lord Chancellor. Watson was acquitted; and the charges against the other 'conspirators' dropped. A year later, Law had only partly recovered. The trial came up at the Guildhall of William Hone, a bookseller, who had published three parodies, the first entitled *The late John Wilkes' Catechism*; the second *The Political Litany* and the third *The Sinecurists' Creed*. On the first day, Hone defended himself so adroitly in a King's Bench presided over by one of Law's puisnes, Mr Justice Abbott, that the Lord Chief Justice himself swore that he would preside in person the following day and see *The Political Litany* condemned, even though *The Late John Wilkes' Catechism* had been absolved. 'I am glad to see you, my Lord Ellenborough,' shouted Hone when the pale hollow-cheeked Law appeared next day.

Lord Chief Justice (Law): I am come to do justice, my only wish is to see justice done.

Hone: It is not rather, my Lord, to send a poor bookseller to rot in a dungeon?

'In obedience to my conscience and my God,' the Lord Chief Justice summed up to the jury, 'I pronounce it to be a most impious and profane libel. Hoping and believing that you are Christians, I doubt not that your opinion is the same.' It was not. The verdict of Not Guilty was followed by a tremendous outburst of applause. Most unwisely Law determined to preside the following day at the trial over *The Sinecurists' Creed*. Hone read out a similar parody composed by Law's own father, the late Bishop of Carlisle.

Lord Chief Justice (in broken voice): Sir, for decency's sake forbear.

Hone courteously withdrew. He was of course acquitted. The Lord Chief Justice kept up a bold front; but the general opinion was that Hone's trial killed him.

> Nature had exhibited evident symptoms of decay before his strenuous and ill-judged efforts on the trial of Hone. His frame had been shaken by violent attacks of gout . . . The fretfulness of his manner, and his irritable temper proved clearly the workings of disease when he occasionally reappeared in the submissive and silent hall . . . To the last he clung to his situation with a sort of desperate fidelity to perform its duties when, as he wrote to a friend, he 'could scarcely totter to his seat.'

It was almost a case of William Murray all over again, particularly as, like Murray with Buller, he had his own favoured candidate for the succession in Sergeant Lens, a King's sergeant, an excellent lawyer and a scholar. At last, on September 18, 1818, he wrote from Worthing his letter of resignation to the Prince Regent. He died in his house at St James' Square – he was the first Lord Chief Justice to move to the fashionable West End – only six weeks later, leaving just under a quarter of a million pounds, a fraction less than his miserly predecessor.

13

Barber's Son, Old Etonian: Abbott and Denman

Who was to succeed the dead Lord Chief Justice? The Attorney General, naturally. But Sir Samuel Shepherd, the Attorney General, was almost stone-deaf. The Solicitor General, Sir Robert Gifford, an obscure figure, was only recently promoted. Sir Vicary Gibbs, Chief Justice of Common Pleas, was dying. Mr Sergeant Lens had been Law's own favourite; but a recommendation from a fading Lord Chief Justice is often the kiss of death, and so it was in Lens' case. Law's successor, who took office on November 4, 1818, was one of his own puisnes, Mr Justice Abbott.

Charles Abbott

The Lord Mayor of London, a man of humble origins, gave the new Lord Chief Justice a dinner at the Mansion House.

'What a country is this we live in!' he exclaimed, passionately. 'In other parts of the world there is no chance, except for men of high birth and aristocratic connections; but here genius and industry are sure to be rewarded. See before you the examples of myself, the Chief Magistrate of the Metropolis of this great empire, and the Chief Justice of England sitting at my right hand – both now in the highest offices in the State, and both sprung from the very dregs of the people.'

'ABBOTT, HAIRDRESSER', read the sign over the door of a small corner house in Canterbury, just opposite the cathedral. 'Shave for a penny – hair cut for twopence, and fashionably dressed on reasonable terms', added the inscription on the sides of the door. Here on October 7, 1762, Charles Abbott was born. As a boy he would deliver wigs frizzed and pomaded by his father to the clergy of the Chapter – a very dull, decent lad, destined, it seemed, to become a barber himself in due course. What saved him from 'the dregs of society' was his admission to King's School, Canterbury. He was quiet, hard-working, and demure. He won a scholarship to Corpus Christi College, Oxford, became a noted classical scholar, and then tutor, for a hundred guineas a year, to the son of Mr Justice Buller, Murray's favourite. It was Buller who pushed him to take up the law. 'You may not possess the garrulity called *eloquence,*' he told the young man, 'which sometimes rapidly forces up an impudent pretender, but you are sure to get early into respectable business at the Bar, and you may count in due time on becoming a puisne judge.' And so Abbott did. As a barrister he was hard-working, and industrious, wrote a book on shipping law that brought him fame, and in 1807 filed an income-tax return of £8,026.5s.0d. As an advocate he was a total failure – husky-voiced, leaden-eyed, expressionless. He married, at the age of thirty-three, a flashy wife of whom he was extremely fond. He nearly finished an obscure career in total obscurity. 'I well remember,' wrote a legal colleague of his, 'in the year 1815 his lamenting to me in a desponding tone that his eyesight was impaired, and that he had some thoughts of retiring altogether from the profession . . . I left him with regret, and under the impression that his health and spirits were declining.' Then, however, fortunately for Abbott, Mr Justice Heath, aged eighty, died and in 1816 he became, at long last, a judge.

His biographer and future successor, Campbell, wrote:

> I happened to be much in his company during the long vacation of 1816. In consequence of a serious illness, then being a desolate bachelor, I had returned to a lonely cottage at Bognor, on the coast of Sussex, and Mr Justice Abbott taking up his residence there with his family, he was exceedingly kind to me. In our walks he talked of literature much more than of law, and he would beautifully recite long passages from the Greek and Latin classics, as well as from Shakespeare, Milton and Dryden. For all modern English poetry he expressed infinite contempt.

Perhaps surprisingly, this rather unpromising man became an excellent Lord Chief Justice – succint, clearly impartial, rapid. As Campbell wrote, 'his pasty face became irradiated and his dim eye sparkled if a new and important point of law was raised.' But, like his two predecessors, Law and Kenyon, he was bad-tempered. 'There is no denying,' added Campbell with condescension, 'that occasionally he was rather irritable and peevish and showed in his manner a want of good-taste and good-breeding.' Or, as Lord Brougham more judiciously put it: 'His temper was naturally bad; it was hasty and it was violent, forming a marked contrast with the rest of his mind. But it was singular with what success he fought against this, and how he mastered the rebellious part of his nature.' Future events were to show that, politically, there was not much to choose between the hairdresser's son and the Bishop's.

Arthur Thistlewood had been one of the 'conspirators' against whom charges had been dropped in the Spa Fields affair, after Dr James Watson was acquitted. A year of subsequent imprisonment for insulting the Home Secretary, Lord Sidmouth, had not improved his temper or quelled his burning desire for a revolution in England. He was released from Horsham gaol on May 28, 1819. The country seemed ripe for the long-awaited revolution. On August 16, a troop of Hussars massacred eleven people, including two women, at a great meeting at St Peter's Field in Manchester. The terrified government pushed through the Six Acts that virtually forbade free assembly, petitioning or a free press. In the circumstances Thistlewood, a slight, soldierly man of about fifty decided that 'a straightforward revolution' was hopeless. In December he formed a secret executive committee of five to plan the assassination of the whole Cabinet at dinner, attack Coutt's bank, set fire to public buildings, seize the Tower or Mansion House and proclaim a provisional government.

The old mad King died on January 29, 1820. The new newspaper *The Times*, announced in its issue of February 22 that a Cabinet dinner would be held the next evening at Lord Harrowby's house in Grosvenor Square. Thistlewood had his attention drawn to this by the only fellow-conspirator he totally trusted, Edwards. It seemed a perfect opportunity. About twenty-five of the conspirators gathered at a loft over a stable in Cato Street on the evening of February 23, to arm themselves with guns, bombs and hand-grenades. There, at 8.30 p.m., they were surrounded by the police. Thistlewood cut his way out with a sword, killing police-officer Smithers and escaped, only to be caught the following morning and to learn that Edwards had all along been a police informer. The trial opened on April 17, and lasted three days. 'That Englishmen, laying aside the national character, should assemble to destroy in cold blood the lives of fifteen persons unknown to them, except for their having fulfilled the highest offices in the State, is,' perorated Lord Chief Justice Abbott inaccurately, 'without example in the history of this country, and I hope will remain unparalleled for atrocity in future times.' Thistlewood was defiant to the last: 'I quit it (my country) without regret. My only sorrow is that the soil should be a theatre for slaves, for cowards, for despots,' he proclaimed.

Three and a half years earlier a barrister in his mid-thirties had defended enthusiastically and well but equally unsuccessfully, three Luddite leaders from Derby who, like the Cato Street Conspirators, though with less excuse, had been hanged. This was Thomas Denman, son of a fashionable London *accoucheur*, unlike Abbott an Old Etonian, and also unlike Abbott, tall, handsome, with an exquisite voice, married to a beautiful wife named Theodosia, and, by 1818, living in fashionable Russell Square. He was a close friend of the extremely talented and quick-witted Scots lawyer, Brougham, founder of the *Edinburgh Review* and a leading Whig M.P. It was to Brougham that Denman owed not only a certain income from journalism but, from January 1819, a seat in the House of Commons as M.P. first for Wareham and then for Nottingham. It was Brougham too who at the end of 1819 told Denham that he could have a general retainer for the Princess of Wales – a few months later, on January 29, 1820, to become the new Queen, Caroline.

Just as Law had made his reputation, and eventually his fortune out of the Warren Hastings Case, so did the much more agreeable and attractive Thomas Denman make his name in the Case of the Delicate Investigation, as it had been called. In this, he was certainly ingenuous. He believed Her Majesty to be, in his own phrase, as pure as driven snow. The Queen, who had for long been living estranged from her husband in Italy, returned to London in triumph on June 6, 1820, escorted by the radical Alderman Wood – 'that beast Wood', as the King called him. She was greeted by extraordinary public hysteria. Posters all over the City ordered the inhabitants to light up their houses in her honour; and her supporters swirled round the West End, breaking the windows of all houses which displayed no lights, two Cabinet Ministers' residences among them.

For months the hysteria continued as Parliament, preparatory to considering a Bill of Divorce, enquired into her conduct. Troops surrounded Westminster Hall, the Duke of Wellington was hissed by the crowd, *The Times* denounced the witnesses against her as a rabble of corrupt Italians. Denman her own Solicitor General made one powerful speech for her defence, then another, and finally on October 24 and 25 concluded with a summing-up that lasted ten hours in which he attacked the King as a Nero (Carlton House was known thereafter as Nero's Palace by impolite society), and, somewhat unfortunately, ended with the inapposite biblical story of the woman taken in adultery.

> Most gracious queen, we thee implore, [summed up the wits]
> To go away and sin no more;
> Or, if that effort be too great,
> To go away at any rate.

Nonetheless, thanks largely to Denman's efforts, the charges against the Queen were, on November 2, dropped and Parliament was hastily prorogued by Lord Liverpool. For three successive nights London was, in every sense, lit up. Cobbett, the great radical, was known to be composing the replies to the addresses of congratulation that now poured in to the Queen. Denman and Brougham were voted thanks and the Freedom of the City. The ruling Tories were in despair: 'One serious insurrection in London and all is lost,' the gloomy Prime Minister, Liverpool, told Chateaubriand. Even the Whig magnates were alarmed. 'The British monarchy is at an end,' thought the Duke of Bedford. It was all, though, something of a false alarm. Much to George IV's relief, the Queen died the following summer. Trade recovered, agitation died down, and the Tories remained in power for another ten years. Denman had a terrible time becoming a K.C.; only when the Duke of Wellington appealed to him in person, did the King consent. 'But by God,' the victor of Waterloo told Denman, 'it was the toughest job I ever had.' All the same, George IV declared he would never admit Denman to his presence. There was another fearful scene, Wellington told Greville, when Denman should, as Common Sergeant, have attended the Council at Windsor. It all had to be put off.

Denman was not a success, either, in the House of Commons where he was thought to be both too much the actor, and too dull. But then nor was Abbott successful in the House of Lords. The Lord Chief Justice, thought a stout Tory was only created a peer after nine years in office. Afraid of the mockery if he called himself simply Lord Abbott, he chose as his title the name of a village in Kent, Tenterden. His only successful speech was his maiden speech, in 1827, on a legal topic. Otherwise his attempts were held to be flat, or even absurd. They were certainly reactionary. Even though the Duke himself was proposing them, he opposed the repeal of the Test Act (which limited official posts to members of the Established Church), the repeal of the Corporation Act (which kept dissenters out of local government) and, horror of horrors, the Catholic Relief Act, 'A measure which I am sure,' he said, 'by a broad and direct road leads to the overthrow of the Protestant Church.'

We now come to that great turmoil in politics that within a few short years put an end for ever to almost half a century of reaction and oppression in England. At the beginning of the year 1830 Wellington and Pitt, firm Tories, appeared in total control of a country whose prosperity was reviving and whose people were passive. Then that summer in swift succession first the despised King George IV died, next within a month a far more reactionary King was chased off the throne of France to be replaced by a middle-class regime. The exultant Radicals in England saw this as the beginning of a second and more successful French Revolution; and indeed the revolutionary fever spread through Switzerland, Germany and Belgium until it infected Southern and Eastern England. Farm labourers, led by the imaginary 'Captain Swing', burnt ricks, destroyed machinery and terrified the countryside in a bloodless *Jacquerie*. Cobbett, the Radical orator, who had lain low for several years, toured Kent, Sussex and Hampshire and loosed broadsides against the ruling classes in his *Political Register* and his cheaper *Twopenny Trash*. In mid-November the Tories fell to be replaced by the Whigs, with as Prime Minister Lord Grey, in Creevey's words 'the best-dressed, the handsomest and apparently the happiest man in the Kingdom'. Thomas Denman and his great friend Brougham were immediately rewarded. Brougham, by far the cleverer of the two, was created a peer and appointed Lord Chancellor. Denman was knighted and appointed Attorney General to the new government. A middle-aged but highly ambitious Scots barrister, John Campbell, was elected Whig M.P. for Salford. 'For God's sake do not become Radical,' he advised his brother. It was typical of the Reformist Whig attitude. Before many months were out the liberal Denman, the defender of the Luddites and the oppressed Queen, was prosecuting Cobbett in King's Bench under the no-doubt beady eye of that robust old Tory reactionary, the hairdresser's lad from Canterbury, Lord Chief Justice Abbott.

Twenty-one years earlier Cobbett had come up before that more ferocious reactionary, Lord Chief Justice Law, for seditious libel, also at King's Bench. He had tried to steal a leaf from Horne Tooke's book, defended himself – badly – and was sentenced to a crushing two years in Newgate. Older now and wiser, Cobbett again defended himself, but with such vehemence and good humour that the papers described it as 'a trial of the government more than of Cobbett'.

'What are my sins? [he cried in his final four-and-a-half hour speech] what are the heinous sins I have committed? Calling upon the government to repeal the hard-hearted laws – hard-hearted laws that drive the labourers of the country to desperation . . . If I am compelled to meet death in some stinking dungeon into which they have the means of cramming me, my last breath shall be employed in praying to God to bless my country and to curse the Whigs to everlasting; and revenge I bequeath to my children and to the labourers of England.

Abbott of course summed up against Cobbett. But, though the jury was out all night and in the end split six-six, Cobbett's master stroke in calling Brougham the Lord Chancellor as his own witness effectively ruined the government's attempt to prove him a rabid revolutionary. There was no retrial. The first Reform Bill, introduced by Lord John Russell, 'a little fellow not weighing above 8 stone', appalled plain John Campbell as he listened: 'I was prepared,' he said, 'to support any moderate measure but this [abolishing most rotten boroughs and reforming Parliament] really is a revolution *ipso facto*.' If it appalled Campbell in the Commons, it can be imagined what was Abbott's reaction in the Lords. 'Corporate rights,' burbled the Lord Chief Justice, 'hitherto held sacred, are now recklessly violated, and I will tell those who despise them that after this precedent the rights of property will be equally disregarded, and liberty and life itself will be sacrificed to expediency, or the appetite of the mob for plunder and blood.' Finally, just before the Reform Bill went through the following year, 'Never, never, my Lords,' he proclaimed, 'shall I enter the doors of this House after it has become the phantom of its departed greatness.' On this he kept, perhaps by *force majeur* rather than total conviction, his word.

In the struggle over the passing of the Reform Bill political passions had flared all over the kingdom. The most serious riots broke out in Bristol, on October 29,1831, directed against the

Recorder of Bristol, Sir Charles Wetherall, M.P., a diehard who had always stoutly opposed Reform. The Mansion House at Bristol was attacked, the Bishop's Palace and the gaols burnt, the cavalry were called in, and the official casualties were given as twelve dead and ninety-four wounded. Next October, Denman as Attorney General led the prosecution of the rioters. The Lord Chief Justice presided; but he was feeling ill and old. On the evening of October 28, the second day of the trial, he had no appetite but fancied some fresh oysters would do him good. In fact, they disagreed with him; he caught a fever and took to his bed. It may have been some consolation to him to learn that twenty-one of the twenty-four indicted were found guilty (four were executed). On November 3, raising his head from the pillow, he was heard to say in, Campbell tells us, a slow and solemn tone, as when he used to conclude his summing-up in cases of great importance, 'And now, gentlemen of the jury, you will consider your verdict.' A few moments later he died. On November 9 the Attorney General was sworn in as his successor.

Thomas Denman

It was just as well that Denman took office when he did, for in all probability he would have been turned out of the Commons by the disgusted electors of Nottingham, where five rioters had been executed. He must have been immensely relieved himself, for he was not by nature a public prosecutor. He was more of a philanthropist and, with eleven children and a doting wife, a family man. He was honourable, witty, and, unlike his more forceful predecessors, pleasant-tempered. Greville might call him 'one of the feeblest Chief Justices who ever presided over the Queen's [as it was about to become] Bench', but, with hindsight, Denman's chief claim to fame, and a most elegant one, was not his period in office but his unceasing efforts to extinguish the slave trade, despite what seemed to be growing public indifference. In an age of law reform he played a decent part, managing to persuade the Lords to pass Bills for the abolition of the death penalty for forgeries, for certain cases of attempts to murder, 'of burglary, robbery, piracy, injuries to houses and ships, offences against the Riot Act, slave-trading, smuggling and violence, rescuing people to execution, seducing soldiers from their allegiance, and administering seditious oaths'.

Although Denman was not a rich man, and had never made a fortune at the Bar, he was raised to the Lords by his friend Brougham despite a feeling in the legal world that it would have been as well to cease this practice, recent Lord Chief Justices not having distinguished themselves as politicians. Furthermore, his salary as Lord Chief Justice, theoretically £10,000, was in fact reduced to £8,000. This was the period when a Court of Appeal was first created and the privileges of sergeants-at-law abolished (so that this order gradually faded away). It was also a period when Peel introduced income tax, and since that time Lord Chief Justices have never, unlike their predecessors, left vast fortunes. Indeed one can date from Denman's years in office the beginning of the period when the Lord Chief Justice's importance, legal, political, social, and financial, began to fade, though of course it was not until the death penalty was totally abolished that the *coup de grâce* was administered to their prestige and power. Since then, the holders have been pale shadows of their potent predecessors.

Denman presided over the legally famous case of parliamentary privilege, of Stockdale versus Hansard, which began on February 7, 1837, lasted for three years, and of which he wrote, not entirely accurately, 'my future reputation depends'. He also presided over the 1842 trials at York Assizes of the Chartists, whose riots were described by Disraeli in his novel *Sybil*. Denman pronounced the appeal judgment favourable to Daniel O'Connell, 'the Liberator', in 1844, in which he first used the now famous expression 'a mockery, a delusion and a snare'. 'Ah,' he said afterwards, 'I am sorry I used those words; they were not judicial.' The Lord Chancellor being ill, the Lord Chief Justice presided as Lord High Steward, over the trial of James Brudenell, Earl of Cardigan, Lieutenant Colonel commanding the 11th Hussars, before his fellow peers in the House of Lords. It was the first trial of a peer since that of the Duchess of Kingston for bigamy; and the prosecutor was John Campbell, the Attorney General.

Arrogance rather than self-confidence was the mark of Lord Cardigan, who had bought his way to command of the 11th Hussars at the age of thirty-nine and spent on it a quarter of his annual income, £10,000 a year. The smartest cavalry regiment in the Army of the new young Queen returned from service in

India to barracks at Canterbury. There in May 1840 an 'Indian' officer, a certain Captain Reynolds, disgraced the standards of the regiment. He placed wine on the mess table in a black bottle instead of a decanter. Naturally enough Lord Cardigan ordered him to be placed under arrest. The 'Black Bottle' affair quickly became notorious, a certain 'H.T.' – Captain Harvey Tuckett – wrote a garbled account of it in the *Morning Chronicle*. Lord Cardigan, having discovered the identity of the writer, called him out; and the duel took place on September 12, 1840 on Wimbledon Common. At the second shot the Captain fell, wounded. News of the duel created immense indignation, prosecution became inevitable, and Lord Cardigan demanded his right to be tried by his peers. The case came up before the House of Lords, Denman presiding, Campbell prosecuting, on February 16, 1841. But it only lasted a day. The defence outwitted the prosecution on a technicality (non-proof of the identity of Tuckett) and Cardigan was declared by all the peers 'not guilty upon my honour' – except for the Duke of Cleveland, who said 'not guilty legally upon my honour'. Thirteen years later, of course, Lord Cardigan was to gain even greater notoriety, thundering into the valley of death at the head of the Light Brigade.

By the spring of 1849 Thomas Denman had had two strokes, could barely sign his name, and was being urged to retire even by his friend Brougham. Lord John Russell, the Prime Minister, had assured Campbell that he would have the post. But though Denman had been spared a complete biography by Campbell, who had spent the years of the Pitt government, while he was out of office, writing *The Lives of the Lord Chief Justices*, he resented several unflattering references to himself that had found their way at various points into Campbell's *Lives*, and he resented even more the thought of Campbell being his successor. 'I begin this memoir,' wrote Campbell in the preface to his final volume of the *Lives of the Lord Chief Justices*, 'at a time when I have the prospect of being myself a CHIEF JUSTICE and when I may calculate upon being subjected in my turn to the criticism of some future biographer.' That was in October 1849. As the autumn dragged into the winter, the newspapers stirred up a controversy on the rival merits of the two men, much to the Englishman's advantage. The *Spectator* even accused Campbell of trying to 'assassinate' Denman by spreading reports that he was unfit to continue in office. The real danger, though, was that Denman would have another stroke, be incapable of resigning and have to be removed by joint address of both Houses of Parliament. It did not happen. He resigned on February 28, 1850. Paradoxically, his health then recovered. In the autumn of 1852, *Uncle Tom's Cabin* came out, and Denman wrote in *The Standard* seven long articles on Negro emancipation, with a bitter attack on his old friend Charles Dickens for the character of Mrs Jellyby in *Bleak House*. This excitement was too much for him. He had a third stroke on December 2 at Nice, but lingered on until September 22, 1854, and was buried in Stoke Albany graveyard. Before he died, he was reconciled with Campbell, who, sure enough, had been appointed Lord Chief Justice in his place.

14

The Biographer and the Baronet: Campbell and Cockburn

'Plain John Campbell', as he loved to call himself, had been promoted to Solicitor General and knighted in 1832 when Denman became Lord Chief Justice. It took him two years more to become Attorney General, thanks to a rather shady man-oeuvre by Lord Chancellor Brougham. He was only two years younger than Denman, canny and resourceful, 'thick-set as a navvy and hard as nails'. He was a minister's son from Fife and had himself been prepared for the ministry until, at the turn of the century at the age of nineteen, and with his father's blessing, he changed his career and entered Lincoln's Inn as a student. It had been a hard, weary slog for him since. At the age of thirty-five, he had set himself to learn to dance 'in order to shine in society', and at the age of forty he had married Mary Scarlett. 'Lucky in nearly everything he set his hand to,' wrote their daughter and his biographer, Mrs Hardcastle, 'John Campbell was never more fortunate than in his marriage.' He was particularly fortunate in that his wife's father was Sir James Scarlett, an enormously successful barrister (he once made £18,500 in a year), the much-resented favourite of Abbott as Lord Chief Justice, and later Lord Chief Baron of the Exchequer and Lord Abinger. No sooner did Scarlett become Attorney General – in 1827 – than his son-in-law became a K.C. Not that John Campbell was undeserving; on the contrary he was extremely hard-working, indeed 'one of the greatest common lawyers of this period'. But he was also selfish and exceptionally pushing, with all the 'hopes and fears of a fighting barrister'. As a young barrister he had often come up before Edward Law, the then Lord Chief Justice, who had terrified him; but Campbell had stood up to him in the end and indeed had used Law's judgments indirectly to further his own career – publishing much-admired reports of the Lord Chief Justice's best decisions, and throwing, legend had it, those improperly ruled into a drawer marked 'bad law'. Whatever else Campbell may have been lacking in – charm and grace, perhaps – it was not self-confidence.

In 1841, the government determined to reward Campbell, who had twice been passed over for Master of the Rolls, probably because he could not be spared in the Commons, with an honour, and a position. His wife had already, much to the mirth of his legal colleagues, been created Baroness Stratheden in her own right. In June, he was himself created Lord Campbell of St Andrews and Lord Chancellor of Ireland. It was an extraordinarily unpopular appointment, an obvious 'job'. Wisely for his reputation, Campbell announced that he would forgo the usual pension of £11,000 attached to the office. Unwisely for his pocket, though; he was only Lord Chancellor of Ireland for six weeks, and then, with the coming to power of Pitt and the Tories, he was out of a job, out of office, out of work and in a comparative sense at any rate, short of money.

What he did then was absolutely admirable. He had, years before, made his living by writing – reporting for the *Morning Chronicle*. He now published his speeches and his autobiography; and then set to work, aged sixty-two, to write first the *Lives of the Lord Chancellors* and then the *Lives of the Lord Chief Justices*. It was an enormous task. He set to, was discouraged by its difficulty and magnitude, gave up, set to again and in one year and ten months, between 1845 and 1847, had in print the first three out of seven volumes of the *Lives of the Lord Chancellors*. Within a month of publication the first edition had sold out, and 2,050 copies of the second edition were sold on the first day of publication. By 1849 he had completed the first three volumes of the *Lives of the Lord Chief Justices*; the fourth volume, on which so much of this present section is based, was not published until 1857; a chatty, lively and often malicious account of the lives of Lloyd Kenyon, Edward Law and Charles Abbott – by that time Campbell himself was Lord Chief Justice.

These were not slim volumes; each was several hundred pages long, of closely printed type, each indeed much longer than this present book. Yet long though they were, Campbell's volumes were immensely popular. Melbourne and Peel, from opposite ends of the political spectrum, both admired them, and Prince Albert found them very readable. 'There is little probability,' wrote a biographer of Campbell (somewhat to the chagrin of at least one reader) 'that they will be displaced by anything more entertaining written on this subject.' The *Lives* may not always have been accurate but they were certainly extraordinarily lively. The greatest resentment and fear was felt, of course, by Campbell's contemporaries. 'I predict,' wrote Lyndhurst, one Lord Chancellor, to Brougham, another, 'that he will take his revenge on you by describing you with all the gall of his nature. He will write of you, and perhaps of me too, with envy, hatred, malice and all uncharitableness, for such is his nature.' He was right enough, though the volume which dealt with Lyndhurst and Brougham was only published posthumously. As another legal colleague, Wetherell, remarked, Campbell's *Lives* added a new sting to death. Brougham got his own back prematurely by commenting on Campbell's performance in the House of Lords – when the Whigs came back in 1846, he had been made Chancellor of the Duchy of Lancaster with a seat in the Cabinet. 'Edinburgh,' said Brougham, 'is now celebrated for having given us the two greatest bores that have ever yet been known in London, for Jack Campbell in the House of Lords is just what Tom Macaulay is in private society.'

John Campbell

The middle of the last century was Palmerston's time. 'Pam', if anyone, was the great symbol of Victorian self-confidence; easy-going, good-tempered, fashionable but hard-working, horse-loving and patriotic, prejudiced to the point of petulance only as far as foreigners were concerned, a Whig as the young Queen was herself, but not really a party man. His favourites were rather like himself. One of his favourites was Alexander Cockburn, heir to a baronetcy, son of a diplomat, the envoy extraordinary and minister plenipotentiary to Colombia, and of his delightful French wife, Yolande de Vignier. Cockburn was forty-five before he was elected, in 1847, as M.P. for Southampton – a small, highly cultivated man, with light red hair and marked angular features, very gay, very polished, very fashionable, witty, courteous, refined, intelligent, passionately interested in music, literature and science, a splendid linguist and suitably for a successful Q.C., melodiously eloquent. He was not particularly hard-working; but, then, he was almost twenty years younger than 'Pam' and Palmerston had not been particularly hard-working when he had first taken office as Foreign Secretary in 1830. Cockburn had been privately educated until he went up to Cambridge, to Trinity Hall of which he became a Fellow, and very nearly Master, the first future Lord Chief Justice to be educated at that legalistically inclined college. He made his name as a barrister in 1843 by defending – he was always best at defences, a characteristic of our nicer type of barrister – the mad McNaughten, who had tried to imitate Bellingham and shoot Mr Peel, then Prime Minister, but instead had killed his secretary. McNaughten, luckier than Bellingham, was acquitted; and the subsequent famous Rules on insanity as a defence against criminal indictments bear his name.

Next year Cockburn appeared in a case that was more to his taste, the famous case of the 1844 Derby winner Running Rein. The greatest of all our racing men, Lord George Bentinck, the last M.P. to appear in the Commons in hunting pink, set out to prove that Running Rein was over age and an imposter. Cockburn had attacked Lord George fiercely and personally but while the trial was on unreservedly withdrew all that he had said in court. It was just as well that he did, for Running Rein was in fact a four-year-old called Maccabeus. 'I don't pretend to know much,' said Lord George, Disraeli's first patron, 'but I can judge horses and men.'

It was in 1850 that Cockburn really endeared himself to Palmerston. Palmerston was a force of nature, almost uncontrollable. The Queen particularly disliked his morals and she and the Prince Consort had refused to speak to their Foreign Secretary for some time. This was less because of his distasteful personal behaviour than his disastrous but infuriatingly popular politics. In the aftermath of the revolutionary spasms of 1848 he had quarrelled with the French, Austrian, Russian and Spanish governments, isolated England diplomatically, and brought Europe to the verge of a major war. Almost the last straw was the order that went out in January 1850 to blockade Greece. King Otto's obstreperous subjects in a fit of anti-semitism had looted the property of a Portuguese Jew living in Athens. Peter – 'Don' – Pacifico claimed exorbitant compensation, £50 for a *lit conjugal* among other lost items. Turned down, he appealed to England on the basis of his birth in Gibraltar. A fleet blockade seemed to the horrified ruling class a dangerous way of collecting disreputable debts.

On June 17, the handling of the Don Pacifico affair was attacked in the Lords – peeresses crowding into the gallery to sit on the floor rather than miss the debate – and the government was defeated. On June 24 the battlefield was transferred to the Commons. The famous Radical, Mr Roebuck, led the attack on Palmerston, followed by Peel, Cobden and Disraeli. On the evening of June 25, Palmerston rose to defend himself in a famous speech that ended at half-past two in the morning, culminating in his demand that a British subject should be able, in whatever land he might be in, to proclaim '*Civis Romanus Sum*', confident that 'the watchful eye and the strong arm of England will protect him against injustice and wrong.' Three nights later, after a long and damaging counter-attack by Gladstone, Alexander Cockburn rose to argue the legal points so eloquently and so successfully that as Peel, who spoke next against Palmerston (and for the last time, as he was thrown from his horse next day and died three days later), put it: 'One half of the treasury benches were left empty, while honourable members ran one after another, tumbling over each other in their haste to shake hands with the honourable and learned member.'

Palmerston's triumph was total. He was the most popular and powerful Minister in Europe. He did not forget his supporters. Cockburn was knighted on July 12 and made Solicitor General. Early in 1851, he became Attorney General, went out with the Whigs in February 1852, came back with the Whigs that same December, was Attorney General to Palmerston as Prime Minister from then until November 1856, very prosperous professionally and very much in demand.

Campbell had become a strong and just judge, though brutal to young barristers, yet with enough of a sense of humour to sub-poena 'Pepper' and 'Mustard' in a dog-biting case, and enough of a sense of responsibility to get no less than three Acts of law reform, each known as 'Lord Campbell's Act' through Parliament. He presided over a fascinating trial in 1852 in which Cockburn defended Dr (later Cardinal) Newman against a libel action brought by the renegade Catholic Achilli, 'a profligate under a cowl', 'a scandalous friar', as Newman had described him. He presided over the first great modern murder case, first of a longer series that were more and more to catch the public's attentions and thus to become associated with the office and position of Lord Chief Justice. This was the trial that lasted for fourteen days, from May 14 to May 27, 1856, the famous prosecution of William Palmer in the Rugely poisoning case, Cockburn prosecuting, Campbell presiding; among the lawyers for the defence was an Irish barrister of thirty-seven, Edward Kenealy, a poet and a linguist. Though the case should normally have been heard at assizes in Staffordshire where the crime was committed, it was transferred for fear of local prejudice to the Central Criminal Court in London – a precedent that was more and more often followed thereafter. In the end, however, 'for the sake of example,' as Campbell put it, Palmer was hanged –hanged by the neck until he was dead – in front of Stafford gaol.

In his diary of June 28, a fortnight after Palmer's execution, Campbell described the case as 'the most memorable judicial proceedings for the last fifty years, engaging the attention not only of this country but of all Europe'. It was a poisoning case: the victim had died by strychnia, or possibly of tetanus. The evidence against Palmer was entirely circumstantial, and inevitably even when the trial was over, doubts remained. 'A most ruffian-like attempt was made by the friends of the prisoner to abuse me,' noted Campbell, 'and to obtain a pardon or reprieve on the ground that the prisoner had not had a fair trial . . . They published a most libellous pamphlet under the title of "A Letter from the Rev. T. Palmer", the prisoner's brother, to Lord Chief Justice Campbell in which the Chief Justice was represented to be worse than his predecessor Jeffreys and it was asserted that there had been nothing in England like the last trial since the "Bloody Assizes".' Certainly Campbell's summing-up, which took two days, and his whole attitude, told against the prisoner. But the real star of the trial was Cockburn. It was said that he had spent days experimenting with chemicals and poisons before the trial and certainly his examination, cross-examination and outlining of the case for the prosecution were deadly. As Palmner, a racing man, put it: 'It was the riding that did it.' It was certainly considered to be the Attorney General's supreme achievement at the Bar.

In November 1856 a see-saw of different appointments began. First Cockburn accepted the post of Chief Justice of the Common Pleas. Greville wrote:

He is very averse to take it, but everyone pressed him to accept it, and after much hesitation and consultation he agreed . . . He gives up Parliament, for which he is well adapted, where he acts a conspicuous part, being a capital speaker, and which he likes and feels that it is his element. He gives up the highest place at the Bar, where he is a successful advocate and makes £15,000 or £16,000 a year, and he sees that he will be obliged to give up his loose habits, and assume a more decorous behaviour which is a great sacrifice to him.

Elsewhere Greville tells of the landlady of the inn who said that he always came with Lady Cockburn – a different Lady Cockburn every time – by complete contrast to Campbell who would invariably bring the same Lady Stratheden.

So his income dropped to £6,000 a year; but not for long. In June 1859, Palmerston was back as Prime Minister, with both Lord John Russell and Gladstone in his Cabinet. Who was to be Lord Chancellor? There were several rivals. Much to the general amazement, Palmerston offered the post to the Lord Chief Justice, though Campbell was five years his own senior and approaching eighty. Even more to the general amazement, Campbell accepted. Cockburn, who had at last succeeded to his father's baronetcy and never wanted to become a peer, took over as Lord Chief Justice.

Campbell was an amazing old man. He took to equity fiercely, at first sitting with two colleagues, like, as he said himself, 'a wild elephant broken in between two tame ones'. He soon speeded up their business. He noted in his journal when war with France was threatening that he was quite ready to volunteer again as he had done against Napoleon in 1803: 'By the blessing of God I could still march twenty miles a day with my musket on my shoulder, my bayonet by my side, and my knapsack on my back.' But the death of his wife in 1860 numbed him. On June 22 he sat in court, attended a Cabinet meeting, walked home, wrote a judgment, had a dinner party, talked to his children, retired to his study. Next morning at 8 a.m. his valet found him there dead in his chair with blood oozing from his mouth, the great artery near his heart having burst.

Alexander Cockburn

Sir Alexander Cockburn, Bt., unmarried, Lord Chief Justice of the King's Bench at £8,000 a year, was meanwhile enjoying himself, as he was to continue to do for the next twenty years. His great relaxation was to cruise in his yacht, the *Zouave*. His greatest political service was to represent Her Majesty's Government at the Alabama Arbitration against the United States' claims. It was held in Geneva; Sir Alexander aired his perfect French; the decision went against him, and the United Kingdom was condemned to pay enormous compensation for the sinking of the *Shenandoah*. All the same, he was again offered a peerage but again declined – the last of our Lord Chief Justices to show this modesty – though he accepted the grand cross of the Bath.

As a judge, and a highly respected and successful judge, dignified, courteous and learned, his great purpose in life was to reserve all the most interesting and notorious cases for his own judgment. He presided over a trial once again involving Lord Cardigan. This time the outrageous Earl was the plaintiff, suing for libel Lord Raglan's nephew, the Hon Somerset Calthorpe, for stating in his *Letters from Headquarters* that after the charge at Balaclava, 'unfortunately Lord Cardigan was not present when most required'. The suit failed. He presided over the action in 1865 in which Mrs Ryves tried to prove she was of the blood royal, the Jamaica rebellion case in 1867 (delivering a masterly six-hour disquisition on martial law), the Roman Catholic convent scandal of Saurin versus Starr, in which a nun sued the mistress of novices for conspiracy, the Derby Will case that ran to four trials, the Clerkenwell explosions case of 1867 in which Michael Barrett, the Fenian, put up such a splendid defence (he was the last man to be publicly executed in England), the fascinating, fashionable libel case of Morrison versus Blecher, the astrologer versus the admiral, the Chelsea Double Murder trial after the killing of the Reverend Elias Huelin and his housekeeper, and the trial of Henry and Thomas Wainwright for the murder of Harriet Lane in Whitechapel Road. But fascinating though all these cases were, undoubtedly the most fascinating – and certainly the longest drawn-out – was that of the Tichborne Claimant.

This extraordinary case is still so well known that it needs only the briefest summary here. The Tichbornes were very wealthy Catholic landed gentry, with estates in Hampshire. The tenth baronet, Sir Roger Tichborne, had drowned at sea. His mother, the old Dowager, believed, despite all the evidence, that her son was alive and living in the Colonies. She advertised in the local newspapers in New South Wales. At Christmas 1866, the Tichborne Claimant reached London; he had been living in Wagga Wagga under the pseudonym of Tom Castro. In fact he was not Roger Tichborne but Arthur Orton, the twelfth son of a Wapping butcher. He managed, despite all appearances – he was twenty-four stone, and totally uneducated – to convince hundreds of witnesses who had known Roger Tichborne as a schoolboy and young Army officer that he was the same man. He brought a case against the trustees of the Tichborne estates. An action of ejectment was the technical term, and, being a civil suit, it came up in the Court of Common Pleas before that Court's Lord Chief Justice, Bovill, on May 11, 1871. It lasted for almost a year.

The Solicitor General, Sir John Duke Coleridge, appeared for the trustees. He spent twenty-two days cross-examining Arthur Orton, and no less than twenty-six days summing-up for the defence – by which time he had been promoted to Attorney General. The stress of the trial ruined the health of Lord Chief Justice Bovill, and eventually, after the trial was over, Sir John Duke Coleridge succeeded to that position too, and a peerage with it. But before that, on March 5, 1872, the jury had halted the trial and non-suited the Claimant. Bovill immediately ordered his arrest on charges of perjury, and Arthur Orton was sent to Newgate.

That was the first of the two Tichborne trials – a great triumph for Coleridge. He was such a melodious speaker, so suave, so impressive a figure of a man, – nicknamed 'Long John' (he was 6 foot 3 inches tall) or 'Handsome Jack' – that the jury was bound to be impressed.

The second of the Tichborne trials began in April 1873. This time it was a criminal case, the trial of 'Thomas Castro' for perjury, and so Lord Chief Justice Cockburn with two of his puisnes presided. Hawkins, who assisted Coleridge in the first trial, led for the prosecution; and Kenealy, who had been junior counsel for Palmer of Rugely, now a Q.C., Doctor of Laws, and a Bencher, conducted the defence. It was a most extraordinary trial; it lasted no less than 188 days. Kenealy based his entire defence on the theory that the Tichborne family and the advisers of the Crown were guilty of wholesale bribery and conspiracy against his client. A lapsed Catholic himself, he mocked mercilessly at the Tichbornes and their relatives the Arundells, launched invectives against the Jesuits of Stonyhurst who had educated Sir Roger Tichborne, and represented his client as debased, depraved and demoralised by their teaching. He called hundreds of witnesses – over 550, on both sides, were heard in all – who still believed that Orton was Sir Roger. He insulted his opponent to the point where Hawkins declared that he would never speak a word to Kenealy again this side of the grave; and in the end he turned on the Lord Chief Justice, though Cockburn had been extremely kind and hospitable to him on his first arrival in London. 'I can only say,' observed Sir Alexander with restraint, 'during the seventeen years I have sat on this Bench, I have never had an unpleasant word from counsel before I had the misfortune to be presiding at this trial.'

Cockburn's summing-up was awaited with immense interest, and not merely by the legal profession. For the Claimant, 'the biggest man in England', was extraordinarily popular. His photograph was all over the shop windows, his face as well known as that of the Prime Minister, Mr Gladstone. Furthermore, he was being tried by a special jury, that is to say by a body of the respectable bourgeoisie whom the people believed, rightly, would be prejudiced against him. Gladstone himself appeared in court, as did various other members of the government – and Gladstone was generally thought to have authorised the vast expense of this second trial. The Lord Chief Justice began his summing-up on Thursday, January 29, 1874, at 10 a.m.

He took twenty days over it; and after the trial he published his notes, with corrections, in two volumes, each of 800 pages. He went over all the witnesses, all the evidence. He referred bitterly to Kenealy's accusations of prejudice. 'We felt it our duty to interpose, and in what way were our remonstrances met? By constant disrespect, by covert allusions to Scroggs and Jeffreys, and judges of ill-repute – as though if the spirit of Scroggs or Jeffreys still animated the Bench in the administration of justice, the learned counsel would not have been pretty quickly laid by the heels and put to silence.'

Almost forty years later, Kenealy's son wrote an account of the trial and remembered how his father had described the summing-up.

Chief Justice Cockburn extended and waved his hand with the gestures and significant looks of a skilled orator; he modulated his tones to be alternately grave, vehement, scornful and pathetic. Every artifice of the sophist and rhetorician was brought into play – and was played to perfection. And when he clenched an argument by striking his desk, and fastened his eyes at the same moment on the members of the jury, we forgot for the instance that he was a judge and saw in him only the expert advocate who moulds juries and to his will by his perfectly tuneful language, and by a flattery and persuasion irresistible. It was impossible not to admire the art and skill. It was impossible also not to wish that it was being used otherwise.

Kenealy was probably exaggerating; but there can be no doubt that Cockburn's summing-up was designed to obtain a conviction. It did. The jury were out for only half an hour. Arthur Orton was condemned to a savage fourteen years' penal servitude (though in fact he was released after ten and died in poverty in Marylebone in 1898). But that was not the end of the affair by any means. Kenealy, who had been formally censured by the jury, set to work after the trial and produced a newssheet called *The Englishman* that attacked Cockburn with almost the spirit of a 'Junius' attacking Murray. It had an enormous circulation. The legal profession took its revenge; Kenealy was, on August 17, 1874, disbenched and disbarred; but the whole affair certainly played a part in Gladstone's defeat in that year's General Election. Kenealy himself was elected as M.P. for Stoke but Disraeli, the new Prime Minister, elegantly if ungratefully rejected his call for a Royal Commission to enquire into the Tichborne Case, praising Cockburn instead as 'a man of transcendent abilities'. On April 23, 1875, Kenealy pressed his request to a division: the Noes had it, by 433 votes to one. Five years later, in the next General Election, he came bottom of the poll; and on April 18 died. A few months later Sir Alexander Cockburn followed him to the grave. Sprightly to the last, he had been sitting all day at the Court for Crown Cases Reserved. He walked home to his house in Hertford Street in Mayfair, worked on an article for the *Nineteenth Century*, had a heart attack in his bedroom as he was about to undress, and in a quarter of an hour, was dead.

15

The Oddest Pair of All: Coleridge and Russell

Despite the somewhat provocative title of this chapter, there was nothing particularly odd about either of the last two Lord Chief Justices of the nineteenth century, taken individually. The oddity lay in the contrast. Coleridge was almost a caricature of an Englishman; Russell every Englishman's idea of what an Irishman should be. There almost seems to be a law of nature in modern times that the Lord Chief Justice should be a very different type of character from his predecessor, as if to prevent type-casting. Homely Ryder, polished Murray, miserly Kenyon, brutal Law, floundering Abbott, pleasant Denman, pushing Campbell, worldly Cockburn – it is a long list of markedly varied personalities. But none presented such a complete anti-thesis as John Duke Coleridge and his successor, Charles Russell.

John Duke Coleridge

When Coleridge was appointed Lord Chief Justice on Cock-burn's death, he was sixty, and Russell was forty-eight. They had at least two other points in common, besides their pro-fession. They were both handsome, though in very different ways, and they were both Gladstonians. But there all resem-blance ended. Coleridge was a cold supercilious man, without the least sense of humour, and a disastrous Lord Chief Justice if only because of his notorious habit of dozing off during trials. Russell was warm-hearted, and hot-tempered, 'an elemental force', Bowen called him, and for the short six years during which he held the office a successful, energetic, Chief Justice.

Coleridge was the son of a judge, educated at Eton and Balliol, distinguished-looking, and well aware of it, arrogant, unctuous, with a majestic rich voice and a delight – from his time at the Oxford Union onwards – in making speeches. 'A silvery mediocrity', Disraeli is said to have called him. Yet there was another side to his character. Among his close friends were Matthew Arnold, Cardinal Newman and Alfred Tennyson. The poet Coleridge was his father's uncle and his background was one of cultured, classical learning, so such friendships could be said to be part of his heritage. What was certainly not, though, was his extraordinary loathing for the aristocracy. He took great delight in suggesting ingenious defences to the poachers who came up before him under the new Game Laws, much to the fury of the Whig and Tory landlords alike. Possibly this was simply because he loathed the country and all its sports, apart from his own family home in Devon, Heath's Court at Ottery St Mary's. But even there the library, seventy-foot long, was his main love. He was a townee, an opera- and theatre-goer, a diner-out in society, twice married, once to Amy, after her death to Jane, both of whom died before him; he was, as might be expected, a difficult man in family life.

Russell on the other hand was a racing man; a great student of form all his life, a friend of trainers, jockeys and book-makers, founder of the Pegasus Club and steward of the first Bar point-to-point. Broad-shouldered, with grey eyes, and crisp chestnut curls, he looked what he was: an Irishman brought up in the open air. He came from County Down, a merchant's son, began his professional life as a Belfast solicitor, switched to the Bar in Dublin, set out for London to make his fortune at the age of twenty-six, and married Eileen Mulholland, his childhood sweetheart, with a thousand pounds from his mother to live on. He had a strong personality, strong opinions on everything, hated fools, loved songs, whist and piquet, spoke well, practised mainly in Liverpool thanks to a Catholic solicitor there, John Yates, a member of the Corporation, and announced that: 'My ambition is to be the first Catholic Attorney General since the Reformation.' By the time he began to make a name for himself with his appearance in 1861 in the Windham lunacy inquiry – the wretched Windham had not only married a prostitute but settled money on her, which seemed cause for locking him up – Coleridge, who also appeared in the case, was a Q.C. Coleridge had made his name by an eloquent speech in a hopeless but popular cause some years earlier, defending two Somerset farm labourers who had murdered a tax-collector. From that time on his path was smooth: 1865 Liberal M.P. for Exeter in his home county, 1868 Solicitor General, 1871 Attorney General, 1873 Lord Chief Justice of the Common Pleas, 1880 Lord Chief Justice of the King's Bench – and that same year the first official Lord Chief Justice of England.

In 1873, as part of the general high Victorian programme of tidying-up the country's administration, the Judicature Act was passed, though it was not to come into operation until 1875 and when it did, Sir Alexander Cockburn did all he could to sabotage its workings. Basically it merged all the main Courts of the country into one Supreme Court of Judicature. It then proceeded to divide the Supreme Court into two new Courts: first a High Court of Justice and then a Court of Appeal. That was all very neat and tidy except that all the old Courts immediately re-emerged under a new guise as Divisions of the High Court: the King's Bench Division, the Common Pleas Division, the Exchequer Division, to say nothing to the equity Courts of Chancery and the rest.

Coleridge put a stop to this as soon as he could. Sir Alexander died on November 20, 1880. Coleridge was appointed on November 24; and five days later 'there was', he writes, 'a council of judges, when we finished our deliberations and concluded by a large majority to abolish the three divisions or, rather, reduce them to one, and to bring down the three chiefs, also to one.' It was said that he could not bear competition and that it was by his machinations that the age-old titles of Lord Chief Baron and Lord Chief Justice of Common Pleas were done away with. At any rate, when he took his seat at Westminster Hall on December 1 as President of the Queen's Bench Division of the Supreme Court of Judicature he was officially, by a patent from Queen Victoria, Lord Chief Justice of England; and so his successors have always for the last hundred years been styled.

The great days of Westminster Hall, historic seat of England's justice, were coming to an end too. On December 4, 1882, Queen Victoria opened the new Royal Courts of Justice just opposite the Temple and two years later all the varied branches of the Supreme Court of Judicature were installed there, including the new Court of Appeal. At first there were four judges only in the Court of Appeal: the Lord Chancellor and his assistant, the Master of the Rolls, the President of the Probate, Divorce and Admiralty Division of the High Court, and the Lord Chief Justice. The original intention of the reformers had been to abolish the appellate jurisdiction of the House of Lords.

Instead, the plan for the clear-cut jurisdiction of a single, small Court of Appeal became hopelessly confused: it expanded downwards to the Court of Criminal Appeal, where the Lord Chief Justice now usually presides, upwards into the House of Lords (particularly after 1913 when many more Lords of Appeal in Ordinary, the first life peers, were created), and across into the Judicial Committee of the Privy Council. Both before and after this the number of judges expanded enormously – before, in 1846 with the creation of the County Courts, afterwards when the number of judges in the Queen's Bench Division was increased first in 1938 to seventeen, and afterwards in 1977 to no less than forty-one. There are scores of judges now where there were once in the common-law courts a simple rounded dozen, and as a result the Lord Chief Justice has become nowadays much more of an administrator, much less of a judge.

In the 1860s, while Coleridge was busying himself in such famous cases as his defence in 1865 of Constance Kent, the twenty-one-year-old who confessed to murdering her baby brother when she was aged sixteen, Russell was laboriously making his way in Liverpool. In 1860 he made £261; in 1865, £2,171; and by the end of the decade he had doubled that. In the 1868 election he stood for Parliament at Dundalk; he was beaten. Next year he faced Coleridge before Cockburn in the convent case, Saurin versus Starr. At the end of the decade he applied three times to take silk but he was not made a Q.C. until 1872. That same year he became a Bencher of Lincoln's Inn and moved to Harley Street. 'Russell,' said a friend, 'if only you could give up your Irish brogue, it would be worth £500 a year.' 'I would not give it up,' said Russell, 'for the additional £500.'
  He did not have to wait long for the extra money. By 1874 his fees were £10,800, and he was beginning to be known in London. Success mellowed him. He had been rough and domineering on his way up; he remained always brusque to solicitors. But they still briefed him, partly because he made such an impression on the court and the jury with his forceful personality and partly because, despite his impatience and his domineering temper, he had a clear head and a kind heart. 'He imposes himself upon the jury and the court,' said Coleridge, who was by no means a fool, 'he is the biggest advocate of the century.' Barry O'Brien, his biographer, once asked him about his methods.
  'An Irish jury enjoys the trial,' he said. 'They can follow every

turn of the game. They understand the points of skill; the play between an Irish witness and an Irish counsel is good fun, and they like the fun and they don't mind the loss of time. They get as good value out of a trial as they would out of the theatre. With an English jury it is different. They are busy men and they want to get away quickly. The great thing in dealing with an English jury is not to lose time. Mere *finesse* they don't appreciate. Go straight at the witness and at the point; throw your cards on the table. It is a simple method, and I think it is a good method.'

At the General Election of 1874 Russell stood again for Dundalk but was again defeated – this time not by a Tory but by Callan, a Home Ruler. In March 1880 he finally got in, after a literal fight on the steps with Callan. He was not at the time a Home Ruler himself. He knew little about the details of Irish history – he was never a bookish man – and he doubted whether an Irish Parliament was necessary. By 1884 he was making £20,000 at the Bar, Dundalk was disenfranchised under the new Reform Act, and he decided to stand for Hackney. In November 1885 he was elected. This was the election that made his fellow-countryman Parnell master of the situation, with eighty-six Irish Nationalists holding the effective balance between the fairly evenly matched Liberals and Conservatives. By January 1886 Gladstone was, with Parnell's support, Prime Minister and Russell fulfilled his ambition. 'Mr Russell,' said the Prime Minister, 'I have advised Her Majesty to appoint you to the office of Attorney General.'

The next few months were the most dramatic in the last hundred years of England's political history. Gladstone, amid phenomenal public excitement, introduced a Home Rule Bill for Ireland, promising to set up an Irish Parliament and an Irish government in Dublin. The Liberals split on the issue; and on June 8 the Bill was defeated by 343 votes to 313. Gladstone decided to dissolve and call another General Election. It resulted in victory for his opponents: 316 Conservatives and 78 rebel Liberals – Liberal Unionists – were elected, as against 191 Liberals and eighty-five Irish Nationalists; and it marked, though that was not clear at the time, the end of the dominance of party politics by the Whigs that had lasted *grosso modo* since the Glorious Revolution of 1688.

So, though Charles Russell was re-elected for South Hackney, his period in office as the first Catholic Attorney General since the Reformation had lasted only a few months. During those months he had thrown himself with extraordinary energy into the campaign for the Home Rule Bill, travelling all over England addressing public meetings and giving by far his best performances in the House of Commons. It was as if, after years of hesitation, he had found his Irish feet at last. It was no use of course; Lord Salisbury was leading a Conservative Unionist government, and his dazzling nephew A. J. Balfour was combating Gladstonians and Parnellites alike in the Commons. Then in April 1887 *The Times* took a hand, an extremely pro-government, pro-Tory hand. It published a facsimile letter, which with other documents it had bought for the enormous sum of £30,000, designed to discredit Parnell, followed by a series of articles on 'Parnellism and Crime', all aimed to help Balfour pilot a new drastic Crimes Act through Parliament.

Charles Stewart Parnell was only forty-one; he had entered Parliament just ten years earlier and in those few years had succeeded in making Home Rule for Ireland, previously thought by English politicians and even by Irishmen such as Russell, to be a mere Celtic fantasy, a matter of practical politics and one almost achieved – that mere shortfall of thirty votes was to bring with it at least a further hundred years of bloody conflict. He had not made himself loved by the English in the process, though in manner he was more English than Irish. Aloof, bushy-bearded, a gentleman, a Protestant, rarely eloquent, impervious to criticism, he had manipulated the English political system in a manner that made him utterly loathed – except of course in Ireland where the whole population, bar the minority in the North-East corner, were solidly behind him. Yet he was careful always to remain, at least officially, a constitutionalist, despite the periodic waves of Fenian violence that swept over Ireland.

Five years earlier the Phoenix Park murders had shocked the whole of the British Isles. On May 6, 1882, a band of assassins, calling themselves 'the Invincibles', hacked to death with long surgical knives Mr Burke the Under-Secretary and his companion, the aimiable and innocent, newly arrived Lord Frederick Cavendish. Even the Irish Nationalists were appalled. 'Early on Sunday morning the 7th,' wrote Sir Charles Dilke M.P., 'Parnell came to see me, white and apparently terror-stricken. He thought the blow was aimed at him and that he himself would be the next victim of the secret societies.' But the facsimile letter which five years later *The Times* published was dated May 1882, apparently written by Parnell, and it certainly condoned the murders. Parnell declared in the House of Commons that the letter was a forgery, and Gladstone and his colleagues at once announced their belief in Parnell's innocence. But a year later, in a connected court action, the matter blew up again and the Conservative Attorney General, Sir Richard Webster, declared that Parnell had not only written the letter of May 15 but other, similar letters too, which he proceeded then and there to read out in court. Next day, Parnell declared in the House that they were all forgeries. *The Times* retorted that it had legal proof that they were all genuine. A *cause célèbre* was blowing up, and on August 11, 1887 a Special Commission of three judges was appointed to enquire into the whole affair and report back to Parliament.

On September 22 what was in effect the State trial of Parnell and sixty-four other Irish Nationalist M.P.s began, with the Attorney General Sir Richard Webster appearing for *The Times* as prosecutor, out to prove that Parnell and his friends were conspirators, hypocrites, corrupt, seditious, and responsible for the wave of agitation and disorder that was then, once more, sweeping across rural Ireland. The specially selected judges were all Webster's sort of men. There was to be no jury; no penalties either of course, bar the total loss of reputation which the government was hoping for. Russell, though he did not particularly care for Parnell as a person, appeared for the Irish, with Herbert Asquith as his junior, a Liberal M.P. then in his thirties. The case dragged on through the wearisome recital of recent Irish history until February 1889, when at long last the story of the famous facsimile letter was due to come up.

In his standard volume of the *Oxford History of England* that covers the period 1870-1914, Ensor refers to 'the dignified phase of English journalism' that 'reigned unchallenged until 1886'. Delane, the great editor of *The Times* had resigned after thirty years; his second successor, a youngish man called Buckle, had to face growing competition not so much from the penny morning papers – *The Times* sold for threepence – as from the sensational weeklies like *Tit-Bits* which had sprung up so successfully. In 'the dignified phase', the law had had an extraordinarily prominent place; the Tichborne Case was probably more fully reported than any lawsuit has ever been, before or after. Barristers and judges became extremely well known, almost heroic, figures. Though Ensor does not specify it, he probably chose 1886 as the moment when *The Times*, with the purchase of the Parnell letters, descended to 'undignified' sensationalism. Buckle, it seems, knew little about the origins of the letters; it was the manager of *The Times*, Macdonald, who had authorised their purchase and printing, convinced that they were the sort of letters that a man of Parnell's stamp would have written. They had come from a certain Mr Houston, secretary of the Irish Loyal and Patriotic League in Dublin; and he in his turn had obtained them from an Irish journalist, a former Fenian, a man of fifty-one, Richard Piggott.

When Piggott went into the witness box on the morning of Wednesday, February 20, he looked a respectable, solid, citizen. Examined by Webster, he gave his evidence clearly and calmly. Russell had been tetchy and ill-tempered for days before he rose to cross-examine Piggott on the Thursday afternoon. But when he rose in court he was calm and self-possessed. His opening series of questions were startling. 'Mr Piggott,' he said, 'would you be good enough with my Lord's permission to write some words on that sheet of paper for me?' 'Will you write the word "livelihood"?' Russell continued, 'Just leave a space. Will you write the word "likelihood"? Will your write your own name? Will you write the word "Proselytism"; and finally (I think I will not trouble you at present with any more) "Patrick Egan" and "P. Egan"?' The last names he uttered with great solemnity. Then carelessly, 'There is one word I had forgotten. Lower down please, leaving spaces, write the word "hesitancy".' Pause. 'With a small "h". Will you kindly give me the sheet?' Sharply. 'Don't blot it, please.'

It was all a trap. In one of the Parnell letters 'hesitancy' had been spelt 'hesitency' – as Piggott had proceeded to spell it. By the time the cross-examination ended and the court adjourned for the weekend, on the Friday, Piggott's credit was utterly destroyed, and the case against Parnell had virtually collapsed. On the Saturday Piggott went to see the leading Radical M.P. Henry Labouchère and confessed that he had forged all the Parnell letters and sold them to Houston for £500. When the court reconvened on the Monday, Piggott had disappeared. The wretched man was traced to Spain; English police officers tracked him down to the Hotel Los Embajadores in Madrid, and there, just as he was about to be arrested on March 5, he blew out his brains.

The sensation can be imagined. Russell went on to sum up the case for the defence in a slow, deliberate speech that lasted six days and finished on April 12, covering the whole of Irish history since the Union, giving the impression that there had been a cut-throat conspiracy of the authorities against the democratically elected representatives of the Irish people. 'When I opened this case, my Lords,' he wound up, 'I said I represented the accusers.' Then, thunderously, pointing to where the Attorney General and *The Times* solicitors were sitting, 'We are the accusers, and the accused are *there*!' Rosebery, Manning, the Lord Chief Justice, even Lord Randolph Churchill, all wrote to congratulate him. 'You have at a bound,' as Rosebery put it, 'passed from solid reputation to supreme eminence.' The editor of the discredited *Times* offered, of course, to resign. If there had been an early election then, Gladstone and Parnell would almost certainly have swept in with a vast majority. But Parnell had, with reason, been somewhat evasive during the case: he had a very different skeleton in his cupboard. It came out all the same the following year when Captain O'Shea sued his wife Kitty for divorce and named Parnell as co-respondent. The subsequent scandal ruined, indeed killed, Parnell, and split the Irish Nationalists to the point where they were ineffective for decades.

This was not the only famous divorce action of the period. In December 1886 Russell had appeared for Lady Colin Campbell in Campbell versus Lady Campbell and (among many other co-respondents) the Duke of Marlborough, a case 'which led to some of the most remarkable revelations a court of law has ever had to listen to'. A few years later, in June 1891, he appeared (again supported by Mr Asquith, who had also distinguished himself as a cross-examiner in the Parnell enquiry) in the most famous of all Victorian society scandals, the 'Baccarat' Case. The trial was presided over by the Lord Chief Justice, in his element. Sir Edward Clarke, Q.C., appeared for the plaintiff, Sir William Gordon Cumming, Bt., who was sueing for libel Mr and Mrs Lycett Green, a Yorkshire M.F.H. and his wife, plus various other guests who had been with him at a Doncaster races house-party at Tranby Croft.

Sir Edward Clarke, describing the opening day of the trial wrote:

[Lord Coleridge] had appropriated half of the public gallery, and had given tickets to his friends. The Prince of Wales occupied a chair at the part of the bench between the judge and the witness-box. Lady Coleridge sat close to her husband's right hand, and had the duty of checking the occasional inclination to sleep which at this time had become noticeable. The rest of the bench was filled by a group of fashionable ladies, in front of whom, and one might fitly say 'close to the footlights', one of the judge's daughters-in-law sat with a sketch book on her knee busily sketching the actors in the drama. Lord Coleridge's angry exclamation, when the crowded Court cheered my opening speech, 'Silence, this is not a theatre' sounded in the circumstances rather amusing.

The high spot of the occasion was, of course, the appearance of the Prince of Wales, who had unofficially 'court-martialled' the Baronet for cheating at cards, in the witness-box. Russell made a brilliant speech for the Lycett Greens, the jury found there was no libel and Sir William was therefore indirectly condemned to a life-sentence as a cad. Lord Coleridge had very wisely confined himself to the judicial side of the affair in his summing-up. It was his last great case. On May 2, 1894 he attended the opening of the Royal College of Music in South Kensington in court dress. He caught a chill, took to his bed and by June 4 he was dead. He ought of course to have retired long before his death, but he openly admitted that he stayed on longer than he should have done, for the money.

As for Charles Russell, he had become Attorney General for the second time when Gladstone returned to power in the General Election of July 1892. But Gladstone, even with his Irish Nationalist allies and that harbinger of days to come, the solitary Independent Labour M.P., Keir Hardie, only had a majority of forty-odd; his second attempt at passing a Home Rule Bill was defeated in the Lords by 419 votes to forty-one. Indeed the whole of that Liberal administration was hamstrung by the Lords' veto, Asquith almost alone distinguishing himself as a young but brilliant Home Secretary. Russell should have been Lord Chancellor; but he was a Catholic, and even now, a hundred years later, in a land of perfect religious tolerance, we cannot have a Catholic as Lord Chancellor. Instead, in May 1894, on the death of Bowen, he was promoted to the new-fangled post of a Lord of Appeal. It was a brief appointment. Only a month later Coleridge died, and Russell became the official Lord Chief Justice of his adopted country.

Charles Russell

In the next General Election, in the spring of 1895, Keir Hardie, symbolically, lost his seat. Lord Salisbury's Tories won a crushing victory, with almost twice as many seats as Lord Rosebery's Liberals; all the same they formed a coalition government with the Liberal Unionists led by that once-dangerous Radical, Chamberlain.

'Pushful Joe' Chamberlain became Secretary of State for the Colonies, and a Liberal Imperialist, not exactly hand-in-hand with Cecil Rhodes, then Premier of the Cape Colony, but certainly closely in touch. President Kruger of the Transvaal glowered at the Uitlanders, the English and cosmopolitan immigrants, whom the discovery of gold on the Witwatersrand had brought flooding in to the primitive, pastoral Boer homeland. Yet the Uitlanders, half the white male population, demanded a say in the running of affairs. Rhodes, with the support not only of his British backers but also of the Cape Dutch, planned a take-over: an uprising of the Uitlanders to coincide with a quick dash by the armed men of his Chartered Company to seize Johannesburg, 'the City of Gold'. As 1895 drew to its close, Dr Jameson, Rhodes' exact contemporary and the chief administrator of the Chartered Company, gathered his striking force on the borders of the Transvaal: 350 Chartered Police, 120 Bechuanaland Police, eight machine-guns, three pieces of artillery.

Then it all went wrong. The Uitlanders failed to rise, the raid should have been called off. But Jameson went ahead on his own initiative. He led his raiders into the Transvaal on December 29. It could never have been a quick dash; there were 180 miles to cover. On January 2, his force was trapped by the Boers at Doornkopf; sixteen were killed before they all surrendered. Rhodes resigned as Cape Premier; Chamberlain, disingenuously but promptly, repudiated the raid; and Jameson and his men were handed over by a wily and apparently magnanimous Kruger to the British authorities for trial.

Five of them, including Leander Starr Jameson himself, were brought back to England and tried before the Lord Chief Justice, two other judges, and a special jury in July 1896. The charge was that of fitting out a warlike expedition against a friendly state in violation of the Foreign Enlistment Act of 1870. It was the only State trial of importance over which Russell presided and all his political inclinations led him to press for a conviction. Unfortunately for his popularity, public opinion was all for an acquittal, inflamed first of all by the Kaiser's 'Kruger telegram' – until then people had thought the worst possible of the French but had imagined that the Kaiser, who was the Queen's grandson, and his people were firmly on the side of the British – and also by an unexpected side-result of the Jameson Raid, the rising of the Matabele in the absence of the Bechuanaland Police.

The trial opened on July 20. Sir Richard Webster, the Attorney General, prosecuting, faced Sir Edward Clarke with, as his junior, Edward Carson. It lasted for nine days. 'These men have done wrong,' wrote *The Times*, 'but they undoubtedly erred from excess of zeal for what they thought the interests of the Empire in South Africa and of their fellow subjects in Johannesburg.' They were indicted on twelve counts. Clarke, inhibited by government directives that forbade him to bring up Chamberlain's collusion, could only emphasise the 'purity' of Jameson's motives. The trial ended on July 28. On that final day, Russell virtually bullied the jury into bringing in a verdict of guilty. Legally, it was undoubtedly correct. Morally, though, it was probably Chamberlain who should have been in the dock and though the sentences were light – Jameson was sentenced to fifteen months in gaol – public opinion was exasperated.

But Russell took his unpopularity lightly enough. His reputation as a judge was growing among his colleagues; he was less impatient and domineering than he had been at the Bar, though, as there, he always drove straight to the point. He served his country well in the Venezuelan boundary dispute, and enjoyed a successful lecture tour in the United States. He had a happy family life, based on his country home Tadworth Court at Epsom, suitably near the Derby course, with his wife and large family. He would sing Moore's Melodies with his sons en route to race-meetings. He was not much of a reader, though, like many Irishmen, he loved *The Count of Monte Cristo* and *The Adventures of Sherlock Holmes*. What he really liked was talking; he even enjoyed making after-dinner speeches, keeping his audience amused, like his predecessor Coleridge, who once rose to reply to a toast at a Balliol dinner with the immortal words: 'I, my Lords and gentlemen, have been asked to respond for Oxford as a whole, and, my Lords and gentlemen, what a whole Oxford is!' Russell was always ready for an informal chat, and even as Lord Chief Justice used to hold open house at lunchtime in his room at the Law Courts.

On July 4, 1900, Russell held a dinner-party in his London house in Cromwell Road. Next morning he left Euston to go on circuit in North Wales in excellent spirits; on the 13th he wrote to his daughter Lilian: 'My dear child, I am really sorry that it did not suit your mother's arrangements or yours and Margaret's to come with me on Circuit. I am sure each of you would have enjoyed this beautiful countryside, full of places of interest. The people too remind me greatly of Irishmen.' On July 18, he felt a little unwell. On July 25, he was back in his home in Epsom; on August 4 he was ill and low. On August 9, the doctors decided to operate. He demanded a diagram, asked a lot of questions, had the last rites, was operated on apparently successfully, slept fitfully, and died at dawn with his wife and children beside him.

Part III

Modern Times 1900-1982

Richard Webster   (Lord Alverstone)
Rufus Isaacs   (Lord Reading)
Alfred Lawrence   (Lord Trevethin)
Gordon (Lord) Hewart
Thomas Inskip   (Lord Caldecote)
Rayner (Lord) Goddard
Hubert (Lord) Parker
John (Lord) Widgery
Geoffrey (Lord) Lane

The Lord Chief Justices of the Victorian Age were a very mixed bunch. But the Lord Chief Justices of modern times have been almost totally disastrous.

This does not apply to the last three Lord Chief Justices, that is to say to Parker, Widgery and the present holder of the office, Lane. All three have, partly by personal preference, partly by force of circumstances, maintained a low profile; and it seems unlikely that we will have a Lord Chief Justice who is important enough, socially or politically, to be classified as a disaster ever again. But their six predecessors, from Webster to Goddard, were an appalling collection of judges that by their combined ineptitudes dragged the office down to absurd depths.

That is not to say that they were corrupt or even incompetent, still less that they were as personalities despicable, though Gordon Hewart, who held office for the longest period this century was generally recognised by the profession as being the worst and most biased Lord Chief Justice since the time of Jeffreys. Goddard, probably the only Lord Chief Justice who is nowadays remembered by the public at all, was in his way a great Englishman, but as a judge extremely controversial and as a political and public figure monstrously outmoded. Isaacs was a phenomenon – but as a party man, a diplomat and indeed a ruler, noticeable in his period as Lord Chief Justice only for a State trial of considerable immorality and for an absenteeism unexampled since the days of the first Chief Justices – if then. Webster and Inskip, the two Tory politicians who held the office, were almost total mediocrities. Alfred Lawrence, the only unpolitical professional lawyer, was an extremely nice man though a remarkably dull judge and in any case was only appointed at the age of seventy-eight and resigned a year later. What a sextet!

It is of course arbitrary to draw a line at the year 1900 and declare 'The Age of Politics' ended. On the contrary, Isaacs and Inskip at any rate were far more important in their political than in their judicial roles. Even Goddard stood for election to the Commons, which he failed to reach, and when he eventually reached the Lords, used that House as a platform from which to fight his rear-guard political and social battles. Since Goddard, all three of the Lord Chief Justices have been members of the House of Lords but, though they have spoken on occasion, have been of no general consequence at all. Inskip was the last actually to be an elected Member of Parliament – and the first Lord Chief Justice ever to have been a Lord Chancellor before: equally undistinguished in either office. One interesting, though minor difference is that whereas the Victorian Lord Chief Justices had a habit of dying in office, all those since 1900 have resigned – Hewart and Goddard with notable reluctance. Only one, Rufus Isaacs, went on to greater things – the most extraordinary figure of them all.

16

The Rise of Rufus Isaacs

Rufus Daniel Isaacs was born on October 10, 1860. His father, Joseph Isaacs, was a prosperous fruit-merchant in the City; his mother Sara Woolf was also the daughter of a Jewish merchant. He was their fourth child and second son. When the ninth child came, the family moved from Finsbury Square to 21, Belsize Park in Hampstead. Rufus had a desultory education, partly in Brussels and partly at University College School until the age of fourteen when he was put to work in his father's firm, M. Isaacs and Sons Ltd., in Moscow House, Eastcheap. He found it difficult to settle down. His father gave him a year as ship's boy on a trading ship that called in at Rio and Calcutta, then eight months' apprenticeship with their trading partners, Junker and Hegnemann of Magdeburg, which ended badly. 'Isaacs secundus,' his schoolmasters had said, 'you will go to the devil!' Instead, thanks to his sister, he went to the Stock Exchange. She was married to Albert Keyzer of the stockbrokers Keyzer and Frederici. On November 3, 1879, Rufus Isaacs applied to be admitted as a member of the Stock Exchange and was; he declared himself, falsely, to be 'of age', though he knew the rules laid down that members must be at least twenty-one. He became a jobber in the foreign market. It slumped. Less than a year later, on August 14, 1884, Mr Rufus D. Isaacs was 'hammered'. His liabilities were £8,000. He decided to leave England and make a completely fresh start in Panama.

So far it is an almost classic black sheep story: failure at two careers, no qualifications, deeply in debt at the age of 24, off to South America – a wandering Jew indeed whose only abilities appeared to be a useful way with his fists (though he had had his nose broken by his angered trainer, Ned Donelly), and an ability, much admired by the girls, to stand on his head in the music-halls and applaud with his feet. He was saved from Panama by his mother's hysterics – retrieved from the boat train at Euston en route to Liverpool seconds before departure.

His weary father decided to try him out on a third career – the law. Rufus took to it like a duck to water, joined the Middle Temple, still the normal home for a Jewish barrister, was called to the Bar on November 17, 1887 and married Alice Cohen on December 8, at the West London Synagogue. She was only twenty-two, rather delicate-looking; her father Albert Cohen, a merchant of German-Jewish background, had been horrified and forbidden the match. They had met at a dancing class; the father thought young Isaacs unstable and unsuitable. Two years later their only child, Gerald, was born. That year Rufus Isaacs earned £750. He was considerably older than most new barristers, but that was by no means a disadvantage. Within a few years he had made his name in commercial cases, heard mainly before the new Commercial Court that the City had insisted be set up, he was making £7,000 a year, and in 1898, just over ten years after being called, he took silk and became a Q.C.

This sudden success was partly due to sheer hard work. Rufus Isaacs did not waste time in drinking or socialising; he always remembered the first advice he had had at the Bar: to be in his chambers by 10 a.m. and not to leave them until 6 p.m. He was normally in bed by nine o'clock in the evening, rose at four in the morning, and did half a day's work before breakfast. He always mastered his papers. Clients trusted him. He was cool, incisive and energetic in cross-examination, the great rival at the Bar of that famous advocate Marshall Hall – but a great friend of his rival too, ready to lend him money when Marshall Hall just after the turn of the century hit a very bad patch. He took silk because he had too much work. He had wanted to try something else earlier on but his wife Alice had dissuaded him. Now all his Stock Exchange debts had been cleared. At the age of forty he turned, for the first time, to politics.

Jews, like Irishmen, Welshmen and Scotsmen, were almost inevitably Liberals in those days; and Rufus Isaacs stood as a Liberal for North Kensington. It was a bad election for Liberals: the Boer War had split them once again, and Campbell-Bannerman, the party's official leader, had been dubbed a 'pro-Boer'. Rufus Isaacs did his best. His election poster, decorated with a Union Jack and a Royal Standard, was also embellished with the letters V.R.I. – which stood, rather unexpectedly, for 'Vote Rufus Isaacs'. But Joe Chamberlain supported his Conservative opponent. Rufus Isaacs lost the seat by 730 votes.

Richard Webster

Meanwhile, on the death of Charles Russell, Richard Webster the Attorney General, Lord Salisbury's appointee, the Conservative M.P. for Launceston, became – after six unwilling months as Master of the Rolls – Lord Chief Justice. He was a real Victorian, 'interested in athletics, glee singing, choirs, missionaries and tracts'. Plenty of exercise, early rising, hard work, no nonsense were his recipes for a successful life. Educated at Charterhouse and Cambridge, son of a Q.C., he had made money and reputation in commercial cases and in particular as counsel for the late Victorian capitalist concerns *par excellence*, the railway companies. He looked impressive – dignified, heavy and stern. He was a devout churchman, singing in St Mary Abbot's choir in Kensington. It was said that the county cricket scores were handed up to him on the Bench. He was a first-rate billiard player, and boisterously genial in social life. He 'looked and sounded like a bluff farmer'. He presided as a totally undistinguished but harmless Lord Chief Justice for thirteen years, retired, wrote an exceptionally tedious autobiography, and died two years later.

As Lord Chief Justice, he judged three famous murder cases and one case of high treason. The first murder case was the Yarmouth Beach Murders, in 1901. Herbert John Bennett had strangled his wife with a bootlace; though he was defended with extraordinary vigour by Marshall Hall, he was found guilty and hanged. The second murder case (and the first to be tried at the new buildings of the Old Bailey, opened in 1907) was that of the murderer of Mr Whiteley, 'the Universal Provider', the apparently genial elderly head of the great store in Westbourne Grove. The third and most notorious of all, in 1910, was that of Crippen. In none of these cases did Webster say or do anything of note. Nor did he do so in the case of Colonel Lynch, the first treason trial to be held for sixty years. Lynch, a British subject but an Irishman, had fought for the Boers. The war being over, he returned to Ireland thinking himself in little danger. Nevertheless in 1903 he was arrested, indicted by a grand jury, tried, found guilty and sentenced to death – the only sentence possible for high treason. The sentence was commuted to imprisonment, and the Colonel was released after eighteen months – a very different fate from that which awaited a fellow countryman of his under the next Lord Chief Justice.

That, however, lies in the future. At this time Rufus Isaacs, shrugging off his election disappointment, was going from success to success at the Bar and rapidly becoming the most fashionable advocate in Edwardian England, with an income that rose to £50,000 a year. There was the libel action of Arthur Chamberlain (Joe's brother) against The *Star* in which the leader of the Bar, Sir Edward Clarke, appeared against him. There was the trial of the Boer lawyer, Dr Krause, for incitement to murder, in which he appeared against Sir Edward Carson, at the time Solicitor General. There was the Liverpool Bank Case (swindling and betting), the Hartopp Divorce Case (high society and scandal) the Taff Vale Case (railwaymen and trade unions), the Gordon Custody Case (bitter and unpleasant) and, above all, the case that finally brought Rufus Isaacs public fame, the Whittaker Wright Case.

Whittaker Wright was a financial genius, a North Countryman, and founder of the London and Globe Finance Corporation with ramifications in Australia, British Columbia, the Yukon and the Pacific. By the time he was fifty his prestige in the City was enormous, and his fortune was made. He had an imposing house in Park Lane, filled with ornate French furniture, a racing yacht *Sybarita* which defeated the Kaiser's *Meteor*, and an enormous mansion in a vast park in Surrey, with stables for fifty horses and over each stall a moulded ceiling depicting a different scene of the chase, and in the landscaped grounds a billiard room beneath an artificial lake. The Marquess of Dufferin and Ava, a former Viceroy of India, had been persuaded to become Chairman of the Board; but it was the benevolent, autocratic, self-confident figure of the great 'W.W.' himself, not the scintillating titles of his associate directors, that made investors clamour to be associated with any, or all, of his projects.

All the wilder was the clamour, therefore, when on December 29, 1900, London and Globe crashed. When the question of a trial arose, Whittaker Wright left the country for America; it took some time to extradite him, and the trial did not come on until January 1904. Rufus Isaacs appeared for the prosecution, arguing basically that Whittaker Wright was not merely a financial manipulator but a downright swindler – whereas Whittaker Wright himself was sincerely convinced that he had done nothing wrong and that his transactions were in the long run for the benefit of mankind, as indeed (they included London's first stretch of Underground) perhaps they were.

The trial evolved into a battle of wits between Rufus Isaacs, cold, dispassionate, logical, conducting his case without notes but with every figure at his fingertips, and the massive figure of the financier, in all the dignity of frock-coat, high-collar and imperial beard. Five hours' masterly cross-examination by Rufus, as all his colleagues called him, made it quite clear that Whittaker Wright had juggled the accounts between his various companies in a totally illegal way. During the weekend following the summing-up speech for the prosecution, the country was in a fever of excitement: which way would the verdict go? It went against Whittaker Wright. The jury was out for only an hour, and the judge sentenced the guilty man to the severest punishment possible, seven years' penal servitude.

After the sentence Whittaker Wright was taken to the room set aside for his use during the trial in the law courts. He had a few words with his solicitor and accountant, smoked a cigar, thanked them in his slow deep voice for all they had done, asked for another cigar, lit it, threw it to the ground, turned purple and collapsed. Within seconds he was dead. For a week he had kept a tablet of potassium cyanide at the back of his tongue, and a bite was all that was needed.

This highly dramatic trial, and above all its sensational and tragic ending, made Rufus Isaacs almost notorious. When he first heard of Whittaker Wright's death, he – like many in the court – assumed that worry caused by the trial had brought about the stroke. It was an admitted relief to hear that it was suicide, and an additional bonus when *The Times* next morning in a leading article referred to his 'exemplary fairness'. In the euphoria of a now blossoming career, Rufus Isaacs decided to stand for Parliament again, this time at a by-election, at Reading.

Reading had been a very swingy seat, now Liberal, now Conservative. The retiring Member was a Liberal, Mr George Palmer of biscuit fame, who had gone deaf; his majority was only 239. For the election campaign, Rufus Isaacs and his wife stayed at a small Temperance hotel in Reading, 'The Lodge'. The hotel was almost the only temperate feature of an extraordinarily vivid campaign. 'RUFUS FOR READING!' proclaimed in bold red letters the candidate's banners. All the youngish Radicals, the left-wing of the Liberal Party, came down to speak for him: Lloyd George, Churchill, Samuel, Montagu. Voting took place on August 4, 1904, and Rufus Isaacs won the seat by a majority of 230.

Soon after his election he bought a country house near his constituency Foxhill, a great place for house-parties and tennis. He – or one of his two chauffeurs – drove a yellow open Renault – too gusty for his wife, for whom he bought a closed

Delaunay-Belleville. He had a small town house in Park Lane. It was a marvellous period for him.

It was also a marvellous period for the Liberal Party. They had the scent of victory in their nostrils and in the General Election held in January 1906, they came back to power with an enormous majority. Two of the most prominent Liberals were lawyers: Asquith, who had been such a successful Home Secretary under Gladstone, and his closest friend, a Chancery barrister named Haldane, fat, clumsy, thin-voiced, highly intellectual, exuberant, generous. They tried to edge the aged Liberal Party leader, Campbell-Bannerman, upstairs to the Lords. He was having none of it; he reacted with surprising vigour, appointed an old pro-Boer Liberal friend of his, Rex Reid (Lord Loreburn), Lord Chancellor and stayed on as Prime Minister in the Commons until, two years later, ill-health forced him out. But Asquith became Chancellor of the Exchequer and heir-apparent; and Haldane, rather amazingly, took on the Ministry of War: quite an achievement, as Asquith remarked, for the pair of briefless barristers they had been.

On the other side of the House were two other famous barristers: One was the neurotic, electric, tall, masterful, Dublin-born Sir Edward Carson, who had been Solicitor General in the fallen Conservative and Unionist government and who now was to be, back in private practice again, Rufus Isaacs' chief rival at the Bar. They were utterly different in style: Carson fierce and emotional, Isaacs suave and coaxing. The other Conservative barrister at only thirty-four roughly twenty years younger than the Asquith/Haldane/Carson age-group, was the handsome, buccaneering F.E. Smith, who had been making £6,000 a year at the Liverpool Bar and had just been elected as Conservative and Unionist Member for the Walton Division of Liverpool. His maiden speech outdid Disraeli's for malice and invective. With his red buttonholes, his enormously long cigars, his soft hat tipped jauntily back on his head he soon became a favourite of the cartoonists; and with his fascinating speeches, of the public.

There was one other extraordinary member of the government who can be described as a lawyer: that was a dapper but fiery young solicitor, the Member for Caernarvon, the partner in the firm Lloyd George and George who became President of the Board of Trade under Campbell-Bannerman and, when Asquith took over as Prime Minister in December 1908, Chancellor of the Exchequer. Winston Churchill succeeded David Lloyd George as President of the Board of Trade.

Asquith, who was ten years older than Lloyd George and twenty years older than Churchill, treated them almost paternally as bright and vivacious lads with a propensity for getting into scrapes. All the same, this Liberal government represented, perhaps more than any of its predecessors, the Non-conformist conscience in power. That was one reason why a Jew like Rufus Isaacs did not appear even to be considered for a government post. Another of course was that he was never a successful House of Commons man. He himself used to say that he was tired out from his work in the courts when he got to the House, but, true though that no doubt was, his over-logical style of speaking did not endear him. Where he did, however, find his niche was behind the scenes, in the smoking-room. He became a great crony of Lloyd George, who was three years younger than him and a cooling, steadying influence.

Lloyd George had two major problems, apart from his political life. One was money, and the other was women. His wife Margaret – 'My dearest little round Maggie' – came from Criccieth, and had all her five children born and brought up in Criccieth. From the time he first became an M.P., in 1890, he lived mainly in London and she and the family stayed mainly in Wales. He was extremely attractive to women and certainly enjoyed affairs with many before his famous liaison with his secretary, Frances Stevenson, that began in 1912 and continued until a year before his death when he married her. But long before that in 1896 a doctor's wife, Kitty Edwards, accused him of having fathered her child, though she later changed her story in the courts. Then there was 'Mrs Tim', his Putney landlady, wife of Tim Davies, the Liberal M.P. for Fulham, and, later on when he was famous, Julia Henry, the American wife of yet another Liberal M.P.: both very attractive women, the second extremely rich.

In 1908 *The People* suggested in a series of articles that Lloyd George was going to be named as a co-respondent, that his friends were desperately trying to stop a case that would ruin him, and, finally, that the husband had been bought off for £20,000.

In the libel action that followed, Rufus Isaacs appeared for Lloyd George, with, as his juniors, not only Raymond Asquith, the Prime Minister's brilliant son – which was not surprising – but also F.E. Smith, which was – particularly as Sir Edward Carson was leading for *The People*. It indicates in a way how like each other Rufus Isaacs, Lloyd George and F.E. Smith were: all very much self-made men, all ambitious, all in their own way men of striking looks (Rufus Isaacs was famous for his 'Red Indian' profile) – and all, as the future was to show, men with more interest in their careers than in their principles.

Mr Justice A.T. Lawrence presided over the trial, on March 12, 1909. He allowed Lloyd George to be called at once, for, as he said, 'The Chancellor of the Exchequer is actually framing his budget and he cannot do his duty to his office or his country with such a charge hanging over his head.' Had Lloyd George read the allegations in *The People*, asked Isaacs.

'Yes.'

Were they true in substance or in fact?

'The paragraphs are an absolute invention. Every line of them.'

Yes. Possibly. But, as a recent biographer John Grigg has shown, there exist two series of letters, now in Earl Lloyd George's collection of family papers, from different women written in early 1908 and early 1909, of which at least one set shows an attempt to blackmail the Chancellor of the Exchequer. There was reason for Lloyd George to be very worried indeed – the Parnell case and the Dilke case showed only too clearly that politicians who broke up other men's marriages could not hope, however brilliant they might be, to stay in public life. There is no knowing now if either Rufus Isaacs or F.E. Smith were aware of how rickety their client's position was; but they must have known the sort of man he was and the sort of life he led. No doubt he was very, very grateful to both of them for their efforts. It was a time when he needed friends.

The Lords threw out the Chancellor of the Exchequer's famous budget on November 30. 'Pure socialism,' Lord Rosebery (though himself a Liberal magnate) called it, 'the end of all, the negation of faith, of family, of property, of monarchy, of empire.' 'Oh these Dukes,' retorted Lloyd George in his notorious Limehouse speech, 'how they harass us!' In the General Election campaign that followed, the most dramatic of Lloyd George's election meetings was that in a huge tram car shed in Reading where he had gone down to support Rufus Isaacs. 'What's the matter with Rufus?' read the election poster this time. 'He's all right!' Northcliffe, now owner of both *The Times* and the *Daily Mail*, wrote to congratulate him as one master of propaganda to another. 'My dear Isaacs, . . . Today I motored through the constituency and was immensely impressed by the brilliance of your poster-artist. He's all right? I never saw such a splendid show.'

When the result was declared in January 1910, Rufus Isaacs

was in again, by 207 votes. This time, and no doubt partially because of his now close association with the Chancellor of the Exchequer, he was offered the post of Solicitor General. The new King, King George V, knighted him, with a charming: 'How much pleasure it would have given my father to do this.'

As Solicitor General Sir Rufus appeared for the Crown in the Archer Shee case, made famous many years later by Terence Rattigan in his play, *The Winslow Boy*. He stuck strictly and legalistically to the rules. Sir Edward Carson, appearing for the family of the young naval cadet who had been expelled from Osborne College virtually without a hearing, threw himself heart and soul into what was more a crusade than a trial. 'This is the case of the grossest oppression without remedy that I have ever known since I have been at the Bar,' he declared. Isaacs was evasive, uneasy, much criticised, and finally over-ruled. He took a summer holiday with his wife in fashionable Marienbad, then returned to London and to promotion: up to Attorney General, with the oily John Simon, aged only thirty-seven, as his Solicitor General. The second election of the year 1910 was looming, and in December he again retained his seat in Reading but only just, by ninety-nine votes.

Before Parliament reassembled in February 1911, Lloyd George invited Isaacs down to Cap Martin; the two were becoming not so much friends – neither of them had friends in the ordinary sense – as intimate associates. Lucy Masterman, wife of another of Lloyd George's advisers, was there too.

'George used to listen interminably to Rufus Isaacs' descriptions of his cases,' she wrote in her diary, 'and appreciated them enormously. But the difference between the two men was very marked. Whenever George began to tell of his experiences among the Welsh preachers, Rufus simply could not understand why he was so interested in them. To him, these things seemed simply ridiculous.' They motored as far afield as Avignon.

It was during these drives, I think, that Rufus Isaacs gave his most amazing exhibitions of vitality. We usually started early in the morning. It was very cold at the time. Rufus was either talking or singing the whole time. Other people fell asleep in turn but never he. Among other things he sang me the Hebrew version of the 'Song of Miriam' which he learned at school. George stared at him open mouthed. 'You are an astonishing fellow. I never knew anybody like you,' was his comment.

Yet there was another side to Isaacs' complex character, a kind of reserve that grew up over the years. 'He guarded jealously his own rigid self-control,' wrote his son, 'and his embarrassed loathing of openly displayed emotions in others was his instinctive reaction against any assault on his own. He hated rows and scenes, for the spectacle of human beings casting aside the decencies of normal intercourse made him acutely uncomfortable, and for the same reason he looked with icy disapproval upon eccentricities of dress or behaviour.' Yet Sir Rufus' 'icy disapproval of eccentricities' must have been reserved for his inferiors; else how could he have stomached Margot Asquith, whom he much admired? Or even F.E. Smith with whom, despite their political differences and F.E.'s distinctly individual dress and behaviour, he was on very good terms? In a famous libel action Lever versus The *Daily Mail* (the future Lord Leverhulme versus Lord Northcliffe), F.E. had first been briefed by Northcliffe. He had settled down one evening with a mound of papers, four feet high, two dozen oysters and a bottle of champagne. In the morning his Opinion was ready, short but to the point. 'There is no answer to this action for libel and the damages must be enormous.' Isaacs had nonetheless taken it on, against Sir Edward Carson for Lever. It was a Carson triumph: Isaacs tried to settle for £10,000, Carson drove him up to £50,000. Nevertheless Isaacs had no resentment at all against F.E. for landing him with this impossible case. They were made Privy Councillors together. 'My pleasure is all the greater for your name being in the same list,' wrote Smith. 'There is no better friend than F.E.,' Isaacs always maintained.

A cloud passed over his good relations with Asquith. The ailing Lord Chancellor, Lord Loreburn, resigned. Asquith was cruising on the Admiralty yacht in the Mediterranean at the time, and Rufus Isaacs confidently expected that the position should be offered to him as Attorney General. It was not exactly the right of the Attorney General to be promoted in such circumstances but it had certainly become the custom. Instead Asquith appointed his old friend Haldane. There was a row. The man who smoothed it over was the Liberal Chief Whip, Alick Murray, the Master of Elibank (they all called him 'the Master' *tout court*), a genial fixer, the crony of the whole political world, rotund, cherubic, shrewd, avuncular. He suggested that the Attorney General should become a member of the Cabinet; this was the first time this had ever happened, and so Sir Rufus – slightly suspicious that his Jewishness had been held against him in the question of the Lord Chancellorship – was placated. He was a touchy and emotional man, for all his self-control.

17

'Gehazi'

In 1896, Commendatore Marconi, son of a Bologna business-man and an Irish mother, invented the wireless. He offered his invention to the Italian government. It is something of a Christopher Columbus story. His own people refused; he immediately went to London, the commercial centre of the whole world, took out patents, transmitted signals across the Atlantic, inevitably fell into debt – and finally in the autumn of 1909 via his brother-in-law the Hon Donough O'Brien met an entrepreneur who, he thought, would be just the man to handle the business side of his enterprises. That man was Godfrey Isaacs, Rufus' younger brother. Had it been anyone else, there would have been no trouble, no notorious Marconi scandal.

It was on April 9, 1912 that Godfrey, just back from making an important deal in America, invited Rufus and his other brother, Harry, now the head of the family fruit-merchants, to lunch at the Savoy. He had 500,000 five-dollar shares in the newly formed American Marconi Company to place, and had already placed 400,000 of them. Generously, he wanted to cut his brothers in on a good thing. Harry immediately agreed to take 50,000; Rufus hesitated, the *Titanic* sank, the value of wireless became immediately apparent, English Marconi shares boomed, and on April 17, Rufus agreed to take 10,000 of Harry's shares, which had doubled in value in the meantime. That night, he called round at 11 Downing Street, found Lloyd George in and Alick Murray staying there. He offered them each 1,000 of his own shares, rather in the same spirit as Godfrey had offered them to him; the Chancellor of the Exchequer and the Government Chief Whip, seeing a chance to turn, literally, a quick buck, both accepted.

However, the Postmaster General, Herbert Samuel, another Jew, was negotiating a contract with the Marconi Company – admittedly the English Marconi Company – to establish a chain of wireless stations all over the Empire; and on August 8 the satirical magazine of the period, Cecil Chesterton's *Eye Witness*, published an article headed 'The Marconi Scandal'.

What progress is the Marconi Scandal making? We ask the question merely from curiosity and under no illusion as to the inevitable end of the affair. Everybody knows the record of Isaacs and his father, and his uncle, and in general of the whole family. Isaacs' brother is Chairman of the Marconi Company, it has therefore been secretly arranged between Isaacs and Samuel that the British people shall give the Marconi company a very large sum of money through the agency of the said Samuel, and for the benefit of the said Isaacs.

There was no reference at all to the Chancellor of the Exchequer.

An elaborate, rather too blandly casual exchange of letters followed between Samuel, Isaacs and Asquith: no truth at all of course in any of the insinuations in this 'contemptible rag'. All (Asquith's phrase) 'scurrilous rubbish'. To sue or not to sue for libel? The decision was to let the matter drop. As Samuel put it to Isaacs, 'It would not be a good thing for the Jewish community for the first two Jews who have entered a British Cabinet to be enmeshed in an affair of this kind.'

It was all very well of course for the government to let the matter drop, but the press did not. In the autumn there was a debate on the Marconi contract, and Rufus Isaacs took the opportunity on October 11, 1912, to make this statement to the House.

'Never from the beginning, when the shares were fourteen shillings or nine pounds, have I had one single transaction with the shares of that company. I am not only speaking for myself but I am also speaking on behalf, I know, of my Right Honourable friends the Postmaster General and the Chancellor of the Exchequer, who in some way or other in some of the articles have been brought into this matter.'

Isaacs' statement was technically true; except that to the ordinary man dealings in Marconi shares were dealings in Marconi shares, whether they were in the English or the American companies. However, the statement dampened speculation and comment for a brief time. But a Committee of Enquiry was set up by the House, and by January 1913 Rufus Isaacs and Lloyd George went to see Asquith in his room in the House of Commons, to tell him that they had been 'guilty of an error of judgment' and to offer him their resignations. Asquith seems to have been shocked but not outraged. He gave them a wigging, and refused their resignations.

There again the matter might have been covered up successfully, had it not been for an article from its London correspondent that appeared in *Le Matin* of February 14, 1913, headed *Scandale Financier en Angleterre*. This got the facts all wrong, accused Herbert Samuel and the Isaacs brothers of total corruption, and led at last to a law case. Rufus sued *Le Matin* and soon afterwards his brother Godfrey sued Cecil Chesterton, whose sandwichmen had been marching up and down outside the House of Commons with posters inscribed 'Godfrey Isaacs: Ghastly Record'. The brothers won both cases. What was extraordinary was that they briefed Sir Edward Carson and F.E. Smith to appear for them, and that both these leading Tory lawyers did so. 'I am most deeply grateful to you,' wrote Rufus to F.E., 'for all you have done in my brother's case and for the triumphant result. I thank you very, very warmly and not least for your courage and loyalty. The Bar will ever remember the part Carson and you played in the matter.'

To outsiders, including ordinary members of the Conservative Party, it seemed merely like a mafia of lawyers defending one another. It had come out in the trials, of course, that the Ministers despite their earlier denials *had* been speculating in Marconi shares. It was Winston Churchill, largely, who saved them all; for it was he who had persuaded Sir Edward Carson and F.E. Smith to appear for their rivals (and hence muzzled their own voices in the Commons) and it was he who persuaded Northcliffe, the greatest press lord of the day, to play the whole story down. However even Churchill, another smoother-down and smoking-room operator *par excellence*, could not prevent the hostile questioning of the two Cabinet Ministers by the Commons Committee of Enquiry.

'Sir Rufus Isaacs,' wrote a Labour M.P., Fred Towett, 'was distinctly and obviously distressed, the most successful advocate in all England pleading in his own defence and it hurt him. His pale face was drawn and care-worn . . . There was on the part of the attacking Party a wolfish eagerness to destroy the two Ministers. There were interruptions which seemed like nothing so much as the deep bay of eager wolves in a hungry pack.'

Turmoil broke out in the full House when a Tory M.P. asked the Chancellor of the Exchequer whether 'the Right Honourable Gentleman's salary is not sufficient to prevent him from wrongfully and improperly gambling . . .' With eyes blazing Lloyd George cut his opponent short. That was enough to set the Opposition Benches in an uproar. 'Marconi Swindle!' they yelled, 'Gag! Packed Jury!' Then came a fresh twist that infuriated even Northcliffe, who, like the British public, began to feel that the whole government was involved. The Committee of Enquiry called on the Liberal Chief Whip to appear before them and give evidence. 'The Master of Elibank,' replied the government, 'is detained on business in Bogota.'

'BOG-OH-TA-AAH!' became the mocking rallying-cry of the Tories on every platform, both in the House and outside it. Alick Murray's absence was particularly scandalous since it had come out that some time after his own personal dealings he had invested Liberal Party funds in Marconi shares. Yet even so on June 13 the Committee of Enquiry published the inevitable whitewash report, though with a dissenting minority opinion. A final two-day debate in the House of Commons, on June 18 and 19, wound up the affair officially.

'If you will,' Lloyd George perorated, 'I acted thoughtlessly, I acted carelessly, I acted mistakenly, but I acted innocently, I acted openly and I acted honestly.'

Thirty years later, convalescing in Marrakesh, Churchill would still talk about the affair: 'After luncheon,' Lord Moran, his doctor, wrote, 'Winston wearing an immense sombrero, slumps in a deck-chair and decides with Max that the Marconi case was a squalid business. They go over again how F.E. and Carson rescued Lloyd George . . .'

It was astonishing that the government survived. It could hardly have done so if F. E. Smith and Carson had led a concerted attack on Isaacs and Lloyd George and 'the Master' in the Commons with all the force of their passionate invective. But both were preoccupied with the Irish crisis. The Ulster Unionist Council had appointed Sir Edward Carson their leader and authorised him to plan for a Provisional Government of Ulster. On September 25, 1913 he reviewed 7,000 armed Ulster Volunteers with F.E. – thereafter popularly known as 'Galloper Smith' – acting as his A.D.C. It was an extraordinary situation for two leading advocates to have propelled themselves into. Asquith, a firm constitutionalist, perfectly convinced that no decent House of Commons man could possibly envisage 'direct action', had no notion of how to handle these role-playing prima donnas of the law courts whose passionate oratory had by this stage stirred even themselves.

But what was even more astonishing than the government's survival was Rufus Isaacs' own position. Despite the Marconi Scandal the most extraordinary thing had happened: he was on the verge of being appointed Lord Chief Justice. Naturally this could hardly be without misgivings. Webster was ill, and clearly about to go. From Asquith's point of view the situation was extremely difficult: Rufus Isaacs had already been passed over for Lord Chancellor, and an Attorney General had a much clearer right to the post of Lord Chief Justice if it fell vacant while he was in office. On the other hand King George V found it all 'most embarrassing'. As his Private Secretary put it, 'if the P.M. does not recommend him, it will be tantamount to condemning his action' but 'if Mr Asquith *does* recommend him, he will be equally condemned by the other side.' On the other hand, both King and Prime Minister agreed that he could not remain on as Attorney General, as the government's chief legal adviser, in the Cabinet. All in all, the safest thing to do seemed to be to appoint him, and on October 22 Rufus Isaacs took office.

Rufus Isaacs

Rufus himself must have been extremely nervous at the reception his appointment would get. He motored down two days before to see the retiring Lord Chief Justice, who said a few kind words about the Marconi affair. When he came out, his son Gerald noted, his father was 'for some moments quite unable to speak'. Carson congratulated him. 'My dear Ned,' wrote Isaacs in reply, 'you behaved to me with all that nobility which is characteristic of you – there I must leave it.' Riddell told him he looked like William Murray: 'You have the same high cheekbones and, if I may say so, a nose that looks as if it had had a knock.' He told Riddell (with, I hope, his tongue in his cheek) that he had been looking through Campbell's *Lives of the Chief Justices* and had been 'much impressed by the succession of brilliant men who have occupied the position'. But it was not all such easy going. When Haldane, who as Lord Chancellor had sworn Isaacs in at the Law Courts ceremony of installation, went on to make several complimentary remarks, a barrister interrupted to shout 'Speak for yourself, Lord Haldane!' The Conservative press was scathing. But the bitterest attack of all came from Rudyard Kipling in a poem that he did not dare publish until years later, though it went the rounds in London at once. There is no record of Rufus Isaacs' reaction to it but he must have heard it and he would certainly have known the story of Gehazi, the servant of Elisha, who received the reward for Naaman's work in the vineyard.

> 'Whence comest thou, Gehazi
> So reverend to behold
> In scarlet and in ermines
> And chain of England's gold?'
> 'From following after Naaman
> To tell him all is well,
> Whereby my zeal hath made me
> A Judge in Israel.'

> Well done, well done, Gehazi
> Stretch forth thy ready hand,
> Thou barely 'scaped from judgment,
> Take oath to judge the land,
> Unswayed by gift of money
> Or privy bribe more base,
> Of knowledge which is profit
> In any market place.

So the verses went on, one more scathing than the next. Was Rufus Isaacs fit to become a judge? There is not the slightest indication that he ever put the question to himself. He accepted the post and the by-now automatic peerage, taking the title of his Commons constituency, Reading. The following summer, however, there was to be no annual holiday in Marienbad.

Rufus Isaacs was Lord Chief Justice of England from October 22, 1913 to January 1, 1921. The extraordinary thing about this comparatively long period in office is how little of it he spent doing the job for which he had been appointed and for which he was being paid. Lloyd George kept him occupied with other duties, and duties which Rufus Isaacs generally speaking found more congenial. At first it was a question of helping the Chancellor of the Exchequer understand bills of exchange and the international money market, then of going over to France with him to visit the Front. When Asquith formed a Coalition government and Lloyd George moved to the Ministry of Munitions, Isaacs was appointed head of the Anglo-French Financial Mission to the United States. Thereafter, at Lloyd George's side, he took part in all the negotiations with American visitors to England and in the great political drama, started by the resignation of Sir Edward Carson as Coalition Attorney General, that ended in December 1916 with the forcing out of Asquith and his replacement as Prime Minister by Lloyd George. He tried to persuade Asquith to serve under Lloyd George in a now Conservative-dominated Coalition, as Lord Chancellor.

'I answered,' noted Asquith, 'that I must use preferably plain language since he had raised the subject . . . He and others had better understand clearly and at once that under no conditions would I serve in a Government of which Lloyd George was the head. I had learned by long and close association to mistrust him profoundly. I knew him to be incapable of loyalty and lasting gratitude. I had always acknowledged, and did still to the full, his many brilliant and useful faculties but he needed to have someone over him. In my judgment, he had incurable defects, both of intellect and character, which totally unfitted him to be at the head. The Lord Chief Justice with rather a wry face acquiesced.'

Only the most formal of acquiescences no doubt, for Lloyd George was far more suited to lead a country at war than Asquith; and from Isaacs' point of view, however much respect he may have had for Asquith, Lloyd George was his close associate and indeed by this time his patron. In a sense it was true that Lloyd George 'needed to have someone over him'. That someone, however, was not Asquith but Isaacs who understood him and in many ways guided him. Indeed when Isaacs finally left his side, Sir Alfred Mond, admittedly a prejudiced witness (his daughter had married Isaacs' son) commented: 'It means the end of Lloyd George. Directly Reading's calming influence is withdrawn from him, his power will decline.' And so indeed it did, though no doubt not for that reason alone.

Meanwhile the Lord Chief Justice's astonishing career continued. In September 1917, he was in Washington for the third time, sent there largely on Northcliffe's urging, as High Commissioner to deal with financial affairs and particularly with the President's *eminence grise*, Colonel House. Indeed Isaacs was himself described, justifiably, as Lloyd George's Colonel House. Then in January 1918 he replaced 'Springy' – Sir Cecil Spring Rice, famous for the undiplomatic remark that 'If the President is the Shepherd of his people, then McAdoo (The Secretary of the Treasury) is his crook' – as Ambassador Extraordinary to the United States of America. As Ambassador he remained until

May 1919 when he returned to England to resume his duties as Lord Chief Justice. To sum up, for almost five of the seven years during which he officially held the post of Lord Chief Justice, Rufus Isaacs was in spirit and often in body an absentee landlord – a quite extraordinary state of affairs such as no previous war in which England was involved had ever occasioned.

When he did sit in judgment, he was not a particularly distinguished judge. His great strength had always lain in his head for details (in particular for numbers) and in his cool remorseless cross-examinations: his one great prosecution as Attorney General, that of the arsenic fly-paper poisoner Arthur Seddon, defended eloquently and possibly rightly but unavailingly by Marshall Hall, had been a case in point. To a judge these qualities were not particularly helpful. He was no jurist, and he did not have that burning interest in either the principles of law or the practice and precedents of common law that seems to be indispensable for a great judge. Yet he was, as one might expect, cool and fair – even in the handling of the one great state trial over which he did preside, the trial of Roger Casement.

Sir Roger Casement was tried for high treason before the Lord Chief Justice and two other High Court judges, the ruthless Avory J. and the obscure Horridge J. (cursed with a most unsuitable laughing rictus) in the last days of June 1916. The prosecution was led by F.E. Smith, who had succeeded Sir Edward Carson as Attorney General, the defence by Sergeant Sullivan of the Irish Bar (where they still used that title). The trial opened on Monday, June 26. Rufus Isaacs summed up on Thursday, June 29, the jury retired at almost three o'clock and returned at a quarter to four. The verdict was guilty; the prisoner read a long, passionate and muddled closing speech, the Lord Chief Justice then sentenced him to death. 'To hear the Jew Isaacs pronouncing those dread words,' said Casement's cousin, Miss Gertrude Bannister, 'and ending up with "May the Lord have mercy on your soul" was so awful and revolting to me that I murmured "And may he have mercy on yours".' Sergeant Sullivan appealed on a point of law. The Court of Criminal Appeal, in which Mr Justice A. T. Lawrence sat with four brother judges, heard the arguments of the advocates on July 17 and 18; they dismissed the appeal. Sergeant Sullivan then tried to appeal to the House of Lords; for this the Attorney General refused the necessary certificate. 'You had a good point there,' F. E. Smith is alleged to have told one of the defence lawyers two years later, 'but if I had given my *fiat* and the Lords had quashed the conviction on such a technicality, feeling against Casement was so strong that it might have brought the government down.' The agitation for a reprieve continued. On the night of August 1, the American Ambassador dined at 10 Downing Street. Mr Asquith – he was still Prime Minister at the time – told him that the Cabinet had practically decided not to interfere with Casement's sentence.

Asquith: By the way, have you heard about his diary?
U.S. Ambassador: I have.
Asquith: I should like you to see it.
U.S. Ambassador: I have. What is more I have been given photographs of some of it.
Asquith: Excellent, and you need not be particular about keeping it to yourself.

Next day the Prime Minister personally saw Miss Bannister before the final Cabinet meeting on Casement's case. When it was over, he wrote her the following note: 'It is with sincere pain (and only in compliance with your request) that I inform you that, after very full consideration, the Cabinet today came to the conclusion that there were not sufficient grounds for a reprieve. I need but assure you that I wish it had been possible for them to arrive at a different decision.'

On August 3, at 9 a.m., Roger Casement was hanged in Pentonville prison. Despite Miss Bannister's request for his body, he was buried the same day in quicklime in the prison grounds next to the remains of Crippen and other murderers.

So much for the bare bones, so to speak, of the Casement trial. It will already be clear that, as in almost all treason trials throughout our history, justice was a minor concern of the government of the day and that the result of the trial was almost a foregone conclusion. As in Wilkes' case, the government was unscrupulous in its use of sexual writings to blacken the reputation of the accused. Did the Lord Chief Justice know about Casement's diaries? Almost certainly, though of course only oblique references were made to them in the trial and all lawyers agreed that Rufus Isaacs' summing-up was scrupulously fair, even if it left the jury with almost no option but to bring in a verdict of guilty. But F.E. Smith sent the diaries to Sergeant Sullivan before the trial opened, ostensibly as a gesture of good will. The police had found the diaries, the Attorney General's message went, when searching Casement's Pimlico lodgings; there seemed to be certain passages in them indicating mental instability and the defence might be led to consider a plea of 'guilty but insane'. Sergeant Sullivan waved the file of papers away. 'There is no question of our pleading guilty,' he said. 'I don't see what it has to do with the case. I don't want to read it. Give it them back.' It is of course impossible to believe that F.E. Smith's real concern was to save Casement's life. If Sergeant Sullivan had fallen into the trap and pleaded the diaries as evidence, the prosecution would have been able to introduce other passages and openly prove Casement a rabid homosexual as well as a traitor. It is equally impossible to believe that the Lord Chief Justice was not well aware of all the Attorney General's moves.

Times of course had changed since the days of Popham and Coke. It was not Rufus Isaacs and F.E. Smith who presided over Casement's interrogation, though – traditionally enough – he was imprisoned in the Tower in an airless, verminous cell. He was taken out to be interrogated at Scotland Yard by Basil Thomson of the C.I.D., virtual founder of M.I.5, and Captain Reginald Hall, of Naval Intelligence, undoubted founder of Britain's Secret Intelligence Service. He was interrogated three times, courteously, though both Thomson and Hall favoured a court martial and a quick execution by firing squad. But Sir Roger Casement had been a very distinguished man, famous for his Consular reports on slave labour in the Congo Free State and in the rubber plantations of Brazil. There could be no question of shooting him out of hand.

Was Casement guilty of treason or was he not? He was a British subject, a Protestant Irishman much in the Parnell mould, and an undoubted idealist. He had retired from the Consular Service at the early age of forty-eight a year before the outbreak of war. As an Irish patriot he had travelled to Germany to try to recruit an Irish Brigade from the prisoner-of-war camps there, to assist in the uprising planned for Easter 1916, but without success. Carson's Ulster Volunteers had landed arms in Ulster most successfully; the Irish Volunteers, formed in reaction, were virtually unarmed. Casement came in with a German arms vessel, the *Aud*. It was intercepted and sunk. He swam ashore in Kerry and was there arrested. In actual fact his intention in coming to Ireland in person had been to contact the leaders of the newly formed Irish Republican Army and to persuade them to call off the hopeless rising. Was he a traitor or was he a patriot? George Bernard Shaw, his fellow Irishman, advised Casement to admit all the facts, defend his conduct as an Irish Nationalist, and claim to be treated as a prisoner-of-war. Those were Casement's own inclinations; he was convinced that the British government, following the execution of Padraic Pearse and the other 'Easter Martyrs' would not want to hang him and thereby create another martyr, but merely to discredit him. But his counsel for the defence disagreed.

It had been difficult for Casement's solicitors to find an eminent barrister prepared to undertake his defence. It is simply not true, now or then, that lawyers accept any brief any more than that London taxi-drivers accept any fare, whatever the theory of the matter may be. Sir John Simon (whom Asquith had nicknamed 'The Impeccable') refused. Gordon Hewart, the other prominent practising K.C. now so many were in official wartime posts, also turned the brief down. Sergeant Sullivan had almost no experience of the English Bar; he first met Casement on June 12, and they immediately found that they totally disagreed on the right line for the defence. Sergeant Sullivan wanted an entirely technical defence, calling no witnesses and only allowing Casement to make an unsworn statement from the dock – in which case he would not be subject to cross-examination. Casement wrote despondently to his solicitor:

> The tribunal I am before here in London can only give one verdict – judge, jury, prosecution are all one – and to take this case to them with any hope of acquittal or annulment or pleas of error or on technical grounds is comparable to referring the question of the keeping of Lent to a jury of butchers ... In any case, as G.B.S. says, I have nothing to lose – I've lost it already – and the only thing to fight for now is the case of others, not my life or fate at this trial.

All the same Casement gave way, and Sergeant Sullivan prepared the technical defence. It was this: that Casement was charged under Edward III's Treason Act of 1381, but wrongly charged. For the Statute defined treason as 'levying war against the King or being adherent to the King's enemies in his realm giving them aid and comfort in the realm or elsewhere.' Forget the words 'or elsewhere', and it will be immediately clear what Sergeant Sullivan's line was: that Sir Roger Casement had not been in the King's realm – indeed he had been in Germany – and so was not guilty of treason within the meaning of the Act. What of 'or elsewhere'? Well, argued Sullivan, that only applied to 'giving them – the King's enemies – aid or comfort'; a traitor still had to be inside the realm, that is to say inside the jurisdiction – as for instance Philip Howard was when he prayed as a prisoner in the Tower for the success of the Spanish Armada. That could, indeed had been, construed as giving the King's enemies 'aid and comfort' but if Philip Howard had been in Spain and done the same thing, then he was not guilty of high treason because under mediaeval law there was no such offence as treason outside the realm.

The trouble with this line of argument was that it had not been applied in the most recent well-known treason trial, that of Colonel Lynch, who had fought for the Boers and that it went against both Coke and Hale's expoundings of the common law. But Sergeant Sullivan argued when the case went to appeal that the Lords of Appeal should treat these comments as mere expressions of personal opinion, that there had been no recorded decisions of treason outside the realm before 1903, and that the Lynch case had been wrongly decided. During the argument that followed it turned out that Mr Justice Darling and Mr Justice Atkin had been to the Public Record Office and examined under a magnifying glass the Parliamentary Roll on which the Norman-French statute had been originally inscribed. They had found breaks in the form of transverse lines, the mediaeval scribe's equivalent of commas. They concluded that the statute basically read 'levying war against the King or being adherent to the King's enemies in his realm or elsewhere' and that the phrase 'giving them comfort', was definitely a subordinate, explanatory clause. And this indeed would seem to be the common-sense point of view, though heaven knows there have been prisoners enough who have been convicted or acquitted on even more trivial technicalities. But it is hard to disagree now with the deadly conclusion of F.E. Smith's 'hanging' speech for the prosecution.

'I have, I hope, outlined these facts without heat and without feeling. Neither in my position would be proper, and fortunately neither is required. Rhetoric would be misplaced, for the proved facts are more eloquent than words. The prisoner, blinded by a hatred to this country, as malignant in quality as it was sudden in origin, has played a desperate hazard. He has played it and he has lost it. Today the forfeit is claimed.'

It is harder to appreciate F.E. Smith's comment in an interview he gave on January 14, 1918: 'Nothing,' he said, 'gave me greater delight than the execution of Casement.'

18

The Hewart Intrigue

In January 1919, Rufus Isaacs was back from America, in Paris for the Peace Conference staying with the British delegation at the Hotel Majestic. One day he and his son went out for a walk in the Bois and ran into F. E. Smith, who had just been appointed Lord Chancellor, and with him Gordon Hewart, who had stepped into F.E.'s shoes as Attorney General. As they walked along, Smith or rather Lord Birkenhead as he had now become (at forty-six the youngest Lord Chancellor since Jeffreys), began to bemoan the fact that he would never conduct a case in court again. 'Look here,' interrupted the Lord Chief Justice, 'you and I are both too young to be stuck for the rest of our lives as Judges. Let's go back to the Bar.'

It seemed a splendid idea, though unprecedented – not that they were the sort of pair to be worried by that. As the whole group were discussing it with animation, they stepped off the kerb, no doubt looking the wrong way as Englishmen in Paris tend to do, and were nearly run down by a large car coming round the corner. 'Good God!' cried F.E., 'The Lord Chancellor, the Lord Chief Justice and the Attorney General; what a bag! And how grieved the Bar would have been!'

As Gerald Isaacs put it, 'The incident at least served to remind them that their reappearance as competitors in the courts might not be too welcome to their successors.' His father was, he found, very depressed in 1919 and 1920 – not only depressed but restless and irritable. He was bored with being a judge. He hated even the physical inactivity of sitting on the Bench, complaining to Gerald that it made him feel as if he were only fit to be wheeled up and down the sea-front at Brighton in a bath chair. His wife's health was bad, he had sold Foxhill, he no longer had the excitement of elections to look forward to or the to-ings and fro-ings of active diplomacy (also he undeniably missed those smart uniforms in which he had looked so well). His golf-companions, Lloyd George and Riddell, found that he was losing his old spring and vitality. The beginning of the Michaelmas Law Term in 1920 coincided with his sixtieth birthday. 'The zest had gone out of his life,' wrote Gerald, 'and he could see nothing ahead of him but stagnation and decay.' Or as Gordon Hewart with greater precision put it, he 'had learned to enjoy the glitter of diplomacy' and was longing to get back to it.

Gordon Hewart was the latest of Lloyd George's minor cronies, at this time just fifty years old, an ugly, hard-working Lancashire man, small, bulky, with a head too big for his body. He was a tailor's son from Bury (a step up, certainly, from a barber's son from Canterbury), educated at Manchester Grammar School, then at Oxford. He had tried his hand at freelance Radical journalism on coming down, writing rather brilliant attacking sketches and articles for the *Manchester Guardian* and for *The Star* as well as for his local Bury paper. He had married, switched to the law, was called to the Bar in 1902, practised in Manchester, lived in suburban bliss in Didsbury, and was soon earning £7,000 a year. 'Never neglect the little fishes' was his motto for success: he was adroit and subtle as well as industrious.

He first stood for Parliament in a Manchester by-election in June 1912. C.P. Scott was chairman of his election committee and threw all the weight of the *Manchester Guardian* behind him. It was a rowdy election. F.E. came down to support, vigorously, the Conservative candidate. 'Smith is a gentleman of certain intelligence and some education,' said Gordon Hewart reproachfully. 'He had not therefore the usual excuse of those who employ Tory Billingsgate.' He lost. He took silk. He moved to London and next year, in East Leicester, he tried again. Parliament was preoccupied with the Marconi affair, the country with the heat wave and Ascot races. Ramsay MacDonald disowned the Socialist candidate, and on June 27, 1913 Hewart was elected, though the Liberal majority had fallen by over 4,000 votes. It was hardly a triumph and he did not at first do particularly well in the House. But his legal practice in London was successful, Lloyd George knew of him, and when Lloyd George ousted Asquith in December 1916 he invited Hewart to become Solicitor General. Hewart had been very much an Asquithian but he had no compunction in accepting. He now found himself F. E. Smith's number two in the Tory-dominated Coalition government; they were both Lancashire men, both opportunists, they got on excellently, and Hewart's public speaking much improved, as his combative natural self-confidence asserted itself.

1918 meant, inevitably, a General Election. Lloyd George

leading his Liberals and Bonar Law leading the Tories went to the country hand-in-hand, swept to victory as leaders of a continued Coalition government, and as a result presented the kingdom with that disastrous parliamentary majority described, so fairly and unforgettably, as being composed of 'hard-faced men who have done well out of the war'. Asquith and his Independent Liberals were almost eliminated; and Asquith himself lost his seat. Gordon Hewart, however, was re-elected. Lloyd George was impressed with Hewart's astuteness, he knew that he himself would be largely involved in European politics and often abroad, and he wanted Hewart to run the House of Commons for him, as a Coalition Liberal. This involved removing the obvious chief government spokesman in the Commons, F.E. Smith, a Conservative. So the Prime Minister had offered F.E. the Attorney Generalship again, but without a seat in the Cabinet. F.E. to Lloyd George's delight refused it on those terms. 'Then how about the Woolsack?' suggested the Prime Minister insidiously. F.E. accepted the tempting bait, went to the Lords, and by doing so, indirectly ruined his own political career, to die, out of office and out of spirits, a few years later at the age of fifty-eight.

As Attorney General, Gordon Hewart established himself in the legal profession – there were successful prosecutions of murderers, often ex-Army officers, and of the unctuous Charles Farrow, of Farrow's Bank – in London's social life, and in the political world. At the time he had a sense of humour, unusual in a lawyer, and always a help in the Commons. On one occasion Horatio Bottomley, whose war-profiteer activities were common knowledge, brought up the question of the Kaiser's trial.

Bottomley (indignantly): Are we to understand that His Majesty's government is unwilling to prosecute this male-factor because he is highly placed?

Hewart (equably): No, Sir. The Honourable Member is not entitled to suppose anything of the sort. His Majesty's Government is prepared to prosecute *any* malefactor, however highly placed. (Sitting down, but then half rising again), The Honourable Member must not be impatient!

This was the sort of easy mastery that made Hewart indispensable to Lloyd George in the House. But Hewart coveted the position of Lord Chief Justice. In the ordinary way he knew that he had no chance of achieving it: Rufus Isaacs was only ten years older than he was, and in the prime of life, judicially speaking. Only if he died or retired while Hewart was Attorney General would Hewart have any claim to the succession. Death seemed hardly on the cards, except perhaps by a fortunate motor-accident; retirement was the last thing in the mind of a man as restless and vigorous as Rufus Isaacs. But it was precisely because Isaacs was so restless and vigorous that Hewart had hopes. It was common knowledge that Isaacs had been angling for the continued Ambassadorship to the United States, or the Ambassadorship to France, which had fallen vacant. But Lord Carson, the Foreign Secretary, would have none of it.

However an even more glittering prize than the Embassy in Paris was looming. Lord Chelmsford, Viceroy of India, was about to retire. Fortunately from Rufus Isaacs' point of view, his wife's mother had died in October 1920 at the age of eighty-one. His wife Alice used to visit her almost every afternoon, and it would have been impossible to persuade Alice to go and live abroad for five years if old Mrs Cohen had still been there; for Rufus was devoted to Alice. Indeed Alice's own ill-health was a great worry. On the other hand India, the Viceroyalty, a new field for his talents, what an opportunity at the age of sixty! Austen Chamberlain had refused; the new Secretary of State for India, Edwin Montagu, in any case wanted for Viceroy a man with political instinct, not a mere administrator however efficient, and Lloyd George agreed. The choice was Rufus Isaacs, if he would accept; failing him, Winston Churchill.

Rufus wanted to accept, but there was a difficulty. He had always lived extravagantly, and he would need money when he had to retire. He had not been long enough Lord Chief Justice to earn his pension, and the Viceroyalty however prestigious, lasted for only five years. What was he to do, how was he to live when he came back from India?

Lloyd George and he, the old cronies who had seen so many financial waves pass over their heads in previous times, cooked up, it seems, a splendidly disreputable scheme, though they were now Prime Minister of the United Kingdom and Lord Chief Justice of England respectively. The plan was this: that Rufus should become Viceroy, an elderly judge should be put in as a stop-gap Lord Chief Justice for five years, then when Rufus came back to England – after all, he would be only sixty-five – he would resume his post as Lord Chief Justice: better by far that, in any case, than a once-and-for-all payment (even if it could be obtained) for the Lord Chief Justice could go on and on until he died of old age. Lloyd George was quite confident of his ability to find an aged judge: there was Mr Justice A. T. Lawrence, generally recognised as sound, if dull. He had presided over that long-ago libel action where Rufus Isaacs had appeared for the allegedly adulterous Lloyd George, so in a sense 'old Lorry' was a very old friend. He was, admittedly, in his late seventies but at that age Lawrence would be so grateful for the totally unexpected appointment that he would surely agree to any conditions – even the extraordinary one that the Prime Minister intended to impose; that the judge should sign a non-dated letter of resignation which Lloyd George could use at any time.

Such at least appears, from the available evidence, to be the thinking behind the Lloyd George-Rufus Isaacs plan, though how far it was a concoction of Lloyd George's fertile brain and love for complicated intrigue and how far Rufus Isaacs was himself involved are totally unclear. I would myself guess that Rufus Isaacs preserved a cool, rather detached attitude, hoping that it would work out but careful not to become too involved in the wheeling and dealing himself. And yet what seems utterly uncontrovertible is that they both set out to bamboozle the potential fly in the ointment, Gordon Hewart.

The greatest difficulty was that F.E. Smith urged his friend Gordon Hewart in the strongest terms to insist on his right to the succession. As Lord Chancellor, F.E. was rather more than the honorific first lawyer in the land; he was administrative head of the judicial profession, with the right to appoint all judges – bar the Lord Chief Justice. That was the Prime Minister's decision. But the Tory-dominated Coalition government could not afford to ignore the views of a front-rank Tory politician, in favour of a scheme which in any case appeared to be illegal under Section 9 of the Supreme Court of Judicature Act, 1873. For, as F.E. put it to the Prime Minister, judges hold office for life, independently of any political influence; 'The proposal under contemplation, however, would make the Lord Chief Justice a transient figure subject to removal at the will of the government of the day and the creature of political exigency.' However, Lloyd George was not the type of man to be impressed by legalistic or juridical arguments, nor the type of politician to allow himself to be outmanoeuvred by the youngish ex-Galloper. From November 1920 onwards there was an extraordinary amount of coming and going, all aimed at softening up Hewart. He was taken aside by Lloyd George in the Commons, had meetings with Rufus Isaacs in the Lord

Chief Justice's Curzon Street home, was summoned to Downing Street, was promised this, told that, squeezed when F.E. (and an equally indignant Carson) were both abroad, and at last realised that 'from the beginning to the end of these conversations, I had not received a scrap of paper – not even a letter from the Prime Minister or from Rufus for the purpose of making an appointment.' Lloyd George had managed it all with great good humour, flattering Hewart, promising him a great future in the Commons, assuring him he was indispensable, offering him the reversion of the Lord Chancellorship should it fall vacant (as if F.E. would resign or die!), and appealing to his better nature. 'But,' he explained to a baffled and indignant Hewart, 'if Rufus cannot become Viceroy without your claim ing at once to become Chief Justice, then it is very certain that he cannot become Viceroy.' Lloyd George, naturally enough, did not explain the full plan to his subordinate. He merely suggested that an elderly judge should become Lord Chief Justice for a few months, and promised Hewart that he would succeed the elderly judge before the next General Election in any case.

Hewart was no mean manoeuvrer himself. He objected that he himself might die first or his dear old father might die 'in whose lifetime the appointment would be infinitely more valuable in my eyes'. Furthermore – and this was an argument that could not fail to impress Lloyd George – the public, and the profession, would think that he had been passed over. 'Neither personally nor as trustee of the rights of the great office of Attorney General can I assent to that suspicion,' declared Hewart.

It was Rufus Isaacs' turn to play on the Attorney General's nerves. He pretended totally to understand Hewart's position and one morning, 'looking like a man who has just seen a ghost', told Hewart that it was all over: he had breakfasted with Lloyd George and Bonar Law, they had made it clear that Hewart could not be spared in the Commons, therefore he Isaacs had had to accept the inevitable. Another man was going to be appointed as Viceroy; it was very cruel, but there it was.

In the end the combined pressures wore Hewart down. He gave way and accepted what he believed to be Lloyd George's proposal. 'You are a very good fellow, Hewart,' said the Prime Minister, 'as I have always known.' So in January 1921, Rufus Isaacs was appointed Viceroy of India. 'You know what I have really been doing,' Lloyd George had the gall to add, 'is this, my dear Attorney. I have been getting Rufus out of your way.' There was a house-party in honour of the Viceroy-designate at

Chequers. Rufus Isaacs took Riddell's arm after dinner. 'I will never look at a law report again if I can help it! I never want to see another one!' he whispered in his ear.

Alfred Lawrence

It was not however until April that the Viceroy-designate and his wife sailed for the land he had last visited as a ship's boy and Mr Justice A.T. Lawrence was officially promoted. 'You ought to have been the welcomed rather than the welcomer,' said the new Lord Chief Justice rather charmingly when he was congratulated by the Attorney General. He had been seventeen years a High Court judge, two more than were needed for the famous pension. The Viceroy cabled his congratulation from Lahore to 'My dear A.T.' and wrote to Montagu, the Secretary of State for India, rather over casually perhaps, 'I notice that Gordon Hewart has apparently fallen into line and that the P.M. has had his way.'

This was not entirely true. The P.M. had given Gordon Hewart a pledge, guaranteed by his Coalition partner Bonar Law, and he did not in the end go back on it. Possibly with Lloyd George out of sight was out of mind; and Rufus Isaacs in India meant much less to him than Rufus Isaacs in Curzon Street or at Chequers. There was also the undoubted fact that the Viceroy's views on Constantinople and the Turkish problem cabled to Montagu and released by him to the press caused an unholy row. This was not Rufus' fault; Montagu had not been authorised to release the cable and was in fact sacked for doing so. But one can hardly blame Lloyd George, struggling for political survival, if he reflected that had the cable never been written it could never have been published. Furthermore, what was he to do? Out of office, he would have no right to appoint a new Lord Chief Justice and he could hardly see his successor either using the letter signed by Lawrence or, even if it were used, appointing one of Lloyd George's oldest friends, a man who besides would notoriously be filling the office of Lord Chief Justice only to earn the pension. Nobody trusted Lloyd George; but at least to Hewart he kept his word.

As early as the end of 1921 it was obvious that the Coalition government was crumbling. It was the Irish settlement that ruined it, the setting-up of an Irish Free State by Lloyd George and Churchill, with the support of F. E. Smith, and their long-drawn-out negotiations with the terrorists and murderers of Sinn Fein, whom they had so often condemned in public.

On December 14 'King Carson' rose in the Lords to denounce with particular vehemence his old friend F. E. Smith, now sitting close to him on the Woolsack.

'Of all the men in my experience that I think are the most loathsome,' he said, 'it is those who will sell their friends for the purpose of conciliating their enemies.' By January 1922 while Lloyd George was in Cannes, the newspapers were bubbling over with talk of a General Election. 'I shall resign as Attorney General and give up politics altogether if I am not appointed Lord Chief Justice,' Hewart had threatened a little early. And in March the Lord Chief Justice, coming up to London to finish a case adjourned from the previous day, opened *The Times* and read in it of his own resignation. His clerk, Curtis, was furious but he himself did not seem to have been particularly perturbed. He retired to his beautiful home in Breconshire and lived on for a further fourteen years, till at the more than ripe old age of ninety-three when fishing in the River Wye he slipped, fell and was washed away – a rather fine end for one of the longest-lived but shortest in office of our Lord Chief Justices.

Gordon Hewart

Thus as Lloyd George's almost ultimate political appointment, Gordon Hewart became in March 1922 Lord Chief Justice of England. After his swearing in, conducted by F.E. Smith, his successor as Attorney General, Sir Ernest Pollock, addressed the assembly.

'Some of us here,' he proclaimed, 'recall the eloquence of Sir Alexander Cockburn; we admired the scholarship and polished diction of John Duke, Lord Coleridge. These talents we know you to possess. To the learning and quick apprehension of Lord Russell of Killowen, the industry of Lord Alverstone, the patience of Lord Reading we know that you will add the great qualities of your immediate predecessor who through five decades . . .' Etc., etc., etc. Possibly on all such occasions this sort of thing is unavoidable though for blather and hypocrisy the legal profession in its moments of self-congratulation must be unrivalled by any but the clerical. But in the peculiarly undignified circumstances surrounding Hewart's appointment, which must certainly have been known to at least all the senior members of the legal profession present, a display of obsequiousness that would have done justice to Francis Bacon seems even now, even so many years later, extraordinarily out-of-place. Particularly as, even without hindsight, the qualities attributed to the new Lord Chief Justice were so grotesquely inaccurate.

'He has acquiesced without a murmur in a policy that has made a hell of Ireland; he bears his share of responsibility for the harrying and tormenting of afflicted Russians. Seemly work, all this, for a man calling himself a Liberal.' That was the *Daily Mail*'s editorial opinion of Gordon Hewart's role in the Coalition government. It was just as well for him, perhaps, that he was promoted out of politics a few months before the bitterness finally burst into the open, in October 1922.

The pure Liberals, the Asquithian Liberals, felt that the Coalition Liberals under Lloyd George's leadership had betrayed all Liberal principles. But to the general surprise it was the Conservative back-benchers who finally brought down the government. On October 10 the Cabinet had decided to call a General Election and go into it as a united force: the Conservative leaders Austen Chamberlain, Balfour and F.E. were sure they could carry the party with them. But a few days later on Thursday, October 19, came the famous meeting in the Carlton Club when the almost unknown President of the Board of Trade, Stanley Baldwin, stigmatised Lloyd George as 'a great dynamic force . . . a very terrible thing'. The back-benchers voted by 187 votes to 87 to go into the General Election alone. F.E., never a good loser, left the meeting with a dark scowl on his face, knowing that it meant the end of his time as Lord Chancellor. Lloyd George resigned that afternoon, and Bonar Law, promising 'tranquillity', was re-elected Leader of the Conservative Party. He formed a government – the 'second eleven' Churchill christened it; 'second-class brains', F.E. rather more hurtfully called them.

There was certainly one first-class brain there, that of 'a clever lawyer called Pig', as Douglas Hogg K.C. had once been described. He became Attorney General. A much less impressive man took the number-two legal post of Solicitor General. This was Thomas Inskip, a pleasant priggish nonentity who had defeated Ernest Bevin at Bristol Central in the General Election four years earlier. He was the son of a Bristol West Country solicitor, educated at Clifton, then at King's College, Cambridge, where he had managed a Third in Classics. He had been called to the Bar in 1899, and lived a bleak bachelor's existence at the National Club until just before war broke out, he had married Lady Augusta Orr-Ewing, widow of an M.P. and daughter of the Earl of Glasgow. That marriage made his career. He had not been much of a success at the Bar, but he moved to Eaton Square, became a K.C., spent most of the war working under Captain Hall in Naval Intelligence, and so on to Bristol Central and the Solicitorship General. Very much the third eleven was Thomas Inskip, but he was, everyone agreed, a very pleasant fellow, fond of shooting, fishing and sailing and now he had, via his wife, a 'place' in Scotland; also, at 6 foot 3, he was suitably distinguished-looking – indeed he thought everyone shorter than himself somewhat deformed. Furthermore, he was not without ambition. When Baldwin took over as Conservative Prime Minister from a dying Bonar Law and offered this nonentity a puisne judgeship, Inskip refused it; he was hoping, quite rightly as it turned out, for greater things.

Meanwhile the new Lord Chief Justice was disgracing himself in the Court of Criminal Appeal. Sir Henry Curtis Bennett was defending Edith Thompson, who with her lodger-lover Bywaters was accused of murdering her husband. 'You have got to get into the atmosphere of this case,' said Curtis Bennett. 'It is no ordinary case you are trying. These are not ordinary people that you are trying. This is not an ordinary charge of murder. This is not an ordinary charge against ordinary people. It is very difficult to get into the atmosphere of a play or opera, but you have to do it in this case. Am I right or wrong in saying that this woman is one of the most extraordinary personalities that you or I have ever met?' Hewart was having none of this: in his summing-up he called it 'an essentially commonplace and unedifying case', and referred to Edith Thompson's letters as 'a remarkable and deplorable correspondence, full of the most mischievous and perilous stuff'. The general opinion of lawyers was, and is, that Edith Thompson was hanged for her letters, and that she had no idea that Bywaters was going to stab her husband to death on the night of October 3. Both appeals were dismissed. Bywaters in Pentonville constantly asked whether Mrs Thompson had been reprieved. He walked erect to his death on January 9, 1923, not knowing that Edith Thompson, heavily drugged and shaven, was being carried, a moaning wreck, to the gallows in Holloway at the same time. As a fellow judge has written with studied moderation, 'It seems a high price to pay for some letters.'

Hewart gave an even more flagrant example of his moralising outlook and his utter inability to understand modern trends, particularly in sexual matters, very soon afterwards when in February 1923 Dr Marie Stopes, of birth-control fame, sued a young Catholic doctor, Dr Halliday Sutherland, for libel. There was no question of a cool summing-up such as Rufus Isaacs would have undoubtedly achieved. Hewart started off by putting his own views to the jury: 'Sex teaching, yes, but in cold scientific language, not mixing up physiology with emotion, not teaching such truths as need to be taught in the language of adjectives and rhetoric, but with austerity, with coldness, stating the facts and no more.' He was constitutionally incapable, then or later, of keeping his own prejudices out of a case. 'You know the passages, you know the content, you know the circulation of these books. Can you say that they fall short of being obscene publications?' (*Married Love* and *Wise Parenthood* were the books in question, and Hewart had made the point that both had sold extremely well.) 'Upon you in this case falls the guardianship of public morality as far as these publications are concerned.' Even though the jury after four hours awarded Dr Stopes £100 damages (which would at least have saved her from paying the costs of the case), Hewart found for Dr Halliday on various technicalities. He seemed unable to realise that he was now a judge, not an advocate. Even Henry Cecil, author of *The Brothers-in-Law* and usually such a tolerant observer of legal frailties, writes 'He was a shockingly bad judge.' Admittedly the next year Hewart came out with that rightly memorable dictum: 'Justice should not only be done, it should manifestly and undoubtedly be seen to be done.' His greatest friend, that caricature of a hanging judge, Mr Justice Avory, in one of his few jokes from the Bench suggested slily that the Lord Chief Justice had said 'seem' not 'seen'. It was also Avory, and Hewart loved to tell this story, who tipped a railway porter sixpence for carrying a large trunk. 'Is that all you give?' asked the man. 'No,' said Avory, looking him up and down, 'The last time I was here I had occasion to give a railway porter seven years.' A man who enjoys that sort of story has, I would say, not just an appreciation of puns but an authoritarian attitude.

Hewart undoubtedly enjoyed power, position and the comfort that wealth had brought him. He had bought a solid Queen Anne house in Totteridge, ten miles north of London, and lived there with his wife Sara, a sunny-tempered Bury manufacturer's daughter, to whom he was devoted and his surviving but invalid son. When ten years later his wife collapsed and died at a reception at the Mansion House, Hewart was inconsolable. But within eighteen months he had married again – a vivacious young nurse from New Zealand, Jean Stewart. 'I hope to be at the Law Courts on Tuesday,' he wrote to a friend shortly afterwards, 'full of new zeal and New Zealand.' On the other hand a man who can make that sort of pun has mellowed.

What is rather extraordinary is that almost exactly the same thing happened to Rufus Isaacs. He and his wife Alice had decided, rather touchingly, to set about learning to dance again when they went out to India rather than to have to endure endless seated conversations at the endless Viceregal receptions. Alice, though she had been constantly ill in England flourished in India. At one dance in the Viceregal Lodge in Delhi she asked a newly-arrived A.D.C. what was the name of the tune the band had just been playing. At this precise moment the music stopped. '"I shall remember your kisses", your Excellency,' the young man's reply reverberated, '"When you have forgotten my name".' Fortunately both she and Rufus had a strong sense of humour – which helped him with Gandhi. On the other hand, she certainly enjoyed the ceremonial and the magnificence: her shopping trips to the Simla bazaars accompanied by an escort of the Viceroy's bodyguard were famous. There were those who thought that she was, and had always been the spur that had forced her husband to success.

'She was very sweet to me as always,' noted a guest, Lady Lee, 'and is certainly a remarkable woman. Indeed she must always have been the driving force behind Rufus and but for her passionate ambition for him I do not believe that in spite of his ability he would have risen to any heights at all. He himself enjoys life so much that he could have enjoyed it equally without a career, and he has a sweetness of nature which would have been satisfied with very much less. They say he consults her on every question and when he *does* make up his mind, it is often she who has made it up for him.'

It is not surprising perhaps that Alice Cohen, who had risen in her lifetime from plain Mrs Isaacs to the Marchioness of Reading (for Rufus was created a Marquess when they returned to England and Curzon Street after their five years of Viceregal splendour), did not last long back in a cold climate. She died on January 30, 1930, after a long illness and was buried in the Jewish cemetery in Golders Green. Rufus was lonely and depressed; his public career seemed to be at an end, for of course there was no question of ousting Gordon Hewart now, and Lloyd George had been out of office for over seven years. It was some consolation that his son's father-in-law, Sir Alfred Mond, like himself a former Liberal M.P. and a Jew, had found a place for him as a director of the vast conglomerate he was now forming into I.C.I.; and more consolation when Mond, then Lord Melchett, died in the year of Alice's death and Rufus became president of I.C.I. But within less than a year there was even greater consolation: at the age of seventy Rufus married his dead wife's secretary, a woman of thirty-seven, Stella Charnaud.

'I went to lunch by myself with Miss Stella Charnaud,' Lady Lee had noted in her diary, 'who succeeded Miss Fitzroy as Private Secretary to Lady Reading. She is a nice girl, clever and hard-working, whose job is by no means an easy one looking after anyone so ill and yet so imperious as the Vicereine.'

Who knows if Stella Charnaud played the role of Lloyd George's secretary, Frances Stevenson to the ageing Rufus? What Alice and Rufus' son, Gerald, wrote in a discreet reference to his new step-mother is this:

Hitherto he had always looked many years younger than his real age; now he seemed suddenly an old man ... After their return from India, Stella Charnaud had changed her functions and become my father's secretary instead of my mother's. My mother had become deeply attached to her but recognised not only that my father's need took precedence of her own but that Miss Charnaud could find greater scope for her exceptional gifts in his work than in hers ... They were married early in August. The transformation in him was immediate and immense.

There is one more death that occurred about this period and that ought to be recorded. Mollie Schuster was the daughter of yet another of those German-Jewish immigré families who made their way in English life and were honoured by the Liberals. Her father, Sir Felix, a banker, was converted to Christianity and created a baronet. She was musical, rather hysterical and became a bad, embittered mother to her three daughters: it was extraordinary that she chose to marry a rather obscure, rather physically unattractive little man, short, thickset and taciturn, called Rayner Goddard. But he was certainly very, very English; that was perhaps why. His background was surprisingly similar to Thomas Inskip's. His father was a solicitor, a partner in Peacock and Goddard, a stern father who had subjected him to a bracing upbringing. The young Goddard had been educated at Marlborough, which he loved; he had become Captain of the Rifle Corps there, gone up to Trinity College Oxford, won a full Blue for athletics, been called to the Bar in the same year as Thomas Inskip, though he was a year younger, and had practised on the Western Circuit. He married Mollie Schuster in 1906. She died in May 1928 when he was Recorder of Bristol, leaving him with a household of women – three daughters aged twenty, eighteen and fifteen and two unmarried sisters. He never remarried for, wrote one of his daughters, he was 'genuinely frightened of women, though easily influenced and strongly attracted by them'. She also thought that his views on life had remained static, fixed at 1914, rigid and reactionary – though he had been a good warm-hearted father to his three girls, only beating them when they thoroughly deserved it and then only with the flat of his hand. He loved Dickens, Trollope and Hardy. Though he had once done very well in a sensational murder trial in Wiltshire, winning an acquittal, he had since then turned aside to banking law and practice. He had become a good, competent lawyer. He was known as 'Doggie' by his colleagues. He was not in the public eye. The only reason that he consented to stand in the General Election of 1929 was that he had been born and bred in Bassett Road in Kensington, and the sitting Conservative M.P., Sir William Davison, also a barrister had just been divorced. So the good ladies of Kensington persuaded the lonely, widowed Rayner Goddard, Q.C., to stand as an Independent Conservative for the constituency of South Kensington.

This, the May 1929 General Election, was an extraordinarily interesting contest. It was the first time ever that there was a genuine three-cornered contest between the three great parties, each putting up candidates in almost all constituencies, each party led by a well-known politician who had at one stage or another in the past decade been Prime Minister: – Baldwin for the Conservatives (he had just been Prime Minister for a calm five years), Ramsay MacDonald for the Labour Party (he had headed the first Labour government ever, which had survived with Asquith's support for nine months) and Lloyd George for the Liberals (Asquith had at last retired, and for the moment the Liberals were reunited). There was absolutely no knowing who would win, especially as there was a new element – the Flappers' Vote. For the first time women under thirty were to have the vote, and that added five million incalculables to the election. It also made Rayner Goddard extremely sorry he had ever agreed to set foot on the hustings. The Flappers christened him 'the Purity Candidate' and heckled him mercilessly. 'Have you ever committed adultery?' they called. That was Goddard's first and last venture into parliamentary politics. The Independent Conservative came bottom of the poll in Kensington with 6,365 votes, and the poor man retired with relief from the humiliation of public exposure to the comparative peace and quiet of commercial law work and the minor judgments that a Recorder's job involves. 'Quite a few people thought it was a frightfully unhappy incident from Rayner's point of view,' commented an old friend.

The result of the General Election was that for the first time ever the Labour Party won more seats than any other party – 288 as compared to the Conservative's 260. Baldwin at once resigned; Sir Douglas Hogg who had become Lord Chancellor (as Lord Hailsham) shortly before was also out; and so was Thomas Inskip who had stepped into Hogg's shoes as Attorney General. Ramsay MacDonald took over as Prime Minister and Lord Shirley became the first genuinely Labour Lord Chancellor. But before long the tidal wave of the Great Depression was sweeping over the new government. A dramatic run on the pound was followed by a decision to reduce wages and benefits all round. No one protested louder at the thought of any cut in salary – twenty per cent was proposed – than the judges, who 'contended that they had a contract of a very solemn kind under which the government undertook to pay them £5,000 a year,' and that, moreover, as Lord Sankey rather plaintively reported to the P.M., 'it was a contract which was confirmed by Statute: that any diminution of salary was a breach of contract and a breach of faith, and so forth.' More importantly, the cutting of unemployment benefit went against the whole socialist philosophy and on August 23, 1931 nine of Ramsay MacDonald's Cabinet Ministers resigned. At once Ramsay MacDonald followed.

Here was an extraordinary situation. The Liberals had fifty-nine M.P.s, and had been supporting the Labour government. The obvious alternative government was therefore a Conservative government with Liberal support. The King sent for Stanley Baldwin – but it was a Sunday, Baldwin was not at home, and he could not be traced. Lloyd George, leader of the

Liberals, had been ill and was recovering from an operation. Who went to see the King? The wily old newly zestful Rufus Isaacs, who had become Liberal leader in the Lords, and the acting leader of the Liberals, his old friend from Marconi days, Herbert Samuel. What was the result? The formation the next day of a National government, 'to deal with the national emergency that now exists' – to save the pound and balance the budget – with a tiny Cabinet of ten ministers, four Labour (Ramsay MacDonald was retained as a figurehead Prime Minister and Sankey as Lord Chancellor), four Conservative, and two Liberal. And who were the two Liberals? Why, none other than Herbert Samuel and Rufus Isaacs.

So, a few days before his seventy-first birthday, that extraordinary man Rufus Isaacs, ex-barrister, ex-Lord Chief Justice, ex-Ambassador, ex-Viceroy, became one of the key Cabinet ministers in what was in effect a government of national salvation, took over the Foreign Office, and moved into the Foreign Secretary's splendid room overlooking St James' Park. From Lloyd George's point of view what could not be cured had to be endured; and he put a brave face on it all, though he knew that it was a government in which he personally would never have a place. Within a month it was in crisis: the United Kingdom left the Gold Standard; and the Liberals split three ways. A month later the National government went to the country for 'a doctor's mandate': they won an overwhelming victory, 531 seats in all. But of those seats no less than 473 were won by Baldwin's Conservatives. In name it continued to be a National government, right up to and into the Second World War. In fact, however, it was a Tory government, with Labour and most of the Liberals in opposition. But Ramsay MacDonald (who stayed on as figurehead Prime Minister for three and a half years) led thirteen National Labour supporters; and Sir John Simon headed thirty-five National Liberals.

Simon's reward came immediately after the General Election. He was appointed Foreign Secretary – and Rufus Isaacs, too closely linked to Lloyd George for Baldwin's taste, was dropped: dropped on November 9, out of office after only two and a half months, out of office for ever. He took his young wife Stella on a long holiday abroad, to Palestine and Egypt, then the following year to Washington and Ottawa. It was not until June 1934 that he was awarded a consolation prize that exactly suited him: the position of Lord Warden of the Cinque Ports, with its splendid ceremonies, uniforms, flag and castles. He spent most of the last eighteen months of his life at Walmer

Castle. In October 1935 he had a bad attack of cardiac asthma. His old friend and enemy Edward Carson was dying of leukaemia nearby, near Ramsgate. They sent each other messages and good wishes for recovery. Carson died first, before the end of the month; Rufus never realised how ill he was. 'These attacks are a horrid bore,' he told Gerald on the evening of December 29, 'I am afraid that, when I am fit again, I shall have to give up some of my work instead of taking on anything new.' He died the following afternoon. He was cremated at Golders Green. He left £290,487 11s 9d.

19

Inskip for P.M.?

At the conclusion of a smart function in London the toast of 'His Majesty's Judges' was proposed. The Lord Chief Justice rose to reply. 'When I accepted the invitation to respond to this toast,' he said, 'I was not certain at what stage of the evening I should be required to speak.' In fact he had been left to the tail-end, much to his annoyance. 'So I prepared two speeches – a short speech and a longer speech. As the night is young, I propose to deliver them both.' There was almost an audible collective groan. 'I will give you first the shorter speech – "Thank you." Now I will deliver the longer speech. "Thank you very much."'

Hewart could be equally short and snappy in court. 'Counsel for the appellant has raised six points in support of this appeal,' he adjudged on one occasion. 'In the first point there is nothing, and the same applies to the others. Five times nothing are nothing. The appeal is dismissed.'

Brevity and a mastery of the English language were his good points as a judge. The other side of the coin was a delight in caustic comments, directed mainly at barristers to many of whom he would take a personal and ill-concealed dislike, for no apparent reason. Occasionally his unpleasing irony was turned on the accused. 'Rust,' he told a wretched young man who had been acquitted in the face of his summing-up and to applause from the public gallery, 'you have been extremely fortunate in your jury.' During the summing-up itself he would insist on total silence and often order the doors of his court to be locked until he had finished. He could hardly bear to be contradicted or, worse still, found wrong on points of law. 'Why on earth did you differ from me yesterday?' was the phrase with which he would greet judges from the Court of Appeal if they dared to overturn his judgments. His temper and his behaviour were becoming so notoriously bad that the weaker-minded among his colleagues would avoid him for fear of a scene. Insomnia and illness increasingly kept him, to the relief of many, away from the courts. When he was in court, it seems true to say that his aim was to see justice done. But his methods became more and more deplorable; and were deplored.

From the start of a libel action in which William Cooper Hobbs, a former solicitor's clerk, sued the *Liverpool Evening Express* for accusing him of blackmail, Hewart took a violent dislike to the plaintiff. Sergeant Sullivan (who also disliked his client) wrote of the Lord Chief Justice's 'continuous snarl' when Hobbs came to give evidence. Then Hewart attempted to bring the case hurriedly to a close.

Sergeant Sullivan: Before your Lordship allows that result to be arrived at I must insist upon my right to address the jury.
Lord Chief Justice (losing his temper):   Insist? That is a strange phrase to use to me. Please don't use the word 'insist' to me.

In a hostile atmosphere the court listened to Sergeant Sullivan's speech, often rudely interrupted by Hewart. The jury awarded one farthing damages. Hobbs was suing fifteen newspapers in all, and next day the case to be heard was that against the *Nottingham Journal*. Sergeant Sullivan asked, very reasonably, that a new jury should be empanelled. The Lord Chief Justice refused. At that Sergeant Sullivan gathered up his papers, bowed stifly, and followed by his junior and his client left the court. 'It looks like part of a transparent manoeuvre,' commented Hewart.

Late that evening, after he had entered judgment for the *Nottingham Journal*, a mere formality in the circumstances, he learnt that Sergeant Sullivan had immediately gone to the Court of Appeal and had been granted leave to appeal over the refusal to empanel a new jury. Worse was to follow. Sergeant Sullivan appealed for a re-trial in the *Liverpool Evening Echo* case on the grounds that the Lord Chief Justice had prejudiced its conduct, misdirected the jury and sanctioned defamatory statements by the defending counsel, Birkett. This time Hewart had, as he realised himself, gone too far. The Court of Appeal ordered a new trial, though 'with regret'. The case never actually came to trial again; it was settled out of court; but Hewart's reputation suffered.

Norman Birkett, a fashionable, rather pleasantly suave Liberal lawyer, had very nearly become Solicitor General in the first, brief National government – in which Rufus Isaacs had been Foreign Secretary. But Thomas Inskip, the Conservative, took the post instead, though he had formely been Attorney General, even though therefore this was a demotion, a step down the ladder. Birkett in any case lost his seat in the General Election that followed and, disillusioned, gave up political life. On November 5 and 6, 1934 he appeared for the radical London paper The *Star*, in a case tried by the Lord Chief Justice. On the other side the counsel for the plaintiff was Sir Patrick Hastings, also a disillusioned politician – he had been Attorney General in the first brief Labour government, and it was his unwise decision to prosecute the editor of the *Workers' Weekly* for incitement to mutiny, the so-called 'Campbell Case' that had brought that government swiftly tumbling. Hastings was fierce, beetle-browed, biting. He appeared, surprisingly enough in view of his past record, for Sir Oswald Mosley. On the other hand it was perhaps not as surprising as all that. Mosley had been the great white hope of the Labour Party and had left it only when appalled by his comrades' lack of vision.

Hewart had as a young man written for The *Star* himself. He had been a Liberal M.P. like Birkett, a Liberal Attorney General and a Lloyd George nominee as Lord Chief Justice. On the other hand he and Hastings – and indeed Mosley – had certain characteristics in common: vigour, a delight in invective, and a propensity to attack, however different their political views, at least officially, had become. The point at issue was whether Mosley had or had not claimed that he and his Fascists 'would be ready to take over the government with the aid of machine-guns when the moment arrived', as The *Star* had reported. Naturally the trial, in the tense atmosphere of a Europe already dominated by dictators and would-be dictators, became a matter of intense public interest. Birkett's purpose in a long, masterly cross-examination was to prove that Mosley intended to overthrow the democratic government of the country by force. But he could not shake the brilliant, agile Sir Oswald.

'Did you or did you not believe him, whatever you may think of his opinions?' Hewart summed up. 'Did it appear to you that he is a public man of no mean courage, no little candour, and no little ability? Did you believe him? He was cross-examined for a long time? Did anything come of it?'

There could be no doubt at all which way the Lord Chief Justice wanted the jury to go. They found for Mosley and awarded the then very large sum of £5,000 in damages. Birkett, shaken, appealed for a stay of execution.

'No, Mr Birkett,' said Hewart, 'Not on any terms whatever. If you want a stay you must go to the Court of Appeal. I entirely agree with the verdict of the jury.'

It could perhaps be argued that this trial showed the Lord Chief Justice's potential for impartiality.

A month later, on December 11, 1934, Hewart adjourned an important case in his court, drove hurriedly to the House of Lords and there, almost incoherent with rage, delivered his maiden speech. The somnolent peers, stirred to a sudden realisation that something most unusual was happening, listened in total silence and with an attention closer than anything Hewart could have hoped for at his own summings-up. It was a sensational speech. In it a long-standing judicial quarrel was brought out into the open. The Lord Chief Justice openly and violently attacked the Lord Chancellor, Lord Sankey, and particularly scathingly and sensationally the permanent head of the Lord Chancellor's Department, Sir Claud Schuster. Schuster (a relative of Mollie Goddard), had been brought into his post almost twenty years earlier transferring from the legal side of the Civil Service and had seen seven Lord Chancellors come and go; he was certainly of enormous backstairs influence. Hewart disliked him thoroughly, always referred to him as 'Shyster' and suspected him, perhaps not without reason, of aiming to set up a continental-style Ministry of Justice.

'I have not been for twelve years the Lord Chief Justice of England with my eyes closed,' Hewart told the astounded Lords. 'That scheme has the strong backing from something that is called the Lord Chancellor's Department. It is perfectly obvious why. If that is done it will no longer be necessary to have in this country a lawyer as head of the judiciary. You might have a successful merchant, and that person would be ignorant of the personnel of the Bar. When a vacancy occurs he would have to turn to somebody to ask whom he should appoint. That person would be a permanent official of the Lord Chancellor's Department. The plan, persistently carried on, is as clear to me as my own face in the mirror.'

The Lords adjourned in a state of shock. Three days later the debate was resumed. Hailsham, with all the pugnacity of his son, attacked Hewart. Then came the current Lord Chancellor, Sankey, whom Hewart suspected of being in Schuster's pocket. Tempers rose, flared, but after three hours of elderly heated debate died down.

'What is the public to make of all this?' asked *The Times*. 'They may say that the question who, if anyone, has insulted whom is of no interest to them; that its public ventilation is unedifying.' Ordinary people were not against Hewart, but, little realising the rivalries and bitter enmities that have always existed at the top of the legal profession and in particular, ever since the days of Coke and Bacon, between the Lord Chief Justice and the Lord Chancellor, they were bewildered. But the Lords did not like Hewart. A friend once asked him if he often went there. 'No, not often,' he replied. 'I went there the other day. The first man I ran into was a man who had been gaoled for issuing a false prospectus, and the second was a man who had been fined heavily for company irregularities. I said to myself, "This is not the House of Lords. This is the House of Frauds!". No, I don't go much.'

He made himself popular in the House of Commons, though, at almost exactly the same time. A.P. Herbert, an old friend of Hewart's, was bringing what was almost as farcical an action as those recorded in his famous fictional accounts of *Misleading Cases* against the Kitchen Committee of the House of Commons. Hewart determined to hear it in his own court. When he had married Jean, he had only asked her for two favours: 'Don't read A.P. Herbert's *Holy Deadlock* and don't play bridge.' The fun came from the fact that the pompous Sir Thomas Inskip, now back as Attorney General, was appearing for the Kitchen Committee and that the whole case was, so to speak, the wrong way round. A.P. Herbert, the individualist, was out to impose the strict enforcement of the licensing laws and Inskip of all men, was arguing that the bars should be kept open at all hours.

As a schoolboy, Inskip had objected to the use of 'language' in the scrum. His parents had not allowed him to attend theatres or dances. So far from reacting against them, he had – after reluctantly abandoning his ambition to become a lay missionary – turned to a life of almost exemplary do-goodings: President of the Lord's Day Observance Society, of the Crusaders Union of the YMCA and of the Church Pastoral Aid Society. His most impassioned speech in the Commons had been in the Prayer Book Debate of 1927. His doctor had sprayed his vocal chords especially for the occasion. 'Well, the day came and it was a day! I have never known anything like it,' he wrote in his diary. Simon congratulated him on 'the most solid and powerful piece of pleading from inside the Church of England that I have come across in the whole controversy.' Everyone, he noted, was very kind. But it was, as things usually were with Inskip, all ineffective. 'When I sat down between the P.M. and Winston, the P.M. said nothing but Winston – who had announced he would vote for the measure – said to me as I sat down, "Well, Solicitor, that's a very fine speech, a fine massive speech" – and he didn't vote.' He was a non-smoker, and almost a non-drinker. Still – despite an extraordinary beginning in which he brought up murder on the floor of the House of Commons –Inskip did win his case against A.P. Herbert. Hewart sat with Avory, and both enjoyed the ponderous schoolboyish jokes they felt fitted the occasion.

So the Commons bars remained wide open, and – *post hoc*, not *propter hoc* – in March 1936 Stanley Baldwin offered Inskip the newly-created post of Minister for the Co-ordination of Defence. 'As regards the Inskip appointment,' noted a General, 'I have only one comment and that is "Thank God we are preserved from Winston Churchill."' That certainly was Stanley Baldwin's reason for an appointment so surprising that, as Michael Foot put it, echoing general public opinion, nothing so extraordinary had been heard of since Emperor Caligula appointed his horse a consul. Inskip was sincere, honest but almost utterly inept. When Baldwin retired he transferred his loyalties without question to Neville Chamberlain, supported appeasement and supported Munich. But, by September 1938, he was becoming doubtful about Simon. 'Simon finished by his usual shower of compliments to the P.M. – all fully deserved but somehow or other coming from Simon's lips they gave an impression of soapiness and flattery which they do not deserve.' And a year later, when war broke out, he had become equally doubtful about Chamberlain. 'I don't like the P.M.'s methods. He is a *"faux ami"* and I think I shall be glad to be out of his inner circle.' The quite extraordinary thing is that by then Inskip was being seriously considered as a possible replacement for Chamberlain, as wartime Prime Minister, that is to say as war leader of Britain and the Empire.

Earlier that year, on January 17, 1939, Neville Chamberlain had sent for him, thanked him for doing a "thankless job" and offered him the Dominions Office, which with some hesitation he accepted. Then the question of Inskip's future career had come up.

'I don't propose to ask Maugham to resign so that I could offer you the Lord Chancellorship,' Chamberlain said. 'He has done very well, and though I gave him no promise I should not like to turn him out before the election. In the ordinary way I should propose – if we come back after the election and I am P.M. – to offer you the Lord Chancellorship then. That will save you from having to make the decision now as to whether you will go to the Lords or continue in the House of Commons. You can then keep open – if you like – your chance of being and I think he always afterwards regretted that he became Lord Chancellor.'

Inskip: Do you mean that you want to keep my way open to become P.M. if I want to take it?
The Prime Minister: Yes, that is what I mean.

This was probably at the time merely Neville Chamberlain's soft soap. He had not the slightest intention of giving up his position, and certainly not to a man like Inskip. Yet, when on Friday, September 1, just after Hitler's invasion of Poland, Chamberlain asked all members of the Cabinet for their resignation, there is incontrovertible evidence that the Duke of Devonshire was urging Inskip on to make a bid for Chamberlain's place. 'I told Eddy I would think about it but there was no certainty that Neville would ask the King to make me P.M., and in any case I had no ambition to be P.M. Eddy said that was one reason why so many people thought I was the man they wanted.'

Admittedly Eddy Devonshire had been Inskip's own Under-Secretary at the Dominions Office, so his move could be considered merely a long-shot attempt to further his own career; but it was not such a long shot as all that. By making Inskip Minister for the Co-ordination of Defence, Stanley Baldwin had virtually appointed him Deputy Prime Minister; and in July 1936, when it became clear that Baldwin would soon retire, Lloyd George, an unbiased witness in this context, estimated that eighty per cent of the Conservative back-benchers would support Inskip for the succession, as opposed to twenty per cent for Neville Chamberlain. So in September 1939 perhaps the Duke was right: perhaps many people in both Houses did feel that Inskip's time had come. But how could such a mediocrity ever have been considered? No doubt his transparent honesty and his loyalty had endeared him to many; also his massive appearance, his height, must have helped to give, literally, the impression of a man of stature. It is awful to think of what would have happened if Inskip had been manoeuvred into the top position. But Chamberlain with his usual brisk administrative efficiency quickly disposed of the threat. On the Friday he had asked for Inskip's resignation. On the Monday, with the war at last officially declared, he sent for Inskip at 7.30 p.m.

'I won't keep you a moment,' he said, 'I want you to become Lord Chancellor.'

'Very well,' said Inskip, and in sixty seconds he was out of the room. He lasted longer than his master. Chamberlain fell on May 10, 1940, the day Hitler invaded the West, Churchill took over as Prime Minister, and the following evening Sir Claud Shuster telephoned shortly before the nine o'clock news to say that Simon's appointment as Lord Chancellor was about to be announced. Inskip was switched back to the Dominions Office again, and, as a sop, offered the Leadership of the House of Lords as well: he made no protest at all. It was of course a time of war. But perhaps Tom Inskip's greatest value to all three Conservative Prime Ministers under whom he served was his immense amenability.

The Lord Chief Justice meanwhile had been becoming even more querulous and quarrelsome. He had quarrelled with Inskip's predecessor and Sankey's successor as Lord Chancellor. 'I am going to see Maugham today,' he told his wife, 'I am going to give him a piece of my mind.' But just as the scene in the House of Lords had ended with handshakes all round (he had even shaken Claud Schuster's hand, though that was probably by mistake), so the quarrel with Maugham died down. 'Well, I saw him,' he told his wife the same evening, 'and I told him. But I really couldn't be angry with him. I've seen nine Lord Chancellors come and go, and I just can't help being sorry for them. After all, they don't last for long but the Lord Chief Justice goes on for ever.'

One thing that absolutely infuriated Hewart was any talk of a fixed retiring age for judges. When Avory died, well into his eighties, he commented sternly, 'He had died as he resolved to die – in harness.' That was said as much for himself as for his old friend. (He also commented, 'No sweeter spirit ever adorned the earth' – an extraordinary summing-up that no doubt would have tickled Avory and amazed the many guilty men he had sentenced to death, if either he or they had been alive to hear it.)

He quarrelled with the judges of Probate, Admiralty and Divorce. The average man, he said, if he rose early, had a light breakfast and brought his mind to bear upon the matter could between Sunday and Monday get up the whole English law on divorce. Those colleagues never forgave the implication that they were useless adjuncts. He nearly quarrelled with Count Grandi, Mussolini's Ambassador, for kissing Jean's hand. 'Damned Italian,' he growled instead. He lost his sense of humour when Low produced a merciless cartoon of him. Next day a young barrister asked Hewart to autograph a copy. 'Get out!' he yelled. 'Get out! You bloody fool!' He quarrelled in February 1938 with an elderly lady who reproached him for having sentenced the 'Mayfair Boys' to be flogged – twenty strokes of 'the cat' and fifteen strokes of 'the cat', the first time he had ever imposed this fearsome punishment. 'Scoundrels!' he retorted. 'Scoundrels, all of them! . . . The fact that they are public schoolboys makes their crime all the worse. They should have known better.' He could relax, but only at the Reform Club or the Savage in the company of male friends, and occasionally on the long sea trips with his wife that became more frequent until the war put a stop to them.

By then his health was failing. Again and again he announced that he would never retire. In January 1940 he confirmed a death-sentence passed on two I.R.A. bombers. He was due to go down to Lewes Assizes to try some more I.R.A. terrorists. A twenty-four-hour police guard was placed on his home. When the time came, he was too ill, and rumours of his retirement increased. In February all the same he took the Kingston Assizes. The barristers saw that he could not concentrate or follow the issues. Breathing was difficult, and he could hardly write. For long periods he sat with his eyes closed, struggling to keep conscious. Finally he muttered to his clerk Skelton, 'I think I am going to faint.' Skelton persuaded him to step down and be driven home.

At home, at Garden Hill, he fought his illness and in May even appeared in court on four separate days. But by September he had been forced to give in. Though he was almost too weak to write, he penned a note to Churchill saying that some time in the near future he intended to retire. But he gave no date. He secretly hoped that he would recover.

That gave one of his many enemies the long-awaited opportunity for an exquisite revenge. One day in October Schuster telephoned him, from the Prime Minister's office, to announce that for convenience's sake his resignation would be announced in the papers the following morning.

'But you cannot do that,' Hewart stammered. 'I have not told any of the judges yet.'

The government could, and did. Inskip was switched around again and at once, without argument, appointed Lord Chief Justice in Hewart's place: the first ex-Lord Chancellor to accept such a move.

Thomas Inskip

Hewart lived on until May 5, 1943. He died as he had lived,

outmanoeuvred. 'Damn,' were his last words, expressive as always, 'it's that cuckoo again.'

Inskip was, by contrast, fair and impartial – but as in all offices totally undistinguished. His own health began to fail towards the end of the war. He resigned on January 21, 1946 and died on October 11 the following year at Godalming. Hewart had left £150,947. Inskip, who had given much away anonymously to charity, left £17,079.

Sir Claud Schuster wrote to his widow:

I have always thought Tom the very model and example of what a lawyer ought to be. *The Times* says he was lucky. I have always thought him the opposite. If he had received the Chancellorship as was his due, when Maugham was appointed, if he had become Chief Justice earlier in times when he would not have been hampered by war conditions, he might have had, indeed I am sure he would have had, in either office a long and fruitful reign. In each case fate was against him. And in addition he had to bear, as he did in silence, the burden of reproaches from ignorant people for the impossible task set him in the Ministry of Co-ordination of Defence.

One wonders what pithy comment Hewart would have made on *that*.

20

Goddard and His Successors

Lord Goddard died on May 29, 1971, at the age of ninety-four. Ten days later Bernard Levin published a long attack on the man, his style, and his work, in *The Times*. It was headed 'Judgment on Lord Goddard'. 'Goddard as Lord Chief Justice,' wrote the notorious columnist, 'was a calamity . . . Goddard's influence on the cause of penal reform was almost unrelievedly malign; with a coarse callousness (his fondness for dirty jokes can hardly have been entirely coincidental) there was not only a desperate ignorance of the springs of human behaviour (including of course his own) but what seemed like a positive pride in his ignorance.' The correspondence column of *The Times* was full of Goddard letters, pro and contra, for days after. It was not Bernard Levin's first or indeed most violent assault. On May 16, 1958, shortly before Goddard's retirement, a book review on a biography of the Lord Chief Justice appeared in *The Spectator*; it was by Bernard Levin and entitled 'Brother Savage'. In it Levin referred to Goddard's 'intellectual megalomania', 'the girlish emotionalism which seems to be his only reaction to such subjects as capital and corporal punishment', and his views in general described as a 'wretched blot on the English legal system'. 'Lord Goddard,' Levin summed up, 'walks hand in hand with ignorance on one side of him and barbarism on the other.'

Previous Lord Chief Justices are history, and readers will regard their antics, foibles or flaws of character with detached amusement or the superiority of modern times. But Goddard is not history. Goddard is still, at least to many of the middle-aged, a folk-hero; his views on hanging, and indeed on birching and buggery, are still shared by a great many of the country's population. The passions aroused by the most famous murder trial over which Goddard presided, that of Craig and Bentley, are not yet dead and gone, unlike Bentley himself (Craig who pulled the trigger and killed P.C. Miles is, through an accident of his date of birth, alive, well, and believed to be living a decent life).

The best biography of Lord Goddard is undoubtedly Fenton Bresler's book, published in 1977; Lord Denning wrote the Foreword to it and summed up in his own way Goddard's merits: first his quickness of perception, next his despatch of business, thirdly his mastery of the court, and fourthly his clearness and forcefulness in speech. He was 'the very embodiment of the common law. He seemed to have it in his bones.' Then there was another thing. 'He looked the part too. His keen brown eyes, his rugged features, his firm mouth and strong chin showed the character of the man. It showed that he was one who would uphold the law. He would "clear out the innocent and convict and punish the guilty". He would stand no nonsense from anyone. He would pronounce the sentence. He would see that it was carried out. All respected him. Some feared him. None dare scorn him.'

Fenton Bresler leaves the last word in his book to Goddard's own daughter, Lady Sachs: 'I am so very glad that one of the more merciful dispensations of Providence has been to enable all of us to forget the last cruel years of extreme old age with its attendant infirmities and to remember with love an able-bodied, mentally vigorous, contentious, cantankerous, prejudiced, fair-minded, infinitely compassionate and lovable human being.'

So there we have the case for the defence. In a way it seems as improbable as the case for the prosecution. Levin, the minor Junius of his day, was out, quite rightly, to deflate the self-righteous, and Fenton Bresler has proved that Goddard was none too scrupulous in his means. But what sort of argument is Denning's statement that Goddard was the embodiment of the common law? It presupposes a premise which many including Levin would contest: that the common law is an excellent thing to be the embodiment of. It is a colleague's argument – as is the reference to Goddard looking the part. Yet, that said, one sees what Denning means: there was a bulldog, Churchillian quality about Goddard that stands out in all his photographs or portraits. As for Lady Sachs, there again one sees what she means – even when she introduces the paradox of Goddard's prejudice co-existing with his fair-mindedness. Mentally vigorous and cantankerous, certainly: but with the phrase 'infinitely compassionate and lovable' filial piety seems to have run off at least the public rails. Perhaps one should settle for a now two-edged phrase, and simply label Goddard, if label there must be, a quintessential Victorian – but without the pomposity. This is therefore the most difficult chapter to write in all this book, especially as only twelve years have passed since Lord Goddard's death. Sixteen pages is too short a space in which to give a reasoned verdict on so controversial a figure. But I must add that, even given ten times the space, I am not sure what my own verdict would be.

Goddard was born on April 10, 1877, a successful Kensington solicitor's son. He was educated at Marlborough, which he always loved, and at Oxford. He practised at the Bar with moderate success. In May 1928 he lost his beloved wife Molly. He never remarried. He was looked after by his three daughters until, one after another, they married and then by a housekeeper. In the spring of 1929 he made his solitary, ignominious incursion into politics as 'the Purity Candidate' in the 'Flappers' Election'. In 1932 he was sworn in as a High Court Judge before Lord Chief Justice Hewart. In 1936 he won a certain notoriety for sentencing Nurse Waddingham to death. In 1938 he was promoted to the Court of Appeal when the number of Appeal Court Judges was increased from five to eight. He was often bored and impatient at having to work as part of a team of three. 'When sitting as an appeal judge he would sometimes say to one of his colleagues "Balls" in a voice I am pretty sure others in court would have heard,' recalled his junior colleague, Lord Hodson. In June 1944 his kinsman, Claud Schuster was retiring after twenty-nine years as permanent secretary in the Lord Chancellor's Department. 'Don't retire or think of retiring,' he wrote with a touch of bitterness to Goddard, 'there is plenty more milk in the coconut.' Next month Goddard was made a Law Lord, a Lord of Appeal in Ordinary and a Life Peer – Lord God-damn, Churchill nicknamed him. He was at the top of his particular tree, restless, under-active, with nothing, despite Schuster's advice, but retirement and death to look forward to. He was, after all, sixty-seven. Then a year later came a dramatic event which affected the country but which he could hardly have expected to affect him in any sense except emotionally: Labour won the General Election. Tom Inskip, the Lord Chief Justice, was ill, ineffective and in any case, as a professional Tory politician, out of sympathy with the new administration and an obvious candidate for retirement. But Goddard was by no means his obvious successor.

The obvious successor was a Labour lawyer. The trouble was that there were so few Labour lawyers of any repute or standing. The veteran turncoat Jowitt had been appointed Lord Chancellor by Attlee. His Attorney General was the immaculate

Hartley Shawcross, fresh from his triumphs at the Nuremberg War Trials. In fact Shawcross, though so comparatively young – only forty-five – was, in the best (or worse) of traditions, offered the post of Lord Chief Justice. 'I don't suppose you'll want it, will you?' said Attlee.

'In fact,' said Hartley Shawcross later, 'I didn't want it. It would be stupid to say that I would never want it at any time. It was about the only judicial appointment I would ever have been likely to accept. But I did not want it then.' He never obtained it later but he did fill other high offices. At the time there were fears of not only a 'Red' government but also of a 'Red' judge, a commissar in scarlet and ermine presiding over what might become a 'people's criminal court'. Extraordinary fears they seem now, though Shawcross was considered rather a militant in his day. Theoretically at any rate an alternative was Sir Patrick Hastings, who had been Attorney General in the short-lived 1924 Labour government. But directly or indirectly Hastings had been responsible for the fall of that government, by agreeing to the Campbell-*Workers Weekly* prosecution. Besides, he had resigned his seat as a Labour M.P. and concentrated on fashionable advocacy and play-writing.

So that left the judges themselves. Mr Justice Travers Humphreys had been virtually acting Lord Chief Justice during Inskip's time; but he was seventy-nine and nobody wanted a repeat of the A.T. Lawrence performance. Goddard eventually emerged, partly because he was extremely popular with his fellow judges, and Jowitt consulted them informally, partly because Hartley Shawcross recommended him, though he hardly knew him and partly because there was a general feeling that the post of Lord Chief Justice should cease to be a political appointment, but most of all because of the need for a firm hand in the actual administration of the criminal law. As Arthur Smith, who had been Goddard's chief clerk, tactfully put it, there was a 'feeling of flatness and inertia, of growing disorganisation, which was prevalent in the Royal Courts of Justice, due partly to the war and partly to the illness of the Lord Chief Justice, Lord Caldecote, (Inskip) who was not able to give the dynamic leadership needed at such a time.'

On January 16, 1946 the Prime Minister wrote to Goddard offering him the post. It came, Goddard told his daughter, as a complete and utter surprise. He wrote back, thrilled, the same day to accept. He summoned Arthur Smith to his house in Chelsea Square. 'I thought that he must want me to do some small job for him. But when I arrived there was an air of suppressed excitement about him which I could not miss. I knew that something tremendous must have happened. He took me into his study and gave me a letter to read. It was from Mr Attlee ... I looked up. There was no doubt about what his answer had been.

'Well, Arthur,' he said, 'so we're both back in harness again. I have a thousand things in mind which I want to do, and I shall need your help. Of course I shan't stay for a day longer than three years.'

Rayner Goddard

Goddard was in fact Lord Chief Justice of England for twelve and a half years, from early 1946 to the middle of 1958 when at last, very reluctantly, at the age of eighty-one, he retired. During those twelve and a half years he did not change. From the very beginning he sped up the work of the courts, took a grip on the whole system of judicial administration and developed a strong and coherent Bench. Five and a half years after his appointment, the Conservatives came back to power and Labour's fallen Lord Chancellor, the ineffable Jowitt, a man of sixty-six, asked Goddard to stand down so that he could replace him. If Inskip the Tory had switched from the Lord Chancellorship to the post of Lord Chief Justice, then why should not Jowitt the Socialist? Goddard refused outright to play any part in creating what would have been an interesting new 'tradition'. He dreaded retirement; he had no other interests in life, bar his family and friends, outside the law. He only retired in the end because he feared he was going deaf and, as Fenton Bresler puts it, 'Rayner Goddard was not the sort of man to wear an artificial hearing aid when performing his duties.' By the time he retired he had become an institution. In the words of the Lord Chancellor of the day, 'Never since the days of Lord Mansfield has a Chief Justice left such an impression on the whole country.'

This was true, not because of his administrative capability or his grasp of the common law, nor even because of his judgments. Goddard became an institution because in the public mind he was identified with the fight against crime, particularly violent crime. In the wake of the war, violence had become commonplace and lawlessness had increased. Goddard fought crime; he fought it in the courts, he fought it in the House of Lords and, with the flair of a natural publicist, he fought it via speeches and quotable quotes in the columns of the press. He became a popular hero; an avenger in ermine. Criminals were said to shudder and turn pale at the thought of appearing before him. Within weeks of his appointment he was using – or, to be accurate, threatening to use – the powers of the Court of Criminal Appeal over which he presided to increase rather than decrease sentences. 'The plausible rogue,' wrote Arthur Smith, 'with a long record of offences of dishonesty who appealed against a sentence of three years had it increased to eight. The young villain of twenty-five who had struck an elderly woman again and again on the head with a rubber cosh "in a way that you would beat a carpet" as the victim described it, and then robbed her, was given ten.' The Lord Chief Justice pushed for – and in 1948 obtained – the institution of the system of Preventive Detention, aimed at dealing with old lags at least three times previously convicted and considered to be beyond reform. As usual, he did not mince his phrases or circumlocute. 'It is a good thing when Preventive Detention is given,' he told a magistrates' meeting. 'If you are giving a sentence of Preventive Detention do not be afraid of giving a long term. It is not the least use unless you do give a long term. That for which you are giving Preventive Detention is not the reformation of the prisoner . . . The whole object of Preventive Detention is to give a longer sentence than you would have given for ordinary imprisonment – not simply for the crime but for the protection of the public.' Courts throughout the country took their cue from the Court of Criminal Appeal. Longer and harsher sentences began to be imposed. Goddard always argued that this had cut the crime wave drastically. His reputation as a stern judge was established.

Preventive Detention was instituted by the Criminal Justice Act of 1948. There were other aspects of this Bill which the Lord Chief Justice liked considerably less. When he rose to his feet shortly before tea-time on April 28, 1948 to make his maiden speech in the House of Lords, he must have known that by the time the following morning's newspapers had been read and digested he would be a national and a highly controversial figure.

'I do not propose,' he said in his opening remarks, 'to follow the Right Reverend Prelate in all his bloodthirsty suggestions.' (The Bishop of Truro had suggested that the death penalty should be widely extended, though the Silverman Amendment in the Commons, suspending the death penalty for five years, had been voted a fortnight earlier by 245 votes to 222.) All the same: 'I know that in uttering this sentiment I shall not have the sympathies of everyone but in my humble opinion I believe that there are many, many cases where the murderer should be destroyed.'

This was a powerful, emotive phrase; one that was often to be remembered and quoted in the long, long controversy that continued before the death sentence was finally abolished seventeen years later. Goddard returned to the attack on June 2, describing the conduct of the Home Secretary, Chuter Ede, in already reprieving existing convicted murderers as 'illegal' and 'altering the law by administrative action'. The Silverman Amendment was killed. This was an initial triumph. The Labour government proposed a compromise, dividing murder into capital and non-capital categories. On July 20, Goddard returned, in masterly fashion, to the attack.

'A few weeks ago,' he said, 'your Lordships rejected by an emphatic vote the clause which was sent up from another place abolishing capital punishment. It was agreed on all hands – it has been conceded in another place and certainly in the public press – that the action of your Lordships was in accord with the opinion of the vast majority of people in this country. If that is so, I ask: what is there to compromise about? With whom are we compromising? Why should there be a compromise?'

Here are rhetorical questions that must appeal to anyone who has ever had to deal with the fudgery of official bureaucracy. The Lord Chief Justice went on to put, with equal conciseness, his view of the ideal in criminal law.

'I believe,' he said, 'that in the criminal law there are three very desirable principles that we should all strive to attain. The first is simplicity, the second is certainty, and the third is that, in its application so far as possible, it should neither be fortuitous or capricious.' Who would argue with that? The proposed compromise was, as Goddard proceeded to show, complex, uncertain and uneven, chancy, in its results. It was thrown out by ninety-nine votes to nineteen, and the government gave way. It was a long time since a Lord Chief Justice had achieved such a double triumph in Parliament. This Lord Chief Justice stood, undoubtedly, for the opinions of the ordinary man in the street; he was not the usual mere last-ditch reactionary in a hopeless cause.

On the other hand there was a hopeless cause that Goddard

did, on this occasion, take up. His support for it in the long run caused his reputation more harm than any other of his actions or attitudes. This was his support for flogging. Admittedly it was nuanced.

'It is proposed in this Bill,' he said in his notorious maiden speech, 'to prohibit any sentence of corporal punishment. May I say at once that if there were a prohibition against inflicting corporal punishment with the "cat", not only I but every judge on the Bench would welcome it. I think that the "cat" is a weapon or instrument which ought not to be used. But are we so certain about the birch? Mind you, when people talk about the birch, it is always thought that they are talking about juvenile offenders. I am not. The birch is an instrument that can be used as a very strong deterrent.' And he went on to argue that in cases involving young men of up to twenty-five or thirty years of age it would be far better to give a short sentence and a whipping rather than a long sentence.

This was the point to which Goddard again returned in the House of Lords in the autumn of 1952 at the height of the cosh-boy menace.

'It has always been said by the advocates of the total abolition of any form of corporal punishment: "Give long sentences." Well, long sentences judges must give. I dislike very much giving long sentences to young men of this age, but if they commit these horrible offences you must punish them, and you must punish them severely: and if the only punishment you can give them is imprisonment you must give them a long term.' Goddard's stand had failed in 1948 and all forms of corporal punishment had been abolished. 'In some cases with young people,' he added with nostalgia and reason, 'I shall very much prefer to be able to give them something which would make them remember it for a considerable time, and a short sentence of imprisonment.'

It was the Lord Chief Justice himself who had re-launched the flogging debate with a speech at the Lord Mayor's Banquet on July 3 that year in reply to the traditional toast of 'Her Majesty's Judges'. It was not the last time he was to use the occasion to utter more than the usual platitudes. Five years later he used it to make the most memorable and pithy statement of his whole philosophy.

'People are constantly asking what is the cause of crime,' he said. 'I do not believe that the psychiatrists alone can provide an answer. Personally I think that human nature remains constant. Those who sit in the criminal courts know that it does not change very much, and must come to the conclusion that the age-old causes of crime are still the desire for easy money, together with greed, passion, lust and cruelty.'

That was how Goddard saw human nature, and that was what he was out to punish. Was he wrong?

He was proved wrong by the test of public opinion – a test which he himself always respected – in the two methods of punishment that he himself favoured. Michael Foot in the *Daily Herald* attacked his utterances on corporal punishment in an article headed *O Wordy Judge*. Taking up Foot's points more soberly but with no less passion Lord Chorley, an official in the Howard League for Penal Reform, addressed a public meeting in London. Said Chorley:

> There can be no doubt that the fact that the Lord Chief Justice has been using his position in the way he has, is one of the main reasons why this agitation for restoration of flogging has become so prominent. Of course it is the tradition of Lord Chief Justices. One hundred and fifty years ago Chief Justice Ellenborough, opposing the reduction in capital punishment, said that nobody would be able to sleep in his bed if a man who stole five shillings' worth of goods out of a shop was not sentenced to death. The Bench in this country has a bad record in this sort of thing. It by no means follows that because the Lord Chief Justice wants to re-introduce flogging it would be a good thing to do so.

What had aroused this ire was neither Goddard's speech at the Lord Mayor's Banquet nor in the House of Lords but his comments at an Old Bailey trial on December 3, 1952, when two young thugs, brothers aged seventeen and fourteen, were up before him. 'Nowadays,' he said, 'the cane is never used at school. It would have done them good if they had had a good larruping. What they want is to have someone who would give them a thundering good beating and then perhaps they would not do it again. I suppose they were brought up to be treated like little darlings and tucked up in beds at night.'

These were doubly unfortunate comments, and by them Goddard effectively scuppered his own cause, firstly because by the use of such an outmoded word as 'larruping' and by the whole tone of his remarks he gave journalists and commentators a field-day: here was an eminently Victorian judge acting more like a propagandist, as Michael Foot put it, than a professional arbiter. Secondly because, as it happened, the two brothers came from a broken home and had been beaten almost every night – the precise remedy which, the Lord Chief Justice alleged, ought to have stopped their crime.

On February 13, 1953, the House of Commons took a free vote on a Private Member's Bill to re-introduce flogging. Sir David Maxwell Fyfe, the Conservative Home Secretary, said that the case for its restoration had not been established; Mr Chuter Ede, his socialist predecessor, justifiably congratulated him on the most courageous speech he had ever heard in Parliament; and by 159 votes to sixty-three the Bill was decisively rejected and the issue, probably finally, closed.

But curiously enough, it was also Sir David Maxwell Fyfe who, indirectly and, as it were, against his will, had written the virtual *finis* to capital punishment by refusing to recommend a reprieve for the 'murderer' Bentley. Bentley had been hanged a fortnight earlier, on January 28, 1953, despite Nye Bevan's emotional outburst in the Commons, an outburst which reflected the feeling of most people in the country: 'A three-quarter witted boy of nineteen is to be hung for a murder he did not commit and which was committed fifteen minutes after he was arrested. Can we be made to keep silent when a thing as horrible and shocking as this is happening?' The Lord Chief Justice was the judge who condemned Bentley to death; the evidence is confused and contradictory as to whether Goddard expected or indeed wanted Bentley to hang. On balance it seems that he probably did – *pour décourager les autres*. But the decision and the controversy it aroused – plus other anguishing cases of the time – eventually led, with only muted opposition from Goddard, to the passing of the Homicide Act in 1957 (a compromise solution of the sort he had once so pungently criticised) and, after his retirement but before his death, to the total abolition of the death penalty. So, once again, by his own actions Goddard had indirectly helped to bring about exactly the opposite result to that which he would have desired. It is a paradox of his career.

It would probably be fair to describe Lord Goddard as the last of the hanging judges. He exhibited no glee in sending murderers to the scaffold, though he often used to tell the tasteless story of how he left Winchester Assizes, after sentencing three prisoners simultaneously to be hanged, to be greeted in the streets by a barrel-organist singing the famous words of the Eton Boating Song: 'We'll all swing together.' He showed no signs of regret, still less of remorse. 'Murder is a crime *sui generis*,' he used to say. 'It stands by itself, the man who commits the supreme crime should pay the supreme penalty.'

This went not only for men but in Goddard's view for women, foreigners, the insane and youths. 'I see no reason,' he told the Royal Commission on Capital Punishment which was set up after the government's defeat in 1948, 'why a woman convicted of murder should not hang equally with men.' Admittedly when, as a High Court Judge, he had sentenced Nurse Waddingham to death, he had sat with bowed head and spoken in choking tones. But when in the Chalk Pit Murder Case in 1946 he sentenced the ex-Minister of Justice for New South Wales, Ley, to death, he felt not the slightest remorse, though he admitted that Ley was a pathological case. 'I think it very proper that he should have been hanged,' he told the Royal Commission. When he was taxed with the medical view, which put the blame on Ley's distorted personality, 'If that is the medical point of view,' he retorted, 'I am afraid, frankly, that it does not appeal to me at all. If that is the case, I think it is one of the reasons why he should have been put out of the way.' When in March 1950 he sent down Klaus Fuchs for fourteen years for treachery, he imposed the maximum term and, from the tone of his summing-up, clearly regretted that he could not impose a more final sentence – as the German-born atom spy indeed expected. As for Craig, aged sixteen, there can be no doubt of Goddard's – or most of the country's – opinion. Craig was the youth who pulled the trigger and killed P.C. Miles; Bentley was hanged in effect for shouting 'Let him have it, Chris' when already under arrest, and despite the jury's recommendation of mercy.

At the end of that famous trial Arthur Smith placed the black cap upon the Lord Chief Justice's head.

Derek William Bentley,' said Goddard, 'you are nineteen years of age. It is my duty to pass upon you the only sentence which the law can pass for the crime of wilful murder. The sentence of the Court upon you is that you be taken from this place to a lawful prison, and thence to a place of execution, and there you suffer death by hanging, and that your body be buried within the precincts of the prison in which you shall have been last confined before your execution; and may the Lord have mercy upon your soul. Take him down.'

Christopher Craig, you are under nineteen but in my judgment and evidently in the judgment of the jury you are the more guilty of the two. Your heart was filled with hate, and you murdered a policeman without thought of his wife, his family or himself; and never once have you expressed a word of sorrow for what you have done. I can only sentence you to be detained until Her Majesty's pleasure be known. I shall tell the Secretary of State when forwarding the recommendation of the Jury in Bentley's case that, in my opinion, you are one of the most dangerous young criminals who has ever stood in this dock . . . Take him down.

That was on December 12, 1952. Despite the jury's recommendation Bentley was hanged at 9 a.m. on the morning of January 28, 1953 at Wandsworth Prison by Albert Pierrepoint.

God knows that Labour M.P.s, from Sydney Silverman upwards and downwards, must have bitterly reproached Attlee and Jowitt for appointing such a forthright reactionary as Goddard to the post of Lord Chief Justice. Particularly, no doubt, when in November 1946, less than two years after his appointment, he presided over the libel case brought by Harold Laski, the Chairman of the National Executive Committee of the Labour Party against the *Newark Advertiser*. That case ruined Laski politically and psychologically (and, very nearly, financially); it would be hard to argue that Goddard was impartial. Yet Laski's real enemy was not the judge but the bitingly effective 'Pat' Hastings, appearing for the defendant newspaper. It was not so much that the Lord Chief Justice was politically prejudiced: it was more that he could not bring himself to accept that this was a political trial that required long answers and careful shadings of opinion. Laski thought Goddard was villainously biased in his summing-up. But when next year Bessie Braddock, the well-loved Labour M.P., unsuccessfully sued the *Bolton Evening News* for a much less offensive (and totally unpolitical) libel, Goddard told Arthur Smith that she was the best witness he'd ever heard – straightforward, frank and fearless, speaking without fear or favour. 'I remember thinking,' commented Arthur, 'that it was a pity Mrs Braddock could not have given Professor Laski a few lessons before he went into the witness box, with such disastrous results to himself.'

In the defence of the freedom of individuals and of the courts, Goddard was, in the best tradition, ruthless. He sent down Sylvester Bolam, the Editor of the *Daily Mirror*, for three months for publishing a 'Vampire Killer Caught' front-page story about the acid-bath murderer, Haigh, before Haigh had been duly tried and convicted; the press were very wary of anything approaching contempt of court thereafter. He and his six fellow judges of the King's Bench Divisional Court virtually did away with National Registration Cards – identity cards on the European system that had survived since the war – by their ruling in July 1951, in the case of *Willcock* versus *Muckle*. In the same court he ordered the release on a writ of *Habeas Corpus* of Kathleen Rutty who had been certified by local authority psychiatrists as a 'high-grade mental defective'. 'Persons of whatever age,' Goddard laid down, 'are not to be deprived of their liberty and confined in an institution merely because doctors and officials think it would be good for them.' This was the sort of case with which, Arthur Smith writes with obvious sincerity, 'the Chief was tremendously happy'.

By early 1958, Goddard knew that he ought to be retiring soon. Ought he indeed to have retired much earlier? In a book published in 1961 entitled *Miscarriages of Justice*, the author, a Gray's Inn barrister, C. G. L. Du Cann writes:

> For High Court Judges there is no retiring age, and there is a strong disposition to take full advantage of this wretched fact. Octogenarians cling to office like limpets to a rock . . . A recent Lord Chief Justice, Lord Goddard, held grimly on to his office as an octogenarian . . . Flatterers – legal, journalistic and political – encourage the old men to remain on the Bench by a fulsome admiration of their supposedly undiminished powers and by over-valuing long experience of legal work. Decayed old men, anxious to remain, grow cunning in hiding both their physical and mental deterioration and the erosion of the inexorable years.

Certainly there is truth about the flattery. In June 1958, on behalf of the assembled Queen's Bench judges, at the beginning of the Hilary Term, Mr Justice Finnemore urged Goddard not to consider retirement 'not only because we respect and admire but rather because we love you'. Fulsome, certainly; and irrelevant to justice or efficiency. But in fact was Goddard as good a judge at the end as at the beginning? Or, to take Du Cann again, could this judgment be applied to him?

> The arteries of the mind, like the arteries of the body, tend to harden. Sympathy and imagination atrophy. The quickness of apprehension, so necessary in a judge, perceptibly slows. Continued and concentrated attention becomes fatiguing. The memory weakens. Old men get garrulous. Judges of the passing generation tend to be out of touch with the new-coming one. Promotion to the Bench is blocked by late-stayers.

The test for Goddard came a month later, in July 1958, in his last great case, the *Isis* trial at the Old Bailey of two Oxford undergraduates who had published an article seriously contravening the Official Secrets Act. Goddard gave the two terrified young men a tremendous wigging, and a very light sentence. He was very calm and very courteous. He treated what was a serious and deliberate, indeed an ideological, offence – it was the time of the Aldermaston marches, the first great wave of the Campaign for Nuclear Disarmament – as an undergraduate prank. He was only a little deaf but in the view of a nineteen-year-old supporter of the defendants, 'the whole thing appeared an upper-class exercise. I remember the interminable discussions about whether *Isis* was still sold on the streets as it had been when Lord Goddard was still there in the Nineties . . . It was all very much removed from the actual crime – "Now you naughty boys, go back to your studies at College!" That sort of air.'

To judge by that comment, there seem to be many of the symptoms of which Du Cann complained: garrulousness, a weakening of the memory, a failure to grasp or get to the point, and certainly the inevitable gap of the generations. Yet the end result was justice of a decent sort; it would be unfair to Goddard to suggest, as has been suggested, that students from a redbrick university would have fared much worse.

Where Du Cann is certainly wrong, though, in this particular case at least, is in the final sentence of his last-quoted paragraph. So far from blocking promotion Goddard was staying on – at least this was certainly one of his motives – to ensure the succession of his own favourite candidate. He sent his letter of resignation in to the Prime Minister, Harold Macmillan, on July 26. It was accepted three days later but even before that the *Evening Standard* had announced, in its edition of July 22, 'Lord Goddard will be succeeded by Sir Reginald Manningham-Buller, the Attorney General.'

'Reggie' certainly wanted it, though he claimed to Fenton Bresler that he did not 'raise a finger to assert the Attorney General's right to the succession'. He was something of a joke figure, thought by many to be the original of Anthony Powell's marvellous fictional creation, the ghastly, pompous, self-satisfied, thick-skinned, blundering successful careerist Widmerpool. But he did not get it (though he did become Lord Chancellor four years later, as Lord Dilhorne). There was a long delay of five and a half weeks before Macmillan announced the successor: it was Hubert Parker, Goddard's 'favourite son', very much a lawyer's lawyer, son of a Law Lord himself, but undistinguished, no better and no worse than several other judges. It is not absolutely clear why Goddard wanted him – they had been out of touch for four years since Parker had gone to the Court of Appeal in 1954 – but it is almost certain that Goddard, like so many of his predecessors, used the threat of staying on indefinitely as a means of pressure on the Lord Chancellor and the Prime Minister. For once, this worked. One can only suppose that Goddard was such a popular figure and so little decayed that Macmillan did not dare to threaten him with a joint address of both Houses of Parliament and forcible ejection, as the younger Pitt had threatened William Murray, Lord Mansfield. Of couse, Macmillan may not have cared much for 'Bullying Manner' either. At any rate on Wednesday, August 20, 1958, during the Long Vacation sitting, Goddard presided for the last time in the Royal Courts of Justice. On September 24 he wrote his last letter in the Lord Chief Justice's room – a warm and brisk letter of congratulation to a fellow judge on his promotion to the Court of Appeal – and on September 29 he formally retired. Characteristically enough, he refused a hereditary peerage on the grounds that as he had no sons he saw no point in it.

A year after Goddard retired Parliament took heed of the criticisms voiced by such commentators as Du Cann. The Judicial Pensions Act laid down that all High Court Judges should retire at the age of seventy-five. There was one senior judge who had no intention of retiring so early: the Master of the Rolls, Lord Denning. He stayed on until he was eighty-nine. But he was appointed a judge before the Act was passed; and to him alone the Act did not apply. There will never – for better or for worse – be a Lord Chief Justice like Murray or Goddard, holding on to office in their eighties, again.

In that year, 1959, Goddard, indomitable after a ten-week cruise around South America, came back to sit in Parliament as a Law Lord, a Lord of Appeal. He lived in a top-floor flat in the Temple, in Queen Elizabeth Building, looked after by a housekeeper and a manservant. The Temple was his home for the remaining long and weary years of his life. He did not approve of the Swinging Sixties. 'Good God,' he said when waitresses first appeared in Inner Temple Hall, 'look at that one over there. Little trollop! Showing far too much leg!'

On May 24, 1965 he made his last speech in the House of Lords to protest against Lord Arran's Bill permitting homosexual behaviour in private between consenting adults. 'There is not a judge who has to go on circuit,' he told the fascinated Lords, 'as I had to go for a good many years, who does not find from time to time in various parts of the country what are generally referred to by members of the Bar as buggers' clubs.' The newspapers were delighted with this latest revelation. Shortly afterwards he bumped into Lord Arran. 'I'm being plagued by letters asking for the addresses of these damned places,' he grumbled.

On Monday, April 10, 1967, his ninetieth birthday, and on the two nights following he was fêted at dinners in Claridges, in the Inner Temple and in the Middle Temple. But he was growing very deaf, living mainly in a wheelchair, feeling gloomy and useless. He lived on for four years more. On the evening of Whit Saturday, May 29, 1971 he died at about 10 p.m. quietly in his bed, in a near-deserted Temple. At his own request there was no memorial service or burial. His remains were cremated in Golders Green crematorium. He would not have resented Bernard Levin's attack. '*De mortuis nil nisi bunkum*', he used to say.

Hubert Lister Parker, John Passmore Widgery, Geoffrey Dawson Lane – there is an air of similarity, almost of interchangeability about the very names of Goddard's successors. They are names redolent of middle-class respectability and they are names that mean almost nothing to the public at large, because they are all three lawyers' lawyers who have played no part at all in politics; because none of them has ever used his position as a member of the House of Lords to air his views; and, most significant of all, because none of them has ever donned the black cap. Indeed with the abolition of the death penalty for murder the office of Lord Chief Justice has become almost unimportant except to those whom it directly affects. It has passed from the public eye into a zone of a dim twilight. What lent the Lord Chief Justice and his colleagues their awesome flavour was, we now see, the power they no longer have – the power to sentence their fellow human beings to death.

Hubert Parker and John Widgery

Goddard lived just long enough to see his own successor Hubert Parker retire. On February 18, 1971 it was announced that

Parker would retire 'to make way for a younger man' – in the event for a lawyer whom he, Parker, had groomed as his successor, Widgery. Parker was only seventy, and history does not record what Goddard thought of this comparative youngster retiring five years before he needed to. Widgery, aged fifty-nine and a man apparently much in the mould of Parker, apparently, too, a competent administrator, was an obvious choice, especially if a lawyers' lawyer and a younger man was again to be appointed. Goddard lived indeed to see Widgery take office in April. In May that year Goddard died; and Parker, aged only seventy-one, died the following year, in September 1972. Widgery was to carry on till his own retirement in 1980. Like Parker, he died in the year following his retirement, in July 1981.

'The trouble with me is that I'm a dull man,' Widgery once told a friend. Parker too was a dull man, at least by comparison to Goddard. Neither admittedly had much chance to shine. Neither presided over famous trials – except perhaps the trial of the spy Blake whom Parker sentenced to a savage forty-two years. Neither was involved in much controversy or excitement, private or public. Neither came out with a memorable phrase or an amusing epigram – except perhaps again Parker's somewhat alarming statement that the courts 'have a positive responsibility to be the handmaiden of administration rather than its governor'. Both indeed showed rather too clearly their inclination to be handmaidens of the administration or, as Bacon had more pithily put it, lions beneath the throne, in the two official and non-judicial Committees of Enquiry over which they presided, in 1971 and 1972 respectively. In the first Parker, who had just retired as Lord Chief Justice, came to the conclusion that neither the Army nor the R.U.C. were guilty of brutality against prisoners in Northern Ireland; Lord Gardiner, a former Lord Chancellor also sitting on the Committee, strongly dissented. In the second Widgery also cleared the Army of blame in the 'Bloody Sunday' enquiry that followed the shooting and killing of thirteen civil rights demonstrators at Londonderry. They were both, from a Conservative government's point of view, safe men and, in the age-old tradition of Lord Chief Justices, upholders rather than challengers of the status quo and conventional wisdom.

'Judges are part of the machinery of authority within the state,' concluded John Griffith in a recent book, *The Politics of the Judiciary*, 'and as such cannot avoid making political decisions.' There is nothing particularly revolutionary or startling about Professor Griffith's conclusions, though he seems to feel that there is. What is certain, and at first rather surprising, is that these two professional lawyers, men bred in the tradition of the law and its at least theoretical tradition of independence, should have been as Lord Chief Justices so much less forceful and independent-minded than many of their political predecessors.

That is not to imply that dull men necessarily make bad judges. If anything, the history of the Lord Chief Justices pinpoints rather the contrary danger, of brilliant men making appalling judges. In the case of these two men, both of whom were Lord Chief Justices for a considerable period, it is generally agreed that one was a success and one was a failure. Parker was the success and Widgery was the failure.

Parker had more self-confidence. He was a calm, logical unruffled man, himself son of a Lord Justice of Appeal, educated at Rugby, Trinity College Cambridge, and Lincoln's Inn, a very hard worker who, like Coke and Isaacs, used to rise at an unearthly hour in the middle of the night to prepare his briefs. What is interesting about an otherwise unremarkable but steadily progressing legal career is that he was for five years Junior Counsel to the Treasury before becoming, in 1950, a puisne Judge of King's Bench. This meant that he was already a virtual, though not a technical, civil servant – a worker for the state, a handmaiden of the administration, imbued with all a well-paid handmaiden's sense of loyalty and duty towards her employers. He made no enemies. As Lord Chief Justice he was, in the phrase of one of his puisnes, 'an absolute sweetie'. He made few close friends either. In contrast to Goddard he did not enjoy, and took almost no part in, the social life of the legal world. At Cambridge he had taken a Double First in Natural Sciences, and only switched to his father's profession because there was no opening for geologists at the time. As Lord Chief Justice he lived with his Kentucky wife (it was a childless marriage) an almost secluded life on a small farm in Dorset, building garden walls, bird-watching, collecting old books and antiques. He was particularly interested in breeding cows. He was, unlike his predecessor, a very tranquil man.

When Parker retired, Widgery had been a judge for ten years and the Lord Chief Justice's puisne for no less than seven. Yet despite his experience Widgery did not have Parker's calmness or confidence. He had been born at South Molton in Devon, the son of a house-furnisher. He was educated at the local elementary school and at Queen's College, Taunton. He did not go to one of the old universities; indeed he went to no university at all. He did not have a distinguished wartime record; he was an officer in a territorial anti-aircraft battalion. He was by training and by profession not a barrister but a solicitor – a member of the 'junior branch' of the legal world. He was not nearly as secure socially as his predecessor had been, in a world where traditional snobbery is rife and social ease or at least social self-confidence is almost essential.

Nevertheless when, immediately after the war, he did become a barrister, his career was extremely successful, mainly in the lucrative but unprestigious field of rating and town-planning cases. Members of the Bar are still extremely discreet, however, about his years as Lord Chief Justice. Apparently what happened was that, conscious of his immense responsibilities, he worked far too hard. He refused to delegate and attempted to do everything himself – judging, administrating, entertaining and being entertained – without a let-up. He fussed and he worried. It is not quite clear whether his physical health collapsed or whether he had a nervous breakdown. Whatever the cause his speech became slurred and inaudible, and his judgments contradictory. In 1979 *Private Eye* reported that Lord Justice Bridge was to become the new Lord Chief Justice because 'the present incumbent has gone mad.' *Private Eye* was wrong on both counts. But, interestingly enough, its legal expert suggested that Widgery had intended to retire in 1978 but learnt that James Callaghan, then Prime Minister, was intending to appoint the Attorney General Sam Silkin in his place.

> Silkin [continued the *Eye*], is the only man in the history of legal conflict to inspire total unanimity of view among all established observers (right and left), journalists, politicians, judges, lawyers and all the strata of English and international society, that as Attorney General he was irredeemably (and sometimes quite spectacularly) dreadful. As Lord Chief Justice he would have been markedly worse . . . Lord Widgery may be mad but he comes from a class that knows its duty. So he stayed.

What was interesting was not so much Silkin's virtues or vices as the suggestion that the Prime Minister was once again considering the 'right' of the Attorney General to the post of Lord Chief Justice. What in fact happened was that Widgery, who had been appointed under the Conservative government of Edward Heath, stayed on till the appearance of another Conservative government, that of Margaret Thatcher. Then he retired.

Like Parker he was married but childless. He was apparently a man without outside interests. The legal world heaved a sigh of relief (as *The Times* obituary a year later delicately put it, 'Unhappily, Widgery's last few years as Lord Chief Justice were marred by ill-health'); and another sigh of relief when Widgery was succeeded not by a politician but by another professional lawyer.

It seems as if a tradition has now been established – and it is probably Goddard's one lasting contribution – that the Lord Chief Justices of post-world war times are always to emerge from the strictly judicial world. Yet it is a 'tradition' that has not necessarily produced better men or better judges than in what professional lawyers now view as the bad old days when professional politicians were preferred.

Geoffrey Lane

The present Lord Chief Justice is a man much more in Parker's mould than Widgery's – public school, a Double First at Cambridge, an active war record as a squadron leader in the R.A.F. He was born in July 1918 and he became Lord Chief Justice on April 15, 1980 – at the age therefore of sixty-one. He was educated at Shrewsbury, like his famous predecessor Judge Jeffreys, and at Trinity College, Cambridge, also like Jeffreys. At Cambridge he read Classics for a year before switching to Law. After the war he decided at first to play safe – he had just married – and to follow a commercial career. But the Bar, however risky, attracted him. He was called at Gray's Inn in 1946. Official sources are discreet about his home, his family and his personal habits, for fairly obvious reasons. His hobbies are traditional enough – gardening and golf. For eight years he sat as a puisne judge of Queen's Bench, a protégé and admirer of Lord Chief Justice Parker. Lord Bridge, tipped by *Private Eye* for the post, a year Lane's senior and like Parker once a Junior Counsel to the Treasury, is still only a Lord Justice of Appeal. Perhaps he was not considered tough enough. Lane is generally considered to be a tough man and a firm administrator. As Goddard after Inskip, so Lane after Widgery – his appointment was welcomed by the Bar as a whole; and, like Goddard, he has taken a grip on a loose and demoralised profession. It is too early to say, some three years later, whether Lane will make a memorable Lord Chief Justice. Certainly in 1982 he became the first Lord Chief Justice for many years to verge on becoming a popular figure. 'Rapists Should Be Jailed, Law Chief Tells Courts', ran the headline on the front page of *The Times* of January 16; and both Mrs Thatcher and the Lord Chancellor, Quintin Hogg (second Lord Hailsham) praised his attitude and echoed his remarks, as rape and the controversy about its fitting punishments suddenly seized public attention in England.

'A sentence of twelve years was wholly appropriate, and might well have been longer,' ruled Lord Chief Justice Lane, refusing leave to appeal to a curate of Caerphilly, convicted of three rapes, one attempted rape, and two cases of causing actual bodily harm. The Court of Appeal (Criminal Division) no longer has the power to increase sentences on appeal by the person convicted as it did in Goddard's day. But the Lord Chief Justice's ruling had the Goddard touch. Have we in Lane, the twenty-fifth Lord Chief Justice since the Glorious Revolution and the ninth this century, a man who will bring the post of the Lord Chief Justice back into the public eye – where over eight centuries of English history it has almost always been? It is not impossible. But it is a question that only future historians of the Lord Chief Justices will be in a position to answer.

Sources, Notes and Further Reading

Bibliographies and meticulous lists of source references undoubtedly add weight to a book. Indeed in recent years they
have tended to add more and more weight to less and less book.
Yet there was a certain contrasting charm in the classical
historians, the first with whom I became acquainted. None of
them would ever give his sources – a tantalising hint here, a
name dropped there, occasionally something more substantial.
Certainly none of them ever considered it necessary to add
bibliographies. Were they any the worse historians for that?
There was, rather, a certain fascination in trying to piece
together the sources for Thucydides or guess at the books that
lay on Livy's work table.

In this thesis-ridden age the pendulum has swung rather too
far the other way. But this book is not a thesis; it is not an
academic study; it is certainly not a legal text-book. There are
no private papers or intriguing primary sources which I have
consulted and to which reference should be made. So there will
be no bibliography; and there will be no exhaustive source
references for every quotation, incident or anecdote. Explanatory footnotes, yes, particularly on personalities or matters
referred to, but not sufficiently explained in the main body of
the book – that seems only fair to the interested reader and adds
texture rather than weight.

As for sources: this book is all based on previously published
material, most of it reasonably easy – for those who would wish
to do so – to dig out. My main source up to and including
Chapter 13 has undeniably been the four volumes of *The Lives
of the Lord Chief Justices of England* by Lord Campbell
(published by John Murray, in the third edition of 1874)
supplemented by the seven volumes of the same author's *Lives
of the Lord Chancellors* (also published by John Murray, in
three series, beginning in 1845). This second set of biographies
includes, somewhat confusingly, the lives of those Lord Chief

Justices, like Jeffreys, who went on to become Lord Chancellor. It is a safe bet that most of the anecdotes, quotations and stories directly relating to the Lord Chief Justices and their trials derive from Campbell's immense and vivid *opus*.

On the other hand I became rapidly aware that, as a contemporary critic – parodying Longfellow – put it:

> Lives of great men misinform us,
> *Campbell's Lives* in this sublime,
> Errors frightfully enormous,
> Misprints on the sands of time.

Furthermore, factual errors apart, there might well be something amiss with the value-judgments of a work which inspired an American compendium in 1856 entitled *Atrocious Judges: Lives of Judges Infamous as Tools of Tyrants and Instruments of Oppression: Compiled from the Judicial Biographies of John, Lord Campbell, Lord Chief Justice of England.*

So, as a check on Campbell's facts and indeed on his prejudices, I used mainly the absolutely invaluable *Dictionary of National Biography* (hereinafter the *DNB*) – usually in the 1921–22 reprint in 22 volumes, occasionally in the most up-to-date edition – as well as Foss' *Biographical Dictionary of the Judges of England* (John Murray, 1870) plus, to some extent, the nine volumes of Foss' *The Judges of England* (also published by John Murray, undoubtedly the great legal populariser of the day, in 1864). For the technicalities I consulted Sir William Holdsworth's *History of English Law* (in the 1966 reprint in 15 volumes) and for the major trials dipped into and out of the closely-printed 33 volumes of C. B. Howell's *State Trials* plus the *New Series* of eight volumes that carried the account up to 1858.

Each of the 20 chapters in this book involved a considerable amount of background reading in the general political history of the time, especially in the Oxford series of the *History of England* and the *Political History* series published by Longman, Green; plus poking around and checking in specialised studies of episodes, lives, incidents, plots, victims, villains and plotters.

In the notes that follow I see no point in mentioning, for instance, Lord Macaulay's *History of England* or Lord Chesterfield's *Letters to His Son* when the main text makes it very clear from which work a long quote comes, and the interested reader can track down its exact provenance for him or herself. As regards 'further reading', it seems insulting to the intelligence of my readers even to suggest Macaulay or Chesterfield, Aubrey or Bacon, Burnet or North, Horace Walpole or Fanny Burney.

Indeed 'further reading' is a choice readers may surely be left to make for themselves on the basis of the allusions in the main text to these and other 'classical' authors or in the references scattered throughout the notes that follow to less well-known writers and their books.

Of the many many books on great judges, famous trials, etc., which I consulted (and of which so vast a selection decorate the shelves of the Oxford Law Library) I must particularly mention two books: *Fourteen English Judges* by the Earl of Birkenhead (Cassell, 1926) – this vivid compendium by 'F.E.' (for whose own legal career see p 234 and following) carries chapters on no less than six Lord Chief Justices: Coke, Hale, Jeffreys, Holt, Yorke and Murray; and also *English Treason Trials* by C. G. L. Du Cann (Frederick Muller, 1964) which has detailed but concise accounts of some major episodes covered in this book: Raleigh's trial, Wentworth's trial, King Charles I's trial, Dame Alice Lisle's trial, the Cato Street Conspiracy, Casement's trial – and the Gunpowder Plot.

1. JESUITS, TREASON AND PLOT

p 4 *Walsingham, with his vast network of spies and informers.*
Walsingham's favourite saying was 'knowledge is never too dear'. He maintained a network of 53 spies at courts throughout Europe.

p 4 *Dr John Storey, who refused to acknowledge the Royal Supremacy.*
Storey, an exile, was a particular *bête noire* of Cecil's. He was lured aboard an English ship in Flanders, kidnapped, tortured, accused of high treason and tried at Westminster Hall in the presence of the highly intelligent Edmund Campion, then aged 32. The trial was apparently so obviously vindictive and unfair that Campion resolved in his indignation to give up his Oxford career, cross the Channel and join the newly-founded English College for Seminary Priests at Douai.

For even more gruesome details of torture, execution and the procedure in criminal trials, see an outstandingly well-researched book, *The Tudor Law of Treason* by John Bellamy (Routledge & Kegan Paul, 1979). Storey was not a young man but, 'when the executioner had cut off his privy members he rushing upon a sudden gave him a blow upon the ears to the great astonishment of all that stood by' (Bellamy, p 205). He had to be held down by four men to be disembowelled.

p 5   *Who were the traitors whom so grim an end awaited? Papists in the main.*
The Lord Chief Justice, the judges and the common law courts had played no part at all in the burning of the Protestant martyrs that began in the previous reign, Mary's, on February 4, 1655 and climaxed with the burning of Archbishop Cranmer at Oxford on March 21, 1656. The Protestant martyrs were accused of heresy, not treason. Therefore they were tried by ecclesiastical courts and handed over to the secular arm on conviction for the punishment of heresy, as laid down by Parliament, burning. However the Catholic martyrs in her sister's reign were accused not of heresy but treason and were therefore tried by the common law courts and hanged, drawn and quartered as traitors. It was Elizabeth's boast that she had never had any subjects of hers suffer death for their religious beliefs.

In point of numbers it has been calculated that 282 Protestant martyrs suffered for their faith under Mary and almost exactly the same number of Catholics (though over a far longer period) under Elizabeth. 25–30 Catholics were martyred under Elizabeth's successor, James I.

p 5   *The comparatively recently founded Society of Jesus, the Jesuits*
Founded in 1540 by the Basque soldier-turned-priest, Ignatius Loyola.

p 5   *Edmund Campion ... was betrayed, paraded through London, racked in the Tower, tried for high treason ... and in November 1581 executed.*
Campion spent a year as a seminarian at Douai before setting off on foot for Rome, where he immediately joined the Jesuits. Two years later, in 1575, two other Englishmen moved on from Douai to enlist with the Jesuits at Rome: Robert Parsons, aged 30, and Henry Garnet, aged 20.

Less than a month after organising a spectacular propaganda coup at St Mary's, the University Church in Oxford, Campion was betrayed by a manservant, a professional informer, and arrested at Lyford Grange near Wantage in Berkshire. In London he was paraded through the streets to the Tower with a paper stuck in his hat, reading 'Campion the Seditious Jesuit', racked four times, taken out between tortures for a public disputation on theological issues with the Dean of St Paul's and other divines, and tried before Sir Christopher Wray, Popham's predecessor as Lord Chief Justice, on November 20, 1581, in the first mass treason trial in English history. The detailed charges were ludicrous, Popham's witnesses for the prosecution utterly discredited, the Lord Chief Justice very courteous – but the end was inevitable. He was executed in particuarly vile circumstances at Tyburn 11 days later. See in particular *Edmund Campion* by Evelyn Waugh (Longman, Green, 1933).

p 5   *Parsons was extremely worried at despatching, as he put it, 'the meekest lamb to cruellest butchery'*
See *Henry Garnet* by Philip Caraman (Longman, 1964), an excellent account and the source for almost all the citations of Garnet's and Parsons' letters in this chapter. The book includes the portrait of Popham of which the original is in the National Portrait Gallery, London. (There is another portrait at Littlecote House.)

p 5   *Topcliffe the priest hunter trapped Southwell one Sunday in June 1592*
Topcliffe was the only man whom the mild Garnet ever criticised as a personality (at least in writing). 'Homo sordidissimus', Garnet called him. Between March 1590 and March 1591 he caught, examined, and helped to prosecute and execute seven priests and three laymen, with whose heads and quarters he adorned the City. The following year he finally trapped Southwell at the Bellamy house at Uxendon, apparently having seduced in prison Anne Bellamy – at least a gentler method of obtaining information than his usual one. For this and Cecil's subsequent comments on what must to us seem a fairly mild torture as tortures go in the twentieth century, see *Robert Southwell* by C. Devlin (p 258). Also for its excellently-written general background *Papists and Puritans under Elizabeth I* by Patrick McGrath (Blandford Press, 1967).

p 6   *The spirited John Gerard*
Gerard wrote the famous *Autobiography of an Elizabethan* in which he vividly describes his escape and subsequent adventures.

p 8   *Within a week Raleigh was in the Tower . . . a hero – as the people with their traditional fickleness soon began to feel – of the great epic just accomplished, the epic of Elizabeth of England.*
Raleigh's reputation had been badly damaged by a pamphlet

written by Robert Parsons accusing him in eloquently vitupera-
tive Latin of being an atheist and a necromancer. He was hated
by the Queen for having married secretly one of her maids of
honour, Bess Throckmorton; by the court because, as Aubrey
put it, 'his naeve was that he was damnably proud', and by the
people for the part they believed him, unjustifiably, to have
played in plotting the condemnation and execution of Robert
Devereux, Earl of Essex, the popular favourite who had sup-
planted him in the Queen's heart.

> Essex for vengeance cries (went the popular rhyme)
> His blood upon thee lies
> Mounting above the skies
> Mischievous Machiavel!

See Lytton Strachey's famous semi-romance *Elizabeth and
Essex*; but also, particularly, *Raleigh and the Throckmortons*
by A. L. Rowse (Macmillan, 1962); and, for the failed Essex
coup in which both Raleigh and the Lord Chief Justice,
Popham, were almost killed, *Sir Walter Raleigh* by Willard M.
Wallace (Princeton, 1955).

p 9   *A very dubious story*
The story was that Popham had acquired the Elizabethan
mansion in return for corruptly arranging the acquittal of its
proprietor, Sir Richard Dayrell (or Darrell) on a charge of
murdering and burning a bastard baby. The only authority for
this is Aubrey's account, written eighty years after Popham's
death. The articles on Popham in the *DNB* and Foss' *Judges*
point out further inconsistencies in this story.

p 10   *thereafter, like Popham, Speaker of the House of Commons*
Popham was elected Speaker for the January 1581 Parliament.
'Well, Mr Speaker,' the Queen asked him, 'what hath passed
in the Lower House?'
'If it please your Majesty,' he replied, 'seven weeks.'
It is Popham's only recorded joke.
Coke was elected Speaker for the far more eventful Parliament that met on February 19, 1593. It was a brilliant assembly
– with, as Members, not only Drake, Grenville, Raleigh, little
Robert Cecil and his dissolute brother-in-law Henry Brooke but
also Cecil's first cousin, Francis Bacon. It was becoming almost
a convention that the Solicitor General should be elected

Speaker and should 'manage' the House on behalf of the Queen and the Council, as Coke did with an obsequious flattery that still sounds repulsive even after so long a time has passed. See especially *Elizabeth I and Her Parliaments* by J. E. Neale (Cape, 1953, 2 vols).

pp 9/10   *one of Walsingham's intelligence agents in Spain*
          wrote to the Council
See Calendar of State Papers Domestic, of 27 April 1602. The Lord High Admiral whom the agent reported the Papists feared as much as Cecil and Popham was Charles Lord Howard of Effingham.

p 10   *Bacon failed to obtain even the junior post . . . 'No man,'*
       he wrote to his patron . . . 'ever had a more exquisite
       disgrace.'
'The attorneyship for Francis is what I must have,' the Earl of Essex had ranted at young Cecil, 'and in that I will spend all my power, might, authority and amity and with tooth and nail procure the same for him against whomsoever'. But Bacon had made – a mistake he was never to repeat – a bold and critical speech against the government in the 1593 Parliament; and Essex' influence was less than Essex thought. In despair Bacon resolved to retire to Cambridge and devote himself to the study of science and philosophy for which he had such a bent; but at the last moment a soothing message from the Queen balmed his ego. He repaid his patron's efforts disgracefully by testifying against Essex at his trial for treason on February 14, 1601. 'Francis Bacon was the last to speak for the prosecution (conducted by Coke) . . . Bacon contributed almost more than any other to his summary conviction.' The *DNB* on Essex.

p 11   *The trial of Sir Walter Raleigh*
A full report of the trial opens Volume II of Cobbett's *Collection of State Trials* (published 1809–1898 London). See also *Raleigh's Trial* by D. Jardine (2 vols, London 1832–1835) and Bowen, pp 190–217 (cf. opening note to next chapter).

p 13   *The Gunpowder Plot*
The most stirring contemporary account is *A Narrative of the Gunpowder Plot* by John Gerard (the MSS is at Stoneyhurst, the Jesuit college in Lancashire). The story is of course told and analysed in all the general histories of the time, of which I have found particularly useful (both for this and for the following

four chapters) *The Early Stuarts 1603–1660* by Godfrey Davies (Clarendon Press, 1959).

p 14   *Thomas Percy, a distant kinsman of the greatest of the Catholic nobles of the North, the Percy Earl of Northumberland*
Thomas Percy, his second cousin once removed and also his Constable at the great Northern fortress of Alnwick, dined with Henry Percy, 9th Earl of Northumberland, on the evening of November 4 at Syon House in Middlesex. It is not strictly true to call the 9th Earl a Catholic. His uncle, 'Simple Thomas', the seventh Earl, had been executed at York after the Rising of the North, proclaiming that he was in life as in death 'a Catholic and a Percy'. His father, 'Cruel Henry', the 8th Earl, nominally a Protestant, had 'committed suicide' in the Tower. The 9th Earl, the 'Wizard Earl', also a nominal Protestant, was as a result of the Plot, tried on June 27, 1606 in Star Chamber for misprision of treason on the grounds that he 'sought to become Chief of Papists' and imprisoned for the next sixteen years in the Tower.

p 17   *Mounteagle's true role is dubious*
He probably betrayed the conspiracy to the Council. For discussion of this point, and references, see his entry in the *DNB*.

2. COKE UNEASY

The Lion and the Throne by Catherine Drinker Bowen (Boston, 1956; Hamish Hamilton, 1957) is a splendidly decorative biography of Coke, tapestry-like in its attention to colourful detail and description. Many of the quotations cited as Coke's or about Coke in this and the following chapter can be found in this book. Its title, like the title of this book, is derived from Bacon's *Essay* (and I would like to add here that, looking back on this book now, I doubt whether 'Lions Under the Throne' is a suitable description of more than a handful of Lord Chief Justices; the true 'lions' being almost invariably the men or women the Lord Chief Justices condemned to death; their judges – if there must be a zoological companion – in too many cases more closely resembled jackals).

    More sober and more analytic is *Sir Edward Coke and the Grievances of the Commonwealth* by Stephen White (Manchester, 1979). I have also used, both for this chapter and indeed for the rest of Part One, *The Stuart Constitution 1603–1688: Documents and Commentaries* edited by J. K. Kenyon (Cambridge, 1966).

p 26   *The wretched Robert Devereux, third and last Earl of Essex ... was ... (according to his young wife) impotent.*

It eventually came out that the delectable young Frances had had a wax figure made of him and had stuck in its 'privity' a thorn from a tree 'that bore leaves but no fruit.' No wonder the wretched Earl, the son of Elizabeth's doomed favourite, apparently genuinely castrated by these witchcraft tricks, turned against favourites, courts and kings, and became, much later, Parliament's most eminent general in the first years of the Civil War. For a vivid account of Frances see *Black Sheep* by Christopher Simon Sykes (Chatto & Windus, 1982) – Chapter II, 'Loose Living'.

p 28   *extraordinarily attractive young page*
This was George Villiers, the future Duke of Buckingham.

p 29   *what one commentator has called his 'grim pedantry'*
The writer of the biography of Coke in the *DNB*.

p 32   *The other eleven judges of the common law courts usually ... 'turned obsequious' when pressed. Coke would not.*

Bacon was always having to pen notes to the King on his plans to deal with the Lord Chief Justice, though never with much optimism: 'Neither am I wholly out of hope that my Lord Coke himself, when I have in some dark manner put him in doubt that he shall be left alone, will not continue singular.'

p 34   '*... not falling upon any of those things which he could not but know were offensive*'
It was just as well that Coke had not put together the twelfth part of his *Reports* (which were printed after his death: see p 51). It would certainly have been seen to be offensive and would probably have landed Coke firmly in front of Star Chamber, where indeed Bacon suggested that, but for the King's mercy, he deserved to be.

p 36   *made an offer for the post of Lord Treasurer*

The Lord Treasurer, Thomas Howard Earl of Suffolk, was the father of the poisonous Frances. Discredited by this connection, he had been fined £30,000 on trumped-up charges and sent to the Tower.

p 37　*The Oxford Peerage suit*
Henry de Vere, eighteenth Earl of Oxford, had died in 1626. Despite the Lord Chief Justice's apostrophic address, the court ruled in favour of the heir male, Robert de Vere, who succeeded to the title; but *his* heir Aubrey died without male issue. The earldom of Oxford therefore lapsed – to be revived by Queen Anne for Harley and, much later, by George V for Asquith, whose grandson is the present holder.

3. COKE TRIUMPHANT

p 41　*Coke objected*
Coke had already clashed, when in office, with George Villiers. The Lord Chief Justice had in his gift one great legal sinecure worth about £4000 a year: the Clerkship of Enrolments of King's Bench. Since 1497 it had been bought by successive generations of the Roper family until it had come to be known as 'Roper's Office'. But in 1606 a rising young barrister and future Lord Chief Justice, Robert Heath, had moved in on the Roper monopoly. Heath was virtually ousted by the first favourite, Ker, in 1612. On Ker's fall, the King had tried to transfer the patronage to his new favourite Villiers. Coke had jibbed; his more amenable successor Montagu agreed, for 'consolation' of £500 a year. See *The King's Servants*, an excellent analysis of this and many other offices, by G. E. Palmer (Routledge, 1974).

p 46　*'Sir', said Bacon . . . 'I cannot help myself.'*
Bacon's corruption was of a rather absent-minded, in some cases trivial, sort. He was accused of having accepted 'in a cause between Reynell and Peacock £200 in money and a diamond ring worth £5 or £600.' It does not sound an enormous sum or a very convincing evaluation.

p 46　*as Bacon had been – after only one day – released.*
King James remitted most of Bacon's penalties but excluded him from further public office. Bacon continued to live in

splendour and to write till his death in 1626. *Francis Bacon* by Mary Sturt (Kegan, Paul 1932) is a decent straightforward biography. More stimulating is *The Martyrdom of Francis Bacon* by Alfred Dodd (Rider & Co, no date). Chapter II begins: 'Francis Bacon was the concealed child of Queen Elizabeth Tudor via Robert Dudley, Earl of Essex.' I know of no major modern biography or study, though this 'greatest Englishman', this 'immortal genius', (*per* Dodd), certainly deserves one. At the end of his life Macaulay apparently expressed regret for only one of his works: over-critical his *Essay on Bacon*.

p 46 *Coke had mortally offended the King's sense of his own*
      importance once again
Parliament had reconvened on November 12. On November 27 Coke made a savage anti-Spanish speech, much approved. But then 14 Points of Grievance, two Petitions and a Protestation followed – all drawn up or inspired by Coke. Parliament was adjourned on December 18. Coke was thereupon summoned before the Council and accused of ignoring instructions not to discuss matters that pertained only to his Prince. Consignment to the Tower followed.

p 47 *the Lord Treasurer, Lionel Cranfield, a deeply unpopu-*
      lar City merchant . . . one of Coke's bitterest enemies
      during his disgrace,
Cranfield was sentenced on May 13, 1624 to lose all offices, to be incapable of public employment for the future, to pay a fine of £50,000 and never to come within the verge of the Court. He was released from the Tower on May 28, pardoned on April 8 next year, but not allowed to resume his seat in the Lords (as Earl of Middlesex) until the Civil War was looming. He died in 1645.

p 50 *But Coke was not one of those M.P.s He never took his*
      seat in the January 1629 session, though he was sum-
      moned.
'He did not come: the Commons Journal has no explanation.' Thus Bowen, p 451, – with no further attempt at explanation herself. It all seems very odd for such a devoted Parliament man as Coke. There must have been a reason.

p 52 *'We will never see his like again . . . Praise be to God.'*
Widew's comment, quoted in *Sir Edward Coke* by S. E. Thorne (Selden Society, 1952, p 4).

4. KING'S MEN

p 54　*they laid it down that torture itself was illegal*

Torture, or at least systematic state torture, had a mercifully short life in English history. It had been unknown in mediaeval times. Thomas Cromwell, Henry VIII's chief minister, introduced it for examining friars 'with pains'. In Mary's reign it was used against witches and horse-thieves; in Elizabeth's almost exclusively against seminary priests and Jesuits.

There were three instruments of torture in use: the brakes, a form of iron contraption that kept a man twisted in a circle, the manacles, and the rack. Apart from the rack in Topcliffe the priest-hunter's house (and manacles: see p 5) there was only one rack in England, applied by the Rackmaster of the Tower in highly formalized conditions. Coke, conveniently forgetting his own past, had inveighed against torture in his later writings. But it was Richardson and his fellow judges who deserve the credit for outlawing it. Torture has never been used, at least legally, in England since.

p 56　*As for Noy, the Attorney General had gone to extremes that even the Archbishop disapproved*

He denounced Prynne in Star Chamber on June 18 as being beyond saving and moved to deprive him of the privilege of attending Divine Service. This was too much even for Laud. Shortly afterwards Noy fell ill with the stone and died in Tunbridge Wells.

p 57　*wrote the parliamentary lawyer John Selden*

Selden, whom Ben Jonson called 'the lawbook of the judges of England', was famed both as a jurist and an orator. He was M.P. for Oxford University in the Long Parliament, a moderate whose name is preserved in the active legal reformist group, the Selden Society.

p 59　*Thomas Wentworth, Viscount Strafford*

See particularly Dame Veronica Wedgwood's *Thomas Wentworth: First Earl of Strafford 1593–1641: a Revaluation* (Collins, 1961).

p 60　*Archbishop Laud, who was to remain in prison for three years and then suffer exactly the same form of murder,*

Just as Laud had persecuted Prynne when he was in power, so, when the tables were turned and with more fatal results, did Prynne persecute him. Laud was impeached on December 18,

1640 but not tried until 1644. The trial lasted from March 12 to October 11. When it seemed likely that he must be acquitted, Prynne urged the Commons to change the procedure from Impeachment to Attainder. The Bill of Attainder passed the Commons on October 31, but not the reluctant Lords until December 17. On January 7, 1645 Laud pleaded the King's pardon sent up from Oxford under the Great Seal. The Pardon was read out in both Houses but declared of no effect: the King cannot pardon a judgment of Parliament. Laud, aged 72, went to the scaffold on January 10, the third and so far the last Archbishop of Canterbury to be murdered or executed in our history.

p 60   *Legal civil war was now being waged to an extent never previously known in England since the days of the Lords Ordainer*

Thomas of Lancaster, the King's uncle, and his baronial supporters, the Ordainers, had placed King Edward II under the control of a written and very detailed constitution, the Ordinances of 1311. Ten years later the Lords Ordainer were summarily tried for treason on the King's record (i.e. by mere statement of their crimes attested by the King). Thomas was beheaded before his own castle of Pontefract – where the King was himself later to be murdered. The Despensers, father and son, Edward's favourites, had earlier been tried, hanged, quartered and beheaded. Later the savage Roger Mortimer, Earl of the March and the Queen Mother's lover, was arrested by her son, the new King, Edward III. 'Fair son,' said Queen Isabella, 'have mercy on the gentle Mortimer!' Mortimer was tried without even being allowed to appear before his accusers, and hanged at the Elms at Smithfield, on the site later to be known as Tyburn. It was only the passing of the Statute of Treason (see *Introductory Notes* pp ix and x) that put an end to this system of judicial assassination and belatedly reassured the decimated nobility.

p 62   *England's previous great ideological civil war, Earl Simon de Montfort's*

At the focus of this struggle between an absolutist monarchy and a constitutionalist régime stood the figure of the Justiciar. 'A Justiciar (Hugh Bigod) has been appointed and the oppressed are now heard', the reformers, the barons of De Montfort's party, wrote to the Pope in 1258 after their triumphant taming of the power of King Henry III. When, seven years later at the

Battle of Evesham, the Lord Edward – the future Edward I – rescued his father and restored the royal power, both Earl Simon de Montfort and the then Justiciar, Hugh le Dispenser, were killed – the first Justiciar to die violently in office and in battle. The office of Justiciar was thereafter abolished. It had lasted for almost exactly 200 years.

p 63   *All Bankes' property was declared forfeited.*
It was restored to the Bankes' family at the Restoration; and has remained in that family till 1982 when under the will of Ralph Bankes, Esquire, all his property (still including Corfe Castle and vast tracts of Dorset) was bequeathed to the National Trust.

p 63   *more loyal but less fortunate than his predecessor, Lord*
       Chief Justice Fortescue, in the Wars of the Roses
The bloodbath of the Wars of the Roses was, unlike previous civil struggles, in every way ruthless and repulsive. Legal assassination in the form of Acts of Attainder were introduced by the Parliament that met at Coventry on November 20, 1459. (cp *Introductory Notes*, p x). Battles were followed by summary executions. Henry VI's Lord Chief Justice, Sir John Fortescue, was for years loyal to the 'she-wolf of France', Henry's wife, Margaret of Anjou. He fought for Lancaster at the greatest battle, in point of numbers, ever to take place on English soil – the Battle of Towton, on Palm Sunday, 1461. He fled after that disaster with Henry and Margaret to Scotland. After Henry was captured he sailed with Margaret to exile in France. There he wrote a learned and famous dialogue *De Laudibus Legum Angliae* as a guide for the young Prince of Wales. Following the at-first-triumphant Lancastrian return to England, he was captured at the Battle of Tewkesbury where the young Prince was killed.

Then, at long last, Fortescue betrayed the Lancastrian cause. His Attainder was reversed, his lands restored, and he was even admitted to the Council of the Yorkist Edward IV. However in return, under pressure from his treacherous former colleague, Billing, he retracted in writing his arguments in favour of the rights of the House of Lancaster, and argued instead that the Yorkist claim was legally just. He lived on till the age of 90 (local tradition had it) in his manor of Ebrington. He did write in retirement a third book *On the Governaunce of England*, which was by way of being England's first constitutional treatise. It suggested in effect that a King under the Law, ruling in harmony with Lords and Commons – the Lancastrian ideal – was the best system in Europe. Fine hopes for an age that had just begun, in recognisably totalitarian fashion, with a published confession of error and a total change of front by a man once reputed for his unswerving loyalty!

5. COMMONWEALTH MEN

pp 65/66   *So did his two far more bitterly anti-monarchist fellow judges*
Oliver St John, a kinsman and close friend of Oliver Cromwell's, counsel for Hampden in the Ship Money case, Solicitor General and 'manager' for the Commons at Wentworth's impeachment, was Chief Justice of Common Pleas from 1649 to the Restoration. His colleague, Sergeant Wilde, Chief Baron of the Exchequer, had been an active member of the Long Parliament.

p 66   *the most famous trial in English history*
See *The Trial of Charles I* by C. V. Wedgwood (Collins, 1964). Dame Veronica has also written two deservedly popular volumes on the whole period: *The King's Peace* and *The King's War* (Collins, 1958).

p 67   *no Lord Chief Justice has ever suffered precisely the indignity that Lord President Bradshaw posthumously incurred*
But in the popular uprisings of 1381 the then Lord Chief Justice, Sir John Cavendish, a Suffolk man, was caught on Friday, June 14, on the borders of the Fenland at Lakenheath by the East Anglian rebels as he was attempting to escape across the River Brandon. The two local leaders, John Pedder of Fordham and John Potter of Somerton, chose their own peasant Chief Justice who declared 'that in respect of the office of dignity which my Brother Cavendish has so long filled, instead of being hanged he shall be beheaded'. He was beheaded then and there on the river bank, and his head was taken back to Bury St Edmunds where amidst yells and execrations it was set up in the tower pillory. Later it was paraded through the town, side by side with the head of the Prior of Bury's famous monastery. As the Lord Chief Justice and the Prior had been excellent friends in life, their dead lips were held pressed together, as if in a kiss.

On the same day in London Wat Tyler and several hundred Kentish rebels hunted down the Lord Chancellor and the Lord Treasurer and summarily beheaded them on a wooden block on Tower Hill. Fortunately for John of Gaunt, the boy King's uncle and the main object of popular wrath, he was away in Edinburgh; but his palace of the Savoy was sacked.

p 67   *'It seems,' wrote his only moderately sympathetic father the Marquess, 'it is a place entailed upon our familie, for wee have now helde it five generations.'*
Protector Somerset – Edward, first Earl of Hertford and first Duke of Somerset – was executed on Tower Hill on January 22, 1552. His son Edward, Second Earl of Hertford, was three times imprisoned in the Tower by Queen Elizabeth. *His* son, Edward, Lord Beauchamp, (who predeceased his own father) was born in the Tower. The Marquess, *his* son, the lover of Arabella Stuart and therefore imprisoned by King James, had escaped from the Tower and fled to Flanders in 1611. Seven years later, back in London and in favour, he married Frances Devereux, sister of the Earl of Essex. At the Restoration in 1660 he welcomed Charles II on his arrival at Dover on May 26; next day he was created a Knight of the Garter. He became the second Duke of Somerset – a title still held by his descendants.

p 70   *Dom Pantaleone Sa*
This was a murder case that dealt with the niceties of diplomatic privilege, and its outcome exalted the reputation of the Commonwealth of England overseas. Dom Pantaleone Sa, the brother of the Portuguese Ambassador, had shot and killed Mr Greneway in the Strand. He was indicted for murder on July 5, 1654 before a jury composed half of Englishmen and half of foreigners. Lord Chief Justice Rolle gave a fine ruling on the inapplicability of the Law of Nations; and on July 10, despite pressure from several European powers, Dom Pantaleone was driven from Newgate to Tower Hill in a coach and six and there executed. Next day articles of peace with Portugal were signed.

p 71   *In May from Antwerp Sexby the 'agitator' published a pamphlet, which he ironically dedicated to Cromwell, entitled* Killing No Murder
Sexby himself followed his pamphlet over, was arrested on July 24 as he was about to embark for Flanders again, and died, half-mad, in the Tower. But the effects of his pamphlet lived on after him.

p 72   *the void left by Richard Cromwell's disappearance*
Oliver's son was effectively deposed in the spring of 1659, though he did not flee abroad until a year later. After two decades in exile he returned to England, to live out what remained of his life peacefully in the country.

p 73   *the Court retransformed itself without more ado into the Court of King's Bench as it had always been before and has always been since*
Not pedantically true. In the Victorian reforms (see p 210) it became the Queen's Bench Divison of the High Court; and in this reign retains that exact title.

6. LORD CHIEF JUSTICES OF THE RESTORATION

p 76   *a permanent focus of possible rebellion*
The Royalist government had been frightened by a futile Fifth-Monarchy-men uprising some months earlier. This must be their only excuse for the disgraceful affair of Sir Harry Vane's judicial murder.

p 79   *So it was back to high treason not by any overt act but by words alone*
As in the days of the Yorkist Kings, Edward IV and Richard III Sir Thomas Billing, the corrupter of Fortescue (see Note to p 63), was on June 23, 1469 appointed Lord Chief Justice. He became the first and apparently willing instrument in our history of that ghastly thing, a régime of judicial terror under which men were condemned and executed as traitors on the strength of words alone without any overt act. He remained Lord Chief Justice for an amazing seventeen years under continually changing régimes; and set the tone for the tyrannies and subservience of the succeeding Lord Chief Justices under Henry VII and Henry VIII.

p 79   *the notorious witchcraft trial . . . of March 1661*
See Volume VI, *State Trials*, pp 647–702. For the general background see also a fascinating short book, *The European Witch Craze of the 16th and 17th Centuries* by Hugh Trevor Roper (Pelican Books, 1969, reprinted Peregrine, 1978 – from a version first published in a collection of Trevor Roper essays).

p 82 *Roger North . . . prejudiced but so good and vivid a writer*
Roger North's main work is the *Lives of the Norths* – his three brothers. He also wrote an entertaining *Autobiography* and a vast *Examen* of some 700 pages, a vindication of 'the late King Charles the Second and his happy reign'.

p 83 *Bishop Burnet*
Besides his famous *History*, he also wrote a *Life and Death of Sir Matthew Hale*.

p 84   *end with a point that judges of our own day might do well to meditate*
18. To be short and sparing at meals, that I may be the fitter for business.
Posterity ought to know that Sir Matthew Hale would be more than satisfied *re* this point with the present Lord Chief Justice. Lord Lane was kind enough to entertain the present author to lunch in his Inn. Though generously plying his guest with both food and drink, His Lordship ate sparingly and drank – unlike so many of his predecessors – only water.

7. FOAM AND THREAT

> This plot which failed for want of common sense
> Had yet a deep and dangerous consequence
> For as when raging fires boil the blood
> The standing lake soon floats into a flood
> And every hostile humour which before
> Slept quiet in its channels bubbles o'er
> So several factions from this first ferment
> Work up to foam and threat the government
> Dryden, *Absalom and Achitophel*, lines 134–141

So much for the title of this chapter. As for its central figure Anthony Ashley Cooper, he appears in all the political histories and general studies of the period. He merited a biography by Campbell on the strength of his brief tenure of the office of Lord Chancellor. Perhaps the best modern biography is *The First Earl of Shaftesbury* by K. Haley (Clarendon Press, 1968).

p 88   *Therefore the Commons voted them into the Tower and ordered their sergeant-at-arms to see to it.*

At this the Lords ordered *their* Usher of the Black Rod to prevent it. It must have been one of the most splendid quarrels ever to divide the two Houses. Black Rod routed a pusillanimous sergeant-of-arms in the Court of Requests. But next day the Commons struck back: the Speaker himself spied Pemberton in Westminster Hall, had him seized and sent down to Little Ease, the prison of the House of Commons; and from there to the Tower.

p 89   *This was the fifteenth session of the Restoration/Cavalier Parliament*
The same M.P.s had therefore been sitting, on and off, for seventeen years without having to face an election.

p 92   *a young man who had himself attended a Jesuit seminary and been expelled*
Titus Oates was born in 1649. He became an Anglican curate in Hastings and after various malodorous adventures managed to obtain the post of chaplain to the Protestants in the Duke of Norfolk's household at nearby Arundel. He first met Israel Tonge in London in the winter of 1676. They at once formed a plan to exploit the fear of the Jesuits, and, to further it, Oates converted to Catholicism in April 1677 and on June 7 entered the Jesuit *Colegio de Los Ingleses* at Valladolid. Five months later he was summarily expelled for scandalous behaviour.

p 92   *a still mysterious murder, that of Sir Edmund Berry Godfrey*
'The mystery remains unresolved. The most probable theory is that Oates and his desperate associates caused Godfrey to be murdered to give colour to their false allegations, and to excite popular opinion in favour of their agitation.' From Godfrey's biography in the latest edition of the *DNB*.

p 93   *Ashley Cooper was almost certainly not the brains behind the Plot*
North in his *Examen* (p 95) accuses Ashley Cooper of cherishing, but not of starting, the Plot; and this verdict seems to be generally accepted by modern historians.

p 95   *'. . . It is better to be warm here than in Smithfield.'*
Scroggs was referring to the burning of the Protestant martyrs at Smithfield in 'Bloody Mary's' time.

p 97   *But for ten thousand pounds he has done*
       The Pope a great deal of good

The idiotic Portuguese Ambassador visited Scroggs the day
after Wakeman's acquittal to thank him. Hence the rumour of a
large bribe.

p 99   *The fates of Lord Chief Justices Tresilian and Belknap*
       during the reign of Richard II

Sir Robert Tresilian was appointed Lord Chief Justice of
King's Bench within a week of the lynching of his predecessor,
Sir John Cavendish (see Note to p 67). His first task, naturally,
was repression. At Bury St Edmunds he tried at least 17 rebels,
who were executed; at St Albans 15; and at Colchester 19 were
seen hanging from one beam. But recent research in court rolls
and records has put the total number of executions at only
about 110, a tiny proportion of the thousands rumoured at the
time.

Four years later Tresilian, a potential Mussolini to the young
King's Vittorio Emmanuele, organised a *coup* against the Lords
Appellant led by the King's uncle, Thomas of Woodstock.
When the tables were turned, the Lord Chief Justice was
appealed of high treason, tried in his absence, and condemned.
Though no one knew his whereabouts, he was suddenly spotted
by a squire of Thomas of Woodstock in an ale-house right
opposite the gates of the palace of Westminster and identified,
though in disguise. He took refuge in Westminster Abbey but
was dragged out by Thomas of Woodstock in person. 'Ah
Tresilian, Tresilian', Thomas is reported to have said, 'you have
been very foolish to come back to this part of the country, for
you are not loved here, and that will be seen. Look to your
affairs, for I will neither eat nor drink till you be dead.' The
Lord Chief Justice was taken to the Tower, put on a hurdle and
dragged through the streets of the City 'with a wonderful
throng of people following him'. When he got to the gibbet, he
refused to climb the ladder, and had to be beaten up with sticks.
He was hanged naked and the mob, after he had been hanging
there sometime, cut his throat to make sure he was dead. He is
the only Lord Chief Justice in our history to have been judicially
(or at least semi-judicially) executed. His name became a
byword for evil totalitarianism.

Sir Robert Belknap, Chief Justice of Common Pleas, was
extraordinarily lucky to survive both his senior colleagues. A
few days before Cavendish's lynching in the Fens, he himself
had been almost lynched in Essex – only released by infuriated

tax-rioters when he had sworn on the Bible he would never hold a session to punish them. But three of his clerks and three of the local jurors of Brentwood were killed in his presence; their heads were set on poles and paraded around the local villages.

Then, at the time of Tresilian's condemnation, he and his puisnes of Common Pleas were also appealed of high treason; and despite their defence of *force majeure* condemned by the 'Merciless Parliament'. But execution was stayed; Belknap was eventually exiled to Ireland, and then released. The position of Chief Justice of Common Pleas was always much less powerful politically – and therefore much less dangerous – than that of Chief Justice of King's Bench.

p 103   *a Quo Warranto* suit: a challenge by the Crown against the City Charter
Quo Warranto (By What Warrant?) was a recognized form of legal examination by the courts into long-established or newly-claimed privileges.

p 104   *staying with his crony, Tom Thynne, the richest land-owner in the West*
'Tom of Ten Thousand' succeeded in 1670 to the Longleat estates and became Monmouth's 'wealthy western friend'. His 15-year-old wife, Lady Elizabeth Percy, heiress of the eleventh and last Percy Earl of Northumberland (cp Note to p 14), was loved by a Swedish nobleman, Count Königsmark. On the evening of February 12, 1682 Thynne was shot and mortally wounded in his carriage on Pall Mall by three henchmen of the Count's – Vrutz, Stern and Boroski. Monmouth had just left Thynne's coach and the Whigs fanned suspicions that he was the real target. Tried before the Lord Chief Justice and a jury composed half of Englishmen and half of foreigners on February 27, Thynne's murderers were executed on March 10.

8. JUDGE JEFFREYS

Despite the reservations expressed on p 113, *Lord Chancellor Jeffreys and the Stuart Cause* by George Keeton (Macdonald, 1965) is an immensely valuable and well-researched book to which not only this chapter but the preceding and subsequent chapters owe a great deal.

Of the many earlier biographies, *Judge Jeffreys* by H.

Montgomery Hyde (Butterworth, 1948), with an excellent foreword by Lord Birkett, is particularly good on the legal side.

p 111 *Jeffreys ... married his first wife Sarah Neesham in 1667, a year before he was called to the Bar*

That was an unselfish, indeed given the spirit of the time, almost a noble marriage. Sarah, an heiress, had been disowned by her father the Reverend Thomas Neesham precisely because of the proposed match. But George married Sarah all the same, fortune or no fortune. Contrast Coke.

p 115 *On the evening of July 12 Arthur Capel committed suicide in the Tower ... foul play, for once, could not reasonably be suspected*

There *were* suspicions, nevertheless. But Capel had earlier recommended the eighth Earl of Northumberland's policy (cp Note to p 14) of committing suicide to pre-empt Attainder and thereby avoid confiscation of the family estates; he had sent for a razor; and he was very melancholy when last seen alive, being lodged in the same room from which his Royalist father Lord Capel had been led out to execution in 1649 (See p. 66).

p 118 *far fewer executions than there had been in the case of the Popish Plot*

About 35 death sentences were carried out on those involved in the non-existent Popish Plot; Scroggs himself sentenced to death *inter alios* seven Jesuits. The Rye House Plot (which it should again be stressed, *did* exist) led to seven executions and one suicide.

p 119 *'The ring upon that was called his blood stone'*

However Burnet alone of contemporary writers refers to this Judas-like blood stone; and Burnet was notoriously biased, not only against Jeffreys but for Armstrong (who seems to have been the main link between the Whig lords and the Rye House assassins).

p 119 *Fortunately for him that was in the spring of 1684. Had it been a year later ...*

Had it been a year later Titus Oates would have been attacking not a Duke but a King; as Charles II had died in the meantime and the Duke of York had succeeded as James II.

p 120 *Titus Oates was not expected to survive ... but he did*

He emerged from prison after the 'Glorious Revolution' and was received by William of Orange in early 1689. On March 31 he petitioned the Lords, who declared his sentence erroneous (which it was not), illegal (which was doubtful), and cruel (which it was). From August he was paid a pension of £5 a week by the new King. He died on July 12, 1705 at lodgings in Axe Yard.

p 122 *There is enormous controversy about the Bloody Assizes*

As Keeton points out, there are great gaps in the domestic state and private papers covering this period. No doubt many were 'shredded' to avoid compromising the glorious revolutionaries of 1688. See particularly *The Bloody Assizes* by J. G. Muddiman (London, 1929).

p 122 *whichever figure is taken, the number of executions is far less than that inflicted on the defeated rebels in the uprisings against Henry VIII and his daughter Elizabeth*

The Reformation in England led directly to three 'popular' traditionalist uprisings. The first and most famous was the Pilgrimage of Grace that broke out in Lincolnshire and then the North in 1536. The second was the Prayer Book Rebellion of 1549 in Devon and Cornwall. The third was the Rising of the North in 1570.

In none of these did it come to a pitched battle, as in Monmouth's Rebellion. Yet, the leaders apart, (they of course were executed in every case) roughly 250 people were executed by Henry VIII despite promises of pardon after the Pilgrimage of Grace and roughly 800 people by Elizabeth I after the much smaller-scale Rising of the North, in which only five lives had been lost. The Prayer Book Rebellion provoked the greatest bloodbath of all. Herbert and Russell, who repressed it ferociously in the name of the young Edward VI, summarily executed about 4000 rebels. This, though in the same part of the world as Monmouth's Rebellion, has been much less emphasised by historians.

(Kett's Rebellion in Norfolk, coinciding with the Prayer Book Rebellion but more economic than religious, was equally severely repressed by Dudley. There was only one uprising in Mary's reign – Wyatt's Rebellion against the Spanish match – in a way the most directly menacing of all. 3000 Kentishmen were only repulsed at the walls of the City, after a running battle in the Strand in which 50–70 lives were lost. Yet there were only 90–odd executions, and spectacular pardons, in this case.)

These statistics should help to put the 'Bloody Assizes' in perspective, not to excuse them.

9. THE LAST DAYS OF FOUR LORD CHIEF JUSTICES

p 126   *The Lords withdrew for half an hour; and unanimously found Delamere innocent*

An acquittal in a treason trial of great importance presided over by Judge Jeffreys . . . All is not so open and shut in Jeffreys' case as historical mythology would have it.

p 132   *The Lord Chancellor. . . was there to witness the birth but not Princess Anne, away in Bath*

By his first marriage to Anne Hyde James had had two daughters; who on his accession had become Princesses. The elder daughter Mary, married to William of Orange, was of course out of the country. But the second daughter, Princess Anne, was 22 and for her to have witnessed the birth of her half-brother (who by the laws of legitimate inheritance displaced both her and her sister's claims to the throne) would have been conclusive evidence against warming-pans. The Lord Chancellor being Jeffreys, the Lord Chancellor's testimony was suspect.

p 133   *that night several ornate effigies of the Pope . . . were . . . amid great rejoicing, burnt*

James II was more hurt, it was noted, by the insult to his religion than by the acquittal of the Seven Bishops.

p 133   *Jeffreys, like a Justiciar of old, was left to preside at Westminster*

When the King was absent – usually abroad –, the Justiciars had ruled the land. The most spectacular case in English history is that of Richard the Lionheart who paid only two brief visits to England during his reign. Like William the Conqueror, he appointed two co-Justiciars to rule during his absence: an earl and a bishop. But the earl died and Richard replaced him with his greatest personal friend – a diminutive, misshapen, lame Frenchman, William de Longchamps, who became Bishop of Ely. This appointment led to enormous rivalries and troubles while the Lionheart was absent on crusade – and, later, in prison.

p 135   *The Prince was at Abingdon*
William of Orange slept, family tradition has it, at Milton Manor.

p 136   *Farewell Wright, worse than Tresilian*
Hardly. See Note to p 99.

10. KNAVISH TRICKS

The title is of course taken from the second verse of the National Anthem:

> Confound their politicks
> Frustrate their knavish tricks
> In thee our hope we fix
> God Save our King!

Macaulay's *History of England* vividly and in great detail recounts the dramas that follow.

p 143   *This Jacobite 'Assassination Plot'*
See *The Triumphs of Providence* by Jane Garrett (Cambridge, 1980) for a lively narrative of this Plot.

p 143   *Ambrose Rookwood*
Not to be confused with the also-executed Ambrose Rookwood of the Gunpowder Plot (see pp 16 and 17), though they must have been related. This Ambrose Rookwood was born after the Restoration in 1664. He had been a Brigadier in James II's army. See Macaulay, Vol. II, p 564.

p 146   *the Solicitor General accused the Attorney General of corruption*
An unwise move in the sense that even if the Attorney General had to resign, so did the Solicitor General for backstabbing his number one.

pp 146/147   *The new Attorney General Robert Raymond . . . had been rewarded with a knighthood when the Tories came in.*
The Tories basically came in with Queen Anne. They did not last long. See for the subsequent period *The Whig Supremacy 1714–1760* by B. Williams (Clarendon Press, 1962, 2nd edi-

tion). Queen Anne was succeeded by George I, the Elector of Hanover, in 1714; George III, 'Farmer George', succeeded George II in 1760.

p 147   *accused of conspiring to bring in the Old Pretender*
The Old Pretender was the rightful King, James III, who had had the misfortune to be born in Jeffreys' presence (cp p 132 and Note), and who was a tiny baby at the time of the Revolution of 1688. His mother, James II's second wife, was Mary of Modena; he was therefore half-brother to both Queen Mary and Queen Anne. On Anne's death the Tories met in London and decided to proclaim James III King; but his unswerving loyalty to the Catholic religion and his generally bigoted stance made any serious movement in his favour impossible. The Old Pretender died, as he had lived, in exile, in 1766. His son, Charles Edward, 'Bonnie Prince Charlie', the Young Pretender was born in 1720, led in person the '45 (see pp 152–154), and died in 1788.

p 148   *yet another hopelessly corrupt judge, as so many of our
          Lord Chief Justices have been*
Most notoriously in the late mediaeval period. This is particularly true of the first 15 Lord Chief Justices who held office during the successive reigns of the first three Edwards. For example, William Thorpe, one of Edward III's right-hand men, like a Justiciar, virtually governed England while the King was gaining glory at Crécy. He was arrested and removed from his office of Lord Chief Justice in October 1350, tried by a Commission of Five, arraigned by the King himself for the enormity of his offences, confessed to taking bribes, and was sentenced to be hanged. (The sentence was commuted to a year's imprisonment and forfeiture of most of his lands.) Even the admirable Shareshull (cp *Introductory Notes* p ix) had been arrested in 1340 with *all* the other judges. This was fairly typical. By contrast the Justiciars had been far greater men — and therefore of course, though notably less corrupt, far more dangerous to the royal power.

p 152   *How sweet an Ovid, Murray, was our boast!
          How many Martials were in Pulteney lost.*
Ovid was famous for his *Ars Amoris* (the Art of Love), Martial for his epigrams. For Pulteney's talents in that direction see p 149 above. William Pulteney, wealthy, witty, and lazy, became one of the greatest orators the House of Commons had ever heard.

p 153 *Philip Yorke as a Lord Justice was virtually Regent and in the position of a Justiciar of old*

But even Ralph de Hengham, though only a Lord Chief Justice, was appointed Guardian of the Realm for the three and a half years that Edward I was abroad, fighting in Gascony. On Edward's return in August 1289 he and his fellow judges were condemned to perpetual imprisonment in the Tower for corruption (cp notes to pp 148 and 133 above).

p 154 *He died with quotations from Horace and Ovid on his lips*

Not from the *Ars Amoris* in Ovid's case. From Horace, Lovat, with a banality unusual for so quick-witted a man, chose the trite '*Dulce et decorum est pro patria mori*'.

11. WILLIAM MURRAY

Lord Mansfield by Edmund Hewart (Barry Rose, 1981) is a legal biography, that has to some extent replaced C. S. Fifoot's standard biography of Murray – thanks largely to Hewart's discovery of 56 legal notebooks found in an attic in Scone Palace.

p 162 *Earl Ferrers ... tried April 1760 ... drove from the Tower to Tyburn ... the first man to be hanged by a clean drop*

By this time beheading for the nobility had been discontinued. As late as 1820 however, though drawing and quartering had also been discontinued, the Cato Street Conspirators (see p188 and 189) had their heads cut off after death and exhibited to the crowd. By 1783 public executions at Tyburn (where Marble Arch now stands) were replaced by executions at Newgate.

'No Sir,' Dr Johnson told Boswell, 'this is *not* an improvement ... Sir, Executions are intended to draw Spectators. If they do not draw Spectators, they do not answer their purpose.' For all this see *Tales from the Newgate Calendar* by Rayner Heppenstall (Constable, 1981).

p 166 *the still mysterious Junius*

He is generally thought to be the doctrinaire Whig Sir Philip Francis (1740–1818). See Francis' biography in the *DNB* for arguments *pro* and *contra*.

p 167   '. . . *Who was that judge who, to save the King's brother, affirmed that a man of the first rank and quality, who obtains a verdict in a case for criminal conversation, is entitled to no greater damages than the meanest mechanic?*

Junius is referring to the notorious case of the *Earl of Grosvenor v. HRH The Duke of Cumberland*, the King's brother. The letters of HRH to the adulterous Countess were cited in evidence, to the general delight. 'Here I am all by myself at see!' was one of the public's favourites.

p 168   *Miss Elizabeth Chudleigh was renowned for her sex appeal, even in that age of great beauties*

When the question came up of whether this book should be illustrated, almost the only argument in favour of doing so was the chance of including, among the tedious portrait gallery of full-bottomed wigs, the extremely erotic drawing of the full-bosomed Miss Chudleigh in the character of Iphigenia at the Venetian Ambassador's Masque.

For a full account of her trial see *The Trial of the Duchess of Kingston* edited by Louis Melville (1927) – in the Famous Trials series that William Hodge & Co. published so successfully in the heyday of popular legal literature between the Wars.

p 169   *But Junius had in 1772 silenced himself or been silenced*

Junius' last letter, another assault on the Lord Chief Justice, appeared on January 2, 1772. It was rated a failure; and Junius, under that name, wrote no more.

p 170   *except only the Earl of M*

It is 99 percent certain that Lord Camden was referring to Murray here, though there were two other Earls of M in the House. The scene took place on April 7, 1778; Chatham died a month later.

p 171   *Historians are still baffled by the last lurid flare-up of 'No Popery' in London known as the Gordon Riots.*

See in particular *The Gordon Riots: a Study of the Rioters and Their Victims* by G. E. F. Rude (Transactions of the R. Historical Soc., 5th series, Vol VI, 1956). It seems as baffling to outsiders as the passion of Ulster Protestants seem to the easy-going people of England at the present time. The situation, and the reactions, have a certain amount in common: a Protestant

Association, with an M.P. as its leader (though the erratic 29-year-old Lord George Gordon is hardly comparable to the Rev. Ian Paisley), and surprising support from 'the Protestant people'.

p 171 *a Lord Chief Justice torn to bits or strung up like his 'brother Cavendish, in the good old days*
To be precise, merely beheaded. See note to p 67.

p 173 *And in the end it was not the ruling classes who lost their lives but, as inevitably happens in England, the revolutionary mob.*
In the Peasants' Revolt of 1381 (cp notes to pp 67 and 99) the ruling classes *did* suffer but far less than might have been the case – far, far less than in the *Jacquerie* in France. In the past 600 years the 'popular masses' have barely ever threatened the established order at all seriously. The last outburst, the 'Captain Swing' agitation in the countryside and the rioting in the cities at the time of Reform (pp 191 and 193), was easily put down.

12. TWO WHIG REACTIONARIES: KENYON AND LAW

p 176 *the ugly Law … wooed and won … the incredibly beautiful Miss Towry*
It was not this Edward Law but his son, namesake and heir, the second Lord Ellenborough, who wooed and won *en deuxièmes noces* and to his misfortune the notorious Lady Ellenborough, Jane Digby (for some see Sykes' magistral work, already cited in the note to p 26).

p 177 *'Little conversant with the manners of polite society*
The quotation is from Wraxall, *Memoirs*, First Series, p 165, (cited by Campbell, like almost all quotations in this and the next chapter).

p 178 *almost a caricature of a Victorian judge*
It would have been less anachronistic to describe him as a forerunner.

p 180 *the first Parliament of the United Kingdom, with …
Irish members*

Before this, before the aftermath of the Great Rebellion of 1798, Ireland had always had its own Parliament. The subsequent agitation for Home Rule (see especially pp 212, 213, 238, 244, 245 & 254) was essentially for the restoration of an Irish Parliament in Dublin.

p 182   *the enticingly named case of the Hottentot Venus*

It was less melodramatic in fact. Do-gooders bought a writ of Habeas Corpus against the Hottentot's keepers. But the Venus testified that she had been brought to England to be exhibited of her own free will, and the action failed.

p 183   *he utterly opposed Sir Samuel Romilly's efforts to have*
         the total number of offences for which the penalty was
         death reduced to manageable proportions

Until 1826 the official penalty for all felonies bar petty larceny was death. Resistance against change had been fierce. In 1784 the Reverend Martin Maclean had specially denounced in his *Thoughts on Executive Justice* 'the leniency exercised towards horse thieves. The law says *they shall be hanged*.' Of course executions of all felons was impractical. Yet in the year 1785, less than 200 years ago, there were 97 executions in London alone. See especially *Johnson's England* (Clarendon Press, 1933): Chapter 25 in Vol II, 'The Law and the Lawyers' by Sir Frank Mackinnon.

p 183   *within a few years Perceval was himself conducting,*
         rather courageously, the war against Napoleon

And thereby flatly and annoyingly disproving the author's generalisation, 30 pages earlier, *re* the total incapacity of lawyers for managing wars.

p 183   *The trial took place . . . with what was later agreed to*
         be indecent haste

It was all over and done with within a week. The Prime Minister was murdered on Monday; the assassin was tried on the Friday at the Old Bailey and found guilty despite his plea of insanity; and he was hanged the following Monday. Not only indecent but suspicious.

p 185   *'Nature had exhibited . . .'*

The quotation is from Townsend's *Twelve Judges*, Vol I, p 389, cited by Campbell.

13. BARBER'S SON, OLD ETONIAN: ABBOTT AND DENMAN

Abbott's biography is Campbell's last and almost his finest effort. A *Memoir of Lord Denman* was written by J. Arnould.

p 186   *but a recommendation from a fading Lord Chief Justice is often the kiss of death*
Not nowadays, however. Goddard recommended his successor Parker, and Parker recommended his own successor Widgery. The present Lord Chief Justice, Lane, told me that he did not know who recommended him or why he was chosen. The selection is (at least officially) made by the Prime Minister — at the time of Lane's appointment Mrs Thatcher.

p 187   *wrote a legal colleague of his*
Cited by Campbell, who, though he did not write his predecessor's biography, often referred to him. On p 342 of Vol IV of his *Lives of the Lord Chief Justices*.

p 189   *The Case of the Delicate Investigation*
On July 5, 1820 a Bill of Pains and Penalties was introduced into the House of Lords, with the aim of depriving the new King's estranged consort Queen Caroline of her title and of dissolving the marriage on the grounds of her notorious adultery. Brougham acted as the Queen's Attorney General and Denman as her Solicitor General. The Bill was eventually shelved in favour of a trial in Westminster Hall that began on August 19 and lasted for nearly four months of intense excitement.

p 189   *summed up the wits*
The ditty is quoted in the excellent *DNB* biography of Denman.

p 190   *The Lord Chief Justice . . . was only created a peer after nine years in office*
This was insulting. His four predecessors, Ryder, Murray, Kenyon and Law, had been raised to the Lords on appointment. They were of course of far less humble origins.

p 192   *burbled the Lord Chief Justice*
No sillier, however, except in form, than the prognostications of Lord Liverpool and the Duke of Bedford (see above, p 190).

p 195 *an 'Indian' officer, a certain Captain Reynolds*

Reynolds held a commission in the Indian Army and was therefore considered of lower social rank and less versed in gentlemanly etiquette. Duelling as such was not – indeed has never been – illegal in England; but it is treated as attempted murder if injury is inflicted. On the other hand the Duke of Wellington had in 1824 fought a duel when Prime Minister with Lord Winchelsea, and neither was prosecuted.

For a splendid account of the whole 'Black Bottle' affair and of Lord Cardigan's subsequent career, see Cecil Woodham Smith's rightly-renowned *The Reason Why*.

14. THE BIOGRAPHER AND THE BARONET: CAMPBELL AND COCKBURN

p 197 *wrote their daughter and his biographer Mrs Hardcastle*

The Life of Lord Campbell – a selection from his autobiography, diaries and letters – was edited by the Hon. Mrs J. Hardcastle (London, 1881, 2 vols). It is complemented by *The Victorian Chancellors* by J. B. Atlay (Smith, Elder & Co, 1906) – a sequel to Campbell's own work. Vol I has a biographer of Brougham; Vol II of Campbell.

p 198 *wrote a biographer of Campbell (somewhat to the chagrin of at least one reader)*

G. P. Macdonell in the *DNB*. The reader is the writer.

p 199 *though the volume which dealt with Lyndhurst and Brougham was only published posthumously*

This was Vol VIII of the *Lives of the Lord Chancellors* published in 1869. Brougham as a counterblast (though in fact he was much more kindly treated than Lyndhurst) wrote his own, very inaccurate, memoirs: *The Life and Times of Henry Lord Brougham: Recollections of a Long Life* (Blackwoods, 1871, 2 vols).

p 199 *one of his favourites was Alexander Cockburn*

There is a chapter on Cockburn in *Famous Judges and Famous Trials* by Charles Kingston (Stanley Paul, 1923) – and also chapters on his successors as Lord Chief Justice, Coleridge, Russell and Webster.

p 201   *Palmerston's triumph was total. He was the most popular Minister ... in Europe.*

Palmerston was in office almost continuously from 1830 to 1865. His fame extended even to the Russian steppes – out of which a peasant crawled (*per* Turgenev) to ask: Who *is* Palmestron?

p 201   *in which Dr (later Cardinal) Newman faced a libel action bought by the renegade Catholic Achilli.*

In October 1850 the restoration of the Catholic hierarchy in England, labelled 'the Papal Aggression', provoked furious opposition fanned by an apostate Dominican friar, Achilli. Newman attacked him; he bought an action for criminal libel against Newman; Newman pleaded not guilty, with a defence of 'justification' on 23 counts. The case was tried by the Lord Chief Justice at Queen's Bench on June 21–24. Campbell summed up against Newman, who was found guilty and fined £100. But his legal costs came to £14,000 – mainly raised by public subscription.

p 201   *the famous prosecution of William Palmer in the Rugely poisoning case*

See *The Trial of William Palmer* edited by G. H. Knott (Hodge, 1912). Also Holdsworth, Vol XV, p 428 and Atlay, Vol II, p 202.

p 202   *Greville wrote*

In his *Memoirs*, Vol VIII, pp 67 and 68.

p 203   *Much to the general amazement Palmerston offered the post to the Lord Chief Justice ... Even more to the general amazement, Campbell accepted*

When Campbell became Lord Chancellor, Lord Lyndhurst offered him a dinner the night before he was sworn in.

'Thou hast it now,' he quoted with obvious irony, 'King, Cawdor, Glamis, all, As the weird women promised.' (Quoted Hardcastle, Vol II, p 384.)

p 205   *a great triumph for Coleridge*

Though fellow lawyers thought that Hawkins Q.C. who assisted him, an incisive lawyer, could have conducted his cross-examination with twice the success and in half the time and knew that his junior counsel Bowen, who shared Coleridge's chambers had done most of the hard work.

p 206 *Almost forty years later Kenealy's son wrote an account*
       of the trial
The Tichborne Tragedy by Maurice Kenealy (Francis
Griffiths, 1913). There are innumerable accounts of the Tich-
borne case.

15. THE ODDEST PAIR OF ALL: COLERIDGE AND RUSSELL

The Life and Correspondence of Lord Coleridge by his cousin
Ernest Coleridge (Heinemann, 1904, 2 vols) is legal hagio-
graphy, less useful than a number of accounts of Coleridge in
other legal works, e.g. in *The Great Judges* by Gerald Sparrow
(Long, 1974). By way of contrast the *Life of Lord Russell of
Killowen* by his friend and pupil Barry O'Brien (Smith Elder &
Co, 1901; pocket edition Thomas Nelson, 1909) is a splendid
work, and my major source for Russell's life and times,
character and tastes.

p 209 *The Pegasus Club*
The Pegasus Club still organises the Bar Point-to-point and
other legal equestrian events.

p 211 *the Court of Criminal Appeal where the Lord Chief
       Justice now usually presides ... there are scores of
       judges now where there were in the common law courts
       a simple rounded dozen, and as a result the Lord Chief
       Justice has become nowadays much more of an admin-
       istrator, much less of a judge*
In January 1982 I sat in at the Lord Chief Justice's Court in
the Law Courts. This is the Court of Criminal Appeal where on
most mornings the Lord Chief Justice sits with two (variable)
colleagues. Basically, the appeals heard are against sentences
imposed by trial judges. On the morning I was there four cases
were heard. The first (see Note to p281) was an appeal by three
youths who had kicked a fourth to death. The judges heard the
barristers on either side, and then left the court for between five
and ten minutes to consider their verdict. They had, of course,
Lord Lane told me afterwards, previously studied all the papers
– and he added that he was very well aware of the presence of
the families of the youths sitting in court in two massive rows
and had allowed for this in the tone of his remarks.

The next case was an application for leave to appeal by a policeman who had been convicted of shoplifting goods worth £3.10 in Woolworths. That was refused with what seemed to me excessive delicacy; but apparently an obvious ex-policeman had been sitting in court, and for him it was a bitter pill, involving loss of job and of pension rights. The third appeal was by a burglar who had used a toy pistol, against his sentence of two years. This time the Lord Chief Justice, largely because of 'a very moving letter from this man's wife' reduced the sentence – with a stern warning – to 12 months. The fourth was a complicated car theft case where the main witness, back in Australia, had changed his mind. It was ruled to be all very unsatisfactory in five minutes' flat. I recount these cases in some detail partly because they at first sight seemed so trivial for a Lord Chief Justice's attention, and partly because of the surprisingly human side which I had not expected to find.

The day before, in a formal interview, Lord Lane explained the present daily routine of a Lord Chief Justice. Administration takes up most of his early mornings – he arrives at his chambers at 8 a.m. – afternoons and early evenings. He had not spoken in the House of Lords, for instance, because he simply had not had the time (but cp note to p 289); where in Hewart's day there had been four courts in the Old Bailey, there were now 24, and that was typical of the general expansion. There were now 49 Queen's Bench Judges, all of whom had to have their cases allotted and their problems solved, besides the circuit judges. He was, however, almost as scathing as Hewart, though more discreet, about the Lord Chancellor's Department which had 'enormously expanded' and was staffed by 'many unsuccessful lawyers'. But he was, he said, very fond of the Lord Chancellor, Lord Hailsham, a 'super chap'. He spoke forthrightly and firmly. On two points only were his replies hardly convincing: first when he told me that he had 'not the remotest idea' why he had been appointed; and secondly when he said he could not remember how much he earned. It is in fact (in 1983) £52,500.

See also note to p 294.

p 214 *In his standard volume of the* Oxford History of
England 1870–1914
(Clarendon Press, 1936). Ensor was notoriously a conservative historian: 'extremely dignified type of journalism, conducted with a high sense of personal responsibility and seeking to win intelligent readers,' was the way he described that lost Eden.

p 216   *Campbell versus Lady Colin Campbell and (among many other co-respondents) the Duke of Marlborough, a case 'which led to some of the most remarkable revelations a court of law has ever had to listen to.'*
The comment is from Kingston, p 144 (see note to p 199). Unfortunately that author does not elaborate and this author has not tracked down the details. The then Duke of Marlborough was the notoriously depraved eldest brother of Lord Randolph Churchill – i.e. Winston's uncle.

p 216   *Sir Edward Clarke, describing the opening day of the trial, wrote*
Quoted on p xi of *The Baccarat Case* edited by W. T. Shore (Hodge, 1931). *Famous Cases of Sir Edward Clarke* by Derek Walker Smith and Edward Clarke (Eyre & Spottiswoode, 1939) is also relevant.

p 217   *even now . . ., in a land of perfect religious tolerance, we cannot have a Catholic as Lord Chancellor*
This is not, I have found, strictly accurate. Under the Tenure of Office and Discharge of Ecclesiastical Funds Act 1974, the Lord Chancellor may indeed be a Catholic but, if so, his visitational and ecclesiastical functions devolve on the Prime Minister or another Minister. Interestingly, there is no such restriction should he be a Nonconformist or Jew (or indeed a Buddhist, Hindu or Muslim).

p 218   *Dr Jameson, Rhodes' exact contemporary*
See especially *Jameson's Raid* By Elizabeth Pakenham (Weidenfeld & Nicolson, 1960); also *The Boer War* by her eldest son Thomas Pakenham (Weidenfeld & Nicolson, 1979).

p 218   *the Foreign Enlistment Act of 1870*
Unsuccessful attempts are continually being made to use this act to stop would-be British mercenaries and their recruiters from signing up in the United Kingdom. See the present author's *Mercenaries* (Macdonald, 1970).

p 219   *wrote to his daughter Lilian*
Quoted by Barry O'Brien, p 369.

16. THE RISE OF RUFUS ISAACS

In this chapter and the two that follow I have attempted to give some idea of the characters and talents, not only of the Lord

Chief Justices as such, but of the group of extraordinarily talented and variegated lawyers and politicians who formed the ruling class in the immediate pre-War years, and of the atmosphere of easy social intercourse despite the passions that constantly flared.

In this brilliant constellation Rufus Isaacs had a particular and starring place. An enormous amount of the next three chapters is based on the excellent biography *Lord Reading* by H. Montgomery Hyde (Heinemann, 1967). To the work of Mr Hyde, one of the most distinguished legal biographers and writers of this century (with which he is almost co-eval) I owe an enormous debt, not only for this biography.

The other major biography (and it is obvious enough in the text where it is used) is that of Rufus Isaacs, by his son, Gerald, the second Marquess of Reading (two volumes, Hutchinson, 1945). *Lord Reading and his Cases* by Derek Walker Smith (Chapman and Hall, 1934) is more sternly legal.

There is no shortage of general studies of the political history of the period or particular biographies of the personalities involved: of all those I have looked through, one stands out, and that is *David Lloyd George: Tempestuous Journey* by Frank Owen (Hutchinson, 1954); a stimulating and most detached biography to which I would like here to record my debt.

p 226   *Rufus Isaacs lost the seat by 730 votes*
The result, declared on October 5, 1900 was:

W.E.T. Sharpe (C)	3257
Rufus Isaacs (L)	2527
Conservative majority	730

p 227   *Richard Webster 'looked and sounded like a bluff farmer'*
Montgomery Hyde's description, as are almost all the otherwise unattributed descriptions or quotations in the chapters that follow. Webster's 'exceptionally tedious autobiography' (my phrase) is *Recollections of Bar and Bench* by Viscount Alverstone (Edward Arnold, 1914).

p 229   *Rufus Isaacs won the seat by a majority of 230*
Voting took place on August 4, 1904:

Rufus Isaacs (L)	4770
C. E. Keyser (C)	4540
Liberal majority	230

p 230   *The Liberal Party . . . in the General Election held in*

January 1906 came back to power with an enormous majority.

377 Liberals were returned, supported by 53 Labour Members (that figure was almost an equal sensation) plus the usual 83 Irish Nationalists against only 132 Conservatives and a wretched 25 Liberal Unionists. It was a landslide.

p 230 *Asquith ... Haldane ... Carson ... F. E. Smith ... Lloyd George*

There are numerous excellent biographies, contemporary and modern, of all these lawyer-politicians, which it would be *de trop* to list here.

p 231 *In the libel action that followed*

The libel first appeared in the 29 July, 1908 issue of *The Bystander* under the heading 'The Chancellor's Troubles'. 'Rumour is now busy', the column read, 'as to the existence of embarrassment of another kind, which is even less likely to prove of assistance in his career. Mr George has of course been overloaded with flattery of late, especially from the fair sex, which is always difficult for a man of "Temperament" to resist. The matter may of course be kept quiet. *Nous verrons*'.

Lloyd George sued, *The Bystander* settled out of court, but then *The People* picked up the story.

p 232 *As a recent biographer, John Grigg has shown, there exist two series of letters ... of which at least one set show an attempt to blackmail the Chancellor of the Exchequer.*

In *Lloyd George, The People's Champion* by John Grigg (Methuen, 1978): 'and also let me have the two photos of my little son', demands the writer, Mrs G, rather pathetically. Quoted p 237.

p 232 *The most dramatic of Lloyd George's election meetings was that ... in Reading where he had gone down to support Rufus Isaacs.*

Dramatic due to the sudden appearance of two suffragettes who had been hiding dirty and dishevelled under the platform – for no women at all, bar Mrs Isaacs and Mrs George, were allowed in. 'You're a robber, Mr Lloyd George,' cried the first. An excitable old gentleman tried to brain her with his bowler hat as she was being removed.

p 232   *Northcliffe . . . wrote to congratulate him.*
Cited in Vol I, p184 of his son Gerald's biography.

p 233   *The second election of the year 1910 was looming*
The Liberals and the Conservatives were, as a result, exactly balanced with 272 seats each; John Redmond, leader of the Irish Nationalists, and, like Asquith, a devoted House of Commons man, held the balance. Home Rule for Ireland once again became therefore the dominating issue; but this time (cp p 212) the power of the Lords to veto a Home Rule Bill had virtually disappeared. The Conservatives and Liberal Unionists were therefore left without that fall-back protection, and venom grew.

p 233   *Lucy Masterman wrote in her diary*
From *Lucy Masterman* by G. F. G. Masterman (1939) pp 174–183. Quoted by Montgomery Hyde, p 87.

p 234   *'He guarded jealously his own rigid self control,' wrote his son, '. . . He hated rows and scenes, for the spectacle of human beings casting aside the decencies of normal intercourse made him acutely uncomfortable.'*
Vol I, p 207, of Gerald's biography. But it is hard to believe that Rufus really hated melodrama. What did drive him on? What motivated him? According to his son he also hated risqué stories; he was a prude (and certainly there was never a breath of sexual scandal in his life). But if he was a sincere prude and a sincere quietist, how could he have tolerated the company of 'The Goat', as his great crony Lloyd George was nicknamed? There is a puzzle here, the sort of puzzle that recurs all through Rufus Isaacs' life.

p 234   *He was a touchy and emotional man, for all his self-control.*
Rufus Isaacs played golf with Lloyd George and Churchill but bridge with that bridge-fiend, Asquith. Is this significant? Was he all things to all men? Is that an explanation of the apparent contradictions in his character and behaviour?

17. GEHAZI

p 235   *Commendatore Marconi*
See in particular *The Marconi Scandal* by Frances Donaldson (London, 1962).

p 236 *Rufus Isaacs took the opportunity to make this statement to the House . . . Isaacs' statement was technically true.*

Though it reminds one of nothing so much as Profumo's statement to the House in Macmillan's day, that he had had no dealings of any sort with Christine Keeler. That was of course a downright lie.

p 237 *I am most deeply grateful to you, wrote Rufus Isaacs to F. E.*

Quoted by Montgomery Hyde, p154

p 237 *It was Winston Churchill . . . who persuaded Lord Northcliffe, the greatest press baron of the day, to play the whole story down.*

'Winston was very agitated when he came to see me,' Northcliffe told Riddell, another crony of the Chancellor's. 'I did not know till then how much he was attached to Lloyd George.' Quoted by Frank Owen, p 231.

'Sir Rufus Isaacs', wrote a Labour M.P. Fred Towett, 'was distinctly and obviously distressed . . .'

Quoted by Frank Owen, p 233.

p 238 *Thirty years later convalescing in Marrakesh, Churchill would still talk about the affair.*

See p 156 of *Struggle for Survival* by Churchill's doctor, Lord Moran (London, 1966).

p 239 *The Ulster Unionist Council had appointed Sir Edward Carson their leader.*

Tempers had been rising since the famous Unionist meeting at Blenheim Palace the year before, when the Conservative leader, Bonar Law, had declared that he could imagine no lengths of resistance to which Ulster might go which he would not be prepared to support. Half a million people had signed the Ulster Covenant in Belfast, against what Carson dubbed, 'the most nefarious conspiracy that has yet been hatched against a free people'.

p 239 *King George V found it all 'most embarrassing'. As his private secretary put it . . .*

Quoted by Montgomery Hyde, p 162.

p 239 *He told Riddell . . . he had been looking through Campbell's Lives of the Chief Justices*

Montgomery Hyde, p 165.

p 240 Verses from 'Gehazi' by Rudyard Kipling are reprinted from the definitive edition of Rudyard Kipling's verse by kind permission of The National Trust.

p 241 *'I answered', noted Asquith, 'that I must use preferably plain language . . .'*
Asquith Papers, quoted by Montgomery Hyde, p 243.

p 242 *The trial of Roger Casement*
Once again I must acknowledge how much I owe to the same author. From the Introduction to *The Trial of Roger Casement* by H. Montgomery Hyde, (William Hope and Son, 1960) come almost all the quotations that follow: for instance the dialogue between the U.S. Ambassador and Asquith (p 243) was reported to Hyde by one of Sir Basil Thomson's staff who had it from a member of the Embassy. For a more general study see *Roger Casement* by Brian Inglis (Hodder & Stoughton, 1973).

pp 242/3 *'You had a good point there,' F. E. Smith is alleged to have told one of the defence lawyers two years later.*
Quoted by Hyde, cxxxii. But the story was vehemently denied by F. E.'s son.

p 245 *Allowing Casement to make an unsworn statement from the dock – in which case he could not be subject to cross-examination.*
Casement could not do this now. The right was abolished, despite strong legal protests, by Parliament in November 1982, part of the constant whittling-down of defendants' rights in this country.

pp 245/6 *as for instance Philip Howard was when he prayed as a prisoner in the Tower for the success of the Spanish Armada.*
Philip Howard, Earl of Arundel, had been one of Queen Elizabeth's early favourites despite the execution of his father, Thomas, fourth Duke of Norfolk. He was converted to Catholicism by his admiration for Edmund Campion's behaviour when confronted, after the rack, with the Anglican Divines (see note to p 5.) and was himself sent to the Tower. There, according to his own story, he prayed that there would be no massacre of the Papist prisoners if the Spanish Armada landed its invading force. He was tried for treason by his fellow peers in Westminster Hall on April 18, 1589. 'The fact having

been held by the Judges as established,' wrote Henry Garnet to Claudio Aquaviva, the General of the Jesuits, 'to wit that he had begged prayers, it was a subject of long discussion whether to pray for the fleet was High Treason and many of the Peers declaring they did not agree with this they summoned and consulted the judges whose order, formerly most venerable, is now much held in contempt'. As always, the Lord Chief Justice, Popham, ruled against liberty, and, for the first and last time in English history, prayer was found to be high treason. But the popular uproar was such that Elizabeth did not sign Howard's death warrant. He died eight years later, still in the Tower, at the age of 38.

18. THE HEWART INTRIGUE

For Hewart's life and in particular for the main subject-matter of this chapter, I have taken my facts almost entirely from *The Chief* by Robert Jackson (Harrap, 1959). This is the sole full length biography of Hewart; and the only source for his version of the intrigue.

Hewart himself published three books: *The New Despotism* (Benn, 1929), *Essays and Observations* (Cassell, 1930) and *Not Without Prejudice* (Hutchinson, 1937). They are of only incidental value to a biographer.

p 248   *Or as Gordon Hewart with greater precision put it*
Quoted by Montgomery Hyde, p 313. As in the previous chapters it is obvious which quotations are from Gerald Isaac's biography of his father; and where this is not so, the source is almost always Montgomery Hyde.

pp 248/9   *1918 meant inevitably a General Election . . . Asquith and his Independent Liberals were almost eliminated*
It was Asquith who christened it 'the Coupon election' because all official Coalition candidates had to have a letter of endorsement signed by both Lloyd George and Bonar Law. 474 Coalition M.P.s were elected – 338 Conservatives and Unionists plus 136 Coalition Liberals. 59 Labour and only 26 Independent Liberals formed the Opposition. Gordon Hewart had his 'coupon' for the Coalition Liberals as of course did F. E. Smith for the Coalition Conservative and Unionists.

p 249   *Horatio Bottomley*
The exchange with Hewart is quoted by Jackson, p 87.

p 251   *Lloyd George was quite confident of his ability to find*
        an aged judge
There was Lord Finlay, at 79 a touch older than the eventual
choice, Lawrence. There was also Mr Justice Darling but the
legal profession despised him. He had been appointed for his
social graces by a Tory Lord Chancellor, Halsbury, whose
appointments of judges had almost all been biased by friendship
or politics.

p 251   *Such at least appears, from the available evidence to be*
        the thinking behind the Lloyd George–Rufus Isaacs
        plan.
The evidence is scattered; and the 'plan' was never admitted
by either of the two main participants. For Hewart's evidence
see Jackson, pp 126–144.

p 254   *'I shall resign as Attorney General and give up politics*
        altogether if I am not appointed Lord Chief Justice,'
        Hewart had threatened
Cited Jackson, p 144. I doubt if the threat influenced Lloyd
George as much as his exasperation with Montagu (who had
been extraordinarily scathing, virtually calling him a dictator)
and with anything – *viz* the Viceroy – connected with India.

p 254   *His clerk Curtis was furious.*
Curtis confirmed the story that same morning to Arthur
Smith, Goddard's clerk. See Chapter 20.

p 256   *Edith Thompson who with her lodger-lover Bywaters*
        was accused of murdering her husband
See *The Trial of Frederick Bywaters and Edith Thompson*
edited by F. Young (Hodge, 1923); and, for a more critical
account, the chapter headed 'The Thompson–Bywaters Horror'
in *Miscarriages of Justice* by C. G. L. Du Cann (Frederick
Muller, 1960).

p 257   *as a fellow judge has written with studied moderation*
Gerald Sparrow in *The Great Judges* (John Lang, 1974)

p 257   *Even Henry Cecil . . . writes*
In *Just Within the Law*, (Hutchinson, 1975).

p 258 *'I shall remember your kisses, Your Excellency'* . . .
This splendid anecdote is told by Montgomery Hyde, p 391.

p 259 *at the age of seventy Rufus married his dead wife's secretary, a woman of thirty-seven, Stella Charnaud*
She became a notoriously 'difficult' old lady. She refused to let Montgomery Hyde see Rufus' private papers when he was writing his biography, imposing her own '50-year-rule'. Created a peeress in her own right in 1958 – as Baroness Swanborough – she died in 1971. The present 4th Marquess of Reading is Rufus' great-grandson.

p 260 *wrote one of his (Goddard's) daughters*
Lady Sachs, quoted by Fenton Bresler. See Chapter 20.

p 261 *'. . . frightfully unhappy incident from Rayner's point of view,' commented an old friend.*
Christopher Clarke, quoted by Fenton Bresler. See Chapter 20.

p 261 *as Lord Sankey rather plaintively reported to the P.M.*
From the Sankey Papers, quoted by R. F. V. Heuston. See Chapter 19. 'It is most unfortunate,' added Sankey of Hewart, 'that the Lord Chief Justice had been unable to attend to his official duties. Originally he wrote a letter in which he said, as far as I can remember, that the judges will cheerfully comply with the cuts which the government thought necessary. It is useless for me to disguise the fact that the judges are rather bent upon giving trouble unless their demands are satisfied.' Heuston, pp 513, 514. Not much to choose between judges then and workers now, it seems.

19. INSKIP FOR P.M.?

Almost the whole of my account of Inskip is based on *Lives of the Lord Chancellors 1885–1940* by R. F. V. Heuston (Clarendon Press, 1964), who in his turn based almost the whole of his account on the Caldecote Papers, to which he had access. He devotes the final section of his book (a sequel to Atlay's *Victorian Chancellors* but far more discreet in tone than either that or of course Campbell's *Lives*), pp 577–608, to Thomas Inskip.

p 266   *Sir Patrick Hastings, also a disillusioned politician*
See *Sir Patrick Hastings* by H. Montgomery Hyde (Heine-mann, 1960) with a Foreword by Hastings' contemporary Norman Birkett – for whom see above, p 265.

p 268   *'This is not the House of Lords. This is the House of Frauds.'*
I wrote this paragraph in a week when Lord Kagan, out of gaol, resumed his seat. The place cannot have changed much.

p 269   *noted a General*
An anonymous General – quoted by Heuston, p 589.

p 269   *as Michael Foot put it, echoing general public opinion, nothing so extraordinary had been heard of since the Emperor Caligula appointed his horse a consul*
In *Guilty Men* by 'Cato' (1939). I wrote to Michael Foot to check on this. 'I think,' he replied, 'Churchill did refer to him in these terms and that is where my co-author of *Guilty Men* got the idea. But I think Churchill had also picked it up from someone else as well.'

p 269   *'I don't propose to ask Maugham to resign so that I could offer you the Lord Chancellorship . . . It is a choice Hailsham had to make, and I think he always afterwards regretted that he became Lord Chancellor.'*
Lord Maugham, Somerset Maugham's elder brother, was Lord Chancellor from March 1938 to September 1939. Doug-las Hogg, first Lord Hailsham, had been Lord Chancellor before him, from June 1935. Hogg's son Quintin, second Lord Hail-sham, is the present Lord Chancellor – a Tory like his father and, like his father, once a potential Prime Minister.

p 273   *Sir Claud Schuster wrote to his widow*
Quoted by Heuston, p 606.

20. GODDARD AND HIS SUCCESSORS

p 275   *The best biography of Lord Goddard is undoubtedly Fenton Bresler's book*
One biography was published just before Goddard's retire-ment. This was *Lord Goddard* by Glyn Jones and Eric Grim-

shaw (Allan Wingate, 1958). It was this biography that was reviewed by Bernard Levin in *The Spectator* (see p 274 above). I have used it sparingly.

A far more personal biography was published the following year: *Lord Goddard* by Arthur Smith (Weidenfeld & Nicolson, 1959). Arthur Smith was Goddard's clerk; and therefore tended to be both well-informed and respectful. It is fairly clear from citations in this chapter what I owe to Arthur Smith.

Lord Goddard by Fenton Bresler (Foreword by Lord Denning) was published by Harrap in 1977. It is the first critical biography, full of vivid detail, and I have largely based my account of Goddard on Mr Bresler's work. The many quotations not attributed elsewhere have almost always been taken from his book; and I would like here to acknowledge my debt and express my thanks to him.

p 275 *Fenton Bresler has proved that Goddard was none too scrupulous in his means*
Fenton Bresler contacted Bernard Levin to try and get him to substantiate the facts on which he based various of his criticisms of Goddard; but met with a distinctly unsatisfactory response, as he recounts in his book.

p 276 *The veteran turncoat Jowitt had been appointed Lord Chancellor by Attlee*
William Jowitt had sat in two Parliaments as a Liberal. He decided to join the Labour ranks to qualify for the post of Attorney General under Ramsay Macdonald. Norman Birkett refused to follow him – though he *nearly* accepted the post of Solicitor General in the National Government of 1931.

p 277 *'In fact,' said Hartley Shawcross later, 'I didn't want it.'*
Quoted by Fenton Bresler, p 13.

p 281 *'. . . Well, long sentences judges must give . . .'*
Three youths kicked another to death in a fight outside a discotheque. They were sentenced by the trial judge to four, six and seven years' imprisonment; and in January 1982 appealed to the Court of Criminal Appeal against their sentences. 'The effect of heavy terms of imprisonment on young men such as these,' said the present Lord Chief Justice, 'is almost catastrophic, especially at their time of life, but we have other things to consider.' In view of the prevalence of this kind of violence, 'any sentence passed must have, inbuilt, a measure of deter-

rence.' It seems to me that Lane is definitely in the line of Goddard – and that is intended neither as praise nor as criticism.

p 283   *–plus other anguishing cases of the time –*
In particular that of Ruth Ellis, the last woman to be hanged; and of Evans, almost certainly wrongly executed for the murder of his wife.

p 286   *Miscarriages of Justice*
For C. G. L. Du Cann's book see note to p 256. The relevant chapter is entitled 'The Case of Derek Bentley'.

p 288   *But it is almost certain that Goddard ... used the*
                threat of staying on
He virtually admitted as much to Fenton Bresler. See Bresler, pp 297–8.

p 289   *because none of them has ever used his position as a*
                member of the House of Lords to air his views
I asked Lord Lane in January 1982 if he was intending to make his mark in the House of Lords, like Goddard. He admitted he had not done so. Two months later, on March 25 – *post hoc? propter hoc?* – the *Daily Telegraph*'s front-page headline announced: 'KID-GLOVE' SENTENCES WARNING. Lane had spoken out in a House of Lords law-and-order debate the day before, condemning 'acquisitiveness, greed'; plus violence on television and pornographic literature. The 'No kid gloves' – and long sentences – were suggested for recidivist burglars only; in general *à la Goddard* he came out against long sentences very firmly.

p 290   *'. . . the trouble with me is that I'm a dull man,'*
                Widgery once told a friend
Quoted in *The Times* obituary. It was published a year later (see p 293 below) because *The Times* had been on strike.

p 290   *the spy Blake whom Parker sentenced to a savage*
                forty-two years
Lord Lane, despite his general views, sentenced the spy Prime to a barely less savage 35 years plus a further three on sexual offences charges in 1982. Prime pleaded guilty to seven counts against the Official Secrets Act; the trial lasted, therefore, only for one day, November 10; much of it was held *in camera*.

p 290   *in a recent book*
The Politics of the Judiciary by Professor J. A. G. Griffith (Manchester, 1981, 2nd edition). I asked Lord Lane what he thought of the Professor's point. The first part was right, he said, the second part was rubbish.

p 293   *What was interesting was not so much Silkin's virtues*
        or vices as the suggestion that the Prime Minister was
        once again considering the 'right' of the Attorney
        General to the post of Lord Chief Justice
I wrote to James Callaghan, who was Prime Minister at the time, to ask what had been in his mind but received only an unhelpful and evasive reply from an assistant.

p 293   *The present Lord Chief Justice ... was educated at*
        Shrewsbury, like his famous predecessor, Judge Jef-
        freys, at Trinity College, Cambridge, also like Jeffreys
A coincidence I rather tentatively mentioned to him – only to find out that, though not exactly emphasising the point, he was very well aware of it.

p 293   *– his appointment was welcomed by the Bar as a*
        whole –
And, rather surprisingly, even by notably left-wing barristers; perhaps because, although obviously a natural conservative, Lane is not a natural prosecutor. At a private meeting of about 100 barristers (including my informant) held at the Old Bailey on October 21, 1981 he suggested that prosecuting counsel should prune documents, cut the length of opening speeches, shorten their interminable cross-examinations, and concentrate on major charges and major criminals only. He was 'appalled' (*per* the Legal Action Group's December bulletin) when asked from the floor if this might not upset prosecuting solicitors. 'In his day solicitors did as they were told and barristers had the last word.'

p 294   *Have we in Lane ... a man who will bring the post of*
        Lord Chief Justice back into the public eye?
This appears (in early 1983) to be happening, at least to a limited extent. It is impossible to say that Lane has impinged as yet on the general consciousness: yet he has had his headlines both in the popular and in the serious press; he has had his photograph, both wigged and unbewigged, on the front pages. He has pronounced publicly on rape, law and order, and

treason; and he has not been seriously criticised either by the left or by the right. He has shown himself to be no pawn of the Establishment. As Chief Coroner of England, it was he who in July 1982 ordered a new inquest in the notorious (thanks to *Private Eye*) case of the dead nurse, Helen Smith. He is, to meet, an impressive man: sharp, accurate, a little frightening as is only to be expected, but good-humoured, almost genial when relaxed; very conscious of the dignity of his office, and very proud of it too. He has not yet however been involved in a case that has caught the popular imagination: as for instance the trial of the traitor Anthony Blunt might have been if Blunt had come to trial and pleaded not guilty. When such a case does occur, the Lord Chief Justice will be, in a sense, face to face with the verdict of history himself.

Index